Created and Directed by Hans Höfer

INSIGHT GUIDES
JORDAN

Edited by Dorothy Stannard
Photography by Lyle Lawson

Editorial Director: Brian Bell

APA PUBLICATIONS

ABOUT THIS BOOK

Stannard

Although Jordan has been drawing intrepid Western visitors for well over a century, it is a relative stranger to modern tourism. Only in the past few years have tour companies and the Jordanians themselves woken up to the fact that Jordan is the Middle East's most exciting travel destination after Egypt. A small country, packed with culture, sights and natural beauty – desert canyons, lush valleys, Red Sea coral reefs, Roman ruins, Crusader castles and the famous rock-carved city of Petra – yet practically uncharted by any guidebook, it was also perfect territory for *Insight Guides'* award-winning recipe of hard-hitting text and eye-catching photojournalism.

The task of editing such a guide was thus an exciting challenge to editor **Dorothy Stannard**, who had already edited and written various Insight titles on North Africa. She is also a long-term addict of Cairo – a boat and camel-ride away from Jordan across the Gulf of Aqaba. She flew to Amman to tap into the expertise of an established network of writers who had made Jordan their home.

Lawson

Stannard began by enlisting as photographer **Lyle Lawson**, who had just finished taking the pictures for two very different Insight titles, *Baltic States* and *Normandy*. Lawson, who had previously undertaken shoots in Turkey and Yemen, spent almost two months travelling through Jordan, Syria and the West Bank, by four-wheel drive, train and taxi and even by helicopter and hot-air balloon. She concedes that the stunning results of her trip are partly thanks to the tireless efforts of her fellow contributors, who made time in their busy schedules to drive her to out-of-the-way places and provided valuable introductions to local society.

Lalor

One such contributor was **Paul Lalor**, who for the purposes of this guide records Jordan's history since its creation as a modern state in 1922. Lalor, an Irishman whose doctorate in Middle East Studies from Oxford University led to employment as a consultant and journalist on Middle Eastern matters, says he fell in love with Jordan because of the warmth of its people and the underestimated beauty of its countryside. He also also wrote the feature on Palestinians living in Jordan and a portrait of Glubb Pasha, plus the Places chapter on the Ottoman-style town of Salt. Lalor teamed up with Greek fellow-Arabist **Floresca Karanasou** to write the chapter on Amman, a convivial modern city which they now call home. Karanasou, who also compiled the fact-packed Travel Tips section, lived in other parts of the Arab world while researching for her PhD in modern Middle Eastern history and learning Arabic.

Karanasou

Khouri

A key contributor to the Places section is **Rami G. Khouri**, a Palestinian-Jordanian native of Nazareth and resident of Amman who is general manager and owner of Al Kutba Publishers in Amman (Al Kutba was the Nabataean goddess of the scribes). Editor-in-chief of the *Jordan Times* for seven years, Khouri writes extensively in the international press and is president of the Jordanian Friends of Archaeology Society and a founding member of the Petra National Trust. As well as writing about the Royals and tackling the chapters on the Jordan Valley and The North, Khouri takes readers on an in-depth tour of Petra.

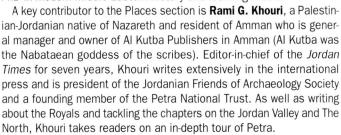

Shahin

Mariam Shahin, a former colleague of Rami Khouri's and currently a

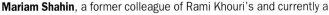

Salti

journalist at the *Jordan Times*, wrote the feature on the lives of ordinary Jordanians and the Places chapters on the West Bank and Aqaba. Born in Berlin but raised in Canada and France, she moved to Jordan in 1986. She travels frequently to the West Bank and Iraq for several international publications. She has also co-produced political and cultural documentaries for Canadian and German TV.

Rebecca Salti fleshes out some of the cultural aspects of Jordan, in particular the country's thriving handicrafts and the lifestyle of the Bedouin. Salti, who is director of Save the Children in Amman (though she trained as a journalist), has been instrumental in resuscitating traditional crafts in Jordan, in particular rug-making among the Bani Hamida Bedouin. An American married to a Palestinian, Salti also casts her eye over the activities of fellow non-Jordanians for a chapter on Amman's energetic expats.

Taylor

Jane Taylor, a writer, photographer and television producer who has lived in Amman since 1989, contributed the chapters on Wadi Rum and East of Azraq as well as a brief portrait of Burckhardt, the Swiss explorer who discovered Petra in 1812, and also contributed some of the photographs in the Wildlife chapter. Her previous books are *Testament to the Bushmen* (with Laurens van der Post), *Imperial Istanbul* and *High Above Jordan*, a collection of aerial photographs of the country which appeared in 1989. Her latest book, *Petra*, is an attempt to capture in both text and photographs something of what Edward Lear called Petra's magical condension of beauty and wonder".

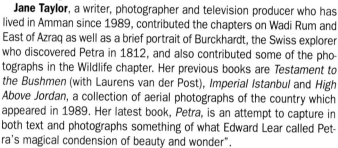

McQuitty

The King's Highway, a beautiful route snaking south along the crest of the Mountains of Moab, has been captured by **Alison McQuitty**, an archaeologist who has lived and worked in Jordan for 12 years. At present she is carrying out research at Oxford University based on the results of her excavations of a multi-period village site near Kerak.

Watson

Another archaeologist is **Pamela Watson** (pictured below in "working gear"), an Australian who has lived and worked on and off in Jordan since 1980 and has travelled widely in the neighbouring regions – hence her piece on Syria for this book. At present Watson is assistant director of the British Institute at Amman for Archaeology and History.

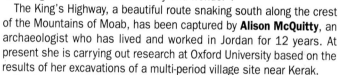

Adding insights from outside Jordan is **Rowlinson Carter**, a regular Insight contributor who worked in Jordan as a cameraman during Black September in 1970. Carter, who believes history should be about people rather than dates, was the ideal person to delve into Jordan's distant past. Other contributors based outside Jordan include **Peter Vine**, a writer and publisher living in Ireland who visits and writes about the Middle East frequently and here writes about Jordan's wildlife, and **Roger Williams**, a UK-based journalist who here shares his passion for the work of the Orientalist artist David Roberts.

Thanks also go to everyone at the Ministry for Tourism in Amman, **James Smith** of Jasmin Travel, **Widad Kawar** and staff at Al Aydi, who lent rare examples of regional costumes to be photographed, and Stephanie Genkin, an American writer and Middle East specialist who helped compile the Travel Tips. Proof-reading and indexing were completed by **Carole Mansur**.

CONTENTS

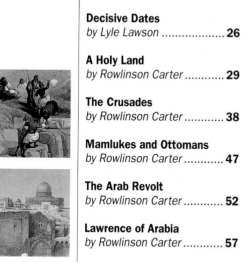

__Preceding pages__: shouldering responsibility; wrestling with a hot-air balloon.

CONTENTS

THE SANDS OF TIME

Jordan is a 20th-century creation in an ancient cockpit of history. Called Transjordan in 1919, it rose out of the detritus of the Ottoman Empire after World War I, between the Jordan River and an arbitrary line running through the sands of the Arabian desert. Although the throne was brand-new, its first occupant, the present King Hussein's grandfather, traced his line to the Prophet Mohammed.

A sharp contrast between the fertile Jordan Valley and the desert hinterland has been at the bottom of Jordan's history from the earliest times. The valley was busy, the desert remote. It is conceivable that the first stirrings of distinctly human activity in the East African Great Rift Valley two million years ago gradually worked north via the Red and Dead seas when these were dry extensions of the same geological rift. In any case, stone tools found at Pella suggest that a comparable level of human activity had been attained in the Jordan Valley some 800,000 years after the original rumblings in Africa. Of parallel social developments in the desert, if indeed there were any, we know nothing.

An astounding milestone in human development was achieved at Jericho in 7000 BC. Beneath the walls which famously came tumbling down in the Old Testament were other walls of immense archaeological significance: the first evidence of nomads abandoning their traditional way of life in order to practise systematic agriculture around a permanent home. Out of that particular acorn grows the whole idea of towns, city-states, statehood, cash economies and so forth – the checklist of urban civilisation. This pioneering effort proved to be way ahead of its time and, as far as Jericho was concerned, it was put on ice for a few thousand years.

In the meantime, civilisations flourished in Egypt and Mesopotamia on the strength of rivers which took care of agricultural necessities, thereby creating societies with a previously unknown commodity, surplus labour. The Jordan River was not as generous but its valley served as a landbridge between Egypt and Mesopotamia, Africa and Asia, and Arabia and Europe. Crowded in biblical times with a tongue-twisting cast of Canaanites, Hittites, Perizzites, Girgashites, Amorites, Jebusites, Edomites and so on, this busy thoroughfare was subjugated at various times by the Egyptian, Assyrian, Babylonian, Persian, Macedonian, Roman, Byzantine, Arabian, Mamluke and Turkish empires. For a while, even Genghis Khan's grandson considered adding it to the Mongol Empire. Similar thoughts occurred to Napoleon and Hitler.

Jordan enters recorded history shortly before its absorption into the Egyptian Empire. Tribal anarchy and famine drove the Hebrews under Abraham to Egypt. Four centuries later, by which time the Egyptians had imposed a measure of law and order in the Promised

Land, Moses led them back. Focusing on these migrations, the Bible loses sight of ancient trade imperatives. Eastern silks, spices and other things unobtainable in the Mediterranean basin could be shipped up the Red Sea, but the more reliable route, avoiding reefs and pirates, was overland by camel caravan from Yemen.

Petra, the outstanding historical site in Jordan, grew rich on this developing trade, as did Mecca further south and Palmyra to the north. Rabbath Ammon, now Amman, also prospered in this period, as did Gerasa, now Jerash. Petra eventually folded under the advance of Rome, and when Rome itself collapsed, its inheritance passed to the Graeco-Roman Eastern Empire, or Byzantium. Jordan was farmed out to the Ghassanids, Christian vassals of Byzantium, before being conquered by the Arabs in the 7th century and becoming part of an Islamic Empire later dominated by the Turks.

In the meantime, the desert hinterland was ignored or positively avoided by these transient empires as it was by the indigenous population of the Jordan Valley. The desert tribes, on the other hand, were perpetually engaged in a warlike ritual over this "wild land of blood and terror". In the words of T. E. Lawrence many years later: "Each hill and valley in it had a man who was its acknowledged owner and who would quickly assert the right of his family or clan to it, against aggression. Even the wells and trees had their masters…" Others were allowed to drink from the wells and make firewood of the trees, but no more than was absolutely necessary. To overstep the mark was an act of war. The ritual was, Lawrence wrote, a kind of "crazed communism".

The distinction between valley and desert people has by no means disappeared. The former, taller and more heavily built, are believed to be basically the Canaanites of old with an uneven sprinkling from passing empires. The desert tribes are an almost pure strain, ethnically indistinguishable from the desert populations of Syria and Saudi Arabia. Consensus says that the valley Arabs have been receptive to cultural currents swirling around the Mediterranean basin while their desert counterparts have stuck steadfastly to their own traditions.

The population of Transjordan, as created in 1919, was predominantly (about 75 percent) of desert tribal origin. The subsequent absorption of the West Bank and the influx of Palestinian refugees during the 1948 and 1967 wars put the desert tribes and the mixed population of "valley" and "coastal" peoples on a roughly equal numerical footing. These statistics would, of course, have to be revised if the present negotiations over the future of the West Bank reach a successful conclusion. The political debate bristles with contemporary rhetoric; in the shadows, though, the course of Jordan's history swings, as always, on a pendulum between the stark contrasts of desert and sown.

Right, the desert hinterland, once "a wild land of blood and terror".

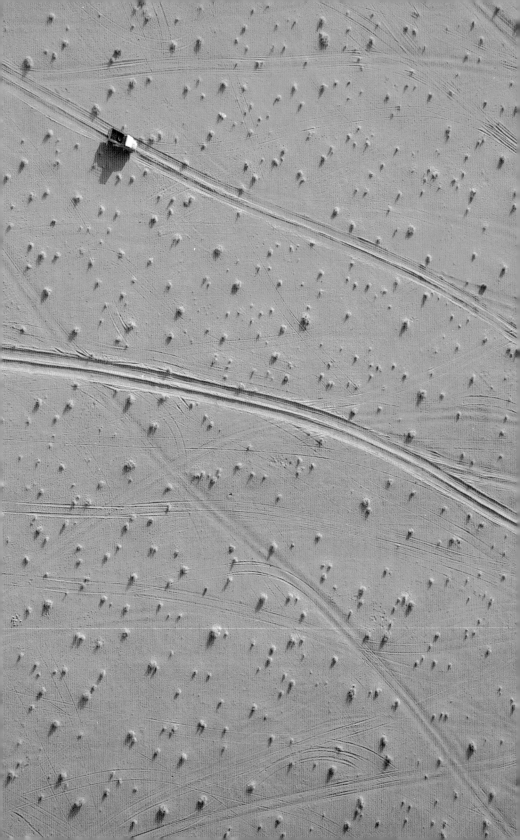

9000 BC: First inhabitants settle on the West Bank of the Jordan River near modern Jericho.
4000–3100 BC: Copper Age; human settlements near Irbid.
3000–1550 BC: Early Bronze Age; Amorites and Canaanites arrive in Jordan.
1550–1200 BC: Bronze Age.
c. **1280 BC:** Moses leads Israelites out of Egypt; 40 years later they settle east of the Jordan River.
c. **1225 BC:** Joshua captures Jericho; Palestine is divided among the 12 tribes of Israel.
1200 BC: The Philistines begin using metal in their weaponry, gaining a fighting advantage.

c. **1000 BC:** David proclaimed King of the Israelites; conquers Jerusalem, makes it his capital.
960–922 BC: Reign of Solomon. Expands kingdom through treaties and marriages, and builds the first Temple in Jerusalem. The kingdom is divided on his death into Judah in the south and Israel to the north.
722 BC: The Assyrians, led by Sargon II, destroy the Kingdom of Israel, replacing the Jews with settlers from Syria and Babylonia.
612 BC: The Babylonian army under Medes captures Nineveh, the Assyrian capital.
597–587 BC: Jerusalem, Palestine and Jordan fall to the Babylonian King Nebuchadnezzar.
539 BC: Cyrus II takes power in Persia (modern Iran) and allows Jews to return to Jerusalem.

538 BC: Nabataeans establish a kingdom based at Petra in southern Jordan.
332–1 BC: Alexander the Great conquers Syria, Palestine and Egypt.
323 BC: Alexander dies and his Middle Eastern domain is divided: Ptolemy I given Egypt and parts of Syria, and Seleuces is granted Babylon.
198 BC: The Seleucid army under Antiochus III defeats the Ptolemies' army; both states are consolidated under the Seleucid flag.
188 BC: Antiochus III is defeated by the Roman army; Roman Empire absorbs his kingdom.
170 BC: Antiochus IV sacks Jerusalem.
167 BC: Jews revolt under Judas Maccabeus.
64 BC: Damascus falls to Pompey's Roman army. Palestine falls in 63 and is renamed Judaea.
63 BC–AD 106: The Decapolis, or the League of 10 Cities, formed in the area.
40 BC: Parthian kings of Persia and Mesopotamia invade the Decapolis; Mark Antony leads the army which repels them.
37 BC: In Rome, Herod the Great is proclaimed King of Israel; Temple rebuilt in Jerusalem.
c. **4 BC–AD 39:** Life of Jesus Christ.
AD 66: Jews revolt against Romans.
AD 106: Nabataean Kingdom incorporated into the Roman Empire.
132: Second revolt by Jews fails.
325: Constantine, the Byzantine Emperor, converts to Christianity.
525–565: The reign of Justinian. Churches are built at Christian holy sites.
629: Byzantines and Arabs battle for the first time near Kerak; Mohammed takes Mecca.
638: Jerusalem falls to Muslim Arabs led by Caliph Omar.
642: Arabs conquer Egypt.
658: Omayyad dynasty founded in Damascus. A brilliant period in arts and architecture ensues.
750: Omayyads overthrown by Abbasids who move the caliphate to Baghdad.
980: Fatimids rule from Cairo.
1095: Pope Urban II launches first Crusade.
1099: Crusaders conquer Jerusalem; fortresses built in Far'un (an island near Aqaba), Wadi Moussa (Petra), Kerak and Shobak.
1250: Mamlukes take power in Cairo. They eventually rule over an area from Egypt to Syria.
1516: Syria and Palestine are absorbed into the Ottoman Empire.
1901: The Jewish National Fund is created to buy Arab lands for Zionist settlements.
1909: Revolt by the Young Turks in Istanbul encourages nationalistic feelings among populations under Ottoman rule.
1914–18: World War I; the Ottoman Empire joins

the war at the end of 1914, siding with Germany.

1916: The Arab Revolt. Emir Feisal, son of the Sherif (ruler) of Mecca, takes up leadership of the Arab Pan-nationalist Movement. It joins forces with the British to drive out Ottoman Turks.

1917: British troops occupy Jerusalem and Aqaba.

1918: Ottoman Empire disbanded; Emir Feisal declares Arab independence in Damascus.

1920: The Conference of San Remo reconfirms the secretly negotiated 1916 Sykes-Picot agreement denying the Arabs an independent state and giving Britain a mandate to rule Palestine and France authority over Syria and Lebanon.

1923: Britain recognises Transjordan's independence under its protection, with Abdullah, Feisal's brother, as its king. Feisal is offered the crown of Iraq; the Arab Legion is formed under Major J.B. Glubb (Glubb Pasha), a British officer.

1930s: Large numbers of Jews fleeing from the Nazis arrive in Palestine, sparking riots.

1939–45: World War II; Jordan offers its Arab Legion to fight with the Allies.

1946: Britain gives up mandate. The Hashemite Kingdom of Jordan is created.

1947 (November): United Nations votes for the partition of Palestine; the Hashemite Kingdom of Jordan is created.

1948 (May): Britain's mandate over Palestine expires and its troops withdraw; State of Israel proclaimed; the first Arab-Israeli war begins as the last British troops depart.

1950: Abdullah formally annexes the West Bank into his kingdom.

1951: King Abdullah is assassinated at Al-Aqsa Mosque in Jerusalem.

1952: Hussein is declared king at 17 after his father, Talal, is declared mentally unstable.

1955: Jordan becomes a member of the United Nations; Egypt nationalises the Suez Canal.

1957: Last British troops leave Jordan.

1959: To counter power of Syria and Egypt, Jordan joins in a federation with Iraq.

1957: Disturbances in Jordan and attempt to depose King Hussein.

1958: Iraqi government is overthrown.

1964: Palestine Liberation Organisation and its more militant cousin, the Palestinian National Liberation Movement (Al-Fatah), are formed.

1967: The Six-Day War between Israel and the Arab armies leaves Jordan devastated: Jerusalem and the West Bank are lost.

Preceding pages: statuary at the Roman Theatre, Amman. **Left**, detail at Iraq al-Amir, near Amman. **Right**, sarcophagi dating from the 13th century to the 7th century BC.

1969: Yasser Arafat is elected chairman of the PLO.

1970: King Hussein clamps down on the PLO's growing power, culminating in Black September. The civil war between local Palestinians and the government leaves the PLO routed.

1974: King Hussein recognises the PLO as the sole representative of the Palestinian people.

1980: Jordan backs Iraq in its eight-year war against Iran; Syria goes with Iran.

1984: Women are given the vote.

1988: King Hussein gives up legal and administrative claims to Jerusalem and the West Bank.

1989: Price rises for basic staples as dictated by the IMF as part of an economic recovery package. Bread riots. In Ma'an, 11 people die. In November, the first free elections are held.

1990: Iraq invades Kuwait in August. Large sections of Jordan's population back Iraq.

1991: The Gulf War. Jordan is inundated by fleeing foreign workers and thousands of Palestinians are expelled by Kuwait.

1992: Israeli-Palestinian peace talks begin in Madrid. Law passed legalising all political parties, including the Communists.

1993: Jordan's first multi-party democratic elections are held.

26 October 1994: Jordan and Israel sign peace treaty, giving new momentum to peace process.

Unresolved confusion over names and dates torments visitors hoping to locate historical and biblical references in Jordan, and that has ever been the case. Early travellers, many of them clergymen attached to various Palestine exploration societies, first had to overcome obstructions put in their way by the Turkish authorities who had ruled the Holy Land virtually since the time of the Crusades. First-hand experiences were pooled, so by the end of the 19th century visitors on their way to Jordan – as distinct from Palestine or the West Bank – understood that 96 places mentioned in the Bible awaited them.

Early settlement: Ironically, fixed settlement became a viable proposition in the Jordan Valley not long after Abraham's departure for Egypt to escape the tribal anarchy and famine which had plagued the region. Egypt was on the point of building an empire, and as the imperial frontier pushed towards Mesopotamia, the area it encompassed benefited from unprecedented, if less than perfect, law and order. Bedouin desert tribes remained a law unto themselves, but urban development took root at Madaba in the plain of Moab and at Jerash in the mountains of Gilead.

Under the umbrella of Egyptian security, it was a relatively short step from nomads exchanging their peripatetic existence for permanent homes to the emergence of a host of petty kingdoms with taxing Old Testament names. Edom is among the most memorable if only because its founder, Esau, has always brightened up religious knowledge classes by virtue of being a hairy man whereas his brother Jacob was a smooth one (Genesis 27:11). It may help readers who understandably lose their bearings in the welter of Old Testament names to remember that Kerak is at the heart of ancient Moab, Petra at the heart of Edom.

The whereabouts of Sodom and Gomorrah are more problematical. By tradition these evil twins were devoured in Abraham's lifetime by a storm of fire and brimstone

which deposited the ashes at the bottom of the Dead Sea. Old maps invariably showed them under fathoms of water but still engulfed in flames. In recent time divers carrying extra weights to counteract the excessive buoyancy of the water have scoured the seabed without success. Various theories have put the site of the cities on the Plain of Jordan and the shores of the Dead Sea. Scholars favouring the Lisam peninsula, which juts into the sea below the Mountains of Moab in the east, have been encouraged by the fairly

recent discovery of a necropolis containing some 20,000 tombs, many untouched since the bodies were laid to rest about 2500 BC.

The Exodus: By 1280 BC the Israelites had outstayed their welcome in Egypt and had to embark on the Exodus under Moses. The direct route lay through Edom, but in spite of Moses's promise not to veer left or right from the beaten track of the King's Highway, the Edomites refused to allow him and his party through their territory. The obligatory detour amounted to 40 years in the wilderness – "a frightful desert, almost wholly without vegetation", according to Burckhardt, the 19th-century Swiss explorer who went to

Left, Madaba's 6th-century mosaic map of Palestine. Right, the destruction of Sodom and Gomorrah.

see for himself – and it was only after this tortuous route that the weary refugees were able to climb Mount Nebo in Moab and survey the Promised Land. Moses died in Moab without ever crossing to the West Bank of the Jordan. He was buried in a valley "over against Bethpeor: but no man knoweth of his sepulchre unto this day". While his grave remains a mystery, there is general agreement these days that Mount Nebo is one of three peaks about 10 km (6 miles) west of Madaba.

The Israelites had to fight their fellow Semites for a place in the Promised Land. Battles took place everywhere; the most interesting on Jordanian territory was prob-

ably fought at Amman, then known as Rabbath Ammon, the Ammonite capital. King David of Israel initially approached Rabbath Ammon on the pretext of consoling the Ammonite king on the recent death of his father. The king was not to be comforted by David's thoughtful message. Instead, the messengers were seized and had their beards hacked off, followed by a crude re-tailoring of their clothes which left their buttocks all but exposed. This hideous insult was sufficient cause for war, but David had another reason for ordering battle to commence. The lovely Bathsheba, on whom he had his eye, was inconveniently married to Uriah the

Hittite. David made a point of ordering the luckless husband into the thickest part of the action with the happy thought that he could not possibly survive. Uriah duly perished, David was free to marry Bathsheba, and the son she subsequently bore him was the future King Solomon. David may have delighted in his coup but he was not inclined to show magnanimity towards the conquered population of Rabbath Ammon. They were roasted alive in a kiln.

For all its candour about the human foibles of the Israelite kings, the Old Testament gives a rather partisan account of the wars, with the Israelites enjoying a suspiciously high rate of success. A different flavour is imparted by the Mesha or Moabite stone, a block of basalt inscribed with 34 lines of writing in a script that falls somewhere between ancient Phoenician and Hebrew, which was discovered just north of Jordan's Wadi Mujib in 1868. This is the voice of King Mesha of Moab, crowing about his victories over the Israelites in the 9th century BC. He is particularly pleased about a battle in which he killed 7,000 Israelites, hastening to add, however, that he scrupulously spared the women. He could afford the gesture because, he says, "Israel is laid waste for ever."

Whether or not King Mesha actually checked the run of Israelite military success, there is no disputing the historical fact that the state eventually carved out by David and Solomon became the leading power in the region. Urusalim (Jerusalem) was captured around 1000 BC and replaced Hebron as the capital of the Israelite kingdom.

On the death of Solomon in 922 BC, the kingdom divided into Israel in the north and Judah in the south, the respective capitals being Samaria and Jerusalem. Both kingdoms were overwhelmed by the Assyrian invasion of 722 BC. The Israelites were carried away to captivity in Mesopotamia but, by agreeing to pay tribute, Judah was left intact, albeit as a vassal state. There was no second reprieve, however, when Nebuchadnezzar II of Babylon conquered the empire in 587 BC. Jerusalem was sacked, Solomon's Temple on Mount Moriah was completely destroyed, and the population was carried off to captivity in Babylon.

Cyrus I of Persia conquered Babylon half a century later, whereupon the men of Judah were allowed to return to Jerusalem under

Persian protection. They rebuilt the Temple and fostered special treatment from Persia by remaining aloof from local rebellions against Persian rule. Deir Alla in the Jordan Valley – the "Succoth" where Jacob recuperated after wrestling with an angel – was evidently a Persian settlement, but there are no significant monuments in Jordan of this Persian era.

Alexander the Great, conqueror of Persia and its possessions in 332 BC, was responsible for drawing the Near East into the orbit of Graeco-Western civilisation. Having previously scorned Macedonians as barbaric foreigners, the Greek diaspora was quick to mount the bandwagon of Alexander's aston-

enough to consolidate his colossal empire, he revitalised trade between east and west and for Jordan, straddling a historic trade route, this was bound to be immensely profitable. The key stretch was the overland camel caravan route from Aden and Yemen up the east coast of the Red Sea to Damascus and points beyond.

The first major staging post was Mecca, and its future role at the centre of Islam was not unconnected with its traditional pre-eminence in trade and commerce. Another of the staging posts was Palmyra in Syria, which grew so rich on trade that at a later stage Queen Zenobia presumed to declare war on Rome. In Jordan, the caravans were

ishing military success. Trading posts and settlement followed in the wake of the triumphant Macedonian army. The industrious Greeks were not inclined to stray very far from the coast, but their influence certainly reached into the Jordan Valley. Rabbath Ammon, for instance, acquired a Greek name, Philadelphia. As always, the desert tribes were so remote that they were unaffected by – if indeed they even noticed – a profound cultural transformation on all sides.

Although Alexander did not live long

serviced – and taxed – at Petra.

Petra and the Nabataeans: Very little is known about Petra in the earlier days of ancient Edom. Biblical references to the Edomite capital of Sela probably refer to the western wall of the canyon. The Nabataeans, a tribe of nomads originating in western Arabia, seem to have settled around Petra in the 6th century BC.

They made the most of Petra's strategic position and prospered wonderfully, but in so doing they inevitably attracted dangerous predators, none more so than a certain Antigonus, one of Alexander the Great's Seleucid heirs, for whom the legacy of

Left, Moses surveys the Promised Land. **Above**, the Dead Sea Scrolls.

Babylonia was never enough. His energies were divided between several unsuccessful attacks on Petra and attempts to take a larger slice of Alexander's legacy from the other principal heirs, the Ptolemies of Egypt. The latter had a foothold in Jordan at Gadara, later Umm Qais, a less important staging post than Petra near Lake Tiberias. The Seleucids eventually seized Gadara from the Ptolemies in 218 BC; they were in turn dispossessed by the Jews in 100 BC.

Petra could afford to maintain forces capable of seeing off enemies like Antigonus. It could even afford to buy Roman recognition of its independence when the Roman legions in 63 BC seized Syria and Palestine. Having Petra. Caesar baulked at Petra so she settled for Jericho.

West of the Jordan in the meantime, the Seleucid Antiochus Epiphanus made a searing impact when he took Jerusalem by storm in 170 BC, slaughtering most of the inhabitants and selling the rest into slavery. The Temple was re-dedicated to Jupiter, an outrage which Daniel called "the Abomination of Desolation". The Jewish backlash was led by the Maccabees, a strait-laced sect who caused consternation among the Edomites by insisting on their circumcision. The pious Maccabees later suffered a dramatic fall from grace. "A complete moral collapse," observes an eminent biblical scholar, "none of

reached an accommodation with Rome, the Nabataeans then suffered a terminal lapse of judgment by taking the side of the Parthians in a dispute they were having with Rome. The agreement was torn up and Rome moved in. As the new masters of Petra, the Romans began their customary re-modelling of the place to suit their own taste. If the remnants are impressive today, the impact at the time must have been overwhelming. It is said that Cleopatra, a Ptolemy herself, snuggled up to the balding and rather older Caesar at a formative stage of their acquaintance and suggested that the best way to prove his feelings would be to make her a present of the moral purity of their ancestors." The Maccabees took one of their private arguments for arbitration to the new Roman master of Damascus, Pompey. He lost his temper with the lot of them, battered down the walls of Jerusalem and marched into the Temple. He also overwhelmed the Nabataeans, hoping to replace their efficient trading tentacles with a kind of common market of 10 semi-independent cities, including Amman, which he called the Decapolis.

As there were never enough Roman-born citizens to administer the rapidly expanding empire, even top positions were delegated to local men. Some acquitted themselves with distinction; others, like Herod the Great, were notably poor choices. Herod joined the imperial service as governor of Galilee and in 31 BC was nominated as King of Judaea, in which capacity he effectively ruled the Jordan Valley. His mind was apparently unsettled by something of an identity crisis. He was, it was said, "by birth an Idumaean (i.e. Edomite), by profession a Jew, by necessity a Roman, by culture and by choice a Greek". Soaking in the hot springs at Zarqa Ma'in ("Callirhoe" in the Bible), he concocted architectural schemes which would either intimidate or placate his restless subjects. Machaerus, now known as Mukawir, was one of a string of fortresses serving the first

plan was executed, but John found the whole affair distasteful and said so. For speaking his mind, John was himself thrown into Mukawir and in due course beheaded.

Herod's vindictiveness towards John presaged the acute paranoia which led him to order a general massacre of any segment of society whose loyalty he suspected. By the time he died at Jericho in 4 BC of internal ulcers and putrid sores, Herod had so much blood on his hands that the Jewish historian Josephus omits to mention the apparently trivial matter of Bethlehem's murdered babes.

Herod's successors could be equally uncongenial. Few subjects sympathised with his grandson Herod Agrippa, Caligula's great

purpose; the Wailing Wall around the Temple in Jerusalem was built to please the Jews. As Cleopatra had evidently lost interest in Jericho, he stepped in with an offer to lease it.

Herod's dispute with John the Baptist began and ended at the Machaerus or Mukawir fortress. The origin of their animosity was Herod's thought of incarcerating in Mukawir the wife (one of 10) who was obstructing his designs on her sister. The wife managed to slip away to her father in Petra before the

Left, Roman remains at Petra. **Above**, decorative fragment at Qasr al-Hallabat, a Roman fort turned Omayyad palace.

friend, as he suffered an agonising death, his insides eaten away by worms. Emperor Claudius at once demoted the kingdom to the status of a province under a Roman governor. Pontius Pilate (AD 26–37) then horrified the Galileans by using their blood in sacrifices and the Jews by milking their Sacred Fund to pay for a new aqueduct. As far as Christians are concerned, Pontius Pilate's overwhelming ignominy was of course earned by his role in the Crucifixion. For the purposes of this book, however, the life and times of Jesus must necessarily be confined to the occasions on which he ventured east of the Jordan River.

Jesus Christ: Tracing Christ's movements in Jordan through biblical references is complicated by changes in place-names. The region east of the Jordan River was administered by the Romans as Peraea, one of four divisions of Palestine, but this name does not appear in the New Testament. On the two occasions when Jesus visited the quarter, it is referred to as "the country of the Gadarene", in other words the area around Gadara, or Umm Qais, the trading post which the Jews seized from the Seleucids in 100 BC. On the more notable of Jesus's visits to Gadarene country, he met two tomb-dwellers possessed by evil spirits and cast their demons into a herd of pigs (Matthew 8: 28–34).

Gadara today is only a ruined shadow of the city it was at this period and continued to be until the 7th century. According to the Jewish historian Josephus, Gadara at the time of Christ was predominantly a heathen rather than Jewish city, which would of course account for the presence of a herd of domestic pigs.

While Christ's own preaching was mainly an appeal to Jews to rectify their own religion, St Paul of Tarsus introduced the idea of aiming the Christian message at heathens like the population of Gadara. This new objective was considerably helped by the Jews being preoccupied by rebellion against

Rome, which reached a gory climax in the destruction of Jerusalem by Titus in AD 70, a massacre in which Jewish converts to Christianty were equal victims.

Christianity readily fitted into the Greek intellectual traditions which had prevailed in the Near East since Alexander the Great's conquest. Compared with the struggle for survival in Rome itself, Eastern Christians could indulge in a debate over the extra iota which turned the Greek word Homoousios into Homoiousis. The former meant that Father and Son were "of the same essence"; the latter that they were merely "of like essence". The distinction dug a chasm between the so-called Monophysitic and Orthodox schools of thought. While Constantine's edict of toleration in 324 made life easier for Christians in the Roman Empire as a whole, the debate over the extra iota reached a pitch that saw Christians killing Christians in what had been their original sanctuary. The conflict continued unabated for centuries to come.

Fully occupied by the skirmishes endemic in desert life, the tribes were totally indifferent to both religious schism and the titanic wars between Byzantium and Persia which characterised the 6th and 7th centuries. Their religion remained rooted in the worship of sacred objects and heavenly bodies. The parallel streams of their ritual were bridged by a *sanctus sanctorum*, a large meteorite preserved in a cubicle temple in Mecca, the Ka'aba. The same black stone is the focal point of Muslim pilgrimage to Mecca, but it was no less revered by pagans long before the birth of the Prophet.

Christianity's equivalent to the Black Stone was the True Cross, kept in the Church of the Holy Sepulchre in Jerusalem. When the Persians captured Jerusalem in 614, they burned the church and carried off the cross. Heraclius, the dashing young emperor of Byzantium, avenged the outrage by defeating the Persians 13 years later and personally carrying the recaptured True Cross along the Via Dolorosa to its rebuilt home. Heraclius hoped that in his hour of triumph he could effect a reconciliation between Orthodox and Monophysite leaders. He soon discovered that he was wasting his breath. Nevertheless, his victory over Persia was tantamount to redrawing the map of the Near East, an achievement celebrated by the contemporary mosaic map still to be seen in the Orthodox Church of St George at Madaba, on the King's Highway south of Amman. Otherwise, the fruits of Heraclius's victory were short-lived: inexplicable reports were received of armies advancing on three fronts, and the possibility of the Persians returning could not be ruled out.

The arrival of Islam: The intruders were Muslim Arabs, devotees of the Prophet Mohammed who had died three years before in Medina. To begin with, Mohammed's call to arms against unbelievers was aimed not at Jews or Christians but at the population of Mecca, who had driven the Prophet out of their city early in his career and, moreover,

Most of the tribes of Arabia had submitted to Islam before Mohammed's death in 632, a miraculous show of unity given their backdrop of perpetual anarchy. It is not known whether Mohammed intended to carry his revolution beyond the Arabian peninsula and he left no instructions about his succession. In the event, Abu Bakr, one of his earliest adherents, was proclaimed Caliph, but there were already hints of rival claims which were to spark endless Muslim civil wars and put a chasm between Sunni and Shi'ite sects.

Early in 633, Abu Bakr organised three columns to invade Byzantine territory. One followed the coastal route to reach the plains

monopolised the proceeds of pilgrimages to the Black Stone. Anyone killed on God's behalf, the Prophet promised, could look forward to an eternal paradise of cool streams, delicious fruit and an unlimited number of beautiful virgins. Nomads who knew only the hardship of life in the desert could hardly wait. In the event, Mecca was captured eight years after Mohammed's flight to Medina (the Hegira), and the Black Stone was at once absorbed into the religious ritual of the victorious Muslims.

Left, Byzantine mosaic, Madaba. **Above**, a trade caravan arrives in Aqaba.

of Beersheba. The others skirted the edge of the desert as they advanced north. In early encounters with Byzantine troops, the desert Arabs demonstrated a degree of mobility that made them formidable opponents in open country although they were still patently ignorant of siege warfare. Even so, they were able to capture a number of fortified positions. After decades locked in combat with Byzantine Greeks over the infamous extra iota, Monophysite Christian defenders were not averse to throwing open their gates to fellow Arabs whose commitment to one God, however recent, might well prove compatible with their own.

All through the summer of 636 (Mohammed had been dead for three years), Muslim Arab and Christian Byzantine armies glared at one another along the banks of the Yarmouk River, the boundary between Jordan and Syria. The afternoon of 20 August then produced the kind of sandstorm against which men can only turn their backs and close their eyes. Wheeling to keep the driving sand behind them, the Arab horsemen scythed through the suddenly blinded Byzantines. The extermination of the Byzantine army

Ruling from Damascus, the Omayyad dynasty indulged their nostalgia for life in the desert by building, east of Amman, a string of castles and hunting lodges where they stayed for a few weeks each year. Two of the castles, at Azraq and Hallabat, were built on the remains of Roman forts.

When the Abbasids overthrew the Omayyads in 750 and moved their capital to Baghdad, Jordan was reduced to a backwater whose population reverted to Bedouin ways. As the Abbasids did not retain the Omayyads'

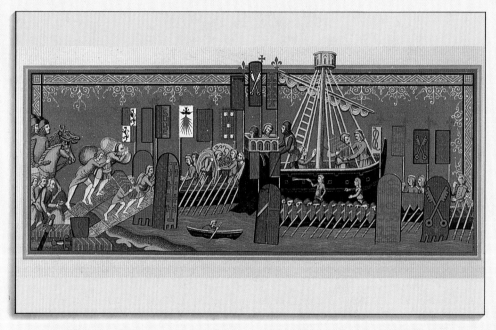

that day ended 1,000 years of Graeco-Roman-Byzantine domination in the region. Within a year, the Arabs controlled most of the Near East, including Jerusalem.

The Arabs were magnanimous victors, eagerly assimilating the unfamiliar skills of their subject peoples and tolerating Judaism and Christianity as long as their adherents paid poll and land taxes.

There appears to have been some reciprocity. Byzantines lent a hand in 691 to the building of the Muslim Dome of the Rock on the spot in Jerusalem from which Mohammed, who actually died in Medina, is believed to have ascended into heaven.

fondness for desert life, the castles and hunting lodges fell into disuse. The change was personified by the Abbasid Caliph Mehedi. When he had to travel through the desert on pilgrimage to Mecca, he made sure that the camel caravan included special containers of snow for cooling his drinks. The desert tribes were incredulous and not a little scornful.

Bedouin misgivings notwithstanding, the Abbasids reached unprecedented levels of artistic and intellectual achievement under Harun ar-Rashid, immortalised in the tales of *Arabian Nights*. Not for the first time, the death of a dazzling leader led to the partition and rapid disintegration of his empire among spiteful sons. Jordan was swept along in a shift of power from the moribund Abbasids in Baghdad to the militant Shi'ite Fatimists in Egypt. Under the Fatimid Caliph al-Hakim at the beginning of the 11th century, the long tradition of Arab religious toleration broke down. He made Christians wear black and hang large wooden crosses from their necks. Jews, too, were ordered into distinctive dress; in the public baths, they had to wear bells.

It was understood at the time that al-Hakim was going mad, the more so when he banned

and, for a while, pilgrims once again made their way to Jerusalem unmolested.

When Christians again found the way barred, those responsible were not Arabs but Seljuk Turks who captured Baghdad in the course of conquering most of Asia Minor. Hordes of undisciplined troops made the pilgrim trail impassable, and in 1069 the Byzantine emperor, Alexius Comnenus, warned that Christianity in the east was imperilled. His call for a Crusade was later endorsed by Pope Urban II.

chess and the sale of female footwear, the latter being his brainwave for sweeping prostitution off the streets. In 1009, however, he went to the lengths of ordering the destruction of the Church of the Holy Sepulchre in Jerusalem. Christians everywhere went up in arms, but the danger of war receded when Hakim went off on one of his constitutional donkey rides at night and to everyone's relief failed to return. Christians rebuilt the church

Preceding pages: siege of Antioch, ancient capital of Syria. Left, Knights of the Holy Ghost embark for the Crusades. Above, Knights of St John charge the Saracens.

The First Crusade consisted of four separate feudal armies. They met up in Constantinople, captured Nicaea in June 1097 after a siege of six weeks and Antioch a year later. Nothing in Europe, however, had prepared the troops for conditions in the desert. Heavy suits of armour offered good protection in battle but were infernos in baking sunshine. Even worse, they were disgustingly impractical for occupants who, to a man, suffered from chronic dysentery. In the circumstances, the Crusaders did not reach Jerusalem until June 1099. The daunting defences seemed to shrink next to the exhilaration of at last being there. "When they heard the name of Jerusalem called," William of Tyre recorded, "they began to weep and fell on their knees, giving thanks to our Lord... Then they raised their hands in prayer to Heaven and, taking off their shoes, bowed down to the ground and kissed the earth." The thoughts of the engineers, though, were on an absence of timber for siege machines without which the city walls looked impregnable.

The solution to the engineers' dilemma was provided, bizarrely, by Tancred, a Norman knight whose dysentery and modesty forced him constantly "to dismount, go away from the group and find a hiding-place". Having withdrawn into a deep recess beneath a hollow rock on one such occasion,

Tancred spotted a large quantity of sawn timber. This windfall went into siege machines which breached the walls of Jerusalem on 15 July 1099.

Godfrey de Bouillon, Duke of Lorraine, was put onto the throne of the proclaimed "Latin Kingdom of Jerusalem" but with famous modesty declined to wear a crown where Jesus had worn thorns. He was thus succeeded by his brother Baldwin I, whose first priority was to secure an adequate coastline and build a line of inland fortresses which would give him mastery over Arab caravan routes. A line of fortresses was called for, but the sight and sound of construction

works warned Toghetekin of Damascus, who had his own ideas about cornering the revenue. In 1108, Toghetekin attacked a recently completed fortress east of Lake Tiberias. Its custodian, Gervase of Basoches, was put to death and his scalp, a shock of wavy white hair, paraded on a pole. Nevertheless, both Baldwin and Toghetekin had greater interests elsewhere, and it made sense to share the proceeds rather than cause them to dry up by turning the trade routes into a battleground. They agreed a truce in northern Transjordan which was supposed to last for 10 years.

It was characteristic of the times that a truce in northern Transjordan in no way inhibited Baldwin and Toghetekin from battling elsewhere. The country between the Dead Sea and the Gulf of Aqaba was important to both of them. For Toghetekin, it was a base from which to raid Judaea; for Baldwin, it was a soft underbelly which the Kingdom of Jerusalem needed to shore up against Egypt's desire to link up with the eastern Muslim world. While the sympathies of the Bedouin population lay with Damascus, the Christians had the support of Greek monasteries in the Idumaean wilderness. Crusaders and Damascenes clashed in Wadi Moussa, near Petra, but again they agreed on a tactical disengagement. The Damascenes withdrew, leaving Baldwin to smoke their Bedouin allies out of their caverns and carry off their flocks.

Baldwin decided in 1115 that the Idumaean country would have to be permanently occupied, and the necessary first step was to build a great castle at one of the few fertile spots, Shobak. He named the castle Montreal, the Royal Mountain, before pushing further south into unknown Arabia until he reached the Red Sea at Aqaba. While the Crusaders bathed their horses in the sea the local inhabitants took to their boats and fled. Baldwin fortified the town with one citadel and built a second on the little island of Jesirat Far'un, which the Franks called Le Graye, just offshore. With garrisons in both strongholds, the Franks dominated the roads to Arabia and Egypt, enabling them to raid caravans at their ease and effectively separating Egypt from the heartland of Islam.

On his return to Jerusalem, Baldwin busied himself administering his kingdom. The most important item of business was the foundation of Military Orders out of monks who since 1070 had looked after poor and sick pilgrims to Jerusalem. Monks based in a wing of the royal palace, the former Al-Aqsa Mosque in the Temple area, adopted a red cross on a white tunic as the insignia of their new order, the Knights Templar. Although the Military Orders owed allegiance to the Pope, they provided the kingdom with a welcome regular army of trained soldiers.

The creation of a regular army went some way towards relieving Baldwin's concern that the influx of Westerners was diluting the warrior and clerical ethos of the kingdom with bourgeois attitudes receptive to the indolent habits of the East. The imperfect truce of the country east and south of the Dead Sea as Muslim caravans found ways of circumventing Montreal, Baldwin's castle, and an increasing number of desert raiders slipped by to attack the coastal plain. It was thus with a view to tightening control along the Dead Sea that the great fortress of Kerak was built. Even so, there was no serious Frank colonisation of the area and the Bedouin tribes continued their traditional nomadic life.

Kerak was built on the crest of a hill, a twilight world of stone-vaulted chambers, halls, corridors and stables behind moated walls. The knights and their ladies lived in silken and fur-lined splendour, drinking the esteemed wine of Palestine out of jewelled

with Toghetekin in Transjordan, for example, required constant vigilance, and at one point the demarcation of a frontier line between their zones of influence involved cutting a castle in half so that by mutual consent it was useless. A fort built by Toghetekin near Jerash was considered altogether out of order and accordingly razed.

Baldwin's death symbolised the supplanting of the pioneer Crusaders by a second generation of newcomers from the West who wished to exercise more systematic control

Left, the first sight of Jerusalem. **Above**, a treaty is made with Saladin.

goblets when they were not riding out with dogs and hawks just as the Omayyads had from their desert castles.

To contemporary Western pilgrims, glimpses of Outremer life in castles like Kerak, to say nothing of Jerusalem, was shocking because of its luxury and licence. "We who had been occidentals have become orientals," Fulcher of Chartres observed. An Arab traveller noted approvingly that on being invited to dinner at the home of an elderly Outremer knight, he was assured that all meals were prepared by Egyptian women and pork never crossed the threshold.

From 1150 onwards, Jerusalem sent increasingly heated messages to the West reporting Muslim encroachment and predicting that another Crusade would soon be necessary, and it was at this point that a cruel young knight named Reynald de Chatillon entered the scene. More than any other single person, Reynald proved fatal to Christian Jerusalem, and tourists visiting Crusader sites in Jordan are likely to hear more of this wretched man than any other Crusader knight.

In November 1160, Reynald went north to plunder the seasonal movement of grazing herds from the mountains to the plain. Slowed down by a huge number of captured cattle, camels and horses, he was himself captured and carried away, bound on a camel, to gaol

Predictably, Reynald wrecked a hard-earned truce between Saladin and the Crusader states. He could not bear to see rich Muslim caravans passing quietly through his domain, and in the summer of 1181 he fell on a caravan on its way to Mecca and made off with its goods. Saladin retaliated by throwing into chains 1,500 Christian pilgrims forced to land in Egypt because of bad weather. Reynald still refused to return the pillaged merchandise and war was inevitable.

Undeterred by news that Saladin was marching north, Reynald launched a fleet (built with timber from the forests of Moab and tested on the Dead Sea) to raid sea-caravans on the Red Sea and to attack Mecca

in Aleppo. There he remained for 16 years.

During Reynald's unlamented absence, the Franks were confronted with their most formidable Muslim adversary to date – Saladin, a Kurdish mercenary who had risen to become vizier of Egypt in 1174. He captured most of Syria in the course of tightening the noose around the Crusader states. Aleppo remained independent, but only because a Frankish army came to its assistance and lifted Saladin's siege. Gumushtekin, the ruler of Aleppo, showed his gratitude by releasing all Christian prisoners from his dungeons. Among those led blinking into unfamiliar sunlight was Reynald de Chatillon.

itself. He captured Aqaba, which had been in Muslim hands since 1170, but the fortress on Ile de Graye held out. While Reynald remained with two of his ships to blockade the island, the rest of his fleet sailed merrily down the Red Sea. They caused havoc by plundering richly laden merchantmen from Aden and India, sinking a pilgrim ship heading for Jedda, setting fire to shipping in almost every port on the Arabian coast, and even sending a landing party ashore to pillage an undefended caravan that had come over the desert from the Nile Valley. The Muslim world was horrified, and even the Frankish princes were ashamed.

Saladin left Damascus in September 1183 with Reynald above all others in his sights. Reynald did not allow his reported advance to interfere with his plans for a gala wedding between his 17-year-old stepson, Humphrey of Toron, and Princess Isabella, aged 11. Distinguished guests, jugglers, dancers and musicians from all over the Christian East arrived at Kerak during the month of November. On 20 November, so too did Saladin.

The Muslim army went to work straight away. They attacked the lower town and managed to force an entrance. Reynald was able to escape back into the castle only because one of his knights single-handedly held the bridge over the moat until it could be destroyed behind him. Reynald repaired to the wedding celebrations which continued in the castle regardless. While rocks were hurled at the walls, the bridegroom's mother personally prepared a selection of tasty dishes which were sent to Saladin with her compliments. In return, he asked which tower the bridal couple were occupying and ordered his siege machines to give it a miss.

The walls of Kerak held out well against the pounding of Saladin's nine mangonels, and on 4 December reports of a Crusader force approaching past Jericho and Mount Nebo persuaded him to lift the siege and return to Damascus. The Franks entered in triumph and at last the wedding guests were free to leave. Saladin tried again the following year, but the result was the same. Under pressure of other business, it then suited both Franks and Saladin to declare a truce.

Peace meant that Muslim caravans could again travel unhindered through Frankish lands, and once again the sight of an enormous pot of gold passing slowly by from Egypt with only a token military escort was more than Reynald could stand. The merchants, their families and all their possessions were diverted into the castle at Kerak. Saladin exploded with rage, Reynald refused to make amends, and war began again.

Saladin assembled around a core of Mamlukes the largest army he had ever commanded. On 1 July 1187, he crossed the Jordan at Sennabra, took Tiberias in less than an hour, and led his army across the hills to Hattin, a village with pastures and plenty of water, where the road descended towards the lake. The Frankish army, including Reynald, approached Saladin's position along a road with no water. On the afternoon of 3 July they gained the plateau above Hattin, but heat and thirst had taken a grievous toll.

The Christians spent a miserable night, racked by thirst and the sound of prayers and songs from the Muslim camp below. To make matters worse, the Muslims set fire to the dry scrub covering the hillside, sending up gusts of choking smoke. The attack began at first light. Not a cat, according to the chronicler, could have slipped through the net. Many of the knights and infantry were slaughtered at once, but the survivors fought with desperate courage. Saladin did not ease the pressure until the Christian King Guy's red tent was overturned.

Saladin greeted the handful of survivors graciously. He seated Guy next to him and offered him a goblet of rose-water, iced with the snows of Mount Hermon. When Guy handed the goblet to the knight sitting next to him, Saladin had a quick word with his interpreter. Under the laws of Arab hospitality, food or drink given to a captive meant that his life was safe. "Tell the King," Saladin said, "he gave that man drink, not I." The man in question was Reynald de Chatillon. Saladin ran through a list of Reynald's crimes but there was not a sign of repentance. He ended the litany with a swipe of his sword, sending Reynald's head rolling. Jerusalem fell to Saladin on 2 October 1187, the news reaching European capitals within days.

A series of misguided Crusades then ensued. The Outremer Franks failed to regain Jerusalem or Transjordan, but they held on to coastal cities for most of the 13th century. They were sustained by the export of coastal products like sugar, taxes on transit trade, and dissension among Saladin's numerous descendants. In 1291, however, Al-Mansur Qalawun, a Mamluke, positioned a huge siege train against the walls of Acre, the main Christian stronghold on the coast, and took it after a desperate fight which saw every last defender killed. The usual cry for a Crusade was heard, but the European heads of state were now completely preoccupied by the Hundred Years' War between France and England. Religious warfare was far from over, but the saga of Crusaders in the Holy Land died in the dust of Acre after 194 years.

Left, Richard the Lionheart and the Master of the Knights of St John at Acre in 1191.

With the expulsion of the Crusaders at the end of the 13th century, Jordan was absorbed into an expanding Mamluke Empire whose foundations rested on the remarkable fact that Mamlukes were white slaves who not only approved of slavery but turned it into a kind of self-perpetuating, oligarchical meritocracy. On this improbable basis, their empire survived for nearly three centuries, and their legacy in Jordan, though modest, does not always get the attention it deserves. The Qalaat ar-Rabad at Ajlun is a fine example of Mamluke military architecture; the Montreal Crusader castle at Shobak is, as it stands, a Mamluke 14th-century restoration of the 12th-century Crusader original.

"Mamluke" means "belonging to", and it was applied in Saladin's day to young boys who were bought or captured abroad in order to be trained for the professional corps of the army. Experience led to a preference for children of the tough Circassian and Caucasian nomadic tribes, hence the tradition that Mamlukes were generally white, even if they adopted Islam and grew up speaking Arabic. Far removed from family and tribal ties, Mamlukes could be relied on to give their masters undivided loyalty.

Unlike domestic slaves, Mamlukes could not be sold on. Servitude was exclusive to the original purchaser, and when he died his Mamlukes were at liberty to market their mercenary services either as individuals or, in cooperation with other Mamlukes, as a private army. These private armies proliferated as Mamlukes grew rich on military plunder and bought their own Mamlukes.

Mamluke armies reached proportions which turned non-Mamlukes into subjects of the former slaves. Individual commanders then competed by any means to get to the top of the tree, which was an unadulterated military dictatorship. The position was not hereditary. Some Mamlukes were eunuchs, and in any case Mamlukes were not, by tradition or taste, the marrying kind. As long as the pool

of small boys was topped up, the system could in theory continue indefinitely. In fact, the Mamluke Empire lasted for nearly three centuries before Mamlukes were reduced to a military caste in Egypt. As such they were still around to fight Napoleon on the banks of the Nile, although the last of their number were massacred soon afterwards, in 1811.

The Mamluke era has been called "a combination of extreme corruption and savage cruelty with exquisite refinement in material civilisation and an admirable devotion to

art". Qalaat ar-Rabad, the aforementioned castle at Ajlun, was a link in the typically ingenious communications network by which the Mamlukes ran their empire from Cairo. Lofts in the castle contained pigeons ready to relay messages attached under their wings. At times they even carried air freight. The story is told of a Mamluke in Cairo who had a sudden craving for Lebanese cherries. The order went off by pigeon; three days later, 600 birds arrived with one cherry each in little silk bags attached to either leg.

Mamlukes could afford such luxuries because, partly through their hold on Jordan, they controlled lucrative trade routes. The

Preceding pages: inscription above the entrance to the Mamluke fort at Aqaba. **Left**, Mamlukes, the Circassian military caste. **Right**, Mamluke warrior dressed for battle.

Portuguese explorer Vasco da Gama eventually wrecked their prosperity by discovering the alternative sea route to India. Five years after his historic voyage in 1498, the Mamluke government in Egypt was bankrupt and unable to maintain an army capable of meeting the growing threat of the Ottoman Turks.

The end of Mamluke rule in Jordan drew nearer with the Ottoman victory over the Persians at Chaldiran in 1514. Ironically, Ottoman success depended on Janissaries who might have been modelled on the Mamlukes themselves. They, too, were foreign boys taken from their parents at a young age and trained as fighters. In their time they were the best infantry in the world. Salim the

Grim, whose grandfather Mehmed II captured Constantinople in 1453, occupied Jordan on behalf of the Ottomans in 1516.

Whereas the Mamlukes had ruled Jordan from Cairo and Damascus, the Ottomans attempted to do so from Constantinople several weeks distant. They saw waging war on Christendom as a pious duty, and it was best discharged going west into Europe. Although the likes of Suleiman the Magnificent built superb monuments in parts of the empire, the area east of the Jordan River was a neglected appendage, administered from Salt.

In the desert, the real rulers were Bedouin who lived on the proceeds of inter-tribal plunder and tolls exacted from travellers. As Lawrence observed of a later period, "camel-raiding parties, self-contained like ships, might cruise confidently along the enemy's cultivation-frontier, sure of unhindered retreat into their desert-element which the Turks could not explore". In the 1880s, the Ottomans entertained hopes of collecting taxes from the tribes, but they came to nothing.

Internationally speaking, the Ottomans could be forgiven for not knowing where they stood in the 19th century. Britain, Turkey's ally against Napoleon, immediately afterwards supported a Mamluke revolt against Turkish suzerainty in Egypt. The British navy sank the Turkish fleet in the interest of Greek independence in 1826, but Britain and Turkey were allies again in the next year against Russia. And so it went.

While relations with Britain were obviously unpredictable, there was at least a constant factor in enmity with Russia. From Catherine the Great onwards, Russian designs on Turkey's Balkan possessions were decked out as a latter-day Crusade: Christians liberating Orthodox believers from the Muslim yoke. The brunt was borne by Circassian Muslims, and it was in these circumstances that Turkey settled Muslim Circassian refugees in Jordan. They revitalised derelict Amman and, with a long tradition as Mamlukes and Janissaries, gravitated towards service in the Ottoman imperial army.

In 1900 the Sultan Abdul Hamid embarked on improving communications between Damascus and the Arabian provinces by building the Hejaz railway line to Medina. It followed the old pilgrim trail to Mecca and thus cut through the heart of Jordan. While it had previously suited Turkey to keep inter-tribal warfare bubbling, stability was now essential to protect the line. A Turkish governor appointed to Kerak in the interest of security was confronted by a tribal rebellion in 1910. This was partly an echo of convulsions in Istanbul following the Young Turk revolution two years earlier, and its successful suppression flattered to deceive. The empire's communications were long and brittle. Moreover, its subject peoples were restless – especially the Arabs.

Left, 19th-century pilgrims dressed for the pilgrimage to Mecca. **Right**, Ajlun Castle, a fine example of Mamluke architecture.

For Hussein, Sherif of Mecca, the apparently terminal condition of the Ottoman Empire, dubbed the "Sick Man of Europe" at the beginning of the 20th century, inspired the dream of a vast Arab confederacy which would recreate the past glory of the Abbasid Empire. He and his sons would rule it as the Hashemite line of the Prophet Mohammed. In February 1914 his second son, the Emir Abdullah, was sent to Cairo to speak to Lord Kitchener, the British Agent and Minister of War. The object of his visit was to find out

Abdullah's suggestion was then held up to the light for closer consideration. If Turkey's Arab subjects were in a rebellious mood, their Islamic loyalty to the Turkish Caliph could conceivably be compromised by a countermand from the Sherif of Mecca. Spiritually, if not temporally, he occupied the rung immediately below caliph. Hussein now procrastinated, holding out for guarantees of his Abbasid dream in return for military support. Before the matter was resolved, British forces suffered a humiliating evacu-

how Britain would react to an Arab revolt against Turkey. Kitchener was interested but, preoccupied with the possibility of war with Germany, non-commital.

Later that year, the Sultan of Turkey could feel British, Russian and French hands tightening around his throat and evoked his authority as Caliph, the spiritual head of Islam, to declare a *jihad* (holy war) on the European powers, in theory making it incumbent on Muslims everywhere to take up arms against them. As each of these powers had huge numbers of Muslim subjects – Britain alone, for example, ruled 70 million in India – the threat was not taken lightly.

ation from Gallipoli and pressure on Hussein increased accordingly.

On 5 June 1916, Ali and Feisal, the Sherif's first and third sons, raised the crimson banner of the Arab Revolt outside Medina. Some 30,000 Arabs assembled in response to Hussein's call. They were all volunteers and aged between 12 and 60.

But a siege of Medina, the terminus of the Hejaz railway from Damascus, was deliberately not pressed, or not pressed with any great conviction. "We must not take Medina," a British adviser mused. "The Turk was harmless there… We wanted him to stay at Medina, and every other distant place, in the largest numbers. Our ideal was to keep his railway just working, but only just, with the maximum of loss and discomfort."

The adviser in question was young T. E. Lawrence, the future "Lawrence of Arabia", and his rank of second-lieutenant belied his true status in British Army Intelligence. Two years earlier, he had posed as an archaeologist to survey a possible invasion route for the British army from Egypt to Damascus. According to his cover story, he was examining the "wilderness" in which Moses

out-of-the-way garrisons while the Arab irregulars fought their way up the Red Sea towards Aqaba, a port ideally placed to receive British arms shipments from Egypt. The positioning of Aqaba's defences presumed that an attack would come from the sea. Instead, Lawrence plotted a loop through the desert which would enable a small number of Arabs to take the Turks by surprise.

Abu al-Lissal had to be taken en route, a test of the fighting qualities of the Howeitat tribesmen and in particular Auda, their great

and the Israelites were obliged to spend 40 years after being denied use of the King's High-way by the Edomites. In 1916, Lawrence was given the responsibility of estimating the leadership qualities of Hussein's three sons and concluded that Feisal was the most promising.

Large numbers of Turkish troops were successfully tied down in Medina and other

Preceding pages: Arab forces on the march. <u>Far left</u>, Sherif Hussein ben Ali, the Emir of Mecca with Sir Ronald Storrs, who became the Governor of Jerusalem. <u>Left</u>, General Allenby. <u>Above</u>, a railway raiding party.

warrior chief. In 30 years of incessant warfare, he was reputed to have killed 75 men with his own hand, and he said he did not count Turks. He had been wounded 13 times and married 28 times. Surveying the Turkish positions in Abu al-Lissal, Lawrence mischievously remarked that from what he had seen of the Howeitat so far, they fired a lot of shots to hit very little. In *The Seven Pillars of Wisdom*, Lawrence described Auda's response. "Almost pale with rage, and trembling, he tore his head-cloth off and threw it on the ground beside me. Then he ran back up the hill like a madman, shouting to the men in his dreadful strained and rustling voice." Lawrence chased after him but all Auda would say was "Get your camel if you want to see the old man's work." The result was a furious downhill camel charge with Auda's men firing from the saddle. Lawrence, up front on his racing camel, shot out of the saddle when his mount tripped. The battle was already over by the time he had recovered his senses. Some 300 Turks were dead and 160 taken prisoner for the loss of two Howeitat killed.

Donning the uniforms of the dead Turks, the Arabs rode down the Negab Pass and across the Guweira plateau towards Aqaba. The surprise assault on the port from the landward side worked to perfection. Turkish

"sharpened to distraction by hope of success." As every fourth or fifth man was a sheikh who would recognise no other sheikh, Lawrence acted as referee. In the course of one operation lasting six days, he had to adjudicate on "twelve cases of assault with weapons, four camel-liftings, one marriage, two thefts, a divorce, fourteen feuds, two evil eyes, and a bewitchment".

The practicalities of war in Jordan had hardly changed since the days of the Crusades or even the Romans. Any spot of intrinsic strategic value invariably boasted some ancient fortification which was either occupied by Ottoman forces or used by Lawrence and his men between hit-and-run at-

outposts were thrown into panic and quick surrender. The Arab force raced through a sand-storm to capture Aqaba and triumphantly splash in the sea.

Victory at Aqaba wrapped up the Hejaz phase of the war. General Sir Edmund Allenby now led the British advance from Sinai to Syria and the Arab troops became his right wing.

While the Arab forces under Feisal's command began to resemble a regular army – they were joined by experienced Arab deserters from the Turkish army – Lawrence's guerrilla strike force revelled in unorthodoxy. "The men were a mad lot," Lawrence wrote,

tacks on the Hejaz railway line. Holed up at one point in the castle at Azraq (begun in AD 300, rebuilt in the 13th century), Lawrence learned "the full disadvantages of imprisonment within such gloomy ancient unmortared places". As the rain came in and the men shivered, "past and present flowed over us like an uneddying river. We dreamed ourselves into the spirit of the place; sieges and feasting, raids, murders, love-singing in the night."

On the other hand, the fall of Jerusalem to General Allenby's army could hardly have deviated further from historical precedents. The mayor first offered the keys of the city to a couple of British army mess cooks who had gone out looking for water and got lost. They didn't want them, nor did two sergeants who came ambling by. The mayor was pleased to find a private willing to accept them, and thus changed hands a prize washed in blood since biblical times.

In the meantime, the Arab army was pushing up through the corn-belt east of the Dead Sea, taking in succession Shobak (where they occupied the old Crusader fort of Montreal), Tafila, Kerak and Madaba. Numbers swelled as more tribes joined the rebellion, the army's backbone being stiffened by artillery and mechanised units. Lawrence had a Rolls-Royce armoured car, although he usu-

inviting for some of the Turkish soldiers, forcing the ladies to take to their heels. The experience brought Lawrence round to the conclusion that behind enemy lines he would in future discard Arab dress, male or female, in favour of British army uniform.

After the capture of Amman, the Arab force began their advance along the gorge of the Yarmouk River, covering the same ground where, in AD636, their ancestors had taken advantage of a sudden sandstorm to overrun the Byzantine army. The Arabs linked up with the British army, took Dir'a, and were then poised for their triumphant entry into Damascus.

By this time it was fairly obvious that

ally kept his Arab mode of dress. "If you can wear Arab kit when with the tribes," he advised his British colleagues, "you will acquire their trust and intimacy to a degree impossible in uniform. It is however dangerous and difficult…"

The use of native "kit" gained an extra dimension when Lawrence hired three gipsy women – and borrowed one of their dresses – for a reconnaissance of Amman. Their appearance in the town proved to be too

Left, General Allenby enters Jerusalem. **Above**, Paris Peace Conference, 1919, with Feisal in the centre and T.E. Lawrence to his right.

Hussein's Abbasid dream would not automatically be granted, so the proclamation in September 1918 of an Arab government under Feisal was an attempt to pre-empt the uncertainty. More powerful forces soon intervened, however, and it was out of the wreckage of the defeated Ottoman Empire and broken Arab dreams that Transjordan came into being.

Five years earlier it was Hussein's son Abdullah who had explored with Lord Kitchener the question of an Arab revolt. On its successful conclusion, it was agreed that Transjordan could be ruled under British tutelage by him.

Lawrence of Arabia – "T. E." (Thomas Edward) to his friends – was a legend before he was 30. In Arab dress, a golden dagger in his belt, Lawrence could mount a moving camel with a kind of pole-vault action using its tail. He was an expert shot with either hand, as useful with a pistol as the lightweight Lewis machine gun packed in a basket on his camel. He picked up a Distinguished Service Order and, but for a technicality, would probably have collected a Victoria Cross as well. Seen against a backdrop of endless desert dunes, the figure of Lawrence was an irresistible antidote to terrible tales of trench warfare on the Western Front.

In due course, the legend attracted iconoclasts, notably a biography by Richard Aldington which implied that Lawrence was pre-eminently a posturing, melodramatic homosexual. The balance swung back with the help of Peter O'Toole's candescent contact lenses in David Lean's 1962 film *Lawrence of Arabia*, but the biggest reassessment of Lawrence's character and motives came with the gradual unpeeling of official British secrets after the statutory 50 years. It seems that Lawrence was more closely attached and loyal to British Intelligence than had hitherto been suspected. His cause was less sincerely Arab independence than a vendetta against French imperial expansion. In his later private life there was, too, the curious business of masochistic rites with a hefty young Scot wielding the birch.

Lawrence was born in 1888 in Wales, the son of an Anglo-Irish landowner called Chapman who had left his wife and four daughters to elope with the girls' governess, Sarah Maden. Both changed their names to Lawrence but never married. Thomas Edward was the second of their four sons, a boy who walked with an unusually alert and brisk step. In conversation, he had the unsettling habit of fixing the other party with an unwavering gaze. A dose of mumps in adolescence probably stunted his growth: his 5 ft 5 inches looked less because of his disproportionately large head.

Left, T.E. Lawrence wearing his characteristic Arab dress in a portrait by Augustus John.

Young Lawrence apparently had some kind of premonition about his future. He toughened himself by sleeping on bare floorboards, bicycling till he dropped and going days without food. An interest in medieval castles led to study of famous battles and hence military strategy. Reflecting on his brilliant military career in the desert, Lawrence liked to say breezily that "of course" he had no army training and had only read "the usual schoolboy stuff". In reality, there was probably not an army general in Britain, let alone a schoolboy, who had trawled through all 25 volumes of Napoleon's dispatches between the textbook strategy of everyone from the Roman Procopius to Clausewitz and Foch.

In 1907, Lawrence won a scholarship to Oxford University and there fatefully caught the eye of D. G. Hogarth, an archaeologist, the Keeper of the Ashmolean Museum and, on the quiet, a British Intelligence expert on the Middle East. Interest in the region then focused on the tottering Ottoman Empire, a tantalising fruit for the European imperial powers. Moreover, the rapid development of the internal combustion engine had put a new complexion on potential oil in the Ottoman provinces. Germany stole a march on rivals by arranging to build a rail-link between Berlin and Baghdad – with an oil concession extending 17 km (12 miles) on either side of the line.

London saw the scheme as a threat to British India, the Suez Canal and its own oil interests. It was therefore not pure coincidence that, at Oxford, Hogarth made preparations for an archaeological expedition to a Hittite site at Carchemish. The site happened to overlook a camp where German engineers were supervising the construction of the Berlin-Baghdad railway. Among Hogarth's recruits was young Lawrence. At Hogarth's insistence, he took crash courses in Arabic and photography, acquiring an early example of a new gadget, the telephoto lens.

When the Carchemish dig closed for the hot summer months, Lawrence roamed farther afield with a young Arab who was known as Dahoum but is thought by some to have been the "S.A." to whom *The Seven*

Pillars of Wisdom was cryptically dedicated. It was on one of these excursions that Lawrence was arrested as a suspected deserter from the Turkish army and held prisoner. Calling at the ruined castle of Azrak during the Arab Revolt, Lawrence pointed out to his driver "what looked like the crumbled mouth of an old well". Visible scratch-marks on the inside were, he said, "some of my attempts to escape". A bribe to one of the guards eventually secured his release.

Lawrence's more notorious arrest interrupted a clandestine reconnaissance of Dir'a during the Revolt. His account in *Seven Pillars* of being led captive to Hajim Bey, the Turkish governor, in order to be beaten and

raped – by the guards if not successfully by the Bey himself – is so effusive in its language and detail that some scholars are inclined to make a connection with his masochistic tendencies in later life. Real, exaggerated or perhaps even imaginary, the Dir'a ordeal apparently contributed to subsequent mental and emotional problems which occasionally made Lawrence suicidal.

It seems that Lawrence was also haunted by having misled the Arabs, Feisal in particular, into believing that they were fighting for a single independent Arab state. He knew all along, it is now clear, about the Anglo-French Sykes-Picot plan to partition the Arab world into British and French spheres of influence. What he disliked most was allowing France any slice of the cake. On the point of deceiving the Arabs, he tried to console himself with the thought that a deception which helped to win the war against Germany and Turkey was better than losing the war.

Nevertheless, the strain of operating under misleading colours took its toll on Lawrence after the Paris Peace Conference. In the face of Zionist pressure at the conference for the creation of a Jewish national home in Palestine, Lawrence came round to thinking that all parties would best be served by a semi-autonomous Arab state under British protection – financed and advised by Zionists! When this was rejected and a large part of the still-born Arab state was given to France, Lawrence tried to disappear from public view by enrolling in the ranks of first the Royal Air Force (as "John Hume Ross") and afterwards of the Royal Tank Corps (as "Private T. E. Shaw").

It was during Lawrence's spell in the Tank Corps that he acquired a small cottage near his base and spun a fantastic yarn about a tyrannical "Old Man" who so disapproved of his past that he prescribed, by post, a series of stern birchings on Lawrence's bared buttocks. A gullible young Scot named John Bruce was prevailed upon to administer these corrective measures. On the other hand, Lawrence remained on good terms with the likes of Winston Churchill and made a genuine contribution to the design of a new generation of speedboat and a device which anticipated the hovercraft.

On 13 May 1935, Lawrence set out from Clouds Hill, his cottage, on some routine errands. He was travelling at moderate speed on his beloved Brough Superior motor-cycle when a cyclist wobbled into his path. In swerving to avoid him, Lawrence crashed and fractured his skull. He died six days later although rumour did its utmost to keep him alive – as a secret agent in World War II, as a recluse living in the international zone of Tangier, and so on. For his army of admirers, a simple motor accident was no way to end the legend.

Left, Lawrence (left) lands in Jerusalem; King Abdullah is on the right. Right, Lawrence astride his beloved motor-bike.

ENTER THE HASHEMITES

When Emir Abdullah arrived in Ma'an by rail from the Hejaz in 1920, Transjordan was teetering on the edge of chaos. The order that had been established by the Ottomans during the second half of the 19th century had broken down in World War I and the efforts of the Emir's brother Feisal to extend his authority from Damascus had been unsuccessful. In July 1920, Feisal's fledgling kingdom fell apart when he was driven out of Syria by the French, who now controlled the country in line with secret wartime agreements with Britain.

fluctuated from day to day. As the Lebanese historian, Kamal Salibi, has put it, "a state of utter lawlessness" prevailed in the countryside.

Within a very short time, Emir Abdullah had restored order and created a state where one had never existed before.

A grand plan: Transjordan was not Emir Abdullah's initial objective and it was never his final one. When he alighted from the train in Ma'an, he announced his intention of marching on Syria to regain it for the

The British, unsure of what to do with Transjordan, had recognised three separate governments, in Irbid, Salt and Kerak, and sent British advisers to each one. The government based in Salt was moderately successful because the local Christians and Circassians continued to pay their taxes and officials appointed by Feisal's short-lived kingdom in Damascus were able to maintain order. But the authority of the administrations in Irbid and Kerak was strictly limited and the country was a patchwork of local sheikhdoms. The Bedouin had begun to raid again and the line between desert and sown

Hashemites. From his point of view, the Arab Revolt had been fought to establish a broad Arab kingdom in the area under his family, which was uniquely qualified to rule on account of its descent from the Prophet Mohammed. Britain had promised to lend its support to this scenario in return for Hashemite backing in World War I.

However, Britain had made conflicting promises during the war. Under the secret Sykes-Picot agreement of 1916, the French were to get Syria and Lebanon and the British were to have Iraq and Palestine. A year later the Balfour Declaration revealed that the British were committed to establishing a

Jewish National Home in Palestine. This carve-up of the Middle East was later ratified by the League of Nations.

So while Emir Abdullah's announcement at the railway station in Ma'an accurately reflected his Arab Nationalist convictions, he must have known that the British would not support him against the French. The sad experience of his brother Feisal had made that clear. The Emir's real aim was to salvage something from the broken promises made by Britain in World War I.

Wary at first, the British quickly recognised that it was in their own interests to back Abdullah. The local administrations established by Feisal from Damascus were largely incompetent and discredited. Abdullah, with British help, would restore order in a territory for which they had no firm plans. Support for the Emir would also help to right the wrongs Britain had done the Hashemites after the Arab Revolt.

On 15 May 1923, therefore, the Emirate of Transjordan came into existence, on the un-

Transjordan, poor, undeveloped and lawless, had not been allocated to anyone in the Great Power land-grab and increasingly it must have seemed like a good starting-point for the Emir's wider ambitions. However, he had very little money and his army was small. His initial objectives therefore were to secure material and moral support from Britain and forge the turmoil that was Transjordan into a state.

Far left, a young Abdullah. **Left**, Abdullah and entourage. **Above**, Abdullah witnesses the establishment of the British mandate in Palestine, July 1920.

derstanding that the country would be closely supervised by Britain on the road to full independence.

The Emir and his aims were also attractive to many of the inhabitants of Transjordan. His Hashemite heritage served him well and he quickly developed links with local Bedouin tribes. Settled communities like the Christians and the Circassians, whose lives were disrupted by persisting lawlessness, also welcomed him. Abdullah consolidated these links by staying with Christian families, such as the Abu Jabers and Sukkars of Salt and with the Circassian Muslim al-Mufti family in Amman. He also lived and held court in

Bedouin-style encampments on the outskirts of Amman and in Shuneh in the Jordan Valley. The Emir's most important card, however, was that he controlled the only military force in the country. He was determined to establish his authority and restore law and order.

In spite of this determination, the Emir's task was not an easy one. As early as 1921, at Kura, near Irbid, a sheikh named Kulayb al-Shurayda led villagers against the Emir's tax collectors. A more serious threat was presented over the next two years by the Adwan Bedouin tribe, who were joined by educated locals from towns such as Irbid, Salt and Kerak.

command of a British army captain, Peake Pasha. Typically, Abdullah tried to solve both rebellions peacefully by personal intervention, and only when all else failed did he order his army into action. It is also a Hashemite hallmark that the leaders of the revolts were later pardoned.

In 1928, partly in response to widespread street demonstrations, a constitution was promulgated and a part-elected, part-appointed parliament was introduced. Its function was largely advisory, but it served the Emir's purpose of bringing Transjordanians into the system and he made sure that it carefully reflected the different constituencies in the country.

The Adwan protested against the favouritism shown to the Beni Sakhr tribe and the townsmen demanded a more democratic form of government. They also raised the slogans "Transjordan for the Transjordanians" and "foreigners out", reflecting their anger about the way power was being monopolised by Syrians, Hejazis and other Arabs employed by Emir Abdullah in line with his pan-Arab convictions.

If he was to survive and forge a state from Transjordan, the Emir had no alternative but to turn to the British. A new military force, which later became the Transjordanian army (the Arab Legion), was created under the

By the mid 1930s, the Emir Abdullah was able to claim: "We entered Transjordan to find four governments, each one separate from the other...Our first aim was to put the country together and secure its need to achieve unity. And here it is today...enjoying the complete unity to which sister countries in its neighbourhood still aspire."

On 22 March 1946, Transjordan secured its independence. Two months later the title Emir was changed to King and the country was renamed Jordan. Four years later Jordan absorbed the West Bank. Both King and country had come a long way since 1920. But at what cost?

Paying the price: To this day King Abdullah remains a controversial figure in the Arab world. The King's critics accuse him of serving British interests in the region to secure his own survival and aggrandisement. During World War II, Transjordan remained loyal to Britain and helped crush Arab nationalists in Iraq who saw Britain's difficulty as their opportunity.

Admirers of King Abdullah portray him as a pragmatic politician who was years ahead of his time. For them, he correctly evaluated the balance of power in the region from the beginning. Working within the constraints it imposed, he managed to carve out the state of Jordan as a first step towards a larger Arab

argue that the union of the East and West Banks was carried out at the request of the Palestinians themselves at a time when their leadership was in complete disarray.

King Abdullah's critics were in the vast majority during the late 1940s and '50s. Colonial rule was coming to an end throughout the region and governments which were tainted by association with the colonial powers were attacked everywhere. Increasingly, the call was for independence and Arab strength through unity.

The failure of the Arab states to prevent the loss of Palestine, the creation of Israel and the exodus of 700,000 Palestinians from their homeland in 1948 finally blew the lid

Kingdom. As a Hashemite, it is argued, he had more claim to Arab leadership than any other individual or ideology.

Foiled in Syria, the King had turned his attentions towards Palestine, where he recommended a conciliatory course rather than the "all or nothing" approach of then Palestinian leader, Haj Amin al-Husseini, the Mufti of Jerusalem. King Abdullah's admirers point out that had it not been for the Jordanian army in the 1948 war, all of Palestine would have been lost to Israel. They also

off the pot. After 1948, governments were overthrown one after the other in Syria, and the Prime Minister of Lebanon was assassinated in 1951. The next year, King Farouk of Egypt was removed from power by a group of army officers, among them Gamal Abdel Nasser.

It was against this turbulent background that King Abdullah proceeded on his regular journey to Al-Aqsa mosque in Jerusalem for the Friday prayer on 20 July 1951. On his way into the mosque, the King was shot dead by a Palestinian gunman, in the presence of his shocked grandson and eventual successor, Hussein.

Left, inspection of the Arab Legion. Above, the funeral of King Abdullah.

In the Arab world, Glubb Pasha, the British officer who set up Jordan's Desert Patrol and turned them into a crack fighting force, is much better known than Lawrence of Arabia, who is more famous elsewhere. Unlike Lawrence, who loved to "back into the limelight" and exaggerate his role, Glubb was a modest, self-effacing man, who should be measured by deeds instead of words. In fact, Glubb knew the Arabs in a way that Lawrence never did, as shown by his many books and his reputation among the Arabs and beyond.

John Bagot Glubb was born in 1897 into a military family – the son of an officer in the Royal Engineers and an Anglo-Irish mother – in an atmosphere of loyalty to the British Empire and confidence in the future. School at Cheltenham Boys' College led in turn to the Royal Military Academy at Woolwich where he began training as an officer cadet in the Royal Engineers in October 1914. Like many of his class and generation, his fear was that World War I would end before he could participate in it.

Glubb served on the Western Front for nearly three years without serious injury. In August 1917, however, he was badly wounded by shrapnel and part of his chin was blown off. The Bedouin would later nickname Glubb "Abu Hunaik" (father of the little jaw). In Jordan after 1940, he became known as Pasha, an honorary title awarded to senior Jordanian officials.

When the war ended in 1918, Glubb was only 21. Life in a peace-time army was not for him and when the call came for volunteers to serve in Mesopotamia, he jumped at the opportunity. A rebellion against British rule was raging there and experienced officers were needed urgently. So it was that a "very young man's desire for further adventures" led to a lifetime's service in the Arab world.

British policy in Iraq was aimed at securing control at minimum expense. Glubb's particular task was to pacify the desert and guard Iraq's borders against Bedouin raiding from the south. To this end, he developed the revolutionary idea of employing Bedouin to police themselves, setting "a thief to catch a thief" as one colonial official unfairly put it. British military thinking at the time was that it was impossible to organise the Bedouin tribes into a fighting force. Glubb proved them wrong with his small troop of camelmen and armoured cars and by using local spies. With some air support, his force played an important part in dissuading Wahhabi tribesmen, Muslim fundamentalist fighters from what is now Saudi Arabia, from mounting raids into Iraq.

Glubb developed his links and love for the Bedouin in his 10 years in Iraq. In the desert, even the most humble and ignorant knew him (as Abu Hunaik).

Under the 1930 Treaty of Friendship between Iraq and Britain, the number of British officials in Iraq was reduced by 60 percent. Glubb did not have to look around for a job, however, as his services were needed in the Emirate of Transjordan, where tribal raiding had become a serious problem. Employing the tactics that had served him so well in Iraq, he set up the Desert Patrol of the Arab Legion, as the British-officered Transjordanian army was known. Composed only of Bedouin, soldiers of the Desert Patrol had their own distinctive uniforms, comprised of a long khaki coat modelled on traditional Arab garb, a red belt and red and white Arab head-dress (*shimag*).

Within two years, Glubb and his Desert Patrol had brought Bedouin raiding to an end, and the Patrol had begun to evolve into the elite striking force of the Transjordanian army, completely loyal to its commander and the Emir Abdullah. As a result of increasing trouble in Palestine and World War II, the army was expanded and Bedouin were taken on in increasing numbers, comprising some 50 percent of the 7,200 total in 1947.

In recognition of his achievement, Glubb replaced Peake Pasha as commander of the Arab Legion in 1939.

Under Glubb's command, the Arab Legion served with distinction in Iraq and Syria during World War II. During the 1948 war against Israel, the Jordanian army's achievements far outstripped those of any other Arab fighting force. However, in these troubled times, Glubb's dual loyalties, to Britain (blamed by Arabs for the creation of Israel) and to Jordan came under strain.

Winds of change were blowing throughout the region. The cause of Arab nationalism, led by Gamal Abdel Nasser in Egypt, swept through the area. British policy exacerbated the situation. Increasingly, Glubb was castigated as British imperialism's chief agent in the Arab world.

When King Hussein came to the throne in 1953, he was barely 18 years old and he found it difficult to cope with Glubb's patronising and old-fashioned ways (Glubb was 56 in 1953). The King wanted to rule in his own country, and he was also sympathetic to calls for the Arabisation of the army, which was still dominated by British officers. Sadly, Glubb failed to recognise that his time had passed and to take strong hints that he should retire. In March 1956, he was summoned to the Prime Minister's office and told that the King no longer needed his services and that he should prepare to leave the country as soon as possible.

This was a rude awakening for a man who had served in Jordan for 26 years and who had intended to live out his life there. Glubb left the Prime Minister's office and went straight to his house to pack. His wife was surprised to see him back from work so early. Glubb movingly recalled that moment in his memoirs: "My dear," I said, "the King has dismissed me. We leave Jordan at seven o'clock tomorrow morning – and we shall never come back."

Glubb retired to the English countryside in Sussex. Because he had only a small pension

from the British government, he made his living by writing and lecturing. Over the next 28 years he wrote more than 22 books, most of them on Arab history, and spoke at meetings throughout Britain and the United States.

General Sir John Bagot Glubb died in England in 1986 after a long illness. King Hussein delivered the eulogy at his funeral in Westminster Abbey. The King said: "He was a down-to-earth soldier with a heart, a simple style of life and impeccable integrity, who performed quietly and unassumingly the duties entrusted to him by his second country, Jordan, at a crucial moment in its history and development."

Left, Glubb listens to the young King Hussein. **Right**, "father of the little jaw".

King Hussein's father, Talal, was the designated successor to the throne, but in a secret parliamentary session in 1952, he was deposed in favour of his eldest son on grounds of mental illness. As Crown Prince Hussein was not yet 18, a regency council was appointed until he reached the legal age of accession in May 1953.

While King Abdullah had created Jordan, it was his grandson's task to consolidate this achievement. Like his grandfather before him, King Hussein quickly came under at-

For most Arabs, Israel and the imperialist powers were their real enemies, not communism. A policy of "non-alignment" seemed to hold out the promise of real independence for the Arab states. In September 1955 the President of Egypt, Gamal Abdel Nasser, signed an arms deal with Czechoslovakia, signalling that his country would no longer be dependent on military supplies from the West.

Local and regional pressure forced King Hussein to recognise that Jordan was swim-

tack from Arab nationalist forces which were rampant in the 1940s and 1950s. Many Transjordanians were also caught up in the radical politics of the day.

Learning to cope with crises: The first few years of the young King's reign were characterised by riots, demonstrations and general unrest throughout the country. The crowds were protesting in particular against the special relationship with Britain. Matters came to a head in December 1955 as the King leaned towards joining the Baghdad Pact, a British-inspired bloc of countries designed to check the spread of communism into the Middle East.

ming against the historical tide. The young King also seems to have had some sympathy with trends in the region. Following the anti-Baghdad Pact riots of December 1955, the King promised free elections within a few months and in March 1956 he dismissed Glubb Pasha, the British commander of the Jordanian army. A promising young Jordanian officer, Ali Abu Nuwar, was appointed in his place. Despite these moves, the King faced the greatest threat to his throne so far in April of the following year.

"A plucky little King": A familiar combination of local and regional developments were the background to the crisis of April 1957.

The Jordanian elections of 1956 resulted in a radical parliament and government under the leadership of Suleiman Nabulsi. And at the end of the same year, Britain, France and Israel launched the Suez war against Egypt and Gamal Abdel Nasser. The tripartite aggression, as it is known in the Arab world, ended with the withdrawal of the three powers under American pressure. Arabs saw the war as a victory for Nasser and increasing support for him was coupled with a peak of anger against the old colonial powers, Brit-

as Saudi Arabia. He had also shown interest in the Eisenhower Doctrine recently announced by the United States, which promised to give aid to countries struggling against communism.

Differences between the Nabulsi cabinet and the King led to the resignation of the government on 10 April 1957, and the King struggled to form a new cabinet. In this general air of crisis, the new army Chief of Staff, Ali Abu Nuwar, attempted a military *coup d'état*. However, he was known for his

ain and France, and the new enemy, Israel.

In Jordan, differences between the King and the Nabulsi government on the distribution of power and regional and international alignments also reached new heights. Nabulsi and his supporters called for a stronger parliament and for closer links with radical Arab states like Egypt and Syria and with the Soviet Union and China. The King was determined to maintain his authority and leaned towards more conservative Arab states such

Preceding pages: King Hussein's Circassian guards. Left, a reign spanning over 40 years. Above, violence rocks Amman, September 1970.

sympathies with the Nabulsi government and had been under surveillance for some time; the attempt was nipped in the bud by Bedouin units loyal to the King.

Against this background, on 24 April, Nabulsi supporters met in Nablus in the West Bank (still part of Jordan at that time) and called for a general strike and street demonstrations against the regime. This was the last straw for the King and he decided to take firm action. He formed a new government under Ibrahim Hashem, a stalwart of the regime. Bedouin and other loyal troops took to the streets. Martial law and a countrywide curfew were imposed. All political parties were dissolved and leading opposition figures were arrested.

These moves were welcomed by the United States as a necessary step against encroaching communism. The American press carried articles about "the plucky little King". However, Egypt and Syria viciously attacked Jordan, and regionally trends seemed to be in their favour. The media in the West quickly changed their tune.

Only a matter of time: In 1958, Syria and Egypt announced the formation of the United Arab Republic. Feeling surrounded and threatened, King Hussein responded by uniting with his Hashemite cousins in Iraq. But in July 1958, there was a bloody coup in

Baghdad and the royal family was massacred. With radical Arab nationalism triumphant in Egypt, Syria and Iraq, observers predicted that it was "only a matter of time" before Jordan went the same way.

The next few months and years were difficult. In October 1958, the Syrian air force tried to force down a plane piloted by the King. In February 1959, General Sadeq al-Shara'a led another coup attempt, and then in August of the following year, one of the most promising of a new generation of politicians, Prime Minister Haza al-Majali, was assassinated.

However, the King stood fast and through a combination of tough security measures and enlightened policy, both he and the country survived. Democracy was laid to one side for the sake of stability. Jordan was ruled by a government appointed by and responsible to the King. The army was placed under the command of Habes al-Majali, an ultra-loyal supporter of the king, and the intelligence and internal security services were built up. At the same time, a booming economy and relatively free elections in 1961 encouraged increasing numbers of Jordanians to develop a stake in the country and the regime.

By 1964, the Arab regional situation had also improved from the King's perspective. The union between Egypt and Syria had broken up in acrimony in 1961 and attempts at unity between Iraq, Egypt and Syria in 1963 had also failed. Trends seemed to be in the direction of the more inclusive form of Arab unity favoured by the King. Meanwhile the need for united action had become even more pressing. Israel's recently announced national water plan threatened to deprive Jordan of the precious resource and intelligence reports revealed that Israel had developed an atomic bomb.

When Gamal Abdel Nasser called for an Arab summit to discuss these and other issues, King Hussein responded with alacrity. However, the meeting in Cairo in 1964 proved to be the peak of a slippery slope that led to the disastrous 1967 war with Israel.

The road to war: At the 1964 summit meeting it was felt that the Palestinian question was being forgotten by the world and that the Palestinians needed a focus for preserving their identity. The PLO was therefore created, but it was agreed that it should cooperate with Jordan. The summit also made a decision to avoid offensive action against Israel until the Arab states were ready for war. But there were other Palestinian organisations operating in the area, among them Yasser Arafat's Fatah. Their strategy was to take the war to Israel and provoke a conflict which they believed the Arab states would inevitably win. Increasingly, the PLO was pushed to take a similar stand.

Jordan clamped down on the PLO and Fatah, but towards the end of 1966 a number of raids against Israel managed to get through. Just as the King had anticipated, Israel's response was ferocious. Eighteen people were killed in a punitive attack against the West

Bank town of Samu'a on 13 November 1966.

Arab summit resolutions were forgotten in the ensuing wave of anger. Jordan was widely blamed for not arming villagers along the ceasefire line so that they could defend themselves against Israeli attack. Riots flared up in Jordan's major towns.

The Arab states descended into a destructive spiral of outbidding each other in actions against Israel. In April 1967, six Syrian warplanes were shot down by Israel. In May, partly in response to Jordanian accusations of cowardice, Nasser requested UN forces based in Sinai since the 1956 war to withdraw. He also closed the straits of Tiran, which controlled access to the Israeli port of

had lost a large part of its population and the source of 40 percent of its gross national product. The defeat also created the conditions for what was perhaps the greatest ever threat to the Hashemite Kingdom of Jordan.

Black September: The Jordanian army was badly mauled in the 1967 war and the King's authority was openly questioned in its wake. Economically, the country was in a mess and also had to provide for about 350,000 Palestinian refugees from the West Bank. In this climate, Palestinian guerrilla organisations (referred to collectively as the Palestinian Resistance) and political parties banned since 1957 began to operate above ground.

However, the undisciplined behaviour of

Eilat, to Israeli shipping. This was Israel's red line and its forces attacked the Arab states in June 1967.

Despite warnings of certain defeat from people like ex-Prime Minister Wasfi at-Tell, the King seems to have felt that win or lose he had little choice but to join the Arab side.

Within six days, the war was over and the Arabs had been utterly defeated. Jordan was the biggest loser, with Israeli forces in occupation of the West Bank. At a stroke, Jordan

Left, pro-Iraq demonstrations in Jordan during the 1990–91 Gulf crisis. **Right**, discussions with PLO chairman Yasser Arafat.

the Palestinian guerrillas in Jordan's towns and villages alienated many of their supporters. The radical leftist politics of the Popular Front for the Liberation of Palestine (PFLP) and the Democratic Front (PDFLP) frightened the Palestinian and Jordanian middle classes. Jordanians were particularly upset by the chauvinistic behaviour of most of the Palestinian organisations and increasingly took refuge in a new Jordanian nationalism.

By 1970, the Palestinian guerrillas had developed into "a state within a state" and posed an unacceptable challenge to the King's authority. In September 1970 (which Palestinians call "Black September"), the Jordanian army moved against the Resistance. The Arab states forced a ceasefire after 10 days of fighting in which more than 3,000 people were killed according to Palestinian estimates. By then, the army had the upper hand and by July 1971, the Resistance had been forced out of Jordan.

Boom time ahead: During the crisis years, an increasing number of citizens developed a stake in Jordan and a loyalty to King Hussein. As the country entered a more stable phase after 1970, political and economic factors accelerated this process. The 1970s and early 1980s were a boom time. The country benefited from the collapse of Lebanon and the oil boom in the Gulf. By the mid-1970s,

sented all Palestinians, even in the East Bank, there was no room for progress.

Meanwhile the King was coming under pressure to democratise the system in Jordan. He was accused of using the West Bank as an excuse for not holding elections. The *intifada*, which began in 1987, made it clear that the Palestinians of the West Bank looked to the PLO for leadership. More seriously, riots broke out in south Jordan, the heartland of Hashemite support, in April 1989.

King Hussein responded to these pressures. In 1984 the constitution was changed to permit elections without the participation of West Bankers. But the real breakthrough came in July 1988 when the King renounced

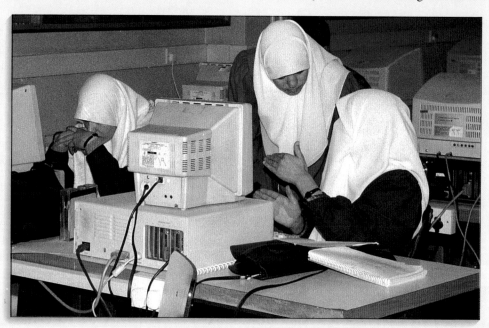

more than 28 percent of the population was working abroad. By 1980, Jordan had a 9 percent growth rate, an average $1,500 per capita income and no unemployment. Palestinians began to invest in real estate in Jordan, a tangible sign of their commitment.

However, the relationship between the PLO (which now represented all Palestinian organisations) and the Jordanian government continued to complicate matters. The two sides got together again towards the end of the 1970s, but efforts to reach a joint position on common problems broke up acrimoniously in 1986. While the King claimed the West Bank and the PLO argued that it repre-

claims to the West Bank. In return the PLO promised to keep out of Jordanian politics. These steps paved the way for a greater degree of democracy.

On 8 November 1989, Jordanians went to the polls in the first free elections since the 1950s. It was also a first for Jordanian women, who had been given the right to vote in 1974. A National Charter was later drawn up by a special commission which stressed national unity and equality of citizenship. A new law legalised political parties.

It was not all plain sailing over the next four years, however. The 1990–91 Gulf War placed King Hussein in a particularly difficult position. In the end, King Hussein's neutrality (he favoured a peaceful resolution of the problem from within the region) and Jordanian public opinion's outright support of Saddam Hussein cost Jordan vital aid and earnings from the Gulf states; on the plus side, however, the King's popularity within Jordan soared as a result of what was seen as a principled stand.

The rising influence of Islamicists was another problem and when, shortly before the 1993 elections, the King changed the electoral law, most observers agreed that this step was aimed at reducing the power of Islamic activists. The changes were criticised for reinforcing tribal and conservative vot-

democratic process demonstrates confidence in the future. It is difficult to overestimate the affection Jordan's citizens feel for their King. When he returned from treatment for cancer in the United States with a clean bill of health in 1992, most of the country came out on the streets to welcome him in a spontaneous outburst of relief and joy.

However, the event also raised uncomfortable questions about life after the King. Will the country survive his demise? Who will succeed him? Questions like these underestimate the achievements of King Hussein and his grandfather King Abdullah and the integrity of Jordan as a state. King Hussein himself once said, "Jordan did not begin with

ing patterns. There were then fears that the election would be cancelled because of the unexpected Palestinian-Israeli peace accord of September 1993. Nevertheless, in November 1993, 800,000 people went to the polls to vote for candidates from some 20 parties. It was widely agreed that the composition of the new parliament reflected the country's respect for the King and his call for moderation.

Future conditional?: Jordan is more stable and united than it has ever been and the

me, and it will not end with me." And Hashemite history suggests that the transition from King Hussein to his brother and designated successor, Crown Prince Hassan, will be smooth.

Those who look far ahead point to some uncertainty about who will succeed Prince Hassan (Hussein's or Hassan's son). Of greater importance is the future role of Jordan's friends in the world. Jordan is a poor country and much depends on the progress of peace in the Middle East. Jordan's future and that of the democratic process rest in the hope that its friends will support its endeavours in years to come.

Left, tradition and modernity comfortably coexist.
Above, campaigning in the 1993 elections.

Take the Bedouins of the biblical desert *wadis*, combine with the peasants and villagers of the hill towns and the Jordan Valley, add a dash of shrewd urban merchants and a sprinkling of Armenian artisans, Druze mountainmen, Circassian warriors and Bahai gentlemen and you begin to have some idea of Jordan's rich ethnic mix.

Lying east of the biblical river that gave the country its name, Jordan is as new as it is old, as rich as it is poor and as powerful as it is weak. It is new in its contemporary framework and composition and rich in its educated citizens. Boasting the highest number of university graduates per capita in the Arab world, for years Jordan received most of its financial capital through remittances from expatriates working in the wealthy Gulf states or in developing Arab countries such as Yemen, Oman and the Sudan.

Its cultural and ethnic multiplicity as well as its relatively flexible political and legal infrastructure has made it unique in the region. In few other countries have Muslim revisionists and Westernised Arabs lived side by side so peacefully. It is home to the full spectrum of Muslim and Christian sects, though the vast majority of people (over 90 percent) belong to the Sunni branch of Islam.

Conservative society: With no outlet to the sea except for the slim port of Aqaba, Jordan's people are conservative in nature and tradition – Jordanians are known even within the Arab world for their more introverted character. That said, they are among the most hospitable people on earth and *marhaba* and *ahlan wa-sahlan*, variations on "welcome", are constant refrains. Formalities and politeness are important social norms, especially with strangers (*franji* or *aganeb*), and intricately bound up with pride and self-esteem. When faced with camera-touting, shorts-clad foreigners, Jordanians are torn between their urge to welcome and the assault on their inherent conservatism.

Amman, the largest and most populated city in Jordan, containing more than 1½ million people, is one of the cleanest and most efficient cities in the Arab world. New arrivals at Queen Alia airport who are familiar with neighbouring Egypt are invariably struck by it being "not quite so oriental" and find in its particular brand of urbanism a sense of brisk progress and change.

But scratch the surface of this modern city, and you will find ancient pride and old allegiances. People born in Amman are still

likely to identify with the town from which their families originally came, and will claim they are from Salt, Jerusalem, Nablus or wherever rather than say they are from Amman. People also identify with the relationship that their forefathers had to the land and will refer to themselves as *fellahin*, meaning farmers or villagers; *Bedu*, meaning Bedouins or *madanieen*, meaning city folk.

A similar regard for heritage is found in the reverence paid to the Bedouin, often considered Jordan's indigenous inhabitants (although they are not the only ones). Clan word carries weight not only locally but also in Amman and six of the 80 seats in parliament are reserved for Bedouin leaders (which makes them over-represented).

Regional differences: Although Jordan is small, it has strong regional differences. Amman's neighbour, Salt, is traditionally hostile to outsiders, and its conservative character is mirrored by its picturesque Ottoman architecture and enclosing mountains, which protect the Saltis and bar the stranger. Many Saltis are senior government functionaries and ambassadors, and two of King Hussein's daughters are married to Saltis.

Known for their haughty pride and stubborn ways, Saltis are the butt of jokes throughout Jordan, as are the people of Tafilie (a region lying between Kerak and Petra), who

their cool heads and sharp tongues as well as the beauty of the women. Their cultural affiliation with Syria has influenced their social and political outlook since the 19th century. Natives of Irbid, Anjara and Ajlun were among the first Jordanians to join pan-Arab political parties in the 1930s. Irbid and Jerash have also witnessed a large influx of Palestinians, who play a major role in the political and cultural life of the north.

The most significant town in southern Jordan is Kerak, whose people are descendants of migrants from the West Bank town of Hebron who came to Kerak up to 400 years ago. Like the Hebronites, the Kerakis are often light-skinned and fair-haired, for many

have a similar reputation. A mixed community of indigenous pastoral Arabs and Kurdish settlers, Tafilie have numbered among them several controversial politicians and one former prime minister, whose nephew is married to another daughter of King Hussein.

Northerners – the residents of Jerash, the industrial town of Zerqa and the University city of Irbid – have a different history from Jordanians to the south. Influenced by Damascene culture and outlook, the northerners are considered shrewder and more business-oriented than southerners. They are frequently fairer and taller, characteristics betraying Syrian origins, and are known for

of them are descendants of Crusaders. For the most part they are Muslims, but the town also has one of the most prominent Christian communities in Jordan. Almost exclusively of Arab origin, they are believed to be one of the oldest Christian communities in the world.

Ma'an, another southern town and a major centre on the north-south trade route for several centuries, retains its links with transport to this day. Over 90 percent of its male population work in the transport sector. When the economy belly-flopped in 1989, Ma'an was the scene of anti-government riots (believed to have triggered democratic changes).

Work and wages: With unemployment running at about 15 percent, and, following the return of some 300,000 expatriates expelled from Kuwait in the wake the 1990–91 Gulf War, a surfeit of professional labour available, work is a question of getting what you can. Though self-employment is the dream of many Jordanians, around 50 percent of the workforce comprises government employees. Their salaries are low – a newly-qualified university graduated teacher and a less educated civil servant who has 10–15 years experience would both earn about £140 (US$210) a month while an assistant professor at the University of Jordan may get £450 ($670) – but come with a raft of benefits, such as cheap health care, subsidised shop-

survive on such salaries, especially when rent on even a small flat in a working-class area is about £60 ($90) a month. Many people, especially civil servants, therefore have two jobs, with writing, running a supermarket, acting as real estate agents or driving taxis being popular ways of moonlighting.

Home and family: Following the influx of expatriates in the aftermath of the Gulf War, rents in Amman tripled and as a result people preferred to take bank loans and buy homes rather than rent. Most families invest heavily in land and property, taking a large mortgage (and then spending up to 30 years to pay it off) or living in inconspicuous homes for years while saving for a villa or a grove of

ping facilities, plus a social security system and pension plan.

Private sector salaries are also fairly low, but again there are attractive fringe benefits. Bank clerks, for example, who earn around £150 ($225) a month, get 14-month salaries as well as health and social security benefits. And large companies often give employees a yearly bonus or gift reflecting profits.

Nonetheless, anyone going to even the smallest shopping centre in Jordan will immediately realise that no family can possibly

Left, home cooking. **Above**, a picnic in Seven Hills park, near Amman.

oranges or olives in the Jordan Valley. Homes are usually built so that further floors can be added when the sons marry, and three- or four-storey homes often contain extended families, who lunch and dine together. As well as solving the problem of affording another home, this family cohabitation takes care of possible social problems. Grandparents act as babysitters and daughters-in-law nurse aging parents. Daughters-in-law are also expected to do most of the cooking, although all female members of the family usually participate in kitchen-related duties. Men hardly ever share in domestic tasks.

The average Jordanian family still has

seven children, and the country has one of the highest birth rates in the world. Though Western-sponsored seminars on contraception are welcomed by the upper classes and condoms and the Pill are available without prescription, greater birth control is not part of government policy. The most that the government has done to encourage birth control is to run a TV campaign promoting breastfeeding – and thus birth spacing.

Family values are paramount and have dictated a particularly strict moral code, to which consecutive waves of political refugees used to a more liberal climate in Palestine, Lebanon and more recently Iraq have had to adapt. Prostitution rings have been invariably a crime of passion, especially in the countryside, and almost always to do with a woman flouting sexual taboos.

Superstitions and the coffee cup: Superstitions and belief in fate ("what is written") and the supernatural are rife. When someone falls sick or has an accident, it is believed to be a result of *rire* (jealousy) and *hassad* (envy). To dispel malevolence and the "evil eye" incense is burned, a lamb is offered to the poor and a blue medallion is worn or hung in the home or car. If a person is believed to be afflicted by the evil eye, he or she will be bombarded with incense and readings from the Holy Koran or Bible. Silver plaques with verses from holy books

closed down, public drunkenness is not tolerated, and gambling is against the law, something which the vast majority of Jordanians want to keep that way. (Plans by oil-rich Arabs to open a gambling casino in the mansion of a late uncle of King Hussein were stopped in their tracks by angry protest.) Even belly-dancing is confined to the large hotels, and the few existing night clubs are watched carefully by the internal police. "Good families" would never give the hand of their daughter in marriage to a man known to frequent such places.

As a consequence of this strict moral climate, Jordan has a low crime rate. Murder is promising fertility, luck, health and a long life guard the bedside of many a Jordanian child. Women consult "coffee ladies", who read their fortune or lack of it in coffee dregs.

Many of the superstitions are religion-related. When, a few years ago, a young Jordanian Christian lost the ability to walk, she swore that she would dress like the Virgin Mary for a year if God restored the use of her limbs. A few months later she was cured and sure enough she walked around in a long robe and wooden cross for a year.

Reported visions of the Virgin Mary are numerous. Muslims and Christians are known to flock to homes of *seiers* or "anointed ones", hoping to catch a glimpse of the most revered woman in Christendom and Islam.

A woman's place: Being a patriarchal society, even in the most educated and Westernised quarters, Jordan is very male-dominated. While two women held ministry portfolios in the early 1980s no woman has become a minister since. However, girls are given a mandatory primary education, most are encouraged to finish secondary school, and more than 50 percent of the 20,000 students at Amman's University of Jordan, established in the late 1950s, are female – even though an education in one of Jordan's three private universities costs about 800 JD (high-flying children from poor families are

single woman to the 80-member house of representatives, men, according to voting results in sexually segregated ballot boxes, were the most likely sex to vote for a female candidate.

But evidence of female submission is not found in veiled faces and modest dress (as recently as 1978 one had to look hard to find a veiled woman walking down the streets of Amman). The revival of the veil has more to do with personal quest and a rejection of Western imperialism. In the aftermath of the war in neighbouring Lebanon and the eight-year Iran-Iraq War people looked to religion in search of peace and tranquillity and many women turned away from the traditionally

eligible for scholarships).

Women have the same political rights as men and according to the Jordanian constitution they have "equal rights". However, a number of laws claiming the Koran as a reference undermine this constitution and liberal thinkers who have lobbied for years to change this anomaly have had no success.

Women are often the most conservative when it comes to changing the sexual imbalance. In the first free election held in three decades in 1989, which failed to elect a

flashy Arab style of dress to a more modest garb. In addition, this change accompanied an economic depression, which often made simple dress an economic necessity, especially for the less well-off.

Marriage, births and deaths: Of all the events that take place in a lifetime, weddings are the most important. In terms of cost they are second only to buying a home (a guest-list can number 200–2,000 people). Indeed men from the middle- and lower-income groups often don't marry until they reach their thirties (even though social and religious custom recommends marriage in the twenties) because they cannot afford to marry before. For

Left, the costly business of weddings. **Above**, Italian fashions for the privileged few.

similar reasons, polygamy has almost died out (less than 1 percent of marriages are polygamous) and rarely found at all in cities.

Most marriages are still the product of family introductions, if not outright matches made by female members of the bride's and/or groom's family, though upper-middle-class Jordanians usually court one another in a Western fashion and in few cases is marriage forced upon an unwilling couple. A suitable groom should have a respected family lineage, wealth, education, be of the same religion as the bride and should not have been married before. The same goes for the bride, but she must also be virtuous. The dowry can consist of presents for the bride's

family to the value of her weight in gold.

About one in five marriages ends in divorce, though in half of these cases it occurs during the period between the signing of the legal contract and consummation, when the couple are "preparing to live together". Though they are legally married and consummation can take place in this period, couples often wait until the night of the "wedding party", which can be a year later.

Divorce for women still carries a stigma and few divorcees remarry. Most divorcees return to their parental homes or to the home of their nearest living male relative, on whom they then depend for their economic sur-vival. Rarely do women live alone. The stigma attached to divorce is intended to discourage marriage breakdown. The motto Jordanian women raise their daughters on is "endurance is a necessary virtue."

Once married, a woman's primary role is to produce children. The birth of a child is the happiest of all occasions and money and time are invested in preparing for a birth. The mother's family is responsible for providing the child's first wardrobe and furniture. A male is almost always preferred as a first child and a woman with many sons is considered more powerful than a women who has mainly daughters. Jordanian mothers thus spoil sons more than daughters and as a result young girls tend to be independent at an earlier age. But children of both sexes are treasured – Jordanian fathers often adore their daughters and ply them with candies and toys – and parents of all social classes value their children's education. Unlike in other developing countries, child vendors are rarely found on the streets during school hours, though many descend upon cars in the afternoon to sell gum, kites or dishcloths.

Male circumcision is an important ritual among Muslim families. At one time it took place at the age of 13, usually at the hand of the local barber, and was followed by a big celebration. Today almost all baby boys are circumcised in a hospital soon after birth.

When a death occurs, the *aza* (condolence period), when respects are paid to the immediate family of the deceased, is another important ritual. It is considered essential to attend the *aza* of a neighbour or colleague and even of relations of neighbours, colleagues, business contacts and in-laws. It takes place in the home of the deceased or that of a relative. Men and women sit in separate rooms – sexual segregation is practised at both Muslim and Christian *azas* – and black, unsweetened Arabic coffee is served. For 40 days after a death, an *aza* is reopened every Monday and Thursday in the original house of the *aza*.

The colour of mourning in Jordan is black. This is contradictory to Islamic custom which dictates that mourning women wear white or beige. Black has been the colour of mourning in Jordan since Byzantine times.

Left, a sweet-toothed nation. **Right**, girls are still the unfavoured sex.

Many Jordanians travelling or living abroad often recount a similar tale: when they tell a foreign person that they come from Jordan, the response is often a polite blank, because the listener cannot quite place Jordan on the map; but when the Jordanian adds "Jordan… King Hussein", the response is always instant recognition.

A reputation for courage: When the young King Hussein assumed his constitutional duties on 2 May 1953, his love of flying, motor-cycling, water sports, racing-car driv-

home. Events in his personal life – in particular the tragic death of his third wife in a helicopter crash and his fourth marriage to Lisa Hallaby (Queen Noor), a beautiful Arab-American whom he met while she was working for Royal Jordanian Airlines in the mid-1970s – fuelled media interest.

But missing from this mediagenic mix are the two crucial factors that explain the domestic popularity of King Hussein and that also define the character of the whole royal family: the force of the king's own charisma,

ing, and amateur ham radio generated a rather adventurous and daring image in the Western press, which in time was complemented by an impressive political courage (he was well-known for incidents in the 1950s and 1960s such as personally confronting a column of troops that was on its way to the palace to seize power, or remaining at the controls of his plane and evading hostile aircraft that pursued him).

He was frequently portrayed as a dashing young Arab monarch who bridged the ways of the Orient and the Occident, who was as comfortable talking to presidents of NATO member states as to Bedouin tribal leaders at

and the personal role that the Royals play in the lives of ordinary Jordanians.

Family values: King Hussein recognised early on that despite the emotional appeal of mid-century pan-Arab ideological currents, the key to the survival of Jordan and its royal family was the improvement of people's daily living conditions, a sense of national and political identity, and hope and security for the future. While balancing the other factors that define modern Jordan – domestic security, pan-Arab ties, Islam, the conflict with Israel, and relations with international powers – the King tries to remain accessible to people and to receive their complaints, suggestions and personal requests, whether through formal gatherings or more informal encounters. Jordanians who feel they have been done an injustice often boast they will take their claim to the King personally – and in many cases, a request for a meeting with him or his aides gets a positive response. In their daily meetings with people, members of the royal family are constantly handed small slips of paper with personal petitions – for help with major problems, such as payment for an operation on a child or a reduction in the sentence of a jailed cousin, to more modest needs such as a pair of eyeglasses or a telephone line to a remote village. Each one of these petitions is read by staff at the royal court and acted on when possible.

Personal charisma is an important element of the King's success. He often goes up in a helicopter after a bad snowstorm or rainfall to check on hard-hit areas, and pays his personal condolences at the homes of Jordanians who have died in the line of duty. In 1992 during the worst snowfall of the century Crown Prince Hassan and some hardy guards and companions trekked out to check on the condition of isolated villages in the south that had been completely cut off.

Along with King Hussein, Queen Noor and the King's brother Crown Prince Hassan, some two dozen active adult princes and princesses carry out public activities. Several are pursuing careers in private business or the armed forces, and most provide patronage for, or actively participate in, the activities of charitable societies. Queen Noor personally instigated the Noor Al Hussein Foundation, focusing on children's and women's needs, the arts, rural development and the environment.

More and more frequently, royal family members can be seen leading charity walks or participating in sports and cultural activities, mixing easily and casually with what they always refer to as "the Jordanian family". King Hussein is very much at home behind the wheel of a rally car, Queen Noor sails and rides and is a regular competitor on

Left, the King and his fourth wife, Queen Noor. **Above**, Crown Prince Hassan.

the tennis courts, and Crown Prince Hassan's athletic abilities include taekwondo, karate, polo, scuba-diving and mountaineering.

The Crown Prince: Crown Prince Hassan, born in Amman in 1947 and married with four children, has been groomed to assume the position of king since his designation as Crown Prince in April 1965. He graduated with BA and MA degrees from Oxford, and has written a number of books on Middle Eastern legal and political issues. Alongside his official duties, he pursues a wide range of

scholarly and intellectual interests.

Both King Hussein and Crown Prince Hassan have spoken in recent years of fulfilling the goals of the Great Arab Revolt by transforming Jordan into a credible example of an Arab/Islamic state based on democratic pluralism and respect for human rights. It is a historical anomaly that a monarch who has reigned for over four decades should be the person driving democratisation. This reflects the King's awareness that the long-term stability and progress of Jordan must rely on the participation of the people rather than on military means, foreign aid, or the personal and political contacts of the monarch.

As amber streaks of dawn illuminate the lilac hills, Fatma, a willowy young shepherdess, herds her flock of sheep and goats out of their corral and down the hill to graze in the nearby valley. While the goats stop to nibble on sprigs of wild thyme, she rests on a boulder, pulls out a twisted roll of black goats' hair from the sack hanging on her wrist and begins to spin.

As she rolls the wooden spindle (*maghzal*) against her thigh to twist the fibres into yarn, Aisha, a 15-year-old girl from the neighbouring tent who accompanies Fatma each day, breaks into song as she darts after the strays who have wandered from the herd. Beco, their sheep dog, bounds after her, adding his voice to Aisha's.

As they follow the flock, the girls are joined by Aisha's mother, Eida, leading her donkey. Water containers are tied to the sides of the animal and one of Aisha's little sisters is perched on top. As Eida stops to fill her jerry cans from an artesian well, two water trucks drive up. Fatma quickly draws her long black *mandeel* across the lower half of her face and tucks it in at the side.

Back at their hillside encampment on the edge of a pine forest Kifaya, Fatma's mother, feeds and waters kid goats. Her long black dress, called a *thaub,* is embroidered with grapevines intertwined with pink and yellow flowers in a pattern from Ramallah. Fatma and Aisha wear the *madraga*, the full-length black gown of another cut worn by the Bedouin women of the East Bank of Jordan. The bright silky blouses of pink and fuchsia worn under their open-necked gowns show off the young women's olive skin and large black eyes.

In 10 days Kifaya will help her daughter set up a loom to weave the 24 skeins of goat hair she has spun since shearing time last spring. Fatma will then weave a long narrow strip to replace one of the seven needed to construct the goat-hair tent her family will pitch ready for the approaching winter at Rama near the Dead Sea.

Each June, when the heat of the Dead Sea

area becomes too intense for the animals, Fatma's family pack up their belongings, load them and their livestock on to two trucks, and move up to the central highlands for better pastures, water and a cooler climate. This summer the family has expanded to three tents – one for each of Fatma's two married brothers and one for her parents, herself and her younger siblings. In summer they use tents of burlap, which are cooler and lighter to transport than the black tent called "house of hair" that they leave in Rama.

On the home front: Once the herd has bedded down for a midday nap in the shade of some pines, the herdswomen return home to find Kifaya baking *shrak*, a Bedouin bread. She plucks a ball of dough off a tray and tosses it from one palm to the other until it becomes a large, paper-thin circle which she deftly throws over the hot *saj*, a wide metal bowl turned upside down on three stones over a fire of brush and goat dung. After just a few seconds the bread is golden-brown and she passes it to Fatma who tears off a piece and scoops up a bite of *rajouf*, a Bedouin dish made of lentils. A meal in itself, the bread is made from the wheat which is grown by the

Preceding pages: leaning on "the house of hair".
Left, face of the Bedu. **Right**, weaving.

family wherever they camp. It is eaten at breakfast and supper with tea or buttermilk.

After the meal, Fatma's brother loads sacks of manure on to a tractor and her mother fills a water trough for the kid goats. Meanwhile her father, known as Abu Musallam, meaning the father of Musallam (the name of his eldest son), opens a silver tobacco case, sprinkles *hisheh*, the locally grown tobacco on to a piece of cigarette paper, rolls it and lights it. Seated on a mattress stuffed with wool from their sheep, he is dressed in an ankle-length gown and the jacket of a grey wool suit. A flowing white *hatta*, folded into a triangle, is draped over his head and held down by a double ring of thick black cord

boards are piled high with provisions and *mansaf* pans (used to prepare the traditional Bedouin feast dish), a hot plate and a large blue barrel of flour occupy one corner. The top of the tent serves as a handy shelf where Kifaya keeps things out of the way, such as her pan for frying eggs and the gazelle's horn she uses to pack down the yarn when weaving. Clothes hang to dry from a guy-rope stretching from a tent pole to a stake in the ground. A white horse ridden by Fatma's brothers is tethered nearby.

"In spring we milk the sheep and goats twice a day. Every year we slaughter a large female goat and make the goatskin into a *si'n* (churn)," Fatma explains. Swung back and

called *aqal*. He sips *miramiya*, a sweet tea flavoured with sage.

At the edge of the courtyard between the tents are two goat pens and an oil drum filled with water. Chickens scurry about among feed sacks, troughs and jerry cans. A clay water pot, butane gas cylinder, large round pan for washing clothes and a kettle black from many fires all have their appointed place in the scene.

Inside, the tent is separated by a curtain. One side is for the men and their guests and the other is where the women carry out the housekeeping and cooking activities. On the women's side a bench and two low cup-

forth from a tripod of poles, this invaluable tool is used by the women to make *saman* (clarified butter) and cheese, some of which the family sells to buy fruit and vegetables. Also made in springtime are *jameed*, yoghurt cakes, which are spread on top of the tents to dry in the sun and used to make the sauce for *mansaf*.

In the evening, Fatma's family and neighbours follow the latest developments in a soap opera about a Jordanian Bedouin family on a TV set hooked up to a car battery.

Kifaya wears a tiny ring in her nose and, like the women on the television series, has two teeth capped with gold. Inside the sash tied around her waist, she carries her coin purse and her *kohl*, the eyeliner worn by Bedouin women and their babies for protection from the elements. Earrings of gold coins dangling from tiny chains add to Fatma's beauty. Aisha, who has learnt a lot of poetry from her grandparents, wears a gold ring delicately inscribed with a verse from the Koran on its coin-shaped surface.

Bedouin females are often given names whose meanings reflect their outdoor lives, such as "Ishbeh" (a blade of grass), "Shatwa" (a spring shower) and "Sharqiya" (the east wind that was blowing on the day she was born). Other names are more prosaic, for example "Kifaya" (meaning that's enough

lies who still move about in tents is a tiny fraction of the whole population. Yet wherever one goes the Bedouins' long narrow tents can be spotted from afar, pitched on remote mountainsides or on the outskirts of cities, whether they belong to the Sirhan tribe in the northeast, the Beni Sakhr in central Jordan, the Howeitat in the south, or to a Palestinian tribe from the Bir Sheba area in Wadi Arabah.

"The nomad by definition keeps moving from one place to the other, following grazing and sources of water," explains Dr Sabri Rbitat, a Jordanian sociologist. "The semi-nomadic people raise crops as well as livestock, and their settlement in villages is sea-

[girls]!), and others, such as Aisha, Fatma and Miriam, the name of Fatma's 10-month-old niece, have religious significance (in this case they are the names of the daughters of the Prophet).

Nomads no more?: There has been massive settlement of the Bedouin over the past decades, a development that reflects both a benevolent government and a desire for a more comfortable lifestyle. Though there are 10 major tribes in Jordan, the number of fami-

Portraits of the Bedouin: Left and right, a man in red and white check *keffiyeh*, tattooed woman near Petra, Adwan siblings.

sonal. After spending the winter in villages, they return in spring and summer to their nomadic lifestyle. As more of their numbers have settled to take advantage of the schools and clinics provided by the government in villages, towns and cities, the lines are no longer clear between urbanism, Bedouin and village life. Today it is individual families who move from place to place, not the tribe. Now the kids are in school and families want electricity. Their needs for life have increased. For them, the Bedouin life is no longer considered comfortable."

The affluent Bedu: But greater comfort and affluence is not merely a case of a Japanese pick-up truck replacing a camel, or the acquisition of a new refrigerator or TV set. There are examples of considerable wealth among the Bedu. Over in Abdoun, the most exclusive part of Amman, Sultan Abdul-Majeed al-Adwan, one of the leaders of his tribe, lives in a sumptuous villa. Hardly a day passes, however, when he isn't visited by members of the Adwan tribe who live in South Shuneh near the King Hussein bridge. They come to ask him a variety of favours, such as to lead their family delegation in the *jaha* (the asking of a bride's hand in marriage) or to represent them in an *atweh*, a tribal method of settling disputes between the members of two families.

Sultan's country residence is a 660-year-old castle, which he inherited from his forefathers, who built it on their lands overlooking the Sail Hisban canyon near Na'ur, and which he renovated in 1993. Lovingly furnished, it gathers together the relics of his family's past – the furniture his grandfather brought from Damascus for his grandmother and photographs of his father, grandfather, and great-grandfather, who lived during the heyday of tribal life in Jordan. On the wall of the courtyard hangs the *mansaf* tray last used by his father to serve 25 sheep on a bed of 200 kg (485 lb) of rice when he was visited by the young King Hussein in 1962.

Sultan explains some aspects of Bedouin etiquette: "If you are a guest, you should approach a tent from behind, and stop before entering, to be polite. The guest is welcome for three and a third days. Then he is no longer welcome. There is a saying that the serpent is more acceptable than the guest who overstays his visit. He is received as a prince, but when he is in the house he is more like a prisoner, he has to be so careful not to look at the wife or the daughter and to be on his best behaviour. When he leaves, they see him off like a minister. It would be impolite to see him off too well, as it would look like the host is glad to see him go!

"When one has many guests, the coffee (poured traditionally from an elegant coffee pot called a *dalleh*) is first offered to the main guest, while tea is offered from the right. If a guest wants more coffee, he holds out his tiny porcelain cup to be served again. Once he has had enough, he shakes it to indicate he wants no more.

"When eating the *mansaf* of bread, meat and rice, one must eat it with the right hand only, never using the left hand which is held behind the back. Everyone gathers around the tray and, without any utensils, uses their fingers to form a ball of rice and sauce into a mouth-sized bite. One should eat only from the food directly before them – not that in front of a neighbour. They should never touch the head of the sheep [placed in the centre of the *mansaf*], because it is the symbol of welcoming the guest.

"If the guest eats all the meat, rice or sauce, it shows he is greedy. If he finishes all the bread, it means the host wasn't as generous as he should have been, as bread is not expensive. So if the guest finishes the bread, it means the host didn't do the job. If he finishes the meat, sauce and rice, the shame is on the guest.

"It used to be that if a man wanted to get engaged to a young woman from outside the tribe, even if the parents agreed, the cousin had priority, even on her wedding day. There was a saying that the cousin brings down the bride from the top of the horse on the bride's way to her wedding. This used to cause a lot of trouble. Now marriages take place without this happening."

Sultan explains the subtle web of etiquette surrounding betrothals and weddings: "The *jaha*, the asking of a bride's hand, is governed by strict protocol. Before going to the bride's family the family of the groom enlists the support of the most respected members of the community. The father of the bride or the head of her tribe welcomes the visitors and one cup of coffee only is poured for the main guest. Determining the identity of this important person is complicated by elaborate politesse. The cup is passed around until someone accepts, with people saying, 'No, it should be so-and-so, not me' and 'No, it's for someone else.' The one who finally accepts the 'cup of the *jaha*' doesn't drink it but begins a speech: 'In the name of God the all-merciful and compassionate, we are the *jaha*. We would like to be your in-laws. We want

eager to be married. They bathed her and put red henna on her palms and the soles of her feet and then took her with them.

"Then the official ceremonial lunch is held on Friday, the day after they have been married. The women are separate and the men sit under a black goat-hair tent. Guests bring a gift (*nuqout*). This used to be a sheep, rice or money. Now it could be a TV, silver or a piece of crystal. They sing and praise the bride and say the groom is a brave man and very generous and that his father is a leader and that he comes from a good strong tribe. Some still celebrate for three nights before the wedding with singing and gunfire, building up to a crescendo the night they bring the

your daughter for our son…' He must never mention the name of the girl. Then he praises the girl's tribe and tells what good friends they are of her tribe or clan.

"In the villages, a group of women go on Thursday afternoon to fetch the bride from her tribe. They used to go on 100 to 200 horses. When the bride saw them coming, she was supposed to run away so they wouldn't make snide comments that she was

Left, Adwan father and son in front of the massive ancestral *mansaf* pan, which was used during a visit from King Hussein in 1962. **Above**, baking *shrak*, the tasty Bedouin bread.

bride. A week later she pays a visit to her parents and takes them a sheep, rice, sugar and clarified butter."

Whether Jordan's tribespeople live in the exclusive quarter of Abdoun in Amman or are camped in remote parts of the desert, whether they originate from a nomadic tribe or, like Sultan, hail from one of what he describes as the "Arab tribes", who were traditionally more settled, living in the same place each summer and another every winter, they still practise to varying degrees some of these customs – and many more. The Bedouin are an essential part of Jordan's rich cultural heritage.

At Umm Qais in the north of Jordan, the site of a Graeco-Roman town, there is a great view over the Sea of Galilee and Tiberias on the other side of the ceasefire line between Israel and Jordan. Cars from many different Arab states – Saudi Arabia, Syria, Iraq and the Gulf states – are parked here nearly every day; they belong to diaspora Palestinians returning to see what was once their homeland. It is a sombre place and tourists often miss the sadness in their haste to view the ruins and eat at Umm Qais's restaurant.

In 1947 there were about 1.3 million Palestinian Arabs living under the British Mandate in Palestine. Two years later, more than 700,000 of them were dispersed through the Middle East, driven from their homes by Israeli forces or in desperate flight from the fighting. When Israel occupied the West Bank in 1967, the last part of historical Palestine, 150,000 existing refugees moved on yet again and another 300,000 Palestinians became refugees for the first time.

Most of these Palestinians settled in Jordan, where they were granted Jordanian citizenship. Some are allowed to visit their homeland – if they have a relative there and the Israeli authorities permit it – but only a small fraction have been given leave by Israel to return to live.

The imprint of Palestine is everywhere in Jordan, but especially in the towns. It is in the accents, the names of shops – the Jerusalem restaurant, the Ramle butcher's – and the crowded refugee camps of Wahdat and Jebel al-Hussein, which have developed into poor neighbourhoods like others in Amman. Palestine is also present in the posh Abdoun area of the capital, amidst the fine mansions funded by money made in the Gulf states.

Many Palestinians have made good. Eager to improve their condition and retrieve what they have lost, they have the highest university graduate rate in the Arab world. Palestinians are to be found at the highest levels in every Arab state and they have contributed enormously to all facets of life in the region.

Preceding pages: Palestinian embroidery. Left, Palestinian man in characteristic black and white *keffiyeh*. Right, Palestinian bakery in Amman.

In Jordan, Palestinians dominate the private sector. One economist estimated that "the proportion of Palestinians in banking is 60–65 percent, in retailing 65–70 percent and in wholesale and import-export 75–80 percent. Only in the government and the army does the proportion fall below 50 percent." The needy among about 1 million Palestinians classified as refugees in Jordan are provided for by the United Nations Relief and Works Agency (UNRWA), which has helped relieve Jordan of the enormous bur-

den. UNRWA has also made a substantial contribution to Jordan's economy.

However, the Palestinian presence in Jordan has also created political problems and this is reflected in the controversy about how many Palestinians there are in this country. Some analysts put the proportion of Palestinians (those who arrived in 1948 and after) at 65 percent of the population. Others claim the number is as low as 35 percent.

In fact, it is impossible to draw sharp lines between who is a Jordanian and who is a Palestinian. Indeed, until relatively recently, the issue would never have been raised.

Under the Ottomans who ruled from the

15th century onwards, there was unrestricted movement throughout an empire that stretched from North Africa to modern Iraq and from Turkey to the Yemen. Links between the east and west banks of the Jordan River were particularly close. Salt had strong socio-economic ties with Nablus, Nazareth and Jerusalem. Kerak was close to Hebron, and in the north, Irbid looked to Beisan, Tiberias and the Galilee.

Famous names: Some of the most famous names in today's Jordan reflect the strength and continuity of these links over hundreds of years. In 1993, the Prime Minister was a Majali, most of whose family migrated from Hebron to Kerak centuries ago. The Nabulsi

family have also played an important role in Jordan's modern history. They moved from Nablus to Salt in the late 19th century and still have relatives in the West Bank.

This close association survived the British Mandate. The Palestinians had more access to education than those east of the Jordan River and many of them found jobs in Emir Abdullah's administration. Peasants on both side of the river continued to cross back and forth in pursuit of seasonal labour.

However, the division of the Middle East into spheres of influence by Britain and France, the creation of the Emirate of Transjordan and Britain's commitment to establishing a Jewish national home in Palestine introduced new realities that contained the seeds of conflict.

Differences appeared and grew wider. Emir Abdullah's primary purpose was to sustain and develop his Emirate. The main objective of the Palestinian leader, Haj Amin al-Husseini, the Mufti of Jerusalem, was to foil British plans to turn Palestine into a Jewish national home. The Mufti adopted a firm anti-Zionist, anti-British stand, while Emir Abdullah recommended a conciliatory line.

The decimation of the Palestinian national movement in the 1936–39 rebellion against the British, and the 1948 war with Israel, permitted the Emir to gather his Palestinian allies in Jericho in 1948, where they agreed to the absorption of areas still held by the Jordanian army (the West Bank) into Jordan. Familiar problems persisted, however. Emir Abdullah and King Hussein concentrated on the consolidation of the Hashemite Kingdom, while most Palestinians wanted to liberate Palestine and return home.

In the 1950s and early 1960s a new Palestinian leadership emerged that eventually coalesced in the form of the PLO, which came into being in 1964. Palestinians everywhere saw this as a welcome sign that they were once more taking charge of their own destiny. The Jordanian government, however, feared the effects of "a dual authority" on its efforts to forge a state out of the Palestinians and Jordanians who made up Jordanian society.

The disastrous defeat in the 1967 war against Israel brought these differences to a head. In the post-war vacuum, Palestinian guerrillas developed their strength in Jordan and soon constituted "a state within a state". In September 1970 all-out conflict broke out between them and the revitalised Jordanian army. By July 1971, King Hussein's forces had driven the guerrillas out of the country.

The PLO's sole right to represent all Palestinians was upheld by the 1974 Rabat Arab Summit. This threatened Hussein's efforts to secure national unity in Jordan and his claim to the West Bank. The PLO and the Jordanian government agreed to meet again at the end of the 1970s, but failed to find a compromise. Successive talks broke up acrimoniously in 1986. The breakthrough came in July 1988, eight months after the outbreak of the *Intifada* uprising in the West Bank and Gaza against

Israeli occupation. Persuaded by clear popular support for the PLO in the Occupied Territories, the King renounced his claims to the West Bank. In return, the PLO promised to stay out of politics on the East Bank.

On the ground today: The question of who is a Palestinian and who is a Jordanian remains one of the most sensitive issues in today's Jordan. Many Palestinians claim that they face discrimination in the army and other sectors of public life. Many Jordanians complain about Palestinian control of the private sector and about how the Palestinian-Israeli conflict dominates their lives.

In general, however, most citizens of Jordan recognise that life under King Hussein is

ever, many Palestinians who arrived in Jordan in 1948 have developed roots here over the last 45 years. The same is true, if to a lesser extent, of those who came in 1967. Businessmen and other well-off Palestinians have a stake in Jordan, as the million-dinar mansions in Abdoun testify. The middle classes have also benefited from the economic booms and even less wealthy Palestinians and refugees would think twice about sacrificing what they have in Jordan for what is currently on offer elsewhere.

Some Jordanian nationalists have called on Palestinians to make a choice between their Palestinian and Jordanian identities. They complain that "the Palestinians want to

better than the alternatives, and all want to put paid to the threat posed by the slogan "Jordan is Palestine", raised by Israelis opposed to the creation of a Palestinian state. The fighting between Palestinian and Jordanian forces in September 1970 showed what efforts to implement such a cynical slogan could lead to. The current democratic process shows both faith in the future and determination to make Jordan work.

Among most Palestinians, the commitment to Palestine remains very strong. How-

Left, Baqa'a refugee camp. **Above left**, sweet seller in Baqa'a. **Right**, aubergine seller.

have it both ways – to retain their rights and privileges in Jordan without jeopardising their national rights in Palestine". However, King Hussein has made it clear that there is no question of asking Palestinians to make such choices at this stage.

If a Palestinian state becomes a reality, Palestinians may choose between Palestine and Jordan. Perhaps some kind of confederation can be worked out between the two states which reflects the historical links between the two banks of the river. If, however, the final status of the West Bank and Gaza remains ambiguous, there may be problems ahead for Jordan and the region as a whole.

Spirits were high as the motley group of joggers gathered under a grove of oaks. A Canadian oilman and a British expert from the World Bank helped a young Jordanian doctor in shorts unload three large tubs of ice and beverages from vehicles, while others unloaded barbecue grills. More cars pulled up, letting out men and women of all ages. It was 6pm and Monday – time for the weekly run of the Hashemite Hash House Harriers. The meeting place for today's run was View Point, a remote spot 15 km (9 miles) outside Amman overlooking the the Dead Sea.

The 70 or so runners assembling at the start comprised a rich assortment of nationalities. Expats from Lebanon, Canada, Switzerland, Iraq, Germany, France, America, Britain and Algeria were joined by native Jordanians. Several sported T-shirts advertising the 330-km (205-mile) Hash relay race from Amman to Aqaba and a 53-km (33-mile) run which 50 members had made to the Dead Sea.

But for many of the runners serious exercise comes second to social intercourse. At the end of this particular run the hungriest put their meat over the hot coals while the others gathered under the trees to toast those who had distinguished themselves and punish those who had not. "Down! Down!" they shouted, as a chap guilty of taking a short cut was made to drink out of his tennis shoe. Amid the din, Maha, a Jordanian MBA graduate, passed out maps to her family's weekend cottage where they were due to meet the following week to race up and down the slopes above the King Talal Dam and toss each other into the pool with their clothes on – a "Hash bash" to bid farewell to departing expat members.

American women and British ladies: A week later another stream of cars followed the same route to View Point. But this time they passed the oaks, continued around the mountain and drove through the gates of an elegant estate. The passengers were women, and they were dressed up. The American Women's Club of Amman had been invited for a

Preceding pages: the Hashemite Hash House Harriers in action. **Right**, home in the hills.

"newcomers' tea" to the palatial home of an American married to a Jordanian.

Though some of the 50 women, many newly settled in Jordan, were having second thoughts about driving so far from "civilisation", their qualms were allayed the moment they reached Rosemary Bdeir's new house perched above the ancient palace of Iraq al-Amir in Wadi as-Seer.

"This beats California!" exclaimed the American wife of an Egyptian posted in Jordan, as she crossed a courtyard complete with swimming pool and colonnade framing perfect views. After sunning themselves on the terrace, the women were invited inside for a briefing on Muslim and Christian cus-

America and Asia. Though social acitivities are high on the agenda – Hallowe'en and Christmas parties for members' children, a Thanksgiving luncheon in November, a Christmas bazaar and a Valentine's Day dance in February – pleasure mixes with serious voluntary work. The community action committee takes members all over Jordan to assess the needs of projects they want to support, from a sanatorium run by an Australian nurse in Mafraq in the north, to a TB clinic being built by a 78-year-old US woman doctor in Ras an-Naqab in the south.

While the AWA is the largest, oldest and best known, women's groups of other nationalities are also active in Amman. The

toms in Jordan, followed by a feast of Arab cuisine. Then they got down to the serious business of visiting. They heard about a Japanese flower-arranging demonstration organised by the Italian Ladies, the need for volunteers at Al-Hussein Society for the Handicapped, the YMCA's search for singers for their Christmas concert, and got first chance to buy tickets for a talent show.

The 30-year-old American Women's Club (AWA) meets every month in the red-carpeted ballroom of Amman's Marriott Hotel. Originally limited to Americans, its membership now includes Jordanians, Europeans, Canadians, and women from Latin

British Ladies, for example, meet each month at the Forte Grand Hotel. They, too, help a number of Jordanian charitable societies, including Father Andrew's School for the Deaf in Salt, and invite speakers, hold luncheons, arrange children's parties and organise carolling at Christmas.

A corner of a foreign field: Formed to prevent their members from feeling isolated in a foreign culture, such clubs are also about creating a corner in expat lives that is forever England/America/Germany or wherever. Every year some of the larger embassies put on a "national week" at one of the hotels with traditional menus, films and events, and festivals and customs of various countries punctuate the social calendar. The Scandinavian Ladies, for example, always gather in a member's home on 13 December to celebrate Santa Lucia and the longest day of the year, with special cakes and with the children wearing wreaths of candles on their heads. On a more regular basis, the German Ladies, famous for their Christmas bazaar, hold a monthly *kaffee klatch* at Amman's Marriott Hotel, while the Greek and the Italian Ladies both hold equivalent occasions at the Philadelphia. The annual three-day Oktoberfest at the Marriott – with barrels of beer and sausages flown in from Germany – is as popular in Amman as the original is in Bavaria.

rope, Korea or Japan, they tend to be men sent to Jordan on 2–3 year contracts and their accompanying family. The majority of women married to Jordanians are American, British or European (with a smaller number from Eastern Europe and Russia), who have invariably met their spouse while he was abroad studying. While most of them are housewives, a number have forged careers in Jordan, as doctors, nurses, teachers, engineers and radiologists. Working expat women include the consuls of Iceland and Nicaragua, the directors of AmidEast and Save the Children, masseuses at the Marriott Hotel and a concert pianist at the Forte Grand. Whether professionals or housewives, these

There is also a certain amount of friendly sparring between the nationalities. The popular Wednesday Quiz Night at the Intercontinental Pub pits the wits of one nationality against the other. While first and second prize might just cover the bar bill, people really come for the pleasure of beating the Aussie table, the Yankees, or the Jordanian gang from International Traders.

Who are the expats? Most of the expat community in Jordan resides in Amman. Whether hailing from America, Canada, Britain, Eu-

Left, playing Little League soccer. **Above**, golf "on the brown".

women serve as a bridge between the expat and Jordanian communities.

Less visible to the average visitor, but of major importance to the Jordanian economy, is another group of expats who are not permitted to bring their families – those doing the low-paid jobs at the other end of the scale. These include some 300,000 Egyptian labourers and tens of thousands of Filipino and Sri Lankan women working as domestics on two-year contracts.

While women lunch and hold charity fashion shows, the social pow-wows of male expatriates tend to revolve around sport, which is all the more appealing in the sunny,

Mediterranean climate. The tennis courts and swimming pools of the Automobile Club, the Orthodox Club, the five-star hotels, and Sports City are used by expats and Jordanians alike, as is a nine-hole golf course, located 15 minutes outside Amman off the airport road. Men and women play on the "brown" rather than the "green", and while it isn't always easy to find balls in the scrub brush and rough terrain, the annual fees – JD200 – are among the most reasonable in the world. Members organise frequent tournaments with hotel-catered lunches under long black Bedouin tents overlooking Amman National Park. Not far from the golf course stables offer riding lessons and, for

some expats, stabling for private horses.

Whether it's the season for soccer in the autumn, basketball in winter, or baseball in the spring, the Amman Little League is a big favourite. Boys and girls between the ages of 5 and 15 take care not to miss the deadline for signing up for try-outs for the mixed sex teams, while parents volunteer to be coaches, "team moms", board members and commissioners. Friday is match day, when the children dress in full uniform, provided by sponsoring companies, and the bleachers resound with multilingual cheering and shouting.

Arts and culture: Like expatriate communities everywhere, Amman's expats are keen supporters of the performing arts. They have put on some of the best plays in town, from *Oliver Twist* to *Charlie Brown*, and the British Airways Players put on dinner-theatre performances in local hotel ballrooms several times a year. But drama is not self-made for want of professional entertainment. International theatre companies include Amman on their tours, and the plush red chairs of the Royal Cultural Centre are frequently filled with theatre-goers of all nationalities attending plays, concerts and sometimes ballets and opera. Larger-scale performances are held at the Royal Palace of Culture.

Nor can Jordan's expats complain about a lack of visual arts. Over the past decade, there have been more art exhibitions per capita in Amman than in any European capital. The ALIA, the Orfeli and the Badia galleries, the Royal Cultural Centre, the National Art Gallery and the Darat al-Funun (Little House of the Arts) put on so many art, sculpture and photographic exhibitions that the *Jordan Times* runs a daily list to keep readers abreast. Since the 1990–91 Gulf War, many well-known Iraqi artists have enriched local art circles.

Diary highlights: Some of the most well-attended events are those that raise funds for charity. The May Fair held each year by the British Ladies in the garden of the ambassador's residence is not to be missed. Medical Aid to Palestine is noted for its walks starting in Amman and ending at a lively country fair. Local handicraft exhibitions are held periodically, the most eagerly awaited being two Save the Children projects featuring embroidered quilts and contemporary Bedouin rugs which are held in old estates that are otherwise closed to the public.

Other popular occasions include the Friends of Archaeology's spring pilgrimage to Pella, a crossroads for different nationalities for centuries, where a talk on the latest excavations is followed by a picnic lunch in flower-filled meadows above a stream, and for the utter hedonists there is the Marriott's annual train ride on the Hejaz railway, kicking off with champagne at Amman's turn-of-the-century station and leading to a banquet with a concert pianist and dancing in the courtyard of a Crusader castle in the desert.

Left, high jinks on the Hejaz railway. **Right**, another genteel luncheon.

To gain an appreciation of Jordan's crafts, especially the feminine arts of embroidery and weaving, there is no better source than Widad Kawar, whose stunning collection of traditional costumes, decorative pieces and Bedouin weavings is a source of inspiration and research for craftsmen, international scholars and modern Arabs seeking to rediscover their heritage.

Originally from Bethlehem, Mrs Kawar began collecting the traditional dresses of her homeland in the late 1950s. The protection of this fragile legacy became even more urgent in 1967, when war accelerated the diaspora of the Palestinian people. Supported by her husband, a Jordanian businessman, she began by collecting heirlooms of women in the refugee camps and moved on to collecting those of women on the East Bank. At the same time she gathered the home-made implements and carpets they used. Exhibited in museums throughout Europe, in Japan and Singapore on a tour that lasted 10 years, the Kawar collection of Palestinian and Jordanian dress and accessories has now returned to Amman, where Mrs Kawar continues the work of cataloguing and conserving the thousands of pieces in preparation for finding a permanent home for them.

Her collection is not only important for its aesthetic value, but for the insights it provides into the everyday lives of women.

Embroidery: While Jordanian men traditionally socialised over coffee, tea and the water pipe, the women were never idle. They plied their crafts, especially embroidery, while visiting one another at home, in courtyards and along footpaths, passing on to the younger generation their proverbs, folklore, and family history as well as their skills.

As a young girl learned the stitches, she was initiated into her culture. Patterns, colours and fabrics revealed her village, tribe, social status, material wealth, and the period in which she lived. Individuality was expressed in the way each woman assembled the pieces of her dress.

Preceding pages: fruit of the loom. Left, examples from Widad Kawar's collection of traditional costumes. Right, dyeing wool.

A young girl's skill in embroidery was noted by the older women and was equated with her capabilities as a homemaker. The finer her stitches, they said, the better her groom. Until recently nearly every Jordanian or Palestinian girl, whatever her social class, embroidered her own trousseau. The six to 12 loosely cut robes she made were worn over a lifetime, and her bridal dress served for many a special occasion – and in some cases was her shroud.

Trousseaus on both sides of the Jordan

River included embroidered cushions as beautiful and varied as the dresses. Today it is the cushions that have carried this art into modern everyday life in Jordan, where in many a home – from simple abodes to the King's palace – the decor is not complete without one or more matching sets. Their colours can range from a riot of red, maroon, purple and pink, spiked with orange, green, and gold, to a more sober combination that emphasises the artistry of the needlework, such as crimson or indigo-coloured embroidery on an off-white background. The simple cross-stitch is the basis for the myriad designs, and the motifs that recur in infinite variety tend to be drawn from nature: trees, flowers, feathers, waves, and geometric triangles or zigzag patterns.

Since the mid-1980s embroidery has embellished articles besides cushions. Elegantly embroidered quilts and matching cushions based on the popular "horse hoof" design hold their own in a Paris home furnishings show; the "tree of life" motif is now embroidered on to large wall hangings; and Oriental village scenes in delicate pastels, complete with a mosque or a church, are recreated in embroidery and appliqué on watered silk.

International recognition: The revival of Jordanian crafts is largely thanks to the patronage of the Noor al-Hussein Foundation,

rated into high fashion. In the 1970s a handful of enterprising women, such as Mariam Abu Laban and Leila Jurius, began to match traditional Jordanian and Palestinian needlework with rich Middle Eastern fabrics, such as striped silk and watered silk, to create elegant gowns and jackets with a modern flair. Other designers followed suit, resulting in collections modelled seasonally on runways at Jordan's luxury hotels. Queen Noor supports this fledgling fashion industry, often wearing such gowns and suits for public appearances at home and abroad.

Weaving: Like embroidery, Bedouin weavings are expressions of a way of life. They serve many purposes in the nomadic

dedicated to encouraging and promoting Jordanian artisans, and to the efforts of non-profit-making organisations. Save the Children's Bani Hamida Women's Weaving Project and Jordan River Designs, which together employ nearly 2,000 Bedouin and refugee women, and the Jerash Women's Society's embroidery and weaving project, initiated by Catholic Relief Services, have put Jordanian crafts on the world map. Upmarket designers, boutiques and home furnishing shops in New York, Paris, London and Germany now carry hand-made products of Jordan.

Traditional crafts have also been incorpo-

environment: the outer walls and room dividers of the tents, the cushions and bedding-bags that comprise the furniture, rugs, saddle-bags, coffee-bags, food containers, and other practical items. All these items are woven by hand out of sheep's wool and goat and camel hair.

It takes at least two months to wash, card, spin, ply, dye the wool, set the loom, weave and sew the pieces together (which more than justifies the high cost of traditionally woven rugs in the shops). Traditionally this process is shared between husband and wife: he shears the wool and washes it; both card and spin the fleece into yarn; and in the past women dyed the wool using bark, earth, indigo, plants and insects as colourants (now the husband delivers the wool to the dyemaster in the nearby town). When the wool is ready, they both set up the ground loom, on which the woman weaves the rug. Sometimes two women sit side by side, passing the shuttle and beating the weft threads into place with the horn of a gazelle. For each rug, a groundloom is constructed anew, with whatever material is available. The stones, sticks and stakes normally used in the loom may be replaced by a shovel and a couple of orange crates or ammunition boxes. To maintain the right tension, the weaver wraps the yarn around her toe in such a way that the

Traditional weaving is encouraged by a number of development projects. Save the Children's Bani Hamida Women's Weaving Project, involving 900 women in 12 villages, the Queen Alia Fund in Sadaqa in the Kerak area, Mleih and Dana in the south strive to revive craft traditions and create jobs and income for rural women at the same time. Under their guidance, the Bedouins' traditional colour combinations – deep-reds, indigo and black, green, orange and mustard and natural sheep colours – have been joined by attractive pieces in a softer palette of modern tones.

Pottery and ceramics: Jordan's natural clay deposits have been utilised for centuries.

rug, the loom and the woman become one. It is sometimes hard to believe that such a simple weaving technique can produce such exquisite pieces.

In towns, male weavers tend to make use of the less strenuous and more expensive upright looms. (The groundloom costs no more than the price of a few tent stakes.) In Madaba a few members of the Ma'ay'a family still continue this long tradition, along with Mr Hayek, whose name means weaver in Arabic.

Left, intricately embroidered quilts are in popular demand. **Above**, appliqué in watered silk.

Archaeological digs are littered with shards dating from prehistoric times, and the early Islamic period witnessed a magnificent blossoming of ceramic arts, as pieces in Jordan's main museums testify. Until recently simple sun-cured pottery, baked in a dung and straw-fired pit, was used for food storage as well as for serving-vessels and oil-lamps. The most common pots were the large coil-and-slab *jarra*, often 75 cm (2½ ft) tall. Once used to store water and olive oil and to pickle and preserve olives, these can now be seen gracing the gardens of elegant villas in Amman.

Today, talented young artisans are bringing new life and a new look to this age-old art form. One of the best modern ceramicists is Mahmoud Taha, well-known for his tile murals. Hazim Zu'bi and sisters Rula and Reem Atalla have introduced designs using contemporary Islamic calligraphy and petraglyph images. Another potter, Maha Faraj, heads the ceramics project of the Queen Alia Fund near the Royal Medical City. In the new tourist village of Taybet-Zaman near Petra, replicas of the delicate rust-coloured pottery of the ancient Nabataeans are now being produced.

Jewellery: Like ceramics, jewellery has a long history in Jordan. Caches of gold jewellery from the 9th to the 5th centuries BC have been found near Petra, and goldwork, cam-

eos and jewellery of copper, bronze, silver, iron, and glass from the later Bronze Age to Roman times have been unearthed near Amman. Today gold jewellery – formerly exclusive to royalty and the upper classes – is collected by rich and poor alike. Most women and some men in all social strata possess at least a few gold pieces (although the Koran discourages men from wearing the precious metal). In Amman's gold *suq* you can see citizens of all walks of life buying and selling the 21-carat jewellery. A nice souvenir is a tiny gold coffee pot (*dalleh*) – a symbol of Jordan – worn on a chain.

Traditionally the silversmith met the de-mands of the common people. Until recently, a Bedouin bride wore her personal wealth in her silver jewellery, and had the right to dispose of it as she liked. As with gold today, the pieces were bought or sold according to the woman's own plans, or the rise or fall in the family's fortunes.

The silver jewellery of the Bedouin comes in dazzling variety: bracelets, chokers, rings, hair ornaments, long chains and rows of coins attached to head-dresses or necklaces. It is embellished by the use of incising, embossing, hammering, repoussé (raised in relief), twisting, and granulation (soldered patterns of tiny silver balls). The latter technique was common in jewellery from the Byzantine period and was reintroduced to Transjordan in the 1920s by silversmiths from the Hejaz. Filigree work probably originated with Yemeni silversmiths working in the area in the late 1800s. Arabic calligraphy is sometimes engraved on flat surfaces, or enhanced with black Circassian enamelled niello decoration. Small pendant ornaments in the shape of fish or crescent moons are made by sand-casting molten silver.

Silver beads are often combined with glass beads or precious stones used as amulets – blue glass from Syria against the evil eye, green malekite from Aqaba or green agate for health, brown agate for warding off evil spirits, and white agate to keep a husband's love alive. Beads of brown and golden amber, rose coral from the Red Sea, mother of pearl, white cowry shells (female symbols) and ancient Venetian glass are often incorporated into Bedouin pieces.

Blown glass: "Hebron glass", named after the West Bank city renowned for this kind of glass, comes in shades of cobalt blue, bottle green, turquoise, amber and rose, and glows like jewels when displayed on a sunny windowsill. Workshops where the skills are practised are found at Na'ur, on the old road to the Dead Sea, in Madaba on the way to Mount Nebo and in the King Abdullah Gardens in Amman where larger items are produced. Originally made from sand, the glass is now made by recycling old bottles.

Basketry: One of the most ubiquitous part-time crafts is basket-making. Baskets and trays are woven for every imaginable use and come in every size. With handles, they are used to store grain or carry fruits and vegetables from market, while a deep laundry basket with lid is large enough for a small child to hide in. Even beehives were once plaited of cane. Today, a basketry project begun by the Bisharat family in the northern village of Mukheibeh, perched high above the Yarmouk River, produces baskets of split bamboo and palm leaves that are sold in flower shops all over Jordan. Large round mats are also woven from bamboo fronds by Druze women in Azraq. Patterned or plain, a hand-woven Jordanian basket makes a lightweight and practical gift.

Wood: Wood has always been scarce in Jordan and the antique wooden parlour chairs, tables, elegant large mirrors, and lovely old bridal chests inlaid with mother of pearl that

shape of a cupcake pan and inherited from Roman times, is still played in some Jordanian villages.

Other crafts: There are a host of other small-scale crafts to be found. A limited quantity of small decorative animal figures are carved out of pink, cream, or white stone by members of the Ta'amreh Bedouin from Palestine (available from the Hands Craft Centre just off Second Circle behind the Lebanese Embassy on Jebel Amman), and beaten brass relief work is done at Kan Zaman, near Amman. Ideal for small presents are bottles filled with intricate patterns of naturally coloured sand, produced in Petra and Aqaba, and soap made of oil extracted

you see in some of the more upmarket shops come from Syria. But traditional implements used to prepare Arab coffee in Jordan were often carved of local cured oak or pistachio. The mortar and pestle (*mihbash* and *yad*), the shallow tray in which the freshly roasted coffee beans were placed to cool (*mabradah*), the wooden mold to stamp bread and cakes, mixing bowls and cooking spoons were all made by local carvers. Some of these antique items are still available. The *mangala*, a game using a wooden board carved in the

Left, reviving an ancient craft. **Above**, a glass-blower in Kan Zaman, near Amman.

from olive pits, which is made by young women in Mahatta camp participating in the Jordan River Designs project. This natural cleanser leaves hair lustrous and softens the complexion, despite Jordan's hard water and desert climate.

For an overview of crafts in Jordan, visit the Folklore Museum of Costumes and Jewellery and the Popular Museum of Bedouin Life, located on either side of the Roman amphitheatre in downtown Amman.

For details of where to buy crafts and telephone numbers to contact workshops and crafts projects, see the *Travel Tips* section at the back of this book.

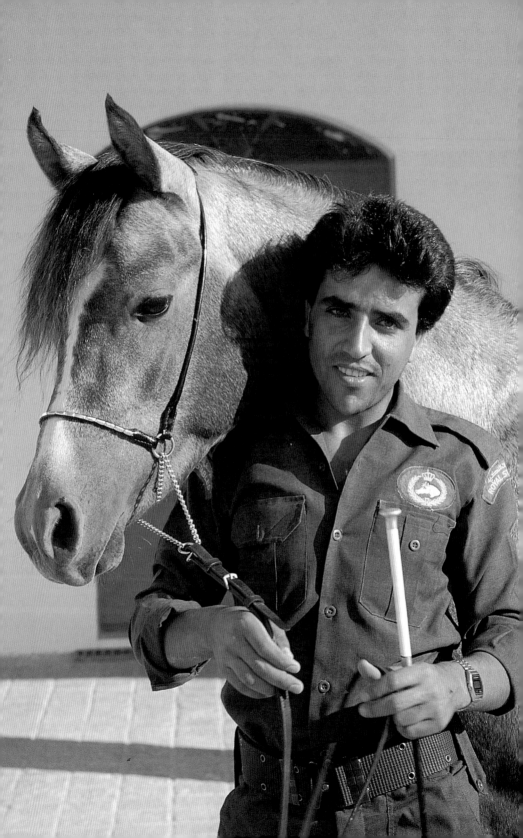

ARABIAN HORSES

Hidden among pine trees, a stone's throw off the road to Fuhays in the suburbs of Amman, is the Royal Jordanian State Stud. It is here, in the buildings and grounds of a low-lying Andalusian-style complex engirdled by pink clematis and cabbage roses, that 135 pure-bred Arabian horses toss their heads and strut their stuff, attended by 40 full-time grooms.

The stables have come a long way since the early 1920s, when the Emir Abdullah brought a small team of Arabs with him from the Hejaz. These horses, augmented by some given to him by local tribes, formed the foundations of today's stock. At the time, Emir Abdullah's interest was recreational rather than ideological, but in the 1960s, when interbreeding with thoroughbreds in the interests of horse-racing threatened to extinguish the purity of the breed in the region, his grandson King Hussein set up an official state stud. First under the management of a European couple, Mr and Mrs Lopez, and now under the hand of Princess Alia, Abdullah's great-granddaughter who traces her consuming interest in Arabians to a childhood love of "a pony and a rocking-horse", the stud has blossomed into a thriving enterprise committed to preserving the local lines and supplying Arab studs all over the world. It is a streamlined and efficient business. The stables have a full-time vet; a team of three farriers; and there is a mountain of paperwork involved in registering new foals. The copious manure from the stables nourishes Amman's finest rose beds.

The Arabian (*equus Arabicus*) is more compact and delicate-looking than the thoroughbred, yet it is famed for its power as well as its beauty, and its most prized asset historically is endurance, a quality that has drawn it close to the Bedouin, its human counterpart in weathering the hardships of the desert. As one early 20th-century traveller noted as he observed a Bedu tending his horse, "The Bedouins seem to belong to the Arabian horse as naturally as the date palm belongs to the sand-dune."

A tribe's horses were its chief pride, its partners in raiding, hunting and war. They were also associated with an important rite of passage. Once a young male Bedu had singlehandedly captured a mare from the midst of an enemy's camp he was admitted to the *mejlis*, the council of men around the chief's camp-fire. As a precaution against such horse rustling, mares were usually shackled at night with a chain and padlock.

As a rule, mares were valued above stallions. Not only did they reproduce, but they

were seen as more manageable in warfare and likely to be quieter when stealth was required and the randy whinny of a stallion could blow a Bedu's cover. It is thought to be for this reason that the blood-line of Arabs is traced through the mares.

Years of working and living together (horses often bedded down in the family tent) forged a bond of affection between Bedouin and horse which transcended usual human/non-human relationships and inspired romantic legends and poetry. The Bedu would refer to their horses as "drinkers of the wind", "the envy of all", and compare them with magic carpets. Myth clouds the truth of the

Arabian's roots. They are believed to have originated either in central Arabia or near the Euphrates River in Mesopotamia some 4,000 years ago, but tradition, based on the fact that the main strains are known as Al-Khamsa (The Five), traces their descent to five horses said to have been owned by the Prophet Mohammed. The Koran itself attributes their source to the south wind: "Then God took a handful of wind and fashioned from it a chestnut horse. He said, 'I have created you, Arabian horse; I have moulded you from the wind; I have tied Good Fortune to your mane; you will fly without wings; you will be the noblest among animals... God then blessed the horse with sign of glory and

and strong). They can be grey (white), chestnut or black, and their colour at birth is no indication of their adult hue.

A superior intelligence makes Arabs unsuitable for polo (they chase the ball) and their independence – perhaps more than their small build – makes them unreliable show-jumpers (though they can jump quite well, they will often refuse). But some strains make good race horses, and all these qualities are prized by part-breeders, who improve the qualities of other breeds by mating them with Arabian stallions. Arabs are known for their prepotency – thus most other warm-blooded breeds contain an element of Arab in their blood, including the English thor-

happiness and marked his forehead with a star, and the horse leaped into space."

Though modern-day breeders talking about Arabs lack such exquisite poeticism, they still talk lyrically of symmetry, harmony, balance and the famous "float", the unique way of moving that brings to mind the magic carpet. The distinguishing physical characteristics of Arabians are pointed ears, a concave face with a broad forehead, a large jaw and small muzzle, a small back (they have 23 vertebrae, instead of the 24 of the non-Arab), long hindquarters which should be level with the back, a high tail, and fine legs (deceptively frail-looking, for they are in fact dense

oughbred and the pedigree hackney – and even if a particular horse lacks some of the classic Arab traits she may still pass them on to her foals.

There are various strains of breed, and the Royal Jordanian Stud has several rare lines, such as Umm Argub and Kehilah Krush. Maintaining these lines has been a delicate and on occasion difficult business. The Hamdani line was almost lost in Jordan when female foals of the stud's only Hamdani mare were sent to Britain and Morocco and the mare went on to produce only male heirs. The stud was forced to buy back a mare.

However, the stud is equally committed to

preserving specifically local lines, even if they are not especially beautiful or prized. The greatest threat to these local lines came immediately after King Abdullah's death. Before the horses' value to the Jordanian heritage was fully realised, the late King's stable was disbanded. When King Hussein began reassembling the stock shortly afterwards, he found the horses dispersed to all corners of Jordan. Though most were found serving with the Royal Mounted Guards and the army, one stallion, Ghazalleh, was found ploughing a field in the Jordan Valley.

Princess Alia believes that some of the horses hired out at Petra are pure Arabs, but their lineage is unrecorded and the tradi-

breeders, some horses are hitting the racetrack. Jordan is planning to host Arab race meetings three or four times a year.

Preparing horses for shows takes up a good deal of the staff's time, especially when making transport and quarantine arrangements for events abroad, but so does day-to-day care. Work begins each day around 7am with grooming and exercise for each horse (only the very young and horses that are heavily in foal are exempt). In keeping with their history, the horses are kept outside as often as possible, for cosseting makes them susceptible to illness. When, during a particularly cold winter, infra-red lamps were rigged up in each of the boxes, all the horses

tional means of tracking a horse's ancestry – verbally from father to son – has broken down. To help improve the general stock at Petra, the Royal Stables lend Petra two stallions a year for mating. The ratio of mares to stallions at the Royal Stables is 5–1.

The horses of the Royal Jordanian Stud are increasingly shown at specialist international shows and Amman itself now holds an annual international show in the grounds attached to the stud. In addition, with renewed interest in Arab registered racing among

Left, awarding marks at the Royal Horse Show.
Above, an Arab stallion poses for the camera.

quickly went down with colds.

Though foals are born throughout the year, the ideal time is as close to the beginning of the year as possible, because a foal born at the end of December will be classed as a one-year-old by 1 January, which would be disadvantageous for race horses where age is crucial. As a rule, horses are not ridden until they are at least three and not used for breeding until they are four. From then on, a mare produces foals every 11 months until her late teens or early twenties, with occasional time off for a rest. The stables' longest-living stallion to date was 33 years old when he died, the sire of a foal just the year before.

For such a small country Jordan encompasses dramatic contrasts. Snow frequently caps hills in winter whilst summer temperatures in the desert may exceed 36°C (97°F). Different areas also experience very different climates simultaneously. While the mountains of Ajlun in the north and Shobak in the south are subject to a Mediterranean climate (hence the snow) the main part of the country basks in a warm desert climate. Between these two extremes there are at least four other climates at work, helping to create a spectrum of wildlife habitats.

Contrary to popular belief, the desert itself is endowed with abundant plants and animals, thanks to a fertile distant past. A drive across Jordan's deserts by four-wheel-drive vehicle, or perhaps over its well-surfaced roads in an ordinary car, is packed with clues to the dramatic changes to natural conditions that have taken place over the years. One only has to stand at the great Omayyad castles at Amra or Kharaneh, both in the midst of arid desert, to realise that the landscape must have been somewhat different when the Omayyad caliphs built here. Great hunters, the caliphs built these castles in the heart of "big-game country", where natural forests provided shade, refuge and food for gazelles and other mammals.

Destruction of tree cover, primarily for wood-burning, was one of the biggest causes of change. Protection of surviving woodlands is therefore a priority of the Royal Society for Conservation of Nature, an organisation that has been active in protecting Jordan's wildlife habitats and setting up wildlife reserves.

The Arabian oryx: Jordan has played a key role in rescuing the Arabian oryx from the jaws of extinction through a captive breeding and reintroduction campaign known as Operation Oryx, in which oryx held at the Shaumari Reserve are bred and swapped with animals from other captive populations in order to maintain a strong blood-line.

Whilst there are currently 143 Arabian oryx at Shaumari, and animals from this

centre are also released into the wild in Oman, the Society has extended the programme to include other threatened animals including the Nubian ibex, the Syrian wild ass (onager), the ostrich, and the common gazelle. The centre at Shaumari, established in 1975, has a total area of 22 sq. km (8½ sq. miles). Apart from the captive breeding programme it is a natural reserve where 11 mammals, 134 birds and 130 plant species have been recorded.

Within only a few miles of Shaumari is the wetland area of Azraq, a magnet for millions of birds as they pass between Eurasia, Arabia and Africa on their seasonal migrations. The sheer variety and abundance of birds is remarkable. At least 120 different species can be regularly seen and the total list of species spotted numbers over 300.

More surprising, however, is the number of waterfowl that congregate in this desert oasis, including teal, gadwall, wigeon, pintail, garganey, shoveler, pochard, and tufted duck. In 1977 the Ramsar Convention declared Azraq to be a wetland of international importance for migratory waterfowl.

Azraq is also an excellent location for close observation of birds of prey such as osprey, honey buzzard, black kite, Levant sparrowhawk, buzzard, short-toed eagle, steppe eagle, spotted eagle, lesser spotted eagle, hen harrier, pallid harrier, marsh harrier, peregrine falcon, red-footed falcon, kestrel and lesser kestrel. Visitors from Europe who are aware of the decline of many of these species will be surprised by their numbers at Azraq. For instance, the corncrake, one of the recent casualties of European agricultural development, turns up at Azraq each year, probably from the steppe-lands of Asia. The Azraq Reserve spreads over a 12-sq. km. (4½-sq. mile) area of pools, marshes, water meadows and salt dunes.

Last leopard: The Wadi Mujib Wildlife Reserve is a wild and beautiful area occupying a 212-sq. km (82-sq. mile) area of steep mountainside and valley, extending from the Dead Sea at 400 metres (1,312 ft) below sea-level to the eastern highlands, which rise 800 metres (2,625 ft) above sea level. Explorations on foot are sometimes rewarded by

Preceding pages: Arabian oryx, rescued from the jaws of extinction. Left, ostrich at Azraq.

sightings of the Nubian ibex, along with a wealth of other fauna, and a long list of plants that includes several rare orchids. Jordan is home to at least 22 species of wild orchids. Many of these are threatened by habitat depletion so care should be taken to leave them undisturbed.

The Dana Wildlife Reserve is in the south of Jordan, where the Shara range reaches 1,300 metres (4,265 ft) and where an exceptionally rugged landscape includes precipitous canyons and deep winding mountain gorges that defeat even the best four-wheel-drive vehicles. Here some of the most exhilarating mountain scenery in Arabia is home to the country's last few leopard and two of

Planned protection: Further plans are afoot to extend wildlife management. A proposed reserve at Burqu' will cover 950 sq. km (367 sq. km) in the northeast of Jordan, close to the borders with Syria and will include the Burqu' Palace within its boundaries. Such a vast area of totally protected habitat is necessary if Jordan's efforts to reintroduce Arabian gazelle, Dorcas gazelle, onager and ostrich to their natural habitats are to succeed. Another desert area earmarked for protection, the Rajil Wildlife Reserve, about 50 km (30 miles) from Azraq in the eastern desert, is an area rich in gazelle, red fox, hare, hyena and wolves as well as desert plants.

At Kerak, the surrounding plateau has a

their prey species, the mountain gazelle and Nubian ibex. Natural woodland on the high ground is formed by pine, oak, and juniper.

Desert places: The southernmost wildlife habitat (excluding the marine life in the Gulf of Aqaba) is Wadi Rum, where huge rocky outcrops of sandstone rise out of a pink desert speckled with Bedouin encampments and covered with a bright blue sky. The designated Wadi Rum Wildlife Reserve covers an area of 510 sq. km (197 sq. miles). Beyond the immediate valley lie range after range of rocky hills inhabited by ibex and gazelle as well as smaller mammals such as hedgehog and porcupine.

wealth of interesting wildlife and a reserve covering 410 sq. km (158 sq. miles) has been surveyed. It has been tentatively named the Abu Rukbah Wildlife Reserve after the main road that passes through the plateau. The elevated, rugged terrain is the perfect habitat for mountain and desert gazelle.

Those interested in desert plants should visit the area of Wadi Bayir, destined to become the Bayir Wildlife Reserve covering an area of 440 sq. km (170 sq. miles). It has a height range of 670–800 metres (2,200–2,625 ft) and is earmarked for the release of Arabian oryx, gazelle, onager and ostrich.

Two other reserves currently on the drawing board include the Jarba Wildlife Reserve, focused on Wadi Jarba, where mountain gazelle will be reintroduced, and the Jebel Mas'ada Wildlife Reserve which will extend over 460 sq. km (286 sq miles) of the Wadi Arabah, including the Mas'ada mountain, in the south of Jordan. This area already includes mountain gazelle, ibex, striped hyena, fox, hare, wolf and badger.

Although the above protected (or soon to be designated) areas offer some of the best wildlife-watching in Jordan it is by no means necessary to follow this trail in order to encounter the country's wild animals and plants. Even roadside verges can offer unexpected rewards, especially for plant-lovers.

stone pathways of Petra, you may well encounter the Petra wall lizard: *Lacerta danfordi,* which suns itself on the rocks in the morning light. A sharp eye is needed to distinguish the Mediterranean chameleon which stands motionless among the branches of bushes, following its prey with its revolving eyes and capturing it on a tongue that is as long as its body. Although there are several poisonous snakes in Jordan, including the horned viper and the Palestine viper, visitors are unlikely to encounter them and there are very few instances of snake bites.

Having climbed Jordan's mountains, trekked across its plateau lands, scrambled up its *wadis* and wandered through its deserts,

Indeed, the national flower of Jordan, the black wild iris, is as likely to be seen growing along the edge of roads running through the plateau lands as it is in wilder locations.

Insects and reptiles: Insect-life is also widely distributed and colourful butterflies, such as the small copper and small tortoiseshell, migrate in large numbers during spring. Look out also for the emerald green grasshopper and its dramatic relative, the preying mantis.

Lizards are frequently seen throughout the country. While walking through the sand-

there is still more wildlife to encounter. There is no better way to cool off after an exhausting day of exploring Petra or Wadi Rum than to swim in the clear waters of the Gulf of Aqaba and admire the northernmost corals and fishes of the Red Sea-Indian Ocean. The hypersaline waters of the Dead Sea, on the other hand, support little life. However, the Dead Sea forms part of the Red Sea Rift, which is itself an extension of the Great Rift Valley in Africa, and as the continental plates gradually move apart, widening the Red Sea, it is likely that the Dead Sea will eventually reconnect with the Gulf of Aqaba and thus become a brand-new haven for marine life.

Far Left, grey heron. **Left**, ibex in Wadi Mujib Wildlife Reserve. **Above**, blue lizard.

The European rush to rediscover antiquities in the 18th and 19th centuries gradually extended to the Orient. Though initially confined to professional explorers, this interest soon spread to dilettantes wealthy enough to undertake the lengthy and costly journeys such exploration involved. The development of the steamship in the early 19th century made such travel much easier (the Red Sea, for example, became navigable in all seasons), and by mid-century touring the Middle East had become a fashionable pastime for adventurous members of the wealthy middle classes. These early tourists were drawn by the sights described in travel literature (a new and booming industry) and by the evocative images of the Orient painted by the artists of the day, who flocked to the region hot on the heels of the explorers.

In the absence of press photographers, it was up to the artists of the day to capture the image of these newly "discovered" places and, via the laborious methods of paintings and lithographs, transmit to the world the wonders they had witnessed. In the early days this was no easy task. In many cases the journeys involved were long and arduous; there was plague and disease, and a high possibility of losing one's baggage and a real possibility of losing one's life.

All these drawbacks were especially true of the rock-carved city of Petra, which had been rediscovered by the Swiss explorer Burckhardt in 1812. The inhabitants of Petra, the Howeitat and Omrah Bedouins descended from the original Nabataeans, were given to such hostility that pictures often had to be made in a great hurry: what a modern photographer might call "snatched". Some of these tribesmen believed that the artists possessed magic powers which enabled them to steal the ancient treasure away, and it was nearly a century before the journey to the city was considered safe.

Any archaeologist worth his salt would

have been able to give a rough impression of a place, but it needed an exceptional draughtsman to convey the full majesty of a site as glorious as Petra. David Roberts was the man to do it: he was the most accomplished draughtsman of his age.

"Painter Davie" came from a humble Scottish family and he was by all accounts an amiable and popular figure, a member of the Royal Academy and a good friend of the great English watercolourist J.M.W. Turner. In 1838 he set out on a tour of the Levant,

starting in Egypt and going up to Jerusalem. His first stop was Cairo where an English traveller, John Pell, took him to meet the French artist, Louis-Maurice-Adolphe Linant. Linant was the first serious artist to have been to Petra, which he had visited 10 years earlier, but his work, which was rather heavy and laboured, had not been widely seen. When Roberts saw Linant's paintings, the scenes bowled him over.

The Scottish academician had been in two minds about taking on the additional hazard and expense of visiting Jeremiah's doomed city, but one look at Linant's drawings convinced him that the rewards would be well

Preceding pages: David Roberts's *El Deir, Petra*. **Left**, local figures ("staffage") were often used to enliven 19th-century picturesque composition, as in this picture of Petra's theatre by Roberts. **Right**, self-portrait by Roberts.

worth the effort. Such a journey, he was instantly convinced, would enable him to return to Britain with "one of the richest folios that ever left the East".

For the journey Roberts was joined by Pell and John Kinnear, an Edinburgh business-man and a keen admirer of Roberts's work. Roberts himself travelled in eastern clothes, which he had bought in order to look less conspicuous when sketching in Cairo.

One month after leaving Cairo they arrived in Aqaba where they were obliged to employ as their escort Sheikh Hussein of the Alowein, who held sway in the lands leading to Petra and had been Linant's guide a decade earlier. But even he seemed unsure that

overawed. "I often throw away my pencil in despair of being able to convey any idea of it," he wrote of al-Deiu.

He spent five and a half days at the site. It was hardly enough. He did not reach the tomb of Aaron on Mount Hor, nor did he get a view of the Royal Tombs from the High Place of Sacrifice. His output was nevertheless prodigious. Petra was ideal for his wonderfully dramatic and romantic style, and he held nothing back. Most of his drawings were, as usual, surisingly accurate.

He had good reason to be satisfied with his results and in good spirits he and his party left Petra and headed for Hebron. There he painted two watercolours of the

he could give the "Franks" full protection against the local Bedouins, and at one point he refused to continue on the journey, declaring his charges to be "all mad" for trying to enter the Wadi Moussa.

Roberts's courage and determination won in the end but the continuing tension of the Arab tribes coloured his first sight of the city and he instantly felt it to be still overshadowed by Jeremiah's curse. However, he wasted no time in making numerous sketches. It took all of his powers to capture the rose-red city's likeness and spirit, although like others who visited it before and after him, there were moments when he felt completely

town he found "almost English" in its cleanliness, and its children, "the most beautiful I have ever seen". But an outbreak of the plague forced them on to Jaffa and Jerusalem where they joined the Easter faithful, visiting the monastery of Saint Saba, Bethlehem, Nablus, Ba'albek and all the other sites on the pilgrims' route.

There was no doubt that his journey did produce one of the richest folios of the region, and Roberts wrote on his return: "My sketches of the East have taken the world of art by storm." They were expertly worked up into watercolours and then lithographs and published in *The Holy Land* in 1842, accompanied by a rather turgid text by an un-worldly Scots cleric, the Rev. George Croly.

Roberts's own reputation has gone up and down according to fashion, suffering most when figurative painting has been out of style, but *The Holy Land* has seldom been out of print and the original lithographs, plates torn from the early editions of the book, are highly priced considering their ubiquity. The 1980s saw a revival of interest in his work and, rather surprisingly, it was not until 1984 that a full biography, an excellent book by by Katharine Sim, was written about a man who is a household name in Scotland.

The next major artist to visit Petra was William Henry Bartlett, in 1845. Bartlett, a

Hebron, he emerged from the Sufa Pass to find a scene of "astonishing beauty" only to remember that his painting equipment was strapped to a camel that had somehow taken a different route through the pass.

But Petra surpassed anything else he saw. And, like Roberts, he felt frustrated when faced with such magnificence. "My art is helpless to recall it to others." Writing to his sister, he described it thus: "All the cliffs are a wonderful colour – like ham in stripes and parts are salmon colour."

Lear was there barely more than half a day when he was seized by local Bedouin tribes-men who sent him packing, robbed of "everything from all my pockets, from dol-

topographic artist who illustrated his own travel books, approached Petra from Egypt via Aqaba. The "marvellous and romantic singularity"of Petra inspired Bartlett's unu-sually detailed watercolour entitled *Princi-pal Range of Tombs*.

After Bartlett came London-born Edward Lear, who made his Holy Land tour 16 years after Roberts and reported conditions that were even worse than in Roberts's time. His first bit of bad luck was when, after leaving

Left, view of Petra from the theatre from *Through Arabia* by M. Léon de Laborde. **Above**, *The Dome of the Rock* by David Roberts.

lars and penknives to handkerchief and hard-boiled eggs." The final indignity came when his major work of the trip, a painting of the eastern cliff entitled *Petra*, was hung in the Royal Academy in London in 1872, above a painting by the American artist, James Abbott McNeill Whistler, of his mother.

"As if in mockery," wrote the critic of the London *Times*, "Petra is placed immediately above Mr Whistler's 'arrangement in gray and black' which, thanks to its broad sim-plicity, would have lost nothing had the two pictures changed places, while, as they hang, Mr Lear's work is entirely sacrificed."

The curse of Jeremiah had struck again.

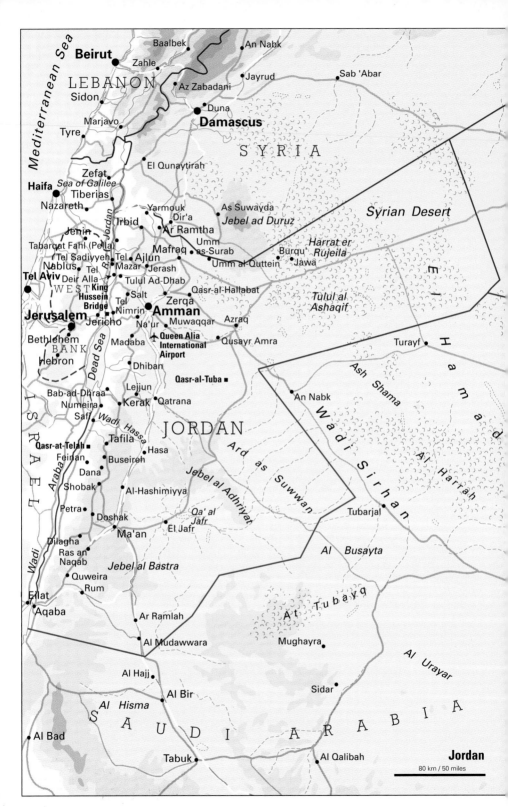

Mediterranean Sea

Baalbek
An Nabk
Beirut
Zahle
LEBANON
Jayrud
Sab 'Abar
Az Zabadani
Sidon
Duna
Marjayo
Damascus
Tyre

S Y R I A

El Qunaytirah

Syrian Desert

Zefat
Haifa Sea of Galilee
Tiberias
Nazareth
Yarmouk
As Suwayda
Dir'a
Jebel ad Duruz
Irbid
Jenin
Ar Ramtha
Harrat er
Tabarqat Fahl (Pella)
Umm
Burqu' Rujeila
Tel Sadiyyeh
Mafraq
as-Surab
Jawa
Nablus
Tel Ajlun
Umm al-Quttein
Tel Aviv Tel
Mazar Jerash
Deir Alla
Tulul Ad-Dhab
W E S T **King**
Qasr-al-Hallabat
Hussein
Tulul al
Bridge
Tel
Salt
Ashaqif
Jerusalem
Nimrin
Zerqa
Jericho
Amman
Bethlehem
Na'ur
Muwaqqar
Azraq
B A N K
Madaba
Qusayr Amra
Turayf
Hebron
Queen Alia
International
Airport
Dhiban
Qasr-al-Tuba ■
Lejjun
An Nabk
Bab-ad-Dhraa
Numeira
Kerak
Qatrana
Saff. Wadi Hassa
J O R D A N
Qasr-at-Telah ■
Tafila
Feinan
Hasa
Dana
Buseireh
Jebel al Adhriyat
Shobak
Al-Hashimiyya
Tubarjal
Petra
Doshak
Qa' al
Jafr
Ma'an
El Jafr
Al Busayta
Dilagha
Ras an
Naqab
Jebel al Bastra
Quweira
Rum
Eilat
Aqaba
Ar Ramlah
At Tubayq
Al Mudawwara
Mughayra
Al Urayar
Al Hajj
Al Bir
Sidar
Al Hisma
S A U D I   A R A B I A
Al Bad
Tabuk
Al Qalibah

Jordan
80 km / 50 miles

I S R A E L
Dead Sea
Jordan
Araba
Wadi
Ard as Suwwan
Wadi Sirhan
Al Harrah
Hamad
Ash Shama

PLACES

A small country carved out of the heart of the Middle East, Jordan offers concentrated pleasures. The Nabataean city of Petra is the outstanding attraction, made all the more compelling by its seclusion. Its slender approach along a mile-long cleft has drawn adventurers (Burckhardt and Lawrence), artists (David Roberts) and poets ("rose-red city half as old as time" J. W. Burgon), not to mention Harrison Ford, Sean Connery and Denholm Elliot when Petra served as a suitably fabulous backdrop for the closing sequence of *Indiana Jones and the Last Crusade*.

But other sights and sensations beckon: the Graeco-Roman ruins of the Decapolis in the north, including Jerash and Pella; the 7th-century Omayyad palaces east of Amman; the ancient King's Highway, which snakes through some of the loveliest country in the Middle East; the pink canyons of Wadi Rum; and the multi-coloured coral reefs off Aqaba. Even Amman, a modern city built on hills, has an appealing energy and friendliness.

Distances in Jordan are short, so a little of everything can be sampled in a week. However, there is plenty to fill a longer stay (Petra alone is worth four days) and there are many incidental delights to be savoured – such as basking in hot springs at Himmeh, tingling in a full-body mudpack at the Dead Sea, or retracing some of the great biblical sites (even non-believers may find they are uplifted by more than soft breezes on Mount Nebo, where Moses surveyed the Promised Land).

The Places section which follows begins with Amman, a comfortable springboard and base, and crosses to its neighbour and rival Salt, an older town with a more Oriental flavour, and then heads north and east. From there it journeys down the length of the Jordan Valley, pausing at the eerie Dead Sea, and then, regaining Amman, meanders along the King's Highway to Petra, via Crusader castles, Byzantine churches and flower-filled *wadis*. From Petra it strikes east to the Desert Highway to explore the Gaudi-shaped desertscapes of Wadi Rum, and ends by dipping into the port-resort of Aqaba on the Red Sea.

Following the chapters on Jordan are short sections on the West Bank and Syria, designed for travellers taking a broader look at the Levant and roaming over its modern borders.

Preceding pages: aerial view of Wadi Rum; the Cardo at Jerash; lush in spring; the Royal Tombs, Petra.

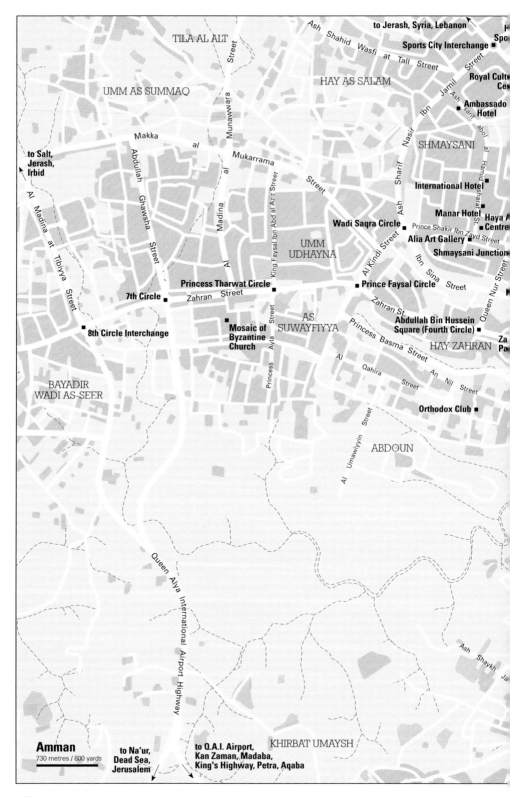

Amman
730 metres / 800 yards

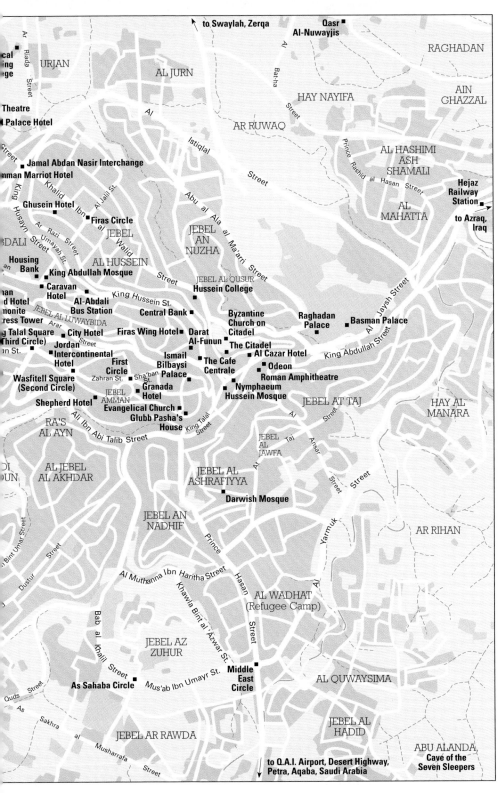

to Swaylah, Zerqa

Qasr
Al-Nuwayjis

RAGHADAN

URJAN

AL JURN

HAY NAYIFA

AIN
GHAZZAL

cal
ing
ge

Theatre
Palace Hotel

AR RUWAQ

AL HASHIMI
ASH
SHAMALI

Jamal Abdan Nasir Interchange
mman Marriot Hotel

Hejaz
Railway
Station

AL
MAHATTA

to Azraq,
Iraq

Ghusein Hotel

Firas Circle

JEBEL
AN
NUZHA

JEBEL

Housing
Bank

DALI

AL HUSSEIN

JEBEL AL QUSUR

King Abdullah Mosque

Hussein College

Caravan
Hotel

an
d Hotel
monite
ress Tower

Al-Abdali
Bus Station

King Hussein St.

Central Bank

Byzantine
Church on
Citadel

Raghadan
Palace

Basman Palace

g Talal Square
Third Circle)
an St.

City Hotel

Firas Wing Hotel

Darat
Al-Funun

Jordan
Intercontinental
Hotel

The Citadel

Al Cazar Hotel

First
Circle

Ismail
Bilbaysi
Palace

The Cafe
Centrale

Odeon

Wasfitell Square
(Second Circle)

Roman Amphitheatre

Granada
Hotel

Nymphaeum

Shepherd Hotel

JEBEL
AMMAN

Hussein Mosque

JEBEL AT TAJ

HAY AL
MANARA

Evangelical Church

RA'S
AL AYN

Glubb Pasha's
House

JEBEL
AL
JAWFA

AL JEBEL
AL AKHDAR

JEBEL AL
ASHRAFIYYA

Darwish Mosque

AR RIHAN

JEBEL AN
NADHIF

AL WADHAT
(Refugee Camp)

JEBEL AZ
ZUHUR

As Sahaba Circle

Middle
East
Circle

AL QUWAYSIMA

Quds Street

JEBEL AR RAWDA

to Q.A.I. Airport, Desert Highway,
Petra, Aqaba, Saudi Arabia

JEBEL AL
HADID

ABU ALANDA
Cave of the
Seven Sleepers

AMMAN

Though most guide books treat Jordan's capital as a base camp for visits to archaeological sites such as Petra and Jerash, **Amman** is a vibrant place with its own monuments, history and pleasures. Situated between the desert and the lush Jordan Valley, with a plentiful water supply, it has always been an attractive place to live.

Trade routes have passed this way throughout history, from Rome to Arabia Felix and from Omayyad Damascus to the holy cities of Mecca and Medina. The building of the Hejaz railway between Damascus and Medina (it reached Amman in 1902) and Emir Abdullah's adoption of Amman as the capital of Transjordan in 1921 marked the city's re-emergence as an important centre.

Nowadays, nearly half of Jordan's population is concentrated in the Amman area. Thanks to the way the city has spread over a number of hills (*jebels*), summer heat is reduced by regular breezes. Most of the houses are a uniform white, in compliance with a municipal law decreeing that buildings should be faced with local stone, but this turns to a mellow gold with age and in the setting sun.

It is difficult to understand Amman's geography from ground level or from maps. The Citadel, which towers over the downtown area and looms large in Amman's history, provides the best historical and geographical introduction. It is also useful to remember that areas in West Amman are located in relation to a number of roundabouts and crossroads on a straight road out of the city. Locals call them circles, and they run from the 1st Circle to the 8th. The "Emirate walk" described later in this chapter begins near 1st Circle, the Jordan Intercontinental hotel is on 3rd Circle, the Abdoun area and its modern architecture lies between 5th and 6th circles and Wadi as-Seer is just beyond 8th Circle.

Early history: There is archaeological evidence of settlement in the Amman area for almost 9,000 years. Ain Ghaz-zal, off the Zerqa road on the outskirts of the city, is one of the largest Neolithic settlements (*c.* 6500 BC) ever discovered in the Middle East. The Citadel hill contains early Bronze-Age tombs (3300–1200 BC), and the site of a late Bronze-Age temple (1300–1200 BC) near the old airport at Marka suggests that these early inhabitants were quite well off.

By the beginning of the Iron Age (1200–539 BC), Amman had developed into the capital of the Ammonites referred to in the Bible. It was here, during a 10th-century siege, that King David of Israel arranged the death of Uriah the Hittite, whose wife he coveted. Fortress towers ringed the outskirts of Amman (today one of the best preserved stands next to the Department of Antiquities' Registration Centre, near the 3rd Circle), but they were little protection against King David's determined attack. His forces toppled the Ammonites and, apart from a brief revival in the 9th and 8th centuries BC, the area was ruled successively by the

Assyrians, Babylonians and Persians for several hundred years.

Amman's history during much of this time is unclear. However, it re-emerged into the limelight during the Hellenistic period, from the 4th century BC. The city was rebuilt and renamed Philadelphia by Ptolemy II (285–247 BC).

The area was conquered by the Seleucids in 218 BC and for two centuries it continued to prosper. In 63 BC, it was absorbed by the Roman Empire and Philadelphia became the southernmost city of the Decapolis, the 10 Graeco-Roman towns in the area. As the Roman Empire extended southward to Petra and beyond, Philadelphia found itself at the centre of the new Roman province of Arabia and of lucrative trade routes running between the Mediterranean and an interior which stretched to India and China as well as routes north and south. The city flourished and impressive monuments were constructed, including the temple of Hercules, the massive walls of the Citadel and the Amphitheatre and Odeon in downtown Amman.

Mausolea like Qasr al-Quwaysmeh, in the village of the same name, and Qasr an-Nuwayjis, about 5 km (3 miles) from Sports City on the Zerqa road, also date from this period.

There were Christian martyrs in Amman during the Roman persecution. Tradition has it that a site near the village of Abu Alanda to the southeast of the city is the "Cave of the Seven Sleepers" mentioned in the Koran. The story goes that seven Christian boys fleeing persecution took refuge in the cave and fell asleep, only to wake three centuries later when Christianity had become the official religion of the Roman Empire based in Byzantium. There are other rock-carved Byzantine tombs in the vicinity.

Amman was a bishopric and the remains of two Byzantine churches can be found on the Citadel and in the garden of Darat al-Funun on Jebel al-Luwaybda. At Swayfieh, near 6th Circle, archaeologists have discovered the mosaic floor of another Byzantine church dating from the 6th century.

The Darwish Mosque, built by a Circassian on Jebel Ashrafiya in 1961.

Philadelphia reverted to its Semitic name, Ammon, under the Islamic caliphate in Damascus and continued to flourish as a trade centre. It was the headquarters of the local Omayyad governor and capital of the surrounding Belqa'a district. The continuity of Amman's history is shown by the Omayyad Palace and other remains on the Citadel, all built on top of earlier structures.

With the shift in political power from Damascus to Baghdad under the Abbasid Caliphate (750–969 AD) and to Cairo under the Fatimids (969–1171 AD), Amman's fortunes declined. Nevertheless, writing in 985 AD, the Arab geographer Muqaddasi referred to Amman as "the sword of the desert". He went on: "Amman, lying on the border of the desert has round it many villages and wheat fields. The Belqa'a district of which it is the capital, is rich in grains and flocks, it also has many streams, the waters of which work the mills. The castle of Goliath is on the hill overlooking the city."

During the Crusades and under the Mamlukes in Egypt, Amman was relegated to the shade by the rise of Kerak in the south. By AD 1321, the Arab traveller Abu al-Fida reported that Amman was "a very ancient town and was ruined before the days of Islam... there are great ruins here and the river al-Zarqa flows through them." It was not until the end of the 19th century that Amman began to regain its former status.

In Ottoman times: Under the Ottoman Empire Amman remained a small backwater, with Salt the main town in the vicinity. In 1806 Amman was reported to be uninhabited, although the ancient buildings were used as temporary dwellings and store rooms by local farmers. There was plenty of water from the stream running through the valley and Bedouin often camped nearby.

Under pressure in Europe in the 19th century, the Ottomans sought to restore their authority to other parts of their empire. This process coincided with the exodus of large numbers of Circassian and other Muslims from the Caucasus in the wake of wars with the Christian tsar based in Moscow. They found ref-

uge in the Ottoman Empire and, with the encouragement of Istanbul, some of them made their way to the area around Amman. The first to arrive – they established the first permanent Circassian settlement on the East Bank of the Jordan river – were from the Shabsugh tribe, and they are commemorated in the names of streets and buildings in downtown Amman today.

The Circassians were mostly farmers, but there were also goldsmiths, silversmiths, leather and dagger craftsmen and carriage-makers among them. Within a few years of their arrival they had built three mills along the river. They also constructed rough roads and used wheeled transport in Amman for the first time in hundreds of years. Local legend has it that they were the first to bring tea to Jordan. With all these talents, the Circassians looked down on commerce, and from the beginning of this century, merchants from Salt, Syria and Palestine moved in to fill the gap.

However, it was the construction of the Hejaz railway which brought Am-

A Circassian guard at the Royal Palace.

THE HEJAZ RAILWAY

Tottering on the brink of extinction for years, Jordan's Hejaz steam railway is set for a revival. The HJR (Hejaz Jordanian Railway), whose work until recently had been reduced to providing a weekly diesel service between Damascus and Amman, have been dusting down their vintage trains for a whole new life as pleasure locomotives. Trains are already being "steamed up" and shunted out for specially chartered jaunts into the desert either for expats on celebratory jamborees or for replays of the Arab Revolt in which horsemen charge the train to the delight of canapé-snacking tourists. Lucrative use in film and television is also being explored following the railway's role in an advertisement for Extra Strong Mints which netted HJR £6,000 (US$9,000) in six days from the British confectioners Trebor.

Construction of the Hejaz railway was begun in 1900 under the direction of the Ottoman Sultan. Though partly motivated by political and economic factors – a railway

seemed like the ideal way of caging Turkey's crumbling empire – the line was designed to transport Muslim pilgrims to Medina in the Hejaz. Prior to the railway's construction the pilgrimage was made by camel, donkey or foot, at the mercy of the beating sun and toll-charging Bedouins. With the railway, the journey from Damascus to Medina was cut from one month to four days.

The railway was built wholly with Muslim funds. Donations poured in from many sources, from the Shah of Iran and the Sultan himself to collections from the poor. Soldiers in the Ottoman army were required to contribute one month's pay to the fund, as well as undertake much of the actual construction work. Up to 5,000 soldiers laboured on the project at one time.

Slowly the track was laid – approximately 1,610 km (1,000 miles) through some of the most difficult and sterile country on the globe. It had to cope with massive swings in gradient from 60 to 90 metres (200–300 ft) below sea level near the Dead Sea to nearly 1,220 metres (4,000 ft) above. A branch line from Haifa connected the railway to the Mediterranean.

The work took eight years to complete and cost an estimated £3 million (US$4.5 million), a figure "strikingly cheap" according to one contemporary commentator. The same [European] source reported that "the railway is up-to-date in every respect. The carriages are of the corridor type and [the pilgrim] can appreciate the luxury, ease and comfort of the Pullman car." A unique on-board feature was the mosque carriage.

During World War I and the Arab Revolt the railway was a vital line of communication for the Turks and a sitting target for T. E. Lawrence and the Arabs. By persistently blowing up trains but never completely severing the line Lawrence and his Arab irregulars drew Turkish attention away from the main battle fronts.

After the war the railway was repaired and where necessary replaced, and it was even expanded in Palestine, but as other forms of travel became easier, it ceased to be profitable. With the creation of Israel in 1948, the network was partitioned and neglected, and in spite of efforts to revive the line, the service continued to dwindle. By the 1960s many locomotives were entombed in sheds or left to rust in sidings. ∎

man to the centre of the historical stage once more. Linking Damascus with Medina, the railway passed through Amman in 1902 and was completed in 1908. The railway changed the exclusively Circassian, agricultural character of the town. Once more Amman became a centre on the route from Damascus to the Holy City and its population began to swell. By 1905 there were 600–700 houses and some 3,000 people in what was becoming a market town and centre with a mixed population.

During the Emirate: When Emir Abdullah arrived in Transjordan from the Hejaz in 1920, it seemed for a while that Salt, the administrative centre of the area under the Ottomans, would become his capital. However, he eventually decided on Amman, marking a crucial stage in the modern history of the city. There were good reasons for choosing Amman. It was at the political and geographical centre of the country and the Hejaz railway linked the Emir with the Hashemite heartland to the south, and with Damascus to the north.

Amman in the early 1920s was described by a British officer as "quite big for this part of the country and built along the bottom of a narrow valley with houses up the side of the hill. The houses are mostly one storey and extraordinary in shape, many of them suggesting a Swiss chalet, and others very much like Irish peasant cottages… with whitewashed outer walls." But there were no paved roads and few services.

A modest start was made at creating an administration. On 11 April 1921, the first Council of Ministers was formed. The Chief Minister set up shop in a small building by the stream, not far from today's much grander Municipality downtown. In 1923, the Emir began to build the Hussein Mosque on a much older Omayyad one, a move which enraged St-John Philby (the father of British spy master Kim Philby), one of Abdullah's advisers at the time. Two years later Abdullah completed the construction of the Raghadan Palace on a hill across from the Citadel.

Amman's main streets were realigned

Canapé-snacking on the Hejaz railway.

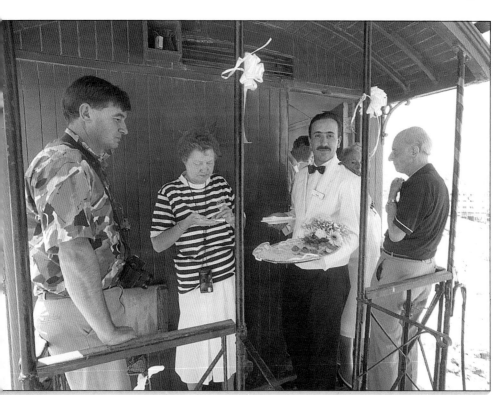

and widened in 1925 and new shops and houses spread along them. Between 1925 and 1927, offices for the Emir Abdullah and the British Residency were built. The telegraph system was reorganised and a bi-weekly motor service was created to connect Amman with Baghdad. Amman's first telephone directory appeared in 1926 and by the following year two newspapers were being published in the city.

The 1927 earthquake encouraged the construction of solid, stone buildings rather than the mud and wood homes preferred by the Circassians. As the *wadi* became more crowded, development began to spread up the nearby hills. Most of the influential people settled on Jebel Amman, near 1st Circle.

The modern kingdom: Despite a process of steady change, until 1948 Amman remained a sleepy capital on the edge of the desert with no more than 25,000 inhabitants. In residential areas, many streets were known by the name of their most important inhabitant. But after the 1948 war with Israel the popu-

lation of Jordan jumped from about 400,000 to 1,300,000 in one year. There was a similar surge in the population of Amman. Better-off refugees in Amman settled in the centre and west of the city, but the vast majority went to camps located in the east

Following Jordan's annexation of the West Bank in 1951, merchants in Amman prospered by serving as middlemen for West Bank importers and between Palestinian producers and Arab markets. Attracted by the opportunities, rural-urban migration enlarged the population still further. By 1967, Amman had about 433,000 inhabitants and this was boosted by the influx of more than 150,000 Palestinian refugees in the wake of the war in that year.

When the job market opened up in the oil-rich Arab states of the Gulf in the early 1970s, the economic boom had enormous consequences on urban expansion in Amman. Between 1972 and 1982, the city grew from 21 sq. km (8 sq. miles) to 54 sq. km (21 sq. miles). Building expanded yet again with the return

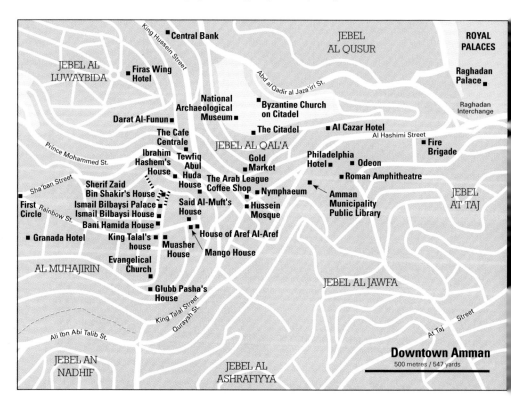

of the 300,000 or more Palestinians and Jordanians expelled from the Gulf and Kuwait after the 1991 Gulf War.

In the process, the city has spilled over and merged with nearby towns like Swaylah, Wadi as-Seer and Rusayfeh. Today the population of the Amman conurbation is estimated at 1.4 million. Unpaved roads have given way to paved streets and highways, and villas and high-rise apartments have replaced earlier simple dwellings. The demand for space has led to former residential buildings becoming centres of commerce. Cake and coffee shops, smart restaurants, hotels and banks have sprung up, especially in the Shmaysani area.

Meanwhile **Abdoun**, off 5th Circle, now boasts some of the best architecture that money can buy. The street leading from the Orthodox Club to the road for 5th Circle is like a gallery dedicated to modern architecture. Nearer the town centre, at Al-Abdali, is the **King Abdullah Mosque** with its distinctive blue dome. This was also built during the early 1980s.

However, like all large cities, Amman has its problems. By the mid-1970s it was divided between an upper-income west with open spaces and good infrastructure and an east with middle- and lower-income neighbourhoods, overcrowding and few facilities. As the city expanded, a lot of much-needed agricultural land was covered by concrete.

Citadel walk: It is appropriate to start a tour of Amman by taking a taxi (it is a tough climb) to the **Citadel**, which not only clarifies the city's history but also gives a sense of its geography, which is confusing at street level. At the top, the Citadel hill looks like a building site. Archaeological digs continue to uncover new evidence of settlement from earliest times down to the recent past. However, the best excavated sites are Roman, Byzantine and Islamic.

Begin with the small, but fascinating **Jordanian Archaeological Museum** which has material from the Palaeolithic period onwards. It has a substantial collection of pottery, small statues, fragments of larger ones and a few coins, but

four exhibits claim special attention.

The first of these is the two wax-like figures discovered at Ain Ghazzal in 1983, and dating to the early Neolithic period (8000–6000 BC). They are reminiscent of the Greek Cycladic statues of the 3rd millennium BC, which so influenced modern sculptors such as Henry Moore. Note, however, that the figures discovered at Ain Ghazzal seem to be much older and more expressive than the Cycladic statues.

The second exhibit of particular importance is a collection of the Dead Sea Scrolls contained in a small alcove on the right at the end of the museum. They were found on the western shore of the Dead Sea in 1952, and one inscribed on metal tells of treasure hidden on the west bank of the Jordan River. Some scholars believe that this may refer to material removed from the Jewish Temple prior to its destruction by the Romans in the 2nd century AD. (All attempts to find this treasure have failed.)

Another alcove on the other side of the room contains two of the most striking exhibits. The first of these comprises four sarcophagi. They are rare examples of burials practised between the 13th and 7th centuries BC. They were discovered in the grounds of the Raghadan Palace in 1966.

Just across from the sarcophagi is the "Amman Daedalus", a Roman copy of a Hellenistic original. The mythical Daedalus built the Minoan Labyrinth in Crete, but he is more famous for the wings he made to enable him and his son Icarus to escape the island. (Icarus's wings subsequently melted when he flew too close to the sun.) The incomplete statue imparts the liveliness and sense of movement characteristic of the finest Greek work.

The Citadel has three archaeological sites which are clear to the layperson. The **Omayyad Palace** and administrative complex, dating from 720–750 AD, is about 40 metres (130 ft) to the rear of the museum. The great audience hall with its cruciform shape and four vaulted chambers leads to a courtyard and colonnaded street running through **At the Citadel.**

the complex, with ruined buildings on either side.

To the left of the museum on the way back to the road lies the site of a small Byzantine church marked out by a number of Corinthian columns and the remains of a wall.

Across the road, on a raised platform, lies the **Temple of Hercules**, dedicated to the Emperor Marcus Aurelius (161–180 AD). Restoration work is in progress and so far two columns have been reconstructed.

Just beyond the temple of Hercules is a platform with a grand view over downtown Amman. Beginning with the walls of the Citadel, immediately to your left, and moving to the right, the eye passes over the small and larger amphitheatre down below. Further to the right along the main streets and hard to make out among modern building is the Nymphaeum. Between it and the twin minarets of the Hussein Mosque, is the black and white Darwish Mosque on the hilltop behind (Jebel Ashrafiya). This mosque was built on the highest point in Amman by a Circassian in 1961. The area around it offers even more stunning views over the city.

On leaving the Citadel, take a left for the main road to downtown Amman. It is downhill all the way and the more athletic may want to walk, but it is also possible to stop a taxi on the main road. The entrance to the **King's Palace**, with Royal Guard sentries in red and white *shireg*, is at the bottom of this road; go right for downtown.

The Roman city centre is mostly under concrete and tarmac nowadays, but the restored large **Amphitheatre** (169–77 AD) conveys a sense of its size and importance. Built into the hillside, it seats about 6,000 people and is still used for performances today. There are three bands of seats: the tiers closest to the arena were for the nobles; the second for the military and the third for the ordinary citizens. Look out for a large stone inscribed with an eye, snake, dagger and bow (just discernible), lying on one side of the arena. This stone once topped the entrance to the amphitheatre and

To the amphitheatre.

symbolised the emperor's protection.

Two small museums at either end of the Roman stage bring the history of Jordan and its capital up to date.

The small **Folklore Museum** tries to present a cross-section of Jordanian life. The statue of a Circassian in traditional dress guards the entrance. Inside, one exhibit shows how rugs are woven, and a display case has samples of different types of embroidery. There are also some old guns and a small display of traditional musical instruments. The latter include the *mihbash* (coffee-grinder), comprising a large wooden pestle and narrow-necked wooden mortar. A good grinder can beat out extraordinary rhythms. Town life is represented by a replica of the living-room of a fine house. The desert and the sown are represented by a Bedouin tent and the plastic camels of a bride and groom, and a small collection of agricultural implements, wooden rakes and threshing boards.

At the other end of the stage is the **Jordanian Museum of Popular Traditions**, opened in 1971 by Sa'adiya at-Tell, the wife of Jordan's then Prime Minister, Wasfi at-Tell. It is an exceptional small museum, this time guarded by the statue of a Bedouin of the Desert Patrol, characteristically dressed in long khaki uniform, ornamental knife and red belt. The collection contains beautifully coloured and embroidered dresses from Jordan and Palestine and some lovely antique jewellery in silver, amber and coral. Look out for the display of heavy silver bracelets and exquisite head-dresses, some of which would not have looked out of place in London's Bloomsbury in the 1920s. A side room contains a collection of mosaics from 4th–6th century churches in Jordan.

The Roman **Odeon** begun in the early part of the 2nd century AD is to the right of the exit from the large amphitheatre. In ruins a short time ago, it has been restored by the Jordanian Department of Antiquities. Over 70 percent of the current building has been rebuilt in a very tasteful way. With 500 seats, it will be a very intimate and comfortable mini theatre when it is completed.

The Hussein Mosque from the Arab League coffee shop.

Turn left along the main street past the Amman Municipality Public Library and keep left at the junction. This is called **Saqf as-Sayl** Street ("the roof of the stream"), so-called because it is built over the stream which was so crucial in Amman's history. The **Roman Nymphaeum** (completed in 191 AD), dedicated to the water nymphs, is about 100 metres (110 yards) further up on the right. The high stone wall on the street is all that remains of the original building.

Turn right after the nymphaeum, past a little shop selling spices and coffee and the colourful fruit and vegetable market, and left at the next intersection for the **Hussein Mosque**. It is decorated in alternating pink and white stone and a plaque on the wall reveals that the original mosque was built by Omar Ibn al-Khattab, the Second Caliph of Islam (634–644) – Emir Abdullah rebuilt on the site and restoration work was carried out by King Hussein in 1987.

Directly opposite is the **Arab League coffee shop**, which is reached via a steep set of stairs round the corner to the right. Customers emerge in a large room filled with men playing cards and backgammon or just talking. The old wooden chairs, marble and smaller brass-topped tables add to its atmosphere. Get a seat near the window just across from the mosque, have a cool drink, coffee, tea or *narghileh* (hubble-bubble) and watch the world go by. Women who would prefer a less masculine domain may prefer to drink and rest at **Jabri's**, which is at the bottom of King Hussein (or Salt) Street, about 200 metres (220 yards) away. Go straight past the entrance to the Arab League coffee shop, take a left along the main street and Jabri's is on the right where the road forks.

The Emirate walk: For a walk through the early modern history of Amman and the Emirate down to modern times, take a taxi to Jebel Amman to where Rainbow Street off 1st Circle comes to an end in a "T" junction. It was to this area that the influential people in the Emirate (including the current King's father and family) moved following the earthquake of 1927. They replaced the old Circassian

offee-shop ursuits.

houses of dried mud and wood with more secure stone houses. The beautiful houses and mansions in characteristic white and sometimes pink stone that are dotted along the route tell the history of Jordan before 1948.

It is appropriate that the first house on the left (as you walk back up Rainbow Street) once belonged to a leading Palestinian historian, Aref al-Aref. He came from Jerusalem in the early 1920s to work with Emir Abdullah and later returned to Palestine to become mayor of Jerusalem. The weathered stone and arched windows are framed by jasmine and a huge date palm tree.

Further up Rainbow Street the **Mango villa** with its curving balconies is next on the left. The present structure dates from the 1950s, but an earlier building is around the corner in Omar Ibn al-Khattab Street. Two brothers, Hamdi and Ibrahim Mango, were cloth merchants, who came to the Emirate from Nablus in Palestine. They made their fortune during World War II, by selling a ship-load of cloth which they had imported just before the war. They were perhaps the first Jordanians to do business with the Japanese.

A little alleyway opposite the Mango villa leads to a small stone house which was home to the daughter of Mirza Pasha, an ex-Ottoman officer who came to Jordan in the early part of this century and became head of the Circassian community. Back on Rainbow Street, the compound on the right belonged to Said al-Mufti, another prominent Circassian who became Prime Minister during the Emirate. Emir Abdullah used to stay at the older Mufti house in the Wadi when he first arrived from the Hejaz. It has been destroyed long since and the current structure dates from the post-1927 period. One of the houses in the compound still has the lines of the old Circassian buildings, with a low roof and long porch.

Turn left along Omar Ibn al-Khattab Street (formerly Glubb Pasha Street). It curves for about 100 metres before coming to No. 40, where high walls on the right surround **Glubb Pasha's house**. Go back along the street for 10 metres,

The birthplace of King Hussein and Crown Prince Hassan (right) and the house of the Muasher family (left).

walk up the stairs on the same side as Glubb's house, and pass the Evangelical church, built in 1949, and the Ahliyah school, which was founded in 1926 by the Christian Mission Society of England. A large mansion on the right belongs to the Muasher family, Christians from Salt who came to Amman in the early years of the Emirate. They had a small grocery business and also made their fortune during World War II.

Just across from the road, near the junction with Rainbow Street, is the house where King Hussein and Prince Hassan were born and lived with their father King Talal. Compared to some of the mansions hereabouts, it is a modest building. The family was relatively poor in those days and Emir Abdullah could accommodate only his immediate family at the Raghadan Palace. Older residents of the neighbourhood still recall how the present King and his family lived there for 17 years, interacting with their neighbours like any other family. Others claim that during the dead of night members of the royal family sometimes come to peek at their former home.

Straight on across Rainbow Street and just past a house of pink stone on the corner, which once belonged to the Mara'i family of Syrian merchants, is what has become known as the **Bani Hamida house**. This is the salesroom and administrative centre of a successful crafts project involving local Bedouin women. Beautiful flat woven rugs and other items are on sale. The house actually belongs to the Qussus family, Christians of the Halassa tribe from southern Jordan (a member of the Odat family was Minister of Justice under Emir Abdullah), but it used to be home to Alec Kirkbride, who was the British Resident in Jordan for many years. Kirkbride's brother and parents lived in other Qussus houses nearby.

The **Bilbaysi house** of white stone, and the **Bilbaysi palace**, of alternating pink and white, are straight ahead. Older residents tell a rags-to-riches tale. They say that old Ismail Bilbaysi, whose family may have come originally from the town of Bilbays in Egypt, was himself

from Nablus. He came to the East Bank in the early 1900s to work on the Hejaz railway as an unskilled labourer. He went on to become a delivery man for Shell (at the time, motor fuel was sold in containers holding 20 litres which required a strong man such as Bilbaysi to shift) and then moved on to selling. In time he became Shell's sole agent in Jordan. He made his fortune from World War II.

The story goes that Bilbaysi accomplished all this without seeing any country other than Palestine and Jordan. When his son later became Jordan's ambassador to Switzerland he invited his father – who had in the meantime developed eye trouble – to Switzerland for the best available care. Ismail was reluctant, but allowed himself to be persuaded. On arrival, he was taken to hospital, where he underwent a successful operation. When it was over, his son tried to persuade him to stay in Switzerland so that he might see some of the country when the bandages were removed. But old Bilbaysi refused and he returned to Jordan where his eyes recovered. So even though he travelled to Switzerland, he never actually saw it.

Bilbaysi built the palace in 1954 and allowed King Abdullah to house his guests here (there was still no room at Raghadan). Locals claim that Rita Hayworth stayed here when shooting *Salomé*. King Abdullah rewarded Bilbaysi by making him a Pasha.

Take the steps down past the high walls to the left, which enclose the **house of Sherif Zaid Bin Shakir**, a relative of the King and ex-Prime Minister and Commander of the Armed Forces. Sherif Zaid's father was one of Emir Abdullah's closest allies during the Arab Revolt. Turn left for about 30 metres and take the stairs down to the next street. The Rashdans house is on the right. The Rashdans were from Irbid in the north and worked in government, reflecting once more Emir Abdullah's efforts to unite all parts of the country.

Go straight down the road for 100 metres, keeping right at the fork, to the **house of Tewfiq Abul Huda**, one of

The coffee ceremony at Kam Zaman.

Emir Abdullah's earliest allies and Prime Minister of Jordan on several occasions. It was built in the style of Lebanese mountain houses in 1927. The mason who planned and constructed the upper storey was a Lebanese Druze, Shekeeb Abu Hamdan. His grandson, an architect, has his offices here now.

Go back towards the fork in the road. A small stone structure in a car park in front is all that remains of the **house of Ibrahim Hashem**. He was also with Emir Abdullah from very early on and locals joke about how he and Tewfiq Abul Huda used to take turns as Prime Minister. Certainly, a lot of important decisions were made in this 50-metre stretch of Amman and it is a shame that cars now park in what was Ibrahim Hashem's living-room. The remaining building is now used as a store room. Unfortunately, there is no law protecting Amman's historical buildings.

Fifty metres down the road to the right, a set of stairs lead down to Emir Mohammed Street. Cross the road and turn right past Omar al-Khayyam Street.

A small alley to the left leads to **Hashem's restaurant**, one of the oldest in the downtown area. It sells Arab fast foods, like *hummus* and *ful* (beans). In the old days, all classes of Jordanians used to meet and eat here; now it caters mainly for Egyptian and local workers.

Emir Mohammed and King Hussein (or Salt) streets intersect a few metres further along the main street. Above, is the **Centrale Café**, one of the oldest coffee shops in Amman and a nice place in which to relax and watch the hustle and bustle of the street. The entrance is via a steep flight of stairs a little way up King Hussein Street, just after two small stalls selling good *shawarma*. Try and get a table outside overlooking the downtown area. Look out for the bullet holes around the window of the Cairo Hotel about 50 metres down the street on the right, a relic of the 1970 conflict between the Jordanian army and the Palestinian Resistance Movement.

Go back to Omar al-Khayyam Street and climb the street past the white "service" taxis. Keep right uphill, then turn to

Arab fast food in Hashem's.

the left. It is a steep climb, but worth it in the end. In front is the restored **Hamud house**, now known as the **Darat al-Funun** (Little House of the Arts), which was once home to Peake Pasha. In the 1920s and '30s Peake used to be woken up every morning by a military band, which echoed through the hills and valleys of what was then a small town.

The house has been beautifully renovated by the architect and artist Amar Khammesh and is now an art gallery containing some of the best work contemporary Arab artists have to offer. All the exhibits are for sale and the artists provide a continuous supply of new material. The small sculpture as you enter the gallery is by Mona Saudi, a leading Jordanian sculptress, whose monumental *Architecture of the Soul* sits outside the Institut du Monde Arabe in Paris. Budding artists and other interested folk can use the library and video-room upstairs. This is one of the most interesting small galleries in the Middle East or anywhere else and sure to breathe life into local and regional contempo-rary art. The garden contains the remains of a Byzantine church where concerts are sometimes held.

Around Amman: Wadi as-Seer is one of the most attractive valleys in Jordan and it also contains one of the most interesting and underrated ancient monuments in the Middle East. The *wadi* lies about 12 km (8 miles) west of Amman, beyond 8th Circle and the village of Wadi as-Seer. The best time to visit the valley is spring, when everything is green and the slopes are dotted with poppies and wild iris, but the scenery is spectacular at any time of the year. The city seems much further away than a few kilometres.

The road winds down the valley to the river and passes through several small villages before reaching **Iraq al-Emir**, the Caves of the Prince. Five hundred metres further on, it ends at **Qasr al-Abd**, the Palace of the Slave, perhaps the most important Hellenistic palace to have survived in the Middle East.

Just south of Amman, on a hilltop 12 km (7 miles) from 7th Circle off the airport road, is **Kan Zaman**, a renovated 19th-century complex of stables, storehouses and residential quarters and now a major tourist attraction. The complex belongs to a prominent Jordanian family, the Abu Jabers, whose forefathers moved from Nazareth to Salt at the beginning of the 19th century. By the middle of the century, they were growing cereals and raising livestock from their hilltop base.

Kan Zaman ("once upon a time") opened in 1989. It combines a turn-of-the-century atmosphere with some of the best food and crafts that Jordan has to offer. The stone-paved courtyard is lined with shops selling handicrafts, jewellery and spices. Visitors can smoke a hubble-bubble at the coffee shop, or eat excellent Arabic food at the restaurant in the renovated stables. Be prepared too for the skirl of bagpipes and to see the waiters dance an Arab *dabkeh* here. There is also a piano restaurant, Al-Baydar ("the Threshing Floor") at the other end of the courtyard, which serves local food cooked in the traditional *tanoor* clay oven.

Left, the coffee-pot as symbol. **Right**, Bedouin rugs for sale in the Bani Hamida House.

SALT

Capital of the Belqa'a region, **Salt** is the most historic town in Jordan. Though practically a satellite town of Amman nowadays, for long periods in history it was the most important settlement between the Jordan River and the desert to the east. Its golden age was at the end of the 19th century and the beginning of the 20th, and it is the legacy of this period that makes Salt unique in Jordan and beyond.

Salt has attracted settlers since the Iron Age at least. The area enjoys a moderate climate, a plentiful supply of water and fertile soil (it gave its name to the sultana, the tasty dried grapes produced here for centuries). Located on the "frontier of settlement", the line between desert and sown, the town provided security from marauding Bedouin. It was also well placed on the north–south trade routes and those running from east to west, linking the interior with Jerusalem, Nablus, Nazareth and the Mediterranean coast. Its mixed Muslim-Christian population and its trading tradition helped create an atmosphere of tolerance and coexistence.

There are Roman tombs on the outskirts of the town, and during the Byzantine period it was known as Saltos Hieraticon. In the 13th century a fortress was built on the site of the citadel by the Mamluke Sultan al-Malik al-Mu'azzam, who was based in Cairo. Destroyed by the Mongols in 1260, the fortress was rebuilt a year later by a second Mamluke ruler from Egypt. Six centuries later, in 1840, it was demolished again by the forces of yet another Egyptian potentate, Ibrahim Pasha. The Citadel is now the site of a large mosque which towers over the modern town.

Throughout this time and with the decline of Amman, Salt played an important role in the region. When the Arab traveller Abu al-Fida visited the town in the 13th century, he described it as a prosperous small town with a castle and numerous orchards. In 1596, officials of the Ottoman Empire based in Istanbul noted that Salt was "the only town in the Belqa'a district". More than 200 years later, the Swiss traveller and Arabist, Burckhardt, described it as "the only inhabited place in the province of Belqa'a. He also recorded that there were 400 Muslim and 80 Christian families in the town at the time.

By the early 19th century, Salt was a well-off frontier town on the edge of the Ottoman Empire and the desert. Useful to all, it was ruled by none. In 1806, the people of Salt were said to be "free from every kind of taxation and to acknowledge no master". Down to the present day, Saltis have a reputation for being stubborn and independent.

The town was also the centre of lucrative trading between the region and urban industries in Palestine. Saltis were the middlemen for the supply of raw materials (3,500 camel-loads annually by mid-century) collected by local Bedouin for use in the tanneries of Jerusalem and the soap factories of Nablus. Raisins and grapes were also exported to Palestine. Travellers of this time write

of a flourishing town with shops stocking cotton from Manchester, England and other goods produced locally. From 1867 onwards, the town's fortunes improved dramatically, and it is this golden age that makes Salt special.

Salt's Golden Age: In the mid-19th century, the Ottomans sought to reassert control over their empire in the Middle East. As part of this process, the Belqa'a region was incorporated into the area governed from Nablus and an administrative officer, with military forces at his disposal, was sent to Salt. The Ottomans also encouraged migration and settlement from other parts of the empire, and as the area became more secure, people flocked in from Nablus, Nazareth, Jerusalem and further afield in search of opportunities in agriculture, trade, construction and government. Soon, officials based in Salt were collecting taxes from the surrounding countryside, as the Bedouin were steadily absorbed into the system.

Salt began to expand and new construction reflected its status. An Ottoman administrative office was built on what was to become the town square three years later in 1869. In 1866, the first modern Christian church was built and the Church Missionary Society set up the first hospital. As trade increased, shops spread along Hamam Street and houses sprang up on the lower slopes of the hills meeting at the town centre.

In the 1870s merchants moved in from Palestine. Families like the Touqans, Nabulsis and Mehyars migrated from Nablus, leading contemporary observers to speak of Salt as a mini Nablus. However, Salt had plenty of homegrown merchants, like the Sukkars, Muashers and Sakets. Another prominent local family, the Abu Jabers, had migrated from Nazareth to Salt in the early 19th century. All of these are well known names in Jordanian public life to this day.

These families celebrated their good fortune by constructing fine houses, most of which have survived. Made from local yellow stone, they incorporate a variety of indigenous and European

Classical flourishes enliven Ottoman architecture.

styles. Typically, they have one to three storeys with domed roofs and inner courtyards. The Abu Jaber mansion, built between 1892 and 1906, has frescoed ceilings painted by Italian artists and is reputed to be the region's finest example of a 19th-century merchant house.

Salt's fortunes declined after World War I. The first blow came when Emir Abdullah chose Amman as the capital of the new Emirate of Transjordan. The irreversible shift in political and economic power concluded with the Arab-Israeli wars of 1948 and 1967, when Salt was cut off from the Mediterranean and its natural markets in Nablus and the rest of Palestine.

For these reasons, Salt's population increased slowly from 15,000 in 1900 to only 50,000 in 1993. Construction matched this pace with the happy result that while reinforced concrete has replaced local stone in many places, the town centre and other buildings remain almost as they were nearly 100 years ago. They provide a rare example of a turn-of-the-century Arab town in the Ottoman Empire.

A walk around Salt: Buildings in Salt climb a tight cluster of hills. Arriving from Amman, one is suddenly confronted by layers of construction rising above. On a hill to the left, just before entering the town, is Salt secondary school, the first of its kind in the country. Built in 1924, it attracted teachers from all over the Arab world and a list of alumni reads like a *Who's Who* of Jordan. Straight ahead, a modern mosque dominates the town centre from the Citadel, the site of the 13th-century Mamluke fortress. Below, older yellow stone houses shine out amidst more modern concrete ones.

Start at **Salt Cultural Centre**, which includes a one-room folklore museum. Turn left at the main entrance and left again along what some know as Sharia al-Dayr (Monastery Street, after the monastery up the road) or Sharia Yarmouk (Yarmouk Street, after the school along the way) or Sharia al-Baladiya (Municipality Street, because it leads to the old Municipality build-

ing). Fifty metres along on the right-hand side is what locals call the **Muasher house**, which marks the true beginning of the walk. A Christian merchant family, the Muashers are long-time residents of Salt from the Dababneh tribe believed to have originated in the Hawran region in the south of modern-day Syria and Lebanon.

In fact, this house also belonged to the Abu Jaber family originally. They built the house at the turn of the century and it was later sold to the Muashers. The house is unmistakable with its intertwined, liquorice-like columns on the second floor.

Walk back along the same street and up towards the town square. Older buildings on the left-hand side belonged to the Hammoud and Nabir families. Note the narrow stairs off the main street leading to other houses up the hill.

The Latin Monastery is on the right-hand side as you approach the square, behind high walls. The complex contains the oldest public building (1871) in Jordan's modern age, a church (1890)

Making repairs.

and a fine courtyard, which was the site of important meetings between local notables and British officials from Palestine in 1921 prior to the establishment of the Emirate. There are two steel doors on the street; ring the bell to see inside.

The large house to the left on entering the square is the **Abu Jaber mansion** mentioned earlier. It s balconies and sheer size make it the most impressive building of its kind in the town. There is talk of turning the mansion into a museum, as part of a broader plan to restore Salt's historic buildings and to turn the town into a tourist centre.

Emir Abdullah stayed at the Abu Jaber house when he first arrived from the Hejaz in March 1921. Locals delight in telling how Abdullah was going to make Salt his capital, but they ran him out of town. According to Saltis, Bedouin from Abdullah's entourage were pestering local women collecting water from a nearby spring. One thing led to another, and irate Saltis drove Abdullah's men from the town by pelting them with stones. The Emir is said to have been so

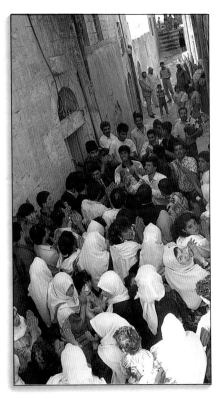

upset by this treatment, which he felt contradicted traditional rules of Arab hospitality, that he went off to Amman and declared it the capital of the Emirate of Transjordan. Relations between Abdullah and his Salti subjects never recovered from the blow, they say.

Keep left up the town square. A small entrance to the left beyond the Abu Jaber building and a row of shops leads up to a number of old houses behind the new government buildings on the square. Climb up the steps to where they fork. The house in front belonged to the Muasher family. The mansion at the top of the stairs to the right was built by the Sukkars, another Christian family from the Dababneh tribe. According to locals, Emir Abdullah also stayed at this house. Note the European-style roof perched on the top storey of the house.

To the right of the Sukkar house, along a small pathway behind the new government buildings, is a one-storey house which belonged to the Khateeb family from Jerusalem. Next door is a good example of the "peasant style" houses which characterised Salt prior to 1860. In ruins in 1993, with an old olive tree in the garden, the lines and structure of the building were clearly visible. It had one storey, and inside, two stone arches supported the remains of a roof of wood and clay.

Continue down the stairs past the house of the Saket family, old residents of Salt, to the town square. Cross the road and go back towards the Abu Jaber house and the modern fountain near the bottom of the square. This may be the site of Salt's first fountain, which is the source of another local legend. The story goes that in the 19th century a mason from the Far family of Nazareth was commissioned to build a fountain, which was to be paid for communally. But when Far finished the job, many Saltis refused to pay their share of the bill. So Far put a plug in the spring and, deprived of water, the defaulting Saltis paid up in due course.

Near the fountain, directly across the square from the steps to the Muasher and Sukkar houses, a small yellow walled lane leads up to the English

A wedding party.

church/hospital/school complex. The first door on the right is to the church, built in 1926. The second one higher up with E.H. (English Hospital?) engraved on it leads to the hospital (1882–1923) and the school. The school, which is no longer in use, is the very yellow building on the left. Sit a while in the old schoolyard and enjoy the view over the town centre. Plans to turn the place into a small restaurant will be welcome news for travellers in need of refreshment at this point.

Go back down the steps and take the second left into Hamam Street. This narrow street is a working market and walking along it is like going back in time. The yellow stone buildings are more than 90 years old, and the ambience goes back hundreds of years. Fruit and spices and other goods are on sale here and 30 metres along, just after a small entrance on the left is the curving facade of the Touqan building. It is said that the Touqans fled from Nablus in the mid-19th century when that town was taken over by the army of Ibrahim Pasha from Egypt, who favoured the Abd al-Hadi family. Fifty metres further on, steps on the left lead to the Nabulsi house, another Nablus family. Note the wooden *mashrabiya* balcony, which allowed women to see out without being seen by passers-by.

Return to Hamam Street and walk along it. Pass a right-hand turn leading to the main street. Next on either side of the road are properties belonging to the Mehyar family, who may have arrived in Salt from Nablus in the 1860s or earlier. A little way along is the carved minaret of the "small mosque", built in 1906. This building, too, reflects the confidence and wealth of the time.

On reaching the main road, turn right towards the **Cultural Centre** and the end of the walk. Just before it on the left is a renovated **Touqan House**, which is now the Municipality building. The entrance hall provides a good example of the domed roofs which characterise these old houses – cool in summer, warm in winter – and upstairs there is a typical interior courtyard.

Talking shop.

NORTH JORDAN

The area of north Jordan and south Syria – roughly from the Jordanian capital of Amman to the Syrian capital of Damascus – was often referred to during the Roman era as the region of the Decapolis, meaning the "10 cities" in Greek. This was a region of great wealth, due to its rich agricultural lands, plentiful water from rainfall and perennial springs and rivers, valuable mineral resources, and its strategic location along some of the most important trade routes of antiquity. The spice, incense, and silk routes all passed through or near the Decapolis.

It is not surprising, therefore, that this region should be dotted with some major archaeological sites, several of which can be visited on a pleasant day-trip from Amman that also takes in the three main topographic and climatic zones of the country – the semi-arid eastern desert, the central highlands, and the Jordan Valley to the west. The four most important sites in the northern highlands and desert plateau are Jerash, Umm Qais, Abila, and Umm al-Jimal (they are joined by the other major northern city of Pella, which is described in the *Jordan Valley* chapter, pages 215–223). These cities all reached their peak during the Graeco-Roman era, but they also flourished during other periods.

In their historical sweep, the antiquities of north Jordan cover a timespan of well over 5,000 years – from the birth of cities in the Early Bronze Age to the Ayyubid/Mamluke settlements of the medieval Islamic era – and almost all major sites continued to be inhabited through the late Ottoman period and into the 20th century.

The area of north Jordan also contains many smaller antiquities sites and areas of natural beauty. The north is the most fertile part of the Jordanian plateau because of its higher altitude and greater rainfall. The best time of year to

Preceding pages: sheep territory. **Left,** Temple of Artemis, Jerash.

visit is the spring, when the plains are covered in wheat and barley and the rolling hills leading down to the Jordan Valley are blanketed in grass. The area is predominantly agricultural, with only a few medium-scale industries and service firms making up the balance of the economy. Many parts of the semi-arid eastern desert fringe turn green in spring, thanks to the seasonal farmers who tap run-off water or underground aquifers.

To help flesh out the history of the region, it's worth stopping for an hour at the small but impressive Jordanian Heritage Museum at Yarmouk University in Irbid, with its excellent overview of the story of human development and civilisation in Jordan during the last half a million years. Hotels at Irbid, Ajlun, Himmeh in the valley, and Azraq (see *East to Azraq*, pages 201–211) can be used for overnight bases. Travellers between Jordan and Syria have to pass through the sole frontier post at the Jordanian town of Ramtha (and the Syrian town of Dir'a). It usually takes about an hour to pass through the border post,

but can require longer if there is a long line of cars (such as during holidays). Traffic is lightest in the early morning.

The Decapolis riddle: The Decapolis itself is something of a riddle, for scholars are not sure exactly what it means. They debate whether the term refers to a formal league or confederation of 10 cities that were bound by commercial, political and security bonds, or to something less systematic. The Decapolis is mentioned in the New Testament as a "region", and Roman era references suggest it may have been an administrative district that was created when the General Pompey conquered the region in 63 BC.

Most scholars now agree that the term Decapolis probably had different meanings at different times. At its height in the Roman period, it was probably a loose association of geographically contiguous Graeco-Roman provincial cities that shared cultural, commercial and political interests. Different lists of Decapolis cities from several historical periods provide the names of more than

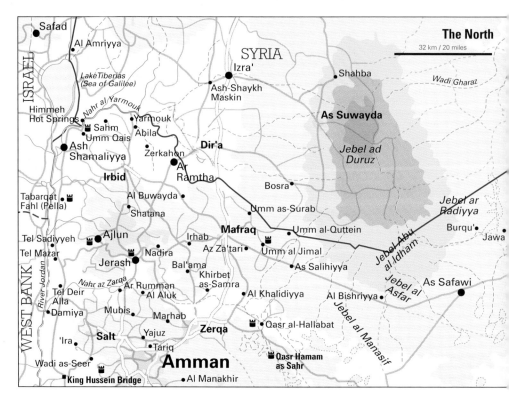

10 cities, indicating that the definition of the region of the Decapolis changed over time.

The most recent scholarship identifies the cities of the Decapolis as: Philadelphia (Amman), Gerasa (Jerash), Pella (Tabaqat Fahl), Gadara (Umm Qais), Scythopolis (Beisan or Bethshean, the only one of the 10 west of the Jordan river), Damascus, Hippos, Canatha, Dium, and Raphana. The first four on this list can be visited in Jordan today, while some of the others are not clearly identified with modern sites. Abila and Capitolias, in north Jordan, are also mentioned on some ancient lists of Decapolis cities.

The term Decapolis has never been found on coins or in inscriptions and literary sources originating within the region of the Decapolis; all ancient references come from literary sources or inscriptions from places further afield.

Magic on the Roman frontier: Often called the "Pompeii of the East" because of its fine state of preservation, **Jerash** retains all the magic and beauty of a rich provincial city along the southeastern frontier of the Roman Empire. Few other Roman era towns in the world are as well preserved or as complete as Jerash. Located 40 km (25 miles) north of Amman, it is Jordan's most visited touristic site – due both to its convenient location and the richness of its antiquities. Not only is virtually the entire ancient city-centre still in place, but the carved architectural details and inscriptions are as fresh today as when they were first chiselled into the soft orange limestone nearly 2,000 years ago.

Graeco-Roman Jerash as we know it today was first built by the remnants of the Hellenistic legions of Alexander the Great in the 2nd century BC. It flourished as a provincial trading city after the Roman General Pompey conquered the land of Jordan in 63 BC. Along with its compatriot Decapolis cities of Philadelphia, Gadara and Pella, Jerash reached its peak in the 2nd century AD, when the Pax Romana (Roman peace) allowed regional and international trade to flourish and encouraged local invest-

Below left, emple of eus, Jerash. ight, the leasure of uins.

ments by wealthy merchants and landowners. It is a fine example of the grand, formal provincial Roman urbanism that is found throughout the Middle East, comprising paved and colonnaded streets, soaring hilltop temples, handsome theatres, spacious public squares and plazas, baths, fountains and city walls pierced by towers and gates.

For the past decade, the Jordanian Department of Antiquities' Jerash International Project has brought together archaeologists and architects from eight countries (the US, France, Poland, Spain, Italy, Australia, the UK and Jordan) to excavate new areas while conserving and restoring monuments. Their work has clarified nagging ambiguities about the earliest (Hellenistic) and latest (early Islamic) phases of the city's life. It confirms that Jerash existed virtually without interruption for over 1,000 years – spanning the Hellenistic, Roman, Byzantine and early Islamic (Omayyad and Abbasid) periods, from the 2nd century BC to the 9th century AD.

Beneath its external Graeco-Roman veneer, Jerash also preserves a subtle blend of the Orient and the Occident, of east and west. Its architecture, religion, languages and even the names of its citizens in antiquity reflect a process by which two powerful cultures initially clashed, but ultimately meshed and co-existed – the Graeco-Roman world of the Mediterranean basin, and the ancient traditions of the Arab Orient. The very name of the city reflects this interaction. The earliest settlement of indigenous Arab/Semitic people, in the pre-classical period of the 1st millennium BC, was called Garshu (as we know from a funerary inscription in Petra in memory of a Jerash trader who died and was buried in the Nabataean capital).

The Hellenistic settlement founded in the 2nd century BC was called Antioch on the Chrysorhoas (or Antioch on the "Golden River", the Hellenistic name of the perennial stream which still runs through the city). Little of the Hellenistic city has been excavated, as most of it was removed when the Romans rebuilt it in the 1st and 2nd centuries AD.

Left, the Cardo, Jerash.

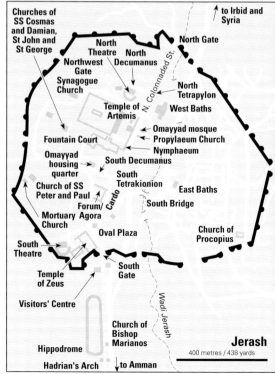

Churches of SS Cosmas and Damian, St John and St George
North Theatre
North Decumanus
to Irbid and Syria
North Gate
Northwest Gate
N. Colonnaded St.
North Tetrapylon
Synagogue Church
Temple of Artemis
West Baths
Fountain Court
Omayyad mosque
Propylaeum Church
Nymphaeum
Omayyad housing quarter
South Decumanus
Church of SS Peter and Paul
South Tetrakionion
East Baths
Forum/ Mortuary Agora Church
Cardo
South Bridge
Oval Plaza
Church of Procopius
South Theatre
South Gate
Temple of Zeus
Visitors' Centre
Wadi Jerash
Church of Bishop Marianos
Hippodrome
Jerash
400 metres / 438 yards
Hadrian's Arch
to Amman

The Romans who came in 63 BC quickly Hellenised the former Arabic name Garshu into Gerasa. At the end of the 19th century, the Arab and Circassian inhabitants of the then small rural settlement in turn transformed Roman Gerasa into Arabic Jerash. In ancient times, the roads linking Jerash with Philadelphia to the south, Bosra and Damascus to the north, and Pella to the west would have been well travelled by local traders, international caravans and Roman legionary troops.

When the Emperor Trajan occupied the Nabataean kingdom in south Jordan, north Arabia and Sinai in AD 106, the area underwent another major reorganisation. Half the Decapolis cities found themselves within the Roman province of Syria, while others, including Jerash, fell under the jurisdiction of the new province of Arabia.

This reorganisation had little impact on the fortunes of these towns, which continued to develop. With peace came local investments in agriculture, industry and services, which in turn boosted both regional and international trade.

As Jerash flourished for more than 200 years thanks to income from exports and taxes from trade, it expanded out towards its meandering city walls, and filled in many of its urban spaces with public structures that still stand. In fact, you sense Gerasa's prosperity even before you arrive at the South Gate, because the first monument you reach on the road from Amman is the triple-gated **Hadrian's Arch**, standing alone some 450 metres (500 yards) south of the city walls. It was built to commemorate the Emperor Hadrian's visit to Gerasa in AD 129, when the city fathers planned to extend the city walls out to link up with the arch, which would form the town's main entrance from the south. The project was never completed, however, and the arch stands virtually on its own now; next to it is the massive **Hippodrome**, which is being excavated, and a cemetery with the remains of a small Byzantine funerary church.

A walk through the ruins: Visitors enter the city today just as the Roman period

n history's ootsteps.

JERASH FESTIVAL

The old Roman amphitheatre at Jerash was packed to the last row on a balmy summer night. A spotlight roamed over the audience who waved and cheered in the sudden limelight. An Algerian flag, in tribute to the evening's performer, flew above the crowd. It looked as if all the *shebab* (youth) of Jordan had come to see Cheb Khaled, one of the most popular singers in the Arab world.

Over 4,000 people had wedged themselves into the intimate confines of the South Theatre on this the last night of the festival. The tiered stone ledges that once held Roman citizens in flowing togas and leather sandals were occupied by modern-day Jordanians sporting Levi's and Reeboks.

When the star finally bounded on to the centre of the stage, the crowd's welcome was deafening. Whole sections leapt up to dance, before Cheb had even finished the opening blast of his most popular hit. During the performance a full moon peeked over the rim of the ancient theatre, as if to see what had disturbed the peace of ruins that had slumbered for centuries.

For two or three weeks every July, the renovated ruins of Jerash come alive with the festival. Performances span many nations and cultures and cover every sphere of the arts from, say, *Rigoletto* performed by an Italian operatic troupe, to modern ballet performed on the steps of the Artemis temple, or the beloved songs of Lebanese singers Fairouz and Ragheb Alameh and *The Taming of the Shrew*, performed by the British Actors' Theatre Co. While Chinese acrobats might spin in circles on bicycles at breakneck speed in the South Theatre, somewhere else in the ancient setting Spanish gipsies sing and dance the flamenco.

On this particular night the audience danced. The previous evening they had sat mesmerised as the Caracalla dancers of Lebanon worked their magic. Women gowned in chiffon and sparkling jewels danced with partners swathed in velvet brocades and Damascene silk, spinning tales of crowded bazaars and mist-filled oases in an oriental version of *A Midsummer Night's Dream*. Earlier in the festival, a full house had wept with laughter at the irreverent political satire of *Welcome Arab Summit*, a play performed in Arabic. Founded by Jordanian actors Nabil Sawalha and Hisham Yanis, the Ahlan Theatre Group poked healthy fun at Arab leaders through the sceptical eyes of the man and woman in the street.

The Jerash festival was inaugurated in 1981 by Queen Noor, who has been its patron and guiding light ever since, and is eagerly awaited every year. Funding is a major challenge to such a small country, yet even during the 1990–91 Gulf War the festival took place. As Mr Akram Masarweh, who organises the event, puts it: "The festival offers an opportunity for Westerners to see Arabic folklore, hear Oriental music and experience Middle Eastern culture. It also provides Jordanians with the chance to see art and cultural events with the West."

But the festival is not just a celebration of performing talent. Jordanian handicrafts are also given their due attention, with wooden craft stalls wedged into every nook and cranny. The Cardo, the ancient avenue of daily commerce, is the perfect showcase for Bedouin rugs, wrought ironwork, blown glass and embroidered gowns. ■

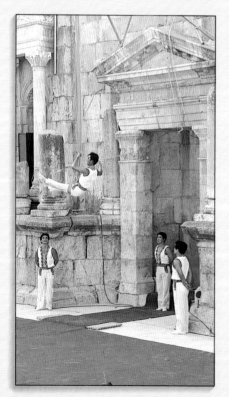

Chinese gymnasts at the Jerash festival.

inhabitants did – through the monumental, delicately carved **South Gate**, now adjacent to the modern visitors' centre and restaurant. The gate has been recently reconstructed by a French-Jordanian team. Immediately inside it is a marketplace with a 3rd-century AD olive press visible in a room now below ground level.

From the South Gate, you walk up into the spacious **Oval Plaza**, a skewed oval-shaped space measuring 90 x 80 metres (295 x 262 ft) in size, with a fine arcade of Ionic columns. These columns retain the 1st-century architectural flavour of the site, which was largely remodelled in the 2nd century with Corinthian capitals and columns replacing the Ionic ones.

The Oval Plaza's non-symmetrical shape is unusual for classical cities, but is explained by its distinct role: it served to reconcile the two different axes of the Cardo and the Zeus Temple, which were aligned neither on a straight line nor at 90-degree angles. The plaza allowed the east-west axis of the Zeus Temple to

fit into the north-south axis of the Cardo and the rest of the city. Visitors who walk into the plaza from the south find themselves naturally turning towards the north, to the start of the Cardo.

High to the west, overlooking the plaza, is the 1st-century AD **Temple of Zeus**; it combines the classical temple look with the oriental tradition of siting cultic installations on hilltops (like the biblical era "high places") and surrounding them with a *temenos* (an enclosed holy precinct). Recent excavations on the terrace in front of the temple have uncovered some pre-Roman, Hellenistic cultic structures, including an open-air altar.

Immediately west of the temple is the **South Theatre**, ancient Gerasa's main gathering place for stage entertainment; it was completed in the early 2nd century AD and could accommodate 3,000 spectators. Inscriptions in Greek give the names of some of the wealthy Gerasenes who donated money to help pay for its construction. Today, with much of its stage area restored, its acous-

The Oval Plaza.

tics as sharp as ever, and some of its seats still "numbered" with engraved Greek letters, the South Theatre hosts the main events at the annual Jerash Festival of Culture and Arts. There is a fine view from the top overlooking the Oval Plaza and much of the city.

The Oval Plaza leads visitors into the 12-metre (39-ft) wide and 800-metre (2,635-ft) long Cardo, the architectural spine and focal point of ancient Gerasa. In the 2nd century, the original Cardo was widened into its present Corinthian configuration (except at its northern end). The city's most important structures were arranged around the Cardo, including markets, temples, fountains and other public buildings.

As you walk up the street, you pass a series of important monuments, most of which are announced by large, thicker columns that stand out above the rest of the street colonnade. Some of the most important monuments which are worth visiting along the Cardo, from south to north, are:

• the large public building with an internal colonnade (perhaps the **Agora**, or **Forum**) recently excavated by the Spanish team;

• the **South Tetrakionia**, the intersection with the South Decumanus which still has the nicely carved bases of four towers;

• the richly carved entrance to a Roman temple which was transformed into a church (now called the Cathedral) in the Byzantine period;

• the **Nymphaeum** (public fountain), with some original coloured paint from the Roman/Byzantine period still clinging to its upper-level niches;

• the stately **propylaeum** (entrance) to the processional way up to the **Temple of Artemis** (daughter of Zeus, sister of Apollo, and patron goddess of the city); her hilltop temple with soaring columns is nestled in a spacious, colonnaded *temenos* measuring 162 x 121 metres (531 x 396 ft), and it was approached via a processional way that started across the river in the area of the modern city;

• the massive **West Baths**, never excavated and still lying as they collapsed

Left, the entrance to the Temple of Artemis. Right, the South Theatre.

during successive earthquakes more than 1,000 years ago;

● the **North Tetrapyla** intersection with the North Decumanus, domed and decorated in the 2nd century AD when the nearby North Theatre complex was built;

● the **North Theatre**, which served as a performance stage as well as the city council chamber; the names of the local tribes represented in the city council are still engraved on the seats in Greek;

● the **North Colonnaded Street**, a stretch of the original Cardo which was never widened or redone in a Corinthian order; it retains the more human-scale dimensions of Jerash during the 1st century AD, and it leads you to the large but ungainly **north gate** (whose strange shape was, like the Oval Plaza, a means of reconciling the different axes of the Cardo and the external road entering Jerash from Pella).

From the Cardo, the Roman town expanded towards the city walls, forming different quarters for housing, commerce and cult. At the height of its prosperity in the 2nd and 3rd centuries

AD, Jerash and its immediate suburbs may have accommodated some 20,000 people. They were served by a splendid array of public facilities including temples, theatres, markets, baths, plazas, fountains, and a hippodrome. The massive east baths, in the centre of the modern town, indicate the extent of the city's spread as well as the monumental size of some of its public facilities.

When The Byzantine Empire and Christianity dominated the region in the 4th century, some of Gerasa's pagan Roman temples were transformed into Christian churches. Many new churches were built from cut stones and columns taken from Roman era buildings that had collapsed from the frequent earthquakes which plagued the region in antiquity. With the discovery of three more churches in recent years, we know of at least 15 churches in Byzantine Gerasa; some of them still sport their fine mosaic floors.

The **complex of three churches** dedicated to St George, St John, and SS Cosmas and Damian, west of the Tem-

estiges
f past
splendour.

ple of Artemis, has the best preserved mosaics from the 6th century AD, including representations of animals and the churches' benefactors and bishops. The foundation remains of one church can be seen on the east side of the city, amidst the modern houses. Some of the church mosaics are also on display in the museum.

Many of the Roman structures were rebuilt or modified in the Byzantine era, when Gerasa ceased to be important for international trade and instead related more to other cities in the region. The city fortunes gradually dwindled, and successive attacks by Persian and Muslim forces in the early 7th century AD saw Jerash's historical course change once again.

After 636, the city fell to the control of Islamic forces emerging from Arabia. It continued to accommodate a small settlement of farmers, traders and potters for another 150 years, as recent excavations have clarified with the discovery of an Omayyad housing quarter off the South Decumanus, a small

mosque across from the Artemis Temple propylaeum, and some pottery kilns; but when the Islamic world's capital shifted from Omayyad Damascus to Abbasid Baghdad in AD 750, Gerasa lost its strategic location on the road between Damascus and Islam's heartland in Arabia. Its fortunes faded slowly thereafter, and the town could support little more than small squatter occupations after the 9th century.

Umm al-Jimal: The easternmost of the major northern cities, **Umm al-Jimal** can be reached by car in 80 minutes from Amman. It is located at the edge of the eastern basalt desert plain, along a secondary road that was close to the junction of several ancient trade routes that linked central Jordan with Syria and Iraq. Remains of the Roman road can still be seen several kilometres (a 10-minute drive) to the west.

The city was inhabited for some 700 years, from the 1st to the 8th centuries AD, in three different stages: a 2nd–3rd century rural village, a 4th–5th century fortified Roman town, and a prosperous

Below left, rebuilding the past at Umm al-Jimal. Right, corbel ceiling, the Old Stables, Umm al-Jimal.

5th–8th century farming and trading city. The key to Umm al-Jimal's success was its inhabitants' ability to store winter rainwater in a series of covered and open reservoirs, which supplied water for human and animal consumption as well as to irrigate summer crops. Such settlements with reliable sources of water and food invariably developed into major caravan stations, as Umm al-Jimal did.

The name Umm al-Jimal can mean either "mother of camels" or "mother of beauty" in Arabic. Its identification with ancient sites is still not determined (Thantia and Surattha have been proposed as possible candidates).

Umm al-Jimal is a dramatic and even chilling sight for visitors, for it rises against the distant horizon like the skyline of a thriving metropolis; on approaching it, however, they soon realise that it is an abandoned ghost town. Visiting Umm al-Jimal in the early morning haze of winter is a particularly thrilling experience, for the black basalt buildings then take on a very eerie character.

A walk through the ruins reveals a wide range of structures typical of a modest provincial town that lacked a formal urban plan – unlike the monumental splendour, architectural extravaganza, and imperial scale of towns such as Jerash, Gadara, and Philadelphia. Among the most interesting structures to visit are the tall barracks with their little chapel, several large churches, numerous open and roofed water cisterns served by conveyor channels, dozens of houses arranged in clusters (often around a common courtyard), the outlines of a Roman fort along the east side of the town, and the remains of several town gates. Many of the structures still stand two storeys high, thanks to the excellent engineering used in antiquity.

Notice the very common "corbelling" technique of long flat slabs of basalt stone laid over intersecting stones to form the roof of a typically long and narrow room or building. Arches were used to make the buildings larger, and nicely designed windows and doors (many still in place) helped to relieve

View of the Barracks, Umm al-Jimal.

structural pressure from the weight of the building material.

Exhilarating Umm Qais: The most dramatically situated Roman era town in Jordan is **Umm Qais** (Roman Gadara). It sits on a long, high promontory overlooking the north Jordan Valley, the Syrian Golan Heights, and Lake Tiberias (Sea of Galilee) to the northwest, about two hours by car from Amman. The view from the site is exhilarating, and is made all the more attractive today by the new resthouse there, with full meal and refreshment service (but no accommodation). Summer dinners on the open terrace are an increasingly popular pastime among Amman residents. Take a powerful pair of binoculars with you to enjoy picking out sites in the distance.

The city was established in the Hellenistic period, and flourished as a strategic trading town for nearly 1,000 years, well into the early and medieval Islamic eras. Its name in Arabic, Umm Qais, is thought to be related to the word *maqass*, which means junction in Arabic; this was an important junction on land trade routes linking the important north-south roads with the east-west passage to the Mediterranean Sea.

Gadara was renowned in the classical era as an inspired city of the arts, famous for its playwrights, poets, satirists, orators, and philosophers. The site is a leading candidate for the location of the New Testament tale of the Gadarene swine (Matthew 8:28), in which Jesus cured two madmen by transferring their demonic spirits into a herd of swine that drowned after stampeding down a mountainside into nearby Lake Tiberias.

Umm Qais today includes two distinct components – the ancient structures and town plan, and the turn-of-the-century Ottoman town clustered on the summit and largely built from stones reused from the classical town. The visitor approaching on the main road from the east passes several tombs from the ancient cemetery and a ruined theatre, before reaching the new resthouse and nearby museum.

Among the most impressive ancient remains are a stunning black basalt thea- **A welcome in Umm Qais.**

tre, the basilica and adjacent courtyard strewn with nicely carved black sarcophagi, the colonnaded main street and a side street lined with shops, an underground mausoleum, two baths, a nymphaeum (public water fountain), a city gate, and the faint outlines of what was once a massive hippodrome. Excavations by a joint German-Jordanian team continue at the site.

Visitors to Umm Qais can also get a feel for life in 19th-century Jordan by strolling among the ruins of the late Ottoman village, with its large houses arranged around central courtyards. Two houses have been restored and are being used again: the museum in Beit Rousan, and the German archaeological dighouse in Beit Malkawi.

Recondite charm: The scattered remains of **Abila** are not frequently visited by international tourists today, but the site is well worth a visit by those who have the time. The large site is located amidst verdant agricultural fields at the modern Ain Quweilbeh spring, a 20-minute drive north of Irbid. While several of its an-

cient structures have been excavated, including churches, aqueducts, tombs, gates and public buildings, Abila is especially fascinating because so much of it remains unexcavated, yet visible on the surface of the ground. The large semi-circular depression in a hillside is where the theatre once stood, the path to the bridge over the stream hints at the route of the Roman road, and the massive column drums and Corinthian capitals scattered incongruously in agricultural fields prod the visitor to imagine the temples, baths or marketplaces that remain buried.

The two hills that make up the site were occupied almost continuously from the Neolithic to the early-Islamic period, roughly from 7000 BC to AD 800. The site also includes an extensive cemetery with some of Jordan's finest Roman era painted tombs, but unfortunately these are not accessible to visitors due to water seepage and the danger of roof collapse. The site flourished for such a long period of time because of its rich water and agricultural resources,

and its strategic location alongside ancient trade routes.

Saladin's castle: One of the best preserved examples of medieval Arab/Islamic military architecture in the entire Middle East is **Ajlun Castle**, formally named Qalaat ar-Rabad. It was built in 1184–85 by Izz ed-Din Ousama, one of the most capable governors of the Islamic leader Salaheddeen (Saladin), who defeated the Crusaders and evicted them from Jordan in 1189; the castle was the base from which Islamic forces defended this region against Crusader expansion.

The castle is very well preserved, and is a popular attraction for Jordanians and foreign visitors alike (beware, it is always crowded on Fridays). Its galleries, towers, staircases, and many chambers are like a medieval maze where visitors can spend an hour or two appreciating the structure itself as well as the magnificent views across the green hills all around. The view from the keep is especially thrilling. Two small hotels nearby are good places to eat, make a refreshment stop, or spend the night.

The minaret in the central mosque in nearby Ajlun town is over 600 years old.

Other sites in north Jordan: There are many other interesting sites in north Jordan that are not usually included in tourist circuits. **Irbid city** itself is worth a visit because it retains the bustle and charm of provincial Middle Eastern towns that have not been totally disfigured by the consumerism and modernism that have made such a big impact on the larger cities. A trading centre to its farming hinterland for thousands of years, Irbid now has nearly 500,000 people and is Jordan's second largest city. Historically, it relied on a combination of agriculture and trading, which are still its main economic activities. There are some fine turn-of-the-century houses and public buildings in the city centre, where a small but rich **museum** can be visited at the office of the antiquities department.

The Decapolis city of **Capitolias** was located on the site of the modern village of **Beit Ras**, astride the road north from Irbid. There are scattered architectural

Restaurant in Ajlun.

194

pieces that can be seen here, along with some tombs, vaults, cisterns, and traces of foundation walls, but no major standing architecture.

About 20 minutes by car north of Irbid is **Zerakhon**, a huge ancient walled city from the Early Bronze Age, recently discovered and being excavated. It has well preserved remains of buildings (including a temple) and an urban water system that was a key reason for the town's existence for 1,000 years in the Early Bronze Age (3300–2200 BC).

Fedein is the ancient name of the walled town that existed at the site of modern Mafraq, between Irbid and Umm al-Jimal. Two distinct periods of ancient urbanism have been identified and excavated: an Iron-Age town with massive fortification walls that still stand several metres high, and a Byzantine/early Islamic walled town with the remains of a church, a beautifully decorated mosque, and other public buildings. Roman milestones from the area attest to its strategic location amidst the roads that criss-crossed northern Jordan

in the classical and early Islamic periods. The site is still being excavated. Between Jerash and Mafraq, the quiet village of **Rihab** contains the remains of a dozen Byzantine churches, some of which are still being excavated.

North Jordan is also home to several other small antiquities sites that were trading towns or security posts in ancient times. **Umm as-Surab**, northwest of Umm al-Jimal, reached the peak of its importance in the Byzantine period, when several large churches were built as part of a monastic complex. One church was converted into a mosque in the early Islamic period. **Umm al-Quttein**, about 40 km (25 miles) by car east of Umm al-Jimal, has remains of four Byzantine churches and a large monastery (ad-Deir), and it once also hosted a Roman cavalry unit. Umm al-Quttein was important historically because of its location at the edge of the settled zone of north Jordan/south Syria, to the east of which lay the more demanding basalt desert environment.

The impressive standing remains of

Levantine landscape round Ajlun astle.

the Roman fortress at **Deir al-Kahf**, half-an-hour's drive east of Umm al-Jimal and near the Syrian border, once formed part of the defensive system along the southeastern frontier of the Roman Empire.

Two fascinating sites are located further east, well off the paved roads and requiring a guide and four-wheel-drive. The remains of the Roman fort at **Burqu'** are interesting mainly because of the location of the site – in the distant, northeastern desert, far from any other town sites and about 25 km (15 miles) north of the road to Iraq. This was one of a series of Roman fortresses that linked the southeastern defensive line of the Roman Empire in the 3rd–6th centuries AD. The troops who manned it survived because of the huge natural pool that formed there every winter, trapping the rainwater for use throughout the dry summer. Bedouin livestockers still bring their herds to drink here in the summer.

Jawa is one of Jordan's most unusual sites, but is also difficult to reach in its isolated desert setting adjacent to Wadi Rajil, well east of Umm al-Jimal and north of the highway to Iraq. In the midst of this barren and inhospitable landscape rises the huge walled town with its central citadel, two city walls, and several residential quarters. It is all the more intriguing because it was first built in the Early Bronze Age, around 3000 BC, and was again extensively used around 2000 BC.

The town's inhabitants survived by building a complex water harnessing system of dams, channels, and cisterns that trapped and conserved the winter run-off from the adjacent wadi (riverbed). This is thought to represent the oldest, largest and most extensive ancient water harvesting system anywhere in the world, with more than 8 km (5 miles) of stone canals and scores of pools and cisterns.

Even more amazing is that the first town built at Jawa was only inhabited for around one generation, and perhaps for as little as 10 years, before its inhabitants appear to have migrated elsewhere (probably to the southwest, in the direction of the verdant region of the Zerqa River and the Jordan Valley).

Further south (15 minutes northeast of Zerqa city) is the large site of **Khirbet as-Samra**; this town was important during several historical periods because of its strategic location astride the main north-south highway linking Petra and Amman, in Jordan, with Bosra and Damascus in Syria. The remains of the Roman highway can be seen near the site, which is located next to the Hejaz railway line (50 km/31 miles or 40 minutes by car from Amman).

The remains of Nabataean/Roman, Byzantine and early Islamic urban structures within a well-defined town wall include houses, gates, eight churches, water works, cemeteries, and other public buildings. The centrepiece at the summit of the site is the large Roman fortress with its corner towers – with a dramatic view in all four directions. Khirbet as-Samra is also interesting for its large early Christian cemetery; hundreds of tombstones are engraved with crosses, in some cases with a rare Aramaic/Syro-Palestinian script.

Left, local dress, Ramtha.
Right, Abila.

EAST TO AZRAQ

Today the area east of Amman is a desert: forbidding black basalt lava wastes in the northeast, plains covered with dark limestone and flint flakes, and a tract of sandy desert along Wadi Sirhan, reaching southeast into Saudi Arabia. At the confluence of these three types of desert stands the much reduced Azraq oasis, its pools filled by a complex network of aquifers fed mainly from the Jebel Druze area of southern Syria (the water taking up to 50 years en route). Surrounding the oasis is the Qa al-Azraq, about 60 sq. km (23 sq. miles) of silt, beneath which lies such a concentration of salt that hundreds of tons each year are collected for both industrial and domestic use.

Lush past: Several hundred million years ago the area, like most of present-day Jordan, lay beneath the sea, which withdrew and re-inundated the land several times. The last inundation probably receded in the Eocene period, which began about 50 million years ago. A mere 1 million years ago, in the Pleistocene era, the broad shallow basin, in which Azraq stands today, was a huge inland lake of about 4,000 sq. km (1,544 sq. miles); then, as the waters slowly receded, the basin became a fertile plain with large swamps and pools and luxuriant vegetation at its centre.

Until only a few decades ago the desert teemed with wildlife. Gazelle, wild ass, ostrich and the magnificent white Arabian oryx roamed freely, preyed upon by wolf, hyena and the Bedouin. Azraq was a paradise of birds and animals, great and small, living in or around its waters or coming from the desert to drink. Some 12,000 to 40,000 years ago rhinoceros and hartebeest also inhabited its marshes; and stones found in a ruined Roman wall, carved with ostrich, snake, fish, hoopoe and wild ass, are eloquent testimonies to the abundance of 2,000 years ago. "Each stone or blade of it," wrote T.E. Lawrence in *The Seven Pillars of Wisdom*, "was radiant with half-memory of the luminous

silky Eden, which had passed so long ago." Today there is little wildlife, and most is protected in reserves. The villain is not climatic change but 20th-century humans, who have cut down trees, overgrazed pasture, pumped water for cities, and hunted with automatic weapons and four-wheel-drive vehicles.

The climate has changed little since the Romans, undaunted by the desert, built a string of forts here – the *limes arabicus* – along the boundaries of their new Arabian province. The two main fort-builders were Septimius Severus (AD 193–211) and, 100 years later, Diocletian. These frontier posts survived into the Byzantine era, some falling into disrepair, others restored for continued service until the Islamic Arab conquest in 636.

From the mid-7th to the mid-8th centuries, when the Omayyad caliphs established their court and the centre of Islam in Damascus, a scattering of settlements were built in the Jordanian desert. Each had a different function – fort, hunting lodge, trading-post, farm,

receding ages: Amra. eft, Qasr al-haraneh. ight, desert looms.

caravanserai or meeting hall – but common to all were the organisation of water and an agricultural base. All were probably intended, whether by the caliph or his local ruler, to maintain regular contact with the Bedouin tribes on whose loyalty the Omayyads depended.

No desert asceticism applied here. The buildings included bath houses, spacious courtyards and great halls for audiences or for entertainment, adorned with columns and carvings, mosaics and frescoes. They were served by sophisticated hydraulic and heating systems, so that the stresses of a hard day's hunting or diplomacy could be soothed by fountains, pools and hot baths.

Around AD 750, when the Omayyads were ousted by the Abbasids and the Islamic capital moved to Baghdad, many settlements in the Jordanian desert fell into disuse and ruin. The abandoned buildings became temporary encampments for Bedouin who lit fires in the decorated halls for heat or to cook food before moving on to deserts new.

In 1896 Alois Musil, an Arabist from Prague, was told by some Bedouin of some richly decorated buildings deep in the desert. Two years later he returned, and within a few days found two of these palaces, Qasr al-Tuba and Qusayr Amra. In the following months and years several more were discovered. None is exactly a palace (the meaning of the Arabic word *qasr*), nor a castle (as they are known in English); but all are charming examples of domestic architecture in Islam's earliest days, taking much inspiration from Byzantine and Persian art, but also showing the beginnings of an individual personality and style.

Visiting the "Desert Castles": Today, with paved roads in place of the ancient desert tracks, some of the better preserved Omayyad palaces, as well as Azraq, can be seen in a day-trip from Amman. The roads form a neat circuit, with Azraq at the eastern end. However, two unusually handsome complexes, Qasr al-Mushatta and Qasr al-Tuba lie outside this circuit (the former near Queen Alia Airport and the latter off the Desert Highway east of Qatrana), and

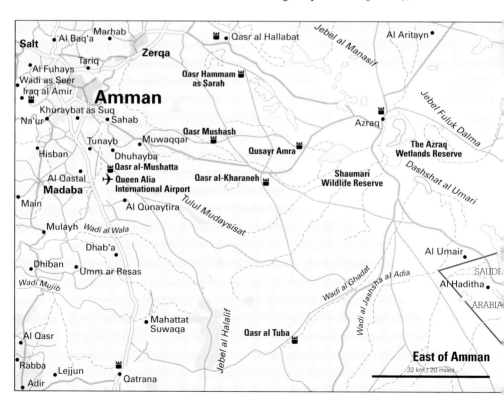

these are covered separately at the end of this chapter.

The suggested route runs clockwise from Amman, but it can equally well be negotiated anti-clockwise. The trip can also be combined with a bird-watching visit to the Azraq Wetlands Reserve, and to the Shaumari Wildlife Reserve, home of the famous Arabian oryx. If more than one day is needed, simple accommodation can be found at Azraq, either in the Government Resthouse (whose large swimming pool is open mid-May to mid-October), at the Sayad (Hunter) Hotel (also with a pool), or at the lodge of the Royal Society for the Conservation of Nature.

Taking the road north out of Amman towards Zarqa, after about 22 km (13½ miles) turn right at the sign to the Syrian and Iraqi borders. After another 12 km (7½ miles) take the right turn to Azraq and the Iraqi border; 7 km (4½ miles) further on, at a junction with a right turn to Azraq, continue straight ahead towards Mafraq. After 6 km (4 miles), a small blue sign points right to **Qasr al-Hallabat**. About 8 km (5 miles) further on, another blue sign points right to the castle itself.

This large desert complex started life as a Roman fort and ended as a luxurious country estate under the Omayyads. The original small fort was built around AD 111–114 to guard Trajan's new road to the south, the Via Nova Traiana; a Latin inscription mentions an extension in the early 3rd century; and another in Greek records a Byzantine restoration in 529.

The Omayyads, not content with mere restoration, virtually demolished the earlier structures to build their estate between AD 709 and 743. It was an extensive complex, of which the castle, the mosque and the bath house are the most rewarding today. There were also a large reservoir, many cisterns and a walled agricultural enclosure.

The castle was lavishly decorated with frescoes and carved stucco, and with lively mosaics of animals and birds, fruits and geometric designs – now removed for safe keeping. Although this

Siphoning scarce resources.

is a limestone area, many of the stones are basalt, and several carry sections of a long Greek inscription – an edict of the Emperor Anastasius I (AD 491–518) reorganising the province of Arabia. As they were all plastered over, they were clearly re-used purely for their architectural value. It is believed they might have been imported to Hallabat by the Omayyads from the ancient basalt city of Umm al-Jimal, some 30 km (18½ miles) to the north.

The mosque stands immediately to the east of the castle, some of its walls still at their full height. The doorway in the north wall, facing the remains of the *mihrab* (niche indicating the direction of prayer) has an attractive cusped arch.

The bath house, known as **Hammam al-Sarah**, 2 km (1¼ miles) to the east of the castle beside the paved road, is a finely built limestone complex, originally finished with marble, mosaics and frescoes. The rectangular audience hall, now just an outline of walls, had three parallel tunnel-vaults, and an alcove with a small room on either side, complete with latrines. A doorway in the north corner leads into the changing room (apodyterium) of the bath house, which doubled as a cool room (*frigidarium*). This opens into the room of medium heat (*tepidarium*) with a tunnel-vaulted recess, and then into the domed hot room (*calidarium*) which has two semi-circular recesses covered with semi-domes. Beyond this was the furnace which sent hot air under the raised floor of the calidarium. This complex is very similar in design to that of Qusayr Amra.

Beside the baths stands a water storage tank into which water was raised from the well (18 metres/59 ft deep) by a pulley system operated by donkeys or horses endlessly walking around a confined circular space. There is also a *mihrab* nearby, the remains of a late Ottoman open-air mosque.

To Azraq: The road running southeast from Hammam al-Sarah turns right and, after 3 km (2 miles), joins the main Zarqa-Azraq road. After 55 km (34 miles) it reaches a junction at Azraq

Inside Hammam al-Sarah.

Janubi (south), one of the two villages of the Azraq complex. Turning left, the tree-lined road to the resthouse can be seen on the left after 2 km (1¼ miles). Azraq Shamali (north) is another 2½ km (1½ miles) further on, with the Sayad Hotel on the left, and, 500 metres (550 yards) further on, is the great black basalt **Azraq Castle**.

Azraq's abundant waters made it as valuable to people as to wildlife. Palaeolithic camp sites have been found in the marshes, with flint tools fashioned by early Stone-Age inhabitants 100,000 years ago. The importance of the oasis continued – for those who later settled here, for the Bedouin who roamed the desert, and for traders, since Azraq stands at the head of Wadi Sirhan, the main caravan route between the Arabian Peninsula and Mesopotamia and Syria.

The first fort here may have been built by Septimius Severus (AD 193–211) as one of the eastern defences of the *limes arabicus*. But the earliest inscription relating to the castle is a dedication to Diocletian and Maximian, joint Emper-

ors from AD 286 to 305. At the same time Diocletian built a new road to Azraq, the Strata Diocletiana, to improve communications between Syria and southern Arabia.

The fort remained in use under the Byzantines, and it was an occasional base for the Omayyads, perfect both for hunting and for meeting the desert tribes. After the fall of the Omayyads, it fell into disrepair and had to be rebuilt in 1237 by the Ayyubid governor, Azz al-Din Aybak, as recorded in an Arabic inscription above the main entrance. It was probably then that the little mosque in the middle of the courtyard was built. How far the castle was remodelled is unclear; plenty of Roman-cut stones were available, and several Roman doors (one weighing 3 tons) were reused exactly in the Roman fashion. They are still there, and still turning on their stone hinges. The Mamelukes and Ottomans also occupied Azraq Castle.

More recently "the blue fort on its rock" was T.E. Lawrence's base for part of the winter of 1917–18 during the

Below left, "Lawrence knew my father": the guardian at Azraq. Right, doorway in Azraq Castle.

Arab Revolt. His office was in the room above the entrance gatehouse. It was from Azraq that Lawrence and his men set out in September 1918 for the final assault on Damascus which marked the collapse of Turkish power and the end of World War I in the Middle East.

Today the castle is less intact than when Lawrence was here, thanks to a severe earthquake in 1927. There is still the shell of an upper storey in some parts, and handsome arched stables with stone mangers and tethering blocks can be explored on the north side. The ancient well is at the bottom of some steps on the east.

Shaumari Wildlife Reserve lies to the south of Azraq, near the main road to Saudi Arabia. A sign 7 km (4½ miles) from the junction at Azraq Janubi points right along a side road; the entrance gates are a further 6 km (4 miles). The visitors' centre has a display of local archaeological finds, a photographic exhibition of flora and fauna, and an audiovisual presentation on conservation in Jordan.

There is a tower for viewing animals in the reserve, including the Arabian oryx, though sightings cannot be guaranteed. The most likely time to see oryx is late afternoon in late summer or autumn, before the rains begin, when there is little natural water and the oryx come to the troughs near the pens. Groups of oryx are occasionally brought to the pens for inoculation.

The Royal Society for the Conservation of Nature (RSCN) was founded in 1966 but, owing to the 1967 Six-Day War and its aftermath, it was not until 1975 that Jordan's first nature reserve was established here at Shaumari on 22 sq. km (8½ sq. miles) of desert. It was designated as a breeding and propagation centre for species that had become extinct or endangered in Jordan, prior to releasing them into the wild.

Specially targeted was the strikingly handsome Arabian oryx (Oryx leucoryx), extinct in Jordan since the 1920s. The once teeming herds had dwindled disturbingly throughout Arabia. The last known wild Arabian oryx were killed

Ostriches and oryx at Shaumari Wildlife Reserve.

by a raiding party in the Jiddat al-Harasis in Oman in 1972.

Already, in 1962, the Fauna Preservation Society and the World Wildlife Fund had launched "Operation Oryx", with a World Survival Herd in Arizona of nine animals donated by Aden, Kuwait, Britain and Saudi Arabia. When numbers grew, sub-groups were established in Texas and California. The RSCN proposed that Jordan should be the first country to reintroduce the oryx into the Arabian desert, and in 1978 four males and four females were sent to Shaumari from San Diego Wild Animal Park. The ruler of Qatar donated a male and two females, and from these 11 animals the Jordanian herd steadily multiplied.

In 1983, when the herd numbered over 30, they were released into the whole area of the reserve. Though zoo-bred, their behaviour showed that they had not lost the millennia-old instincts of the wild. They quickly split into smaller herds and established a hierarchy. Herd growth has continued, and today Shaumari has well over 100 oryx.

Other rehabilitation projects have also been undertaken, notably with the ostrich and the wild ass.

If you leave the reserve after dark, it is not uncommon to see a gerbil, jerboa or hare in the car headlights. But a night drive back to Amman, with heavy trucks thundering along the Azraq-Amman road, is not one of Jordan's more restful experiences.

The **Azraq Wetlands Reserve**, 12 sq. km (4½ sq. miles) of marsh, mudflats and pools, was proclaimed soon after Shaumari. It lies near Azraq Janubi, and visitors should check in first at the RSCN Resthouse, 600 metres (650 yards) towards Amman from the junction in Azraq Janubi, up a drive on the left (south) of the road.

About 300 bird species were recorded here in the 1970s – migrants, residents and seasonal visitors. But since then marshes and birds alike have diminished dramatically as water is pumped to supply the ever increasing demands of Amman.

A visit here can still be rewarding,

Palms in a sadly depleted oasis.

especially in the spring and autumn migration periods when a variety of birds can be seen – bee-eaters, swallows, flycatchers, warblers, wagtails, shrikes, snipe, pipits, hoopoes, larks, sandpipers, plovers, harriers, eagles, chats, ducks, crakes, storks and many more. A faint echo of Lawrence's "luminous, silky Eden" can be heard in the susurrus of wind in reeds, punctuated by the piping and fluting of birds, and the hoarse trumpetings of the marsh frogs. About 100 water buffalo roam the marshes, along with 200 feral horses. Jackals are seen occasionally.

Sensuous frescoes: The main road to Amman divides nearly 9 km (5½ miles) from Azraq, the left-hand fork passing the harmonious stone-built **Qusayr Amra** on the right, after another 17½ km (11 miles). It stands in Wadi Butm, a shallow watercourse (dry most of the year), named after the *butm* (wild pistachio trees: Pistachia atlantica) once numerous here. Qusayr is the diminutive of *qasr*, and this "little palace" is the remains of a larger complex, probably including a fort, agricultural enclosures and living quarters, which was built in 711, under Caliph Walid I.

Today we see an audience hall with three barrel vaults, and an alcove flanked by two small rooms; and a three-roomed bath house, including a domed *calidarium* with under-floor heating. All the walls and ceilings are covered with the vivid frescoes which are Amra's main attraction. Restored in 1971–73 by experts from the Madrid National Archaeological Museum, they are now in passably good condition despite centuries of neglect, smoke from Bedouin fires and grafitti.

The interest is not just for their style (which is mixed), or for their joyous naturalism, but for what they reveal of the brilliant eclecticism of early Arab/Islamic art, drawing from Byzantine and Persian sources; and because they are there at all. The first edict ordering the destruction of images was under Caliph Yazid II (720–24), when these frescoes were sparklingly new. Mercifully they were overlooked – in fact,

Below left, Qusayr Amra Right, frescoes are Amra's main attraction.

destruction was not rigorously imposed in secular buildings.

Here the painters were uninhibited in their depictions of human and mythological life: hunting scenes; athletes in training; the goddesses of poetry, philosophy and history; musicians and dancers; women and children bathers (in varying states of undress); and six figures, believed to be rulers conquered by Walid I – the Byzantine emperor, the Visigothic king of Spain, the Sassanian king and the Negus of Abyssinia (with inscriptions), and two without inscriptions who may have been the emperor of China and the Turkish khan. In addition, there are delicate gazelles, monkeys and birds, and a guitar-strumming bear; and set-pieces of the working life of various craftsmen.

Most interesting of all is the fresco in the dome of the *calidarium*, the earliest known representation of the night sky in the round instead of on a flat surface. The Great and Little Bears, Andromeda, Cassiopeia, Sagittarius, Scorpio, Orion and others are all there – but the artist appears to have copied them from a drawing which he transposed from right to left, thus altering the relationships of the constellations.

About 16 km (10 miles) west of Amra, immediately left of the main road, stands **Qasr al-Kharaneh**, the most complete of the Omayyad castles and the only one that appears military in purpose (though this may be more apparent than real). This great four-square, two-storey structure has round towers on each corner and semi-circular ones in each wall, except on the south where the entrance is. It is built of large undressed stones, with layers of smaller stones between them, and with a decorative line of bricks in an open herringbone pattern running all round the building near the top. Originally it was plastered overall, but most of this has dropped off.

Small holes at intervals in the walls look like arrow-slits, but inside it is clear that they would have given the archers insufficient field of fire, and some would have needed 3-metre (9-ft) giants to reach them. In fact, they were

probably for ventilation and light rather than for battle.

The entrance leads past large stables or store rooms on either side, and into a central courtyard, beneath which was a cistern. Suites of rooms are arranged in the tradional Arab pattern of a large rectangular room, with two smaller square rooms on each long side. Two handsome stone stairways lead to the upper floor, where several rooms still have some of their original decoration of arches and vaults, semi-domes and squinches, and plasterwork medallions, all reminiscent of Sassanian buildings. Above a door in one of the large rooms on the upper floor, a small painted Kufic inscription records the date in AD 710 when the castle was built.

The function of Qasr al-Kharaneh is uncertain. Its large stable area might suggest a caravanserai, but though near a trade route, it is not on it; and with no springs, or other means of storing water, the one cistern could not have supplied a regular traffic of traders. It may have been simply an occasional meeting place for the Omayyad authorities and the Bedouin tribes.

Around 37 km (23 miles) west of Kharaneh is the village of **Muwaqqar**, once the site of a considerable Omayyad settlement, which has now completely disappeared; there is, however, a large ancient reservoir which is still used. Between Kharaneh and Muwaqqar, but some distance north of the main road along an unmarked track, lies **Qasr Mushash**, a very large but very ruined Omayyad agricultural estate, which is strictly for addicts of tumbled stones.

Off the beaten track: The splendid **Qasr al-Tuba**, in Wadi Ghadaf, is one of the hardest of the Omayyad palaces to reach. There is a choice of three routes there, but they all demand a 4 x 4 high-clearance vehicle, a compass and a guide. The route with the least rough driving runs 55 km (34 miles) south of Azraq, along the road that passes the turning to Shaumari. A track to the right leads to the palace. More difficult is a track from Qasr al-Kharaneh leading almost due south to Tuba (47 km/29 miles); criss-

Qasr al-Mushatta.

crossed by other tracks, the route is hard to make out. The third route runs 70 km (43 miles) east from Qatrana on the Desert Highway, half on paved road, half on rough tracks.

Qasr al-Tuba was the first palace found by Alois Musil in 1898, a great architectural skeleton, half lost in the desert sand. It was probably designed as a caravanserai on the trade route between Amman and the west, and Wadi Sirhan and southern Arabia. Wandering in its silent courts, surrounded by the limitless and haunting desert, it is not hard to imagine the men, horses and camels that once filled these ruins. It is thought Qasr al-Tuba was begun in 743–44, at the end of the decadent Caliph Walid II's reign, remaining unfinished at his death.

The complex consists of two symmetrical enclosures, together forming almost a double square – Siamese twins of palaces, each with suites of interconnecting rooms around a central courtyard. A round tower was set at each corner, and semi-circular towers at intervals along the sides. In the north corner the buildings are still nearly intact, including a magnificent barrel-vaulted hall; so too is most of the lower part of the west wall. The rest is an outline of foundations and tumbled walls, the latter originally built of three courses of stone, above which were sun-dried mud bricks. Stone also framed the door arches, and Musii originally found some finely carved stone door jambs and lintels – all these, alas, have long since disappeared.

How they managed for water seems puzzling, but the answer lies in some pools nearby, three huge wells, and the remains of round buildings where donkeys or horses operated a pulley system to raise water from the wells.

Near the airport: The largest and most richly decorated of the Omayyad palaces in Jordan was **Qasr al-Mushatta**, now near the Queen Alia International Airport. It is reached by turning off the highway towards the airport, and turning right just past the Alia Gateway Hotel. The palace stands on the right of the perimeter road, after 11 km (7 miles).

Qasr al-Mushatta is a great square walled enclosure with round towers at the corners and five semi-circular ones on each side, except on the south whose centre was occupied by a monumental gateway. Around this gateway the finest of Mushatta's carvings once stood to a considerable height; but in 1903 the Ottoman Sultan Abdul Hamid II gave them to the German Kaiser Wilhelm II. They can now be seen in the Pergamum Museum in Berlin. A few delicate carvings still bear witness to the palace's original glory.

The interior was never completed and most of it consists of outlines of walls and foundations around a large courtyard. North of this are the remains of the royal audience hall and residence – probably of Walid II, the extravagant and hated caliph who built Qasr al-Tuba, also around 743–44. The audience hall, basilical in form, has a trefoil apse which was once covered by a dome. On either side are barrel-vaulted halls. While stone was used for the outer walls, the whole of this inner palace was built of bricks made of burnt mud.

THE JORDAN VALLEY

The Jordan Rift Valley is the lowest spot on earth – at the Dead Sea it is over 400 metres (1,312 ft) below sea level, and dropping several centimetres per year. For international visitors it is also one of the most fascinating destinations in the entire Middle East.

The valley is not a single, overpowering site like Petra or Jerash; rather, it elicits a mood of quiet fascination mixed with deep spirituality, all enveloped in a dramatic landscape that is enticing for both its physical beauty and its many historical and biblical associations. With many new touristic facilities being added every year, visiting the valley can now be combined with trips to other attractions in Jordan, such as Aqaba, Umm Qais or Jerash.

A great valley is born: The Jordan Rift Valley-Dead Sea region is part of the Great Rift Valley that runs from Turkey to east Africa, which was formed by geological upheavals millions of years ago. The valley in its present form started to take shape between 100,000 and 20,000 years ago, as a result of the contraction of a salt-water sea that originally covered the entire 360-km (223-mile) stretch from the Red Sea port-resort of Aqaba in the south to Lake Tiberias (also known as the Sea of Galilee) in the north. It initially formed an inland lake (Lake Lisan, some 200 km/125 miles long and with a surface water level about 200 metres (656 ft) higher than the present Dead Sea) before shrinking again to leave behind Lake Tiberias and the Dead Sea; these two inland water bodies are surrounded on all sides by dry plains interspersed with side valleys (*wadis*) flowing from the eastern and western highlands.

The Dead Sea today is 80 km (50 miles) long and 14 km (9 miles) wide on average, and reaches depths of 400 metres (1,312 ft). The Jordan River Valley to its north is 104 km (64 miles) long, and near Lake Tiberias it reaches 212 metres (695 ft) below sea level, while south of the Dead Sea the Wadi Arabah rises 400 metres (1,312 ft) on its route south to sea level at Aqaba.

Due to its low altitude, the valley is a natural hothouse characterised by mild winters, hot summers, rich agricultural lands, important mineral resources and plentiful water from the side valleys that flow into it – assets which successive ancient civilisations appreciated and exploited just as we do today. This is why the Jordan Rift Valley is associated with some of the earliest episodes of human civilisation, and why its many antiquities retain the complete story of the development of human culture in this region during the last 15,000 years.

Since the mid-1970s, the valley has benefited from a new programme of integrated rural development, based on exploiting the area's agricultural and mineral resources while providing a full range of social services for its growing population. This is a far cry from the early decades of this century, when the valley was an inhospitable and dangerous place, known more for its malaria and occasional banditry than for its eco-

nomic potential. The valley's permanent farming population of some 40,000 people in the early 1960s was almost totally uprooted during the politically turbulent and violent period of 1967–72. The integrated development effort was launched by the Jordan Valley Authority in 1973 with the aim of encouraging small, family-based farming units to cultivate 50,000 hectares (123,550 acres) of land using drip and sprinkler irrigation.

In the past two decades, the year-round population of the Jordan Rift Valley has quadrupled, to over 170,000. Most of these residents live in some 50 villages that have been provided with all basic services (housing, water, electricity, health care, schooling, telecommunications, roads, government and agricultural extension offices, and social welfare services), prompting private sector investments in farming and service companies.

The **Dead Sea** itself is a destination for visitors from around the world, due to its unique water qualities, climate and historical and spiritual legacy. It sits amidst the dramatic mountains of the biblical kingdoms of Moab, Ammon, and Edom to the east, and the rolling hills of Jerusalem to the west. Visitors enjoy its buoyant, warm water, lounge on the shoreline and cover their bodies with its soothing mud, which is rich in mineral sources.

A four-star hotel and resthouse offer full facilities for dining, sleeping, swimming, and therapeutic treatments for people suffering from skin and other diseases. There is also a modest motel at the **Himmeh** mineral thermal springs in the far north (accessible from Umm Qais: see *North Jordan*), well worth a visit for those who enjoy the special pleasures of soaking or swimming in piping hot mineral water. Arrangements can also be made to swim in the thermal waters at the black basalt Roman period pool at the Bisharat family complex at nearby Mukheibeh.

The Dead Sea and the Jordan River Valley are just a 40-minute drive from Amman along a new highway via Na'ur.

The women's shift at Himmeh hot springs.

Several other roads descend from Salt, Ajlun and the Irbid areas; the southern Dead Sea and Wadi Arabah are accessible from Aqaba or from Kerak (both of which have hotels and resthouses).

A very ancient valley: The valley's water, land and warm climate have encouraged people to live, hunt and farm here since the earliest days of the human saga. There are over 200 known archaeological sites in the Jordan Rift Valley, and hundreds of others await discovery. The oldest evidence for human activity, stone tools discovered in the Wadi Hammeh region in the northern valley, date back almost 1 million years – to a time when the region probably looked very similar to today's savannah grasslands in East Africa.

Evidence of some of the world's earliest camp sites and semi-permanent villages comes from excavations near Pella, dating from the Natufian and Kebaran periods (10,000–18,000 years ago). The advent of year-round farming and livestocking settlements in the Neolithic period (8000–4500 BC), is also attested at several sites, though the most famous Neolithic village in the valley is across the river in Jericho.

Large sites such as Pella and Tell Nimrin show an almost uninterrupted sequence of human occupation going back at least 4,000 years, from the Bronze Age to the present. What follows is an overview of the most important sites that can be easily visited today, from north to south.

Panoramic Pella: Nestled in the foothills of the northern valley, exactly at sea level altitude just above the modern town of Mashare', **Pella** may be Jordan's richest site in terms of its historical sweep and architectural remains. It is also a delightful natural setting of rolling green plains, lush plantations, and forested hills, watered by the perennial Wadi Jirm stream and overlooking the Jordan Valley plain below. On a clear day, you can look across the valley, through the hills of northern Palestine/Israel, and just discern the hills of Haifa on the Mediterranean coast.

The name Pella dates from the Hel-

King Hussein Bridge.

lenistic period, when soldiers of Alexander the Great named their new imperial settlements after the Macedonian birthplace of their leader. The site is known in Arabic as Tabaqat Fahl, the name of the nearby village ("Fahl" retains a linguistic link with the ancient names of Pella and Pihilum). Archaeological excavations have revealed the presence of modest settlements and major walled towns at Pella for most of the past 6,000 years.

The site's impressive continuity is due to its rich natural resources and strategic location at the intersection of major north/south and east/west trade routes. A resthouse overlooking Pella from the east provides a splendid opportunity for rest and refreshments, along with one of the most satisfying panoramas in all Jordan. A 90-minute drive from Amman, Pella can be easily combined in a day-trip with the Dead Sea, Ajlun, Jerash, or Umm Qais.

On the central main mound of the site, where the archaeological dighouse is located, the earliest visible mudbrick house and fortification walls (in the deep trenches on the south side) date from Bronze and Iron Age walled towns, spanning the period 2000–600 BC. The Roman and Byzantine periods are represented by the small theatre adjacent to the stream, the colonnaded civic complex and church above it (reached over a monumental staircase), and the east and west churches.

The remains of domestic houses of the early Islamic (Omayyad) period are well preserved on the central mound; later Islamic structures can be seen at the 9th/10th-century Abbasid domestic area recently excavated in **Wadi Khandak** (in the valley north of the main mound) and in the restored 13th to 14th-century Mamluke period mosque on the main mound.

The entire rift valley is dotted with ancient tells (artificial mounds or small hills formed by the cumulative collapse of successive ancient settlements built of stone and mudbrick). Three of the most striking and substantial can be visited in the centre of the valley (west

Limes leave for market.

of the main road), and some of their excavated walls can be seen (though the sites have not been properly conserved for display). The long double mound of **Tell Saadiyyeh** was an important regional walled town for most of the Bronze and Iron Ages (3300–600 BC) and also had a large caravanserai in the early Islamic period. It has been inconclusively associated with the biblical sites of Zaphon and Zarthan.

The smaller **Tell Mazar** to its south (and visible from the summit of Saadiyyeh) was a substantial settlement in the Iron and Persian periods, from the 11th to the 4th centuries BC. Its name comes from the nearby *mazar* (pilgrimage site), of Abu Obeidah, an early Islamic general and companion of the Prophet Mohammad who died and was buried there in AD 639. This is one of several such sites in the northern valley where companions of the Prophet died and were buried; these are not touristic sites, but pilgrimage sites that reflect the reverence accorded to some parts of the valley by Muslims.

The most dramatic of the three archaeological mounds is **Tell Deir Alla**, towering over the main road at Deir Alla village. Excavations have revealed almost continuous human habitation and use of the site from 1600–400 BC, for purposes such as a township, cultic centre, metalworking, a cemetery, grain storage, farming and a seasonal migration site. The tell rises 30 metres (98 ft) high, with its summit at an altitude of 200 metres (656 ft) below sea level. Some archaeologists believe it is the biblical site of Succoth.

About 7 km (4 miles) east of Tell Deir Alla, enclosed by a meandering, S-shaped bend in the Zerqa River, are the twin hills called **Tulul ad-Dhahab** ("the little hills of gold"). They are not always easy to reach due to the waters of the Zerqa River (the biblical Jabbok). Excavated architectural remains and pottery shards indicate that both hills were fortified settlements in the Early Iron Age and Late Hellenistic/Early Roman periods. Remains of slag and furnaces confirm that iron smelting took place

here, with the ore coming from the nearby Mugharat Wardah mines, 4 km (2 miles) to the north. Scholars in the 19th century identified these twin hills with the biblical sites of Penuel (where, according to the Genesis story, Jacob wrestled all night with an angel) and Mahanaim (where David was told of the death of his son Absalom). Neither of these site identifications has been verified by archaeological evidence.

The area south of Deir Alla (in the hills east of the main road) also has some **dolmens** still in their original position, especially at Damieh, Quttein and Matabi. These structures of four or five stone slabs (often associated with druids in Europe) were Bronze and Iron-Age burials, probably introduced into the area by immigrant populations from other parts of the Middle East. (Those who would like to see a dolmen without leaving Amman can view the dolmen that was excavated in the valley and precisely reconstructed on the campus of the University of Jordan.)

The southern valley: In the southern valley, at the edge of South Shouneh town, is the large site of **Tell Nimrin**, next to the road leading north from the town. Recent excavations have verified that this area has been used as an agricultural settlement almost without interruption for the past 4,000 years.

From the main road, it is possible to see over 12 metres (40 ft) of stratified ancient remains in the exposed archaeological trenches – an unusually deep and rich sequence of historical material that allows scholars to note changes in environmental conditions, land use patterns, and cultural traditions in the same spot over a very long period of time.

The view from the summit of Tell Nimrin has probably barely changed in the last several thousand years; except for the new technology of today, the site still houses a predominantly farming village whose residents use the water from the Wadi Nimrin to irrigate the rich lands around them, while also engaging in some regional trade.

There are several historically interesting sites along the east coast of the

The buoyant waters of the Dead Sea.

Dead Sea, but their remains are too scanty to attract many visitors. One such site is **Zara**, 10 minutes by car south of the Dead Sea Hotel. This was the famous 1st-century BC hot springs complex from the time of King Herod, which is identified on the famous 6th-century mosaic map in Madaba as the "therma Callirhoe" – the same Callirhoe baths mentioned by the writers Josephus and Pliny in the 1st century AD.

Excavations have revealed the walls of several buildings and pool-like structures that can still be seen. Also in this area are two natural pools of hot mineral water adjacent to the roadside, where families and tourists enjoy free swims throughout the year.

The new road which is under construction will soon allow travellers to drive along the entire east coast of the Dead Sea to reach the **Southern Ghors**, an intriguing area along the southeast coast of the Dead Sea with many important historical associations. **Bab ad-Dhraa** and **Numeira** have been excavated in recent years and are plausible

candidates for the sites of Sodom and Gomorrah (in the Genesis accounts, God destroyed Sodom and Gomorrah as a sign of His displeasure with the wickedness of their inhabitants). Bab ad-Dhraa (near the junction of the Dead Sea and Kerak roads) was inhabited for about 1,000 years during the Early Bronze Age, around 3300–2000 BC; for much of that time it was also used as a cemetery by nomads who brought their dead for burial there in multiple shaft tombs and large charnel houses.

Numeira, 14 km (9 miles) to the south, is a large, hilltop walled town that lasted for about a century during the Early Bronze Age III period (c. 2750–2350 BC), before suffering a violent and fiery destruction (to judge from the compelling archaeological evidence of 40-cm/1-ft thick ash layers).

Together with Bab ad-Dhraa and Numeira, the remains of other Early Bronze Age sites in the area can be seen at **Feifa, Khneizira,** and **Safi** – suggesting to some that these five sites may be the best available candidates for the

Dead Sea mud is rich in minerals.

Five Cities of the Plain mentioned in the Book of Genesis, namely Sodom, Gomorrah, Admah, Zeboiim, and Bela (that is, Zoar).

The remains of a medieval sugar mill can be seen at **Safi** (the "Zoar" of the Madaba mosaic map), and large, circular millstones are scattered in several areas throughout the Southern Ghors. About a kilometre east of Safi is a large, hilltop, ancient walled townsite called **Umm al-Tawabeen** (meaning "Mother of Ovens"), which has never been excavated but is fun to walk through, especially for its panoramic view of the southern Dead Sea region.

Northeast of Safi is the recently discovered and excavated **Sanctuary of Lot**. This Byzantine monastic complex had a church with mosaic floors, a reservoir, living quarters, burial chambers, and a cave that appears to have been presented to ancient pilgrims as the place where Lot and his daughters took refuge after the destruction of Sodom.

Some ceramic artifacts found in the cave date from around 3000 BC – the assumed period of the destruction of Sodom. An inscription at the site also mentions Lot by name. The complex appears to have been used from the 5th to the 8th centuries AD. The site is identified on the Madaba mosaic map as the Monastery of Saint Lot. It is easily accessible now by car, and can be visited during the road trip between Aqaba and Amman or Kerak.

Some 9 km (5 miles) south of Khneizira and nearly 2 km (1 mile) to the east are the extensive remains of **Qasr at-Telah**, a large Nabataean complex that includes a caravanserai, a water reservoir, aqueducts, agricultural fields, and houses.

Fifteen minutes to the south by car brings you to the turnoff for **Feinan**, which is half an hour to the east and accessible only by four-wheel-drive vehicle. Feinan is a sprawling copper-mining complex that was one of the biggest in the ancient world. It has been associated with the biblical site of Punon. Several hundred shaft mines in the area were exploited for their rich ore during the 5½ millennia from the Chalcolithic to the Mamluke periods (*circa* 4000 BC–AD 1500).

Still visible above ground today are enormous slag heaps from several different periods, and remains of the large Roman-Byzantine town's water systems, agricultural fields, smelters, water-powered mill and at least two churches.

About 22 km (14 miles) south of the Feinan junction is the modern settlement of **Bir Mathkoor**, with its unexcavated remains of a square Nabataean caravanserai.

A similar structure is visible in outline but is largely buried beneath the sand at **Ghrandal**, further south (near the incongruous Chinese pagoda that was erected as a sign of friendship by the Chinese contractors who built the road in the late 1970s). Bir Mathkoor and Ghrandal were important stops on the caravan routes between Petra and Gaza/Egypt.

A hike down from Petra to either of these ancient spring sites is an exciting day-trip but one which should only be done with an experienced guide.

Left, Lot's church. **Right**, Dead Sea shore.

THE KING'S HIGHWAY

Famed for its scenic beauty, the **King's Highway** winding south from Amman to Arabia is an ancient route. Traders, armies and pilgrims have all left their mark on the landscape. As early as 1200 BC, Moses addressed the Edomites: "Let us pass, I pray thee, through thy country: we will not pass through the fields, or through the vineyards, neither will we drink of the water of the wells: we will go by the king's highway, we will not turn to the right hand nor to the left, until we have passed thy borders." (Numbers 20:17).

Most famously, in the centuries before Christ, the Nabataeans used the route to carry frankincense and myrrh from Southern Arabia up to the Mediterranean and the Hellenistic and Roman world. In AD 106 the Emperor Trajan completed the Via Nova Traiana, running through Syria and down to the borders of Arabia, to facilitate trade and the passage of his troops.

In the 7th century the King's Highway transported Muslim pilgrims on the Haj to Mecca. Under the Ottomans the Haj caravan, transported by camel, would amass at Damascus to be led by an official appointed by the Ottoman sultan. The parallel **Desert Highway** (Tariq al-Bint) was a 16th-century Ottoman creation intended to replace the King's Highway, although water scarcity and the mood of potentially predatory tribes occasionally prompted recourse to the earlier route. Travelling down the Desert Highway during the Haj season today, you will encounter convoys of pilgrim-packed buses sporting flags from as far away as Turkey.

Heading south: Various options for the route south exist and which one you choose will depend on the time available: the winding but scenic King's Highway (250 km/155 miles between Amman and Petra), the duller but faster Desert Highway (265 km/165 miles) or a combination of the two which takes advantage of the good east-west connecting roads. A popular option, which includes the best of the scenery and the major sights, is to drive along the King's Highway via Madaba, Mount Nebo, Umm ar Resas and Kerak and then cross to the Desert Highway for more rapid driving. This route still takes about 12 hours if you want to stop off and see the sights; two days is recommended for a more leisurely tour. There are government resthouses in Madaba and Kerak, with accommodation at the latter. The spa hotel at Zarqa Ma'in near Madaba provides the only alternative accommodation on the King's Highway, although more hotels are planned. Fuel and garage back-up are no problem since the larger towns all boast fuel stations.

Leaving Amman on the airport road, travellers can approach Madaba, 33 km (20 miles) away, either directly or via the ancient biblical site of **Hisban**. To go via Hisban take the Na'ur exit 10 km (6 miles) along the airport road. The pools of Hisban are mentioned in the Song of Solomon: "Thy neck is as a tower of ivory; thine eyes like the fishpools in Heshbon [Hisban]…"(7:4).

The only evidence of Hisban today are the archaeologists' trenches visible on top of a tell crowned by several impressive 19th-century village houses on the right-hand side of the main road. (Tells, formed by the accumulation of debris of successive cities and presenting a layer-cake effect when excavated, are a common sight in Jordan.)

The modern town of Madaba spills on to the rolling Madaba plain, a fertile land planted with wheat, barley and tobacco (the latter picked and dried by encampments of brightly-dressed Pakistanis). The town's skyline of church spires and minarets gives a clue to its history. In common with many of the settlements along the King's Highway, Madaba seems to have been abandoned in the 18th and 19th centuries, but was resettled by Christians from Kerak at the end of the 19th century (it was these Christians who found many of the town's mosaics). Now the town is a thriving market centre for the local Bedouin tribes and it is not uncommon to see camels and sheep being brought to market.

Madaba has early origins in biblical times but it is as the seat of a Byzantine bishopric and the centre of a mosaic "school" that this "City of Mosaics" is most famous. The mosaics, inspired by pattern books circulating in the Byzantine world, were made from local stone *tesserae*. The pattern books ensured a certain amount of uniformity although individual creativity on the part of the craftsman is always evident. Common motifs which look back to the Hellenistic/Roman world include scenes of hunting, fishing and pastoral pursuits; representations of buildings; mythological scenes; marine or riverine scenes; and, most commonly, depictions of animals, including exotic beasts from Africa and Asia, birds and plants. Such motifs are common to all the mosaics along the King's Highway.

During the 7th–8th centuries, the figures of humans and animals in many of the mosaics were obliterated and replaced by carefully made patches of blank *tesserae*. This is more likely to be the result of the iconoclastic movement among Christian communities during

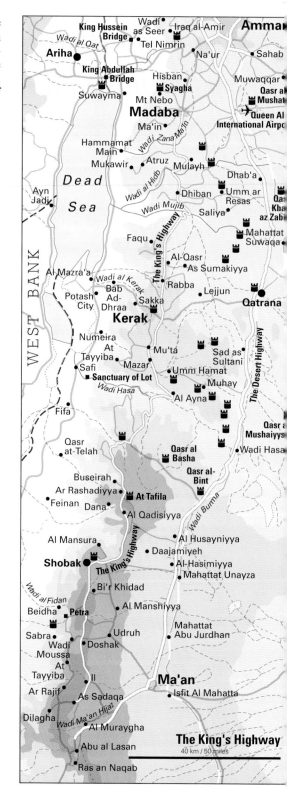

the 7th and 8th centuries than the result of Muslim destruction of figural representation as is commonly claimed.

The first stop in Madaba should be the 6th-century **Madaba Map** found during construction, in 1898, of the Greek Orthodox Church of **St George's**, itself on the site of a Byzantine church. The church stands near the government resthouse in the town centre. Between the gaudy icons of the modern church and covered by a dingy carpet when not on display (if the mosaic is not uncovered permission to pull back the carpet must be got from the attendant in the church) it portrays with delightful realism the physical characteristics of the Eastern Byzantine world, including rivers, valleys, the Dead Sea and its neighbouring hills, and towns. The centrepiece is Jerusalem, including the Church of the Holy Sepulchre. The area depicted stretches from Tyre and Sidon to the Egyptian Delta and from the Mediterranean to the Eastern Desert.

Further along the main road, under an ugly hangar, lies the **Church of the Apostles**. The fine mosaic floors of the body of the basilica-church were completed in AD 578 by one Salamanios (whose name appears around the central medallion). This medallion depicts a personification of the Sea emerging against a background of jumping fish, open-jawed sharks and an octopus. Also housed here for display and safe-keeping are mosaics from Byzantine houses.

The centre of Madaba is the scene for long-term excavation of the main street of the city in classical and early Islamic times (a joint project between the Department of Antiquities and US AID). The various churches and private houses on either side, including the church of the Virgin, the church of the Prophet Elias and the church of al-Khadr are being investigated and restored. The **Madaba Museum**, which is signposted, is worth visiting. It contains mosaics and artifacts removed from other buildings within the city and a large ethnographic section devoted to everyday objects and local traditional costume.

Moses's mountain: "And Moses went

urveying
he scene.

up from the plains of Moab unto the mountain of Nebo, to the top of Pisgah, that is over against Jericho...And the Lord said unto him this is the land which I sware unto Abraham, unto Isaac, and unto Jacob saying, I will give it unto thy seed. I have caused thee to see it with thine eyes, but thou shalt not go over thither. So Moses the servant of the Lord died there in the land of Moab, according to the word of the Lord." (Deut.34:1, 4-5).

Mount Nebo (Arabic: Jebel Siyagha), site of the death of Moses, has been a place of pilgrimage since the early days of Christianity. The standard pilgrimage route included Jerusalem, Jericho, Ain Moussa (the springs of Moses) and Mount Nebo, and ended with a restorative bathe in the hot springs of Hammamat Ma'in. (The facilities at Hammamat Ma'in are now more up-market – the four-star hotel with all spa facilities is signposted Zarqa Ma'in from Madaba – and allow this admirable example to be followed in comfort.)

In AD 394 the intrepid Roman pilgrim Egeria travelled from Jerusalem, over the Jordan River and up the Wadi Hisban and its tributaries to the **spring of Moses** (now marked by a large eucalyptus tree). She then scrambled further up to the **church of Moses**, erected by early Christians. By the 6th century the small, square chapel had expanded into one of the most extensive monastic complexes in the Middle East. Excavations started by the Franciscan Biblical Institute of Jerusalem in 1933 have exposed the three-apse basilica-church (still in use for services) and the monastic buildings surrounding it. (A modern monastery has been built to the southwest of the church.)

The view from the platform in front of the church is stupendous and best seen early in the morning or at sunset. The Promised Land spreads out to the west, the dark-green mass of the Jordan Valley masking the ancient city of Jericho, the roofs of Jerusalem and Bethlehem glinting on the hills of Palestine, and the opaque expanse of the Dead Sea glinting below. The bronze snake on a cross

Archaeology students at Al-Qasr.

230

outside the church was designed by Fantoni of Florence and symbolises the serpent lifted up by Moses in the desert and Jesus on the Cross.

The basilica itself dates from the 6th and 7th centuries, although the earlier chapels, baptistry and memorial to Moses are incorporated into the fabric of the building. The most significant mosaic, dating to AD 531, is that of the old baptistry to the left of the main entrance. The central field enclosed in a plait-border depicts hunting and pastoral scenes including exotic animals – zebra, zebu (humped ox), camel (spotted!), lion and ostrich, all present in Jordan until hunted to extinction in the early part of this century.

Most of the central aisle mosaics have been lifted for preservation and are displayed on the walls of the modern building. The memorial to Moses which the pilgrim Egeria reported probably survives as the raised structure near the pulpit at the east end of the south aisle. Pieces of the mosaic which decorated this early church have been lifted and

can be seen near the altar, including a simple cross. The tombs of early monks are near the chancel and are visible through metal trap doors in the nave.

Madaba and Mount Nebo are home to the most famous mosaics of the area but many others have been found, only a few of which are still *in situ*. Two churches have been excavated in the vicinity of **Ain Moussa**; three in the nearby village of **Khirbet al-Moukhayyat**; and at least five mosaiced structures in **Ma'in**, including churches, a bath and private buildings. Information regarding access is best obtained from the Madaba Museum.

Twenty kilometres (12 miles) southwest of Madaba on the King's Highway is a signpost on the right to **Mukawir**, the site of Machaerus, mentioned in the New Testament as the palace in which Salome danced in exchange for the head of John the Baptist on a platter (Mark 6:21-29). Mukawir lies on a stark promontory (700 metres/2,295 ft) overlooking the Dead Sea and protected on three sides by deep ravines. The royal fortress

Site of Herod's Palace, Mukawir.

on top of the steep hill is that of Herod the Great. It dates to 30 BC and is a replacement of an earlier structure. It is similar to Herod's other mountain-top abodes west of the River Jordan: Herodium, Alexandrum and Masada. The site is undergoing extensive restoration by the Department of Antiquities and the Franciscan Institute although few walls of any height remain standing and the view is the principal reward for climbing to the top. The traces of baths and rooms arranged around a courtyard can be picked out.

Land of Moab: The land through which the King's Highway passes south of Amman is often referred to by its biblical name Moab. Most of the Book of Ruth takes place against the background of this open limestone plateau of rolling rounded hills, which rises from about 900 metres (2,950 ft) to the peak of Jebel Shihan south of the Wadi Mujib. The plateau is full of interest all year round but it is most beautiful in spring (late-March to May), when there is a green fuzz over the hills and scarlet anemones, black irises, wild gladioli, yellow heavy-scented mimosa and fire-station-red poppies border the road, colour the fields and fill the Wadi Mujib.

By summer hollyhocks and caper-bushes take over, against a background of intense activity as first the harvesting – in many cases by hand – followed by the threshing take place. The tinkle of bells heralds flocks grazing the stubble – just one example of the way in which agriculture and pastoralism are intertwined. The same land is used by several interest groups: the nomadic tribes herding sheep, goats and, less commonly, camels, who live in black goat-hair tents; the semi-nomadic tribes who live in village houses for part of the year but exchange these for black tents in the spring and autumn when they follow the grazing and move out to the fields for harvest; and the fully sedentary villagers, who now live in concrete houses but used to build large stone houses where at least half of the space was used for storage of agricultural produce.

Occasionally encampments of smaller sacking or canvas tents are seen on the outskirts of villages. These belong to the gipsies, who carry out dentistry work (putting in gold teeth) and sing and dance at weddings. Gipsies can be distinguished by the vibrantly coloured dresses of the women, for Moabite women traditionally dress in black. The latter are also known for their long braided hair which falls on the front of the dress while their head is covered by a tiny black tulle scarf.

The men of the region are less distinctive and opt for either Western dress or for a long, plainly coloured *dish-dash*. They reserve any form of sartorial individualism for their headcloth *(hatteh/ keffiyeh)*, which varies in design from red-and-white check to snowy white and can be worn at a very rakish angle. On high days and holidays men wear an *abayeh* over the *dish-dash*, a finely woven cloak of wool or linen often trimmed with gold. The status of the man is indicated by his *agal*, the cord which holds the *hatteh* on the head.

Umm ar-Resas can be reached from Madaba directly, from Dhiban or from

The post-office at the bottom of Wadi Mujib.

the Desert Highway, and is signed in all cases. The picture painted by the English writer and traveller C. M. Doughty in 1876 still greets the visitor today: "a rude stone-built walled town in ruins... a quaint tower of fair masonry".

Now one of the centres of the Beni Sakhr tribe, this square walled town, full of a bewildering jumble of stone, was probably built in the Roman period. There is a densely constructed urban district to the north and 2 km (1¼ miles) beyond a tall square tower amongst cisterns. So far the archaeologists have concentrated on the ecclesiastical nature of the site. Four churches have been identified within the walled town, and 12 within the northern district.

Two churches have emerged from the rubble in the southeast of the town, both floored with 6th-century mosaics depicting the familiar repertoire of fruit trees, animals, geometric and floral patterns. Other discernible features amongst the rubble include the three gates and rectangular towers. The most dramatic churches and mosaics are those outside

.eading
he way.

the town perimeter, now sheltered under another ugly hangar.

The mosaics are magnificent. The northern church was constructed in AD 586 and its mosaic depicts scenes of the church's benefactors carrying out daily tasks. In the southeast corner a personification of a Season was protected from iconoclasm by the stone base of a pulpit.

The southern church was floored in two stages. According to an inscription, the mosaic of the presbytery was laid in AD 756 by Etaurachius of Hisban. The main mosaic of the central nave and small lateral nave was remade in 785.

These churches were obviously still in use well into the early Islamic period. A border comprising vignettes of towns encloses an inner frame of Nilotic scenes, with a central panel of hunting, pastoral and harvesting scenes. All figures have been carefully patched during the iconoclastic movement so as to render them unrecognisable. The cities of the east and west banks of the Jordan are shown and named. On the north side from top to bottom are the western cities. From

top to bottom they read: Hagia Polis (Jerusalem); Neapolis (Nablus); Sebastis (Samaria-Sebaste); Kesaria (Caesarea); Diospolis (Lidda); Eleutheropolis (Beit Gibrin); Askalon (Ashkelon); Gaza (Gaza). On the south side from top to bottom are the eastern cities; Kastron Mephaa (Umm ar-Resas); Philadelphia (Amman); Madaba (Madaba); Esbounta (Hisban); Belemounta (Ma'in); Aeropolis (Rabba); Charach Mouba (Kerak).

The two pictures of Kastron Mephaa include the tall square tower, which was initially thought to be a watch-tower. Following the discovery of a 6th-century church at the base of the tower it seems certain that this was the tower of a Stylite, an ascetic monk who spent years on top of this stairless tower meditating and praying.

A grand descent: Nothing prepares one for the plunge into the gash across the plateau which is the **Wadi Mujib**, Jordan's answer to the Grand Canyon. The King's Highway twists and winds its way down 900 metres (almost 3,000 ft) to a small post-office at the bottom of the *wadi*. There are Roman milestones on the southern edge marking the course of the Roman road. A dam is planned, which will detract from the *wadi*'s grandeur but help meet the country's water shortage. It is worth pausing at the vantage-point on the north side of the *wadi* to drink in the view and watch the buzzards soaring at eye level.

Emerging through walls of basalt rock at the top of the *wadi*, the road once again passes through a wide open plateau covered in grain. This is southern Moab, an area known for its independent spirit for centuries. The King's Highway passes through small but thriving villages, all boasting large schools to cope with the expanding population. Several of the villages have standing monuments close to the road. In **al-Qasr** there is an early 2nd-century Nabataean temple which has never been excavated. To the west of the main road in **Rabba** are the well-preserved remains of a Roman temple, probably converted to a church and then reused in the 19th century as a village house.

Highway apple orchards.

234

To get the military permits necessary to travel from Kerak down to the Wadi Arabah via Safi, which you may want to do after visiting Kerak (*see below*), a brief stop should be made at the Army Security near the Prince Ali Hospital just before the main road into Kerak. From here one of the best and most complete views of the castle and town is obtained. The modern town – current population 122,000 – has spilled over the ancient walls and is creeping over the surrounding hills.

Kerak Castle: The site of **Kerak** has always been important because of its strategic position at the head of the Wadi Kerak leading west to Palestine. The visible remains of the castle date mainly from the Mamluke rather than Crusader period.

Originally access was through small man-made tunnels through the rock and these are still visible under an impressive facade linking four square towers above a stone *glacis* (slope, often artificially strengthened), which is being reconstructed by the Jordanian and Czech governments. Now the entrance curls up to the government resthouse with its spectacular view down to the Dead Sea. Kerak, like the other castles in Jordan, is a castle to be explored; there are many dark passages, cavernous holes and the occasional sheer drop (many of them unfenced, so beware). One problem for visitors and archaeologists alike is that the castle has been used and remodelled by successive governments right down to the brief Independent Republic of Moab in 1920, which makes it difficult to sift one period from another.

The steps down to the **Mamluke Lower Court** lead to a **museum** housed in one of the castle's many long galleries and containing artifacts from excavations and early photographs of Kerak taken by England's Edwardian explorer Gertrude Bell. The inner wall of this Lower Court sits on Crusader foundations but is largely Mamluke, while the outer wall is Mamluke, dating to the time of Sultan Baybars, who is also responsible for constructing the towers along the city wall inscribed with his

Looking towards Kerak Castle.

emblem, the lion. Turning sharp left from the entrance, walk up into an impressive two-storey gallery which used to double as a football pitch for the local boys. Look through the narrow arrow-slits on to one of the original Crusader entrances, now a blocked-up doorway in the rough stone wall in a projecting bastion to the east.

Once through this gallery, turn right along a narrow passage past a relief of a male torso which many guides tell you is Salah-ad-Din, better known to the English-speaking world as Saladin, the famous opponent of Richard the Lionheart and Reynald de Chatillon. In fact, this is a fragment of a Nabataean sculpture which was found on the site when the Crusaders started building in 1142. There are side rooms leading off the passageway, including the castle bakery, crucial for sustaining the garrison in times of siege, as were the cisterns.

Emerging from the gloom of the passage, you will find the ruined **Crusader chapel** on the right, and ahead the three-storey Mamluke keep, from which a good view of the castle and its surrounds can be had. The keep lies at the southern end of the citadel and replaces an earlier Crusader construction which would have defended this side against the siege-engines of Salah-ad-Din, which were set up on the high ground opposite. He twice besieged the castle, then occupied by his arch-enemy Reynald de Chatillon, first in 1183 and then in 1184. Reynald had been harrying Muslim caravans and sailing vessels, and had managed to get within one day's march of Mecca. During the siege, Salah-ad-Din suspended his fire on the tower on account of it being occupied by the newly married Isabelle, sister of the King, and Reynald's stepson.

Both sieges were eventually relieved by Baldwin IV marching with a garrison from Jerusalem, and Kerak did not capitulate until 1189.

Turning in the other direction and looking immediately down, you can see the excavated 14th-century reception-hall of al-Nasir Mohammed's palace. Here the Sultan would have received **Wadi Hassa.**

236

guests and supplicants. Its cruciform design with four *iwans* opening on to an unroofed courtyard is typical for that period and it mirrors a similar building at Shobak.

The **town of Kerak**, like Madaba, is a market centre for the surrounding Bedouin and villagers. Also like Madaba, it is a mixed Muslim and Christian town. Six percent of the total population of Jordan is Christian; two-thirds is Greek Orthodox and one-third is Greek Catholic, Roman Catholic, Protestant, Syrian Orthodox or Armenian. To avoid the confusion of celebrating different feast days, the Catholic and Orthodox Christmas and Easter are celebrated alternately by everyone. The Christian population of the Kerak area has a long history pre-dating the Crusades and several of the villages to the north of the town are 99 percent Christian. The Christians, being a minority, are determinedly Christian, and Kerak also has its share of fundamentalist Muslims (recognised by their bushy beards and the disconcerting habit of not acknowledging female customers in their shops).

The main street of Kerak is always bustling with fast-moving pedestrians and slow-moving cars. The modern *suq* is worth investigating; not only for the cool and tranquil interiors of the Ottoman shops but also for the useful items that can be purchased, such as threshing forks, sheep-skins, richly-roasted coffee beans, sacks of unidentified bark for medicinal purposes, goat-bells, blue-beaded Fatima's Hands for warding off the evil eye, rolls of tent-cloth and hand-stitched cotton- or wool-stuffed quilts, bolsters and mattresses. At the top of the main street several eateries offer very tasty *felafel*, *ful*, *humous* and salad, while further down near the mosque the delicious smell of spit-roasted chicken tempts. On the first sharp bend on the road out of town, look out for the dyeing shop with its vats of colour and an Ottoman school built on the orders of Sultan Abdul Hamid in the late 1890s.

For enthusiasts of Roman military history the excavated legionary fortress of **Lejjun** lies equidistant between the King's and Desert Highway and can be easily reached from Kerak. The name Lejjun is very probably a corruption of the Latin *legio*; in this case the legion being Legio IV Martia. The square fortress was probably built in AD 302 during the reign of Diocletian and contains all the usual requirements of a garrison-town: the central *principia* (headquarters), the barracks, defensive towers and a monumental gateway within the wall.

Lejjun was one of the forts which guarded the Eastern *limes* of the Roman Empire, which ran north-south near the line of the Desert Highway. The buildings on the hill above the site belong to the late Ottoman period when a Turkish garrison was stationed here to guard the spring and the communication lines between Kerak and Qatrana. The houses are now used by local Bedouin for storage of their winter tents.

Continuing south along the King's Highway from Kerak, the road passes through the neighbouring towns of **Mu'ta** and **Mazar**, site of the first battle between the Muslims and Byzantium in

AD 632 and of Jordan's third university. The Companions of the Prophet Mohammed who fell during the battle were buried at Mazar, and the town remains an important pilgrimage centre today, though the original commemorative mosque has been replaced by a 20th-century creation.

The road meanders on through rural landscape until reaching **Wadi Hasa**, the ancient boundary between Moab and Edom. Edom was an Iron Age kingdom which differed from Moab in that it was made up of small stretches of cultivatable land between steep little valleys. The side valleys contain traces of the Nabataean terracing which harvested and exploited the water run-off.

On the southern side of Wadi Hasa, on top of a high isolated hill, lies the Nabataean temple of **Khirbet al-Tannur**. The path to the summit is signposted and the sense of achievement at reaching the top is overwhelming. The temple was built in the 1st century BC/AD and dedicated to the gods Hadad and Atargaris, local versions of the main Nabataean gods Dushara and Allat. The whole structure was richly decorated with fine sculpture, which is now in the Archaeological Museum in Amman. Traces of the temple survive in low walls outlining the outer paved courtyard and altar in the northeast corner. A doorway leads to an inner smaller courtyard, in the centre of which stood the shrine and main altar. Animal sacrifices were made on these altars.

The King's Highway climbs out of the Wadi Hasa onto the long plain of **Tafila** where Lawrence fought his only pitched battle against the Turks in January 1918. The region is famous for its olives, a fact readily appreciated when looking at the groves of olive-trees blanketing the side of the *wadi* leading down from Tafila.

After passing the ancient site of **Buseirah**, ancient Bozrah and possible capital of the Edomites, the road passes the ar-Rashadiyya cement works and, just below, the village of **Dana**, an enchanting honeycomb of tightly-knit **Wadi Arabah**

roofs surrounded by fertile orchards. Dana nestles at the head of a magnificent *wadi* running west into the Wadi Arabah which was the site of early copper-mines.

The area is part of a project initiated by the Royal Society for the Conservation of Nature (RSCN) and funded chiefly by the World Bank and UNDP. Plans include the setting up of a nature reserve and research centre to study the local flora, fauna (including the rare ibex) and archaeology. The old village houses are gradually being restored with a view to providing improved accommodation and traditional crafts are being encouraged. At present a camp-site offers the only opportunity to stay in this beautiful and fascinating area.

Shobak Castle lies east of the main road running through Shobak village. The first sight of the castle on its isolated hill is quite breathtaking. As with Kerak, most of the visible defences belong to post-Crusader times. Shobak, or Montreal, was the first outpost of the Kingdom of Jerusalem in Outrejordain and constructed in 1115 by Baldwin I. It was later eclipsed by Kerak when its commander, Pagan the Butler, realised the strategic value of the latter. The castle shares a similar history to Kerak. It was taken over by the Ayyubids and then the Mamlukes, whose extensive reconstruction is recorded in inscriptions on the outer face of the towers. The original entrance to the castle was through a triple gate arranged on a bent axis as found at Ajlun.

The **Crusader church**, with its bird's-eye view of the old village, is above the entrance. Apart from this and several rooms along the arched corridor on the northeast side of the castle there are no other positively identified Crusader buildings. Although the water was usually brought up from springs at the base of the hill, in times of siege a deep and steep passageway within the castle walls led down to the spring. The passageway is still accessible but the steps are very worn and unlit.

A **palace/reception hall**, similar to the one at Kerak, has been excavated. It

was probably built by al-Mu'azzem Isa al-Adil, the Ayyubid governor of this area, at the end of the 12th century. The Ottoman village, including the old post-office and rebuilt rooms used by the village sheikh and more recently by a team of visiting archaeologists, is close to the entrance.

Below Shobak Castle is the domed **shrine of Abu Suleiman al-Dirany**, probably Ayyubid/Mamluke in date. Hennaed hand-prints adorn the internal walls of the shrine, smeared there by women who come to offer prayers for the sick and for fertility.

From Shobak the route to Petra is straightforward. If you arrive towards sunset consider taking a picturesque side road, indicated to Hesha, on the right-hand side shortly after the 20-km (12-mile) sign to Wadi Moussa. The road wiggles up through the original scrub-oak forest and emerges on the escarpment, giving a panoramic view of the rock-massif around Petra and Beidha. The road then snakes down to the modern villages.

The Desert Highway: The alternative to the site-packed journey along the King's Highway is to take the desert route, which is much faster (Amman to Wadi Moussa can be done in 3–4 hours), with dual-carriageway right down to Ma'an. The road has its own appeal but is generally less interesting, with scrub desert stretching either side of the road and occasional glimpses of the Hejaz railway stations (incongruous red-roofed buildings) in the distance.

The major truck-stops of al-Jiza, Qatrana and Hasa were also stops for the Haj caravan and each modern settlement hosts an Ottoman fort which guarded the cisterns and reservoirs so vital to the caravan. The fort at **Qatrana,** built in 1531, has been restored with financial help from the Turkish government. The Petra Resthouse at Qatrana always provides a welcome stop where good and hot meals are served.

Pervasive white dust heralds the phosphate mines at **Hasa**. Phosphate and potash from the Dead Sea are Jordan's most important exports and the old Hejaz railway is still used to transport phosphate down to Aqaba. Apart from the luxurious mine-camp and truck stops, the only "villages" along the Highway belong to recently settled Bedouin who often use the concrete houses and tin shacks for storage rather than dwelling.

Petra is signposted near al-Hashimiyya and again at **Ma'an**. The new road bypasses Ma'an where there is no longer much to see apart from Khoury's Resthouse on the old road to the north of the town, which the Desert Highway now bypasses. It is worth stopping here for a beer or tea and a personal welcome by Khoury, whose pink palace is papered with assorted photographs of Khoury as an actor.

From Ma'an a scenic route to Wadi Moussa is via Il and at-Tayyiba, an old village perched on the edge of the escarpment overlooking Petra and the Wadi Arabah. If continuing down to Wadi Rum the dual-carriageway stops south of Ma'an so that the winding descent of the Ras an-Naqab is a mixture of gasping at the stupendous view and at the oncoming over-laden trucks. **Examples of Ma'an's regional dress.**

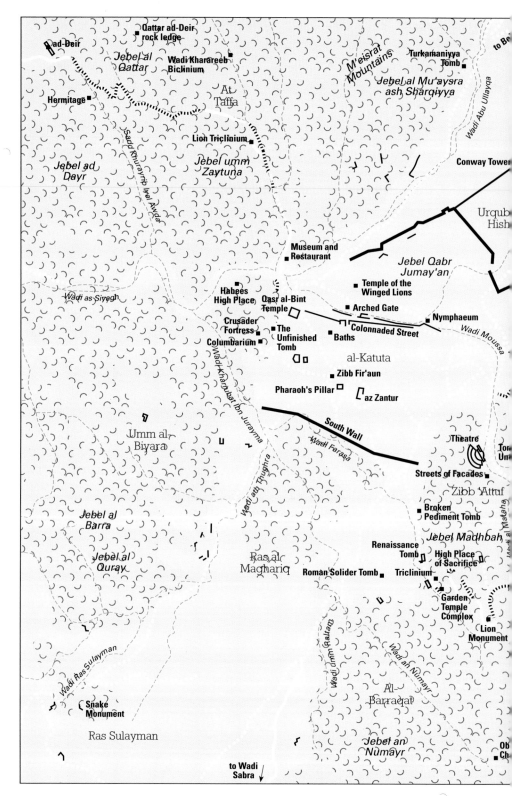

ad-Deir

Qattar al-Deir
rock ledge

*Jebel al
Qattar*

Wadi Kharareeb
Biclinium

At
Taffa

Hermitage

*M'eisrat
Mountains*

Turkamaniyya
Tomb

*Jebel al Mu'aysra
ash Sharqiyya*

to Be

Wadi Abu Ullayqa

Lion Triclinium

*Jebel umm
Zaytuna*

*Jebel ad
Dayr*

Conway Tower

Saad Khurayrib Iwl Awdar

Urqub
Hish

Museum and
Restaurant

*Jebel Qabr
Jumay'an*

Temple of the
Winged Lions

Wadi as Siyegh

Habees
High Place

Qasr al-Bint
Temple

Arched Gate

Nymphaeum

Crusader
Fortress

The
Unfinished
Tomb

Colonnaded Street

Baths

Wadi Moussa

Columbarium

al-Katuta

Zibb Fir'aun

Wadi Kharabat Ibn Jurayma

Pharaoh's Pillar

az Zantur

*Umm al
Biyara*

South Wall

Wadi Farasa

Theatre

Wadi ath Thughra

Streets of Facades

Tor
Un

Zibb 'Attuf

Broken
Pediment Tomb

*Jebel al
Barra*

Renaissance
Tomb

Jebel Madhbah

*Jebel al
Quray*

*Ras al
Maghariq*

High Place
of Sacrifice

Roman Solider Tomb

Triclinium

Mrka al Matana

Garden
Temple
Complex

Wadi umm Rattam

Lion
Monument

Wadi Ras Sulayman

Snake
Monument

Ras Sulayman

Wadi ah Numayr

*Al
Barraqat*

*Jebel an
Numayr*

Ob
Ch

to Wadi
Sabra

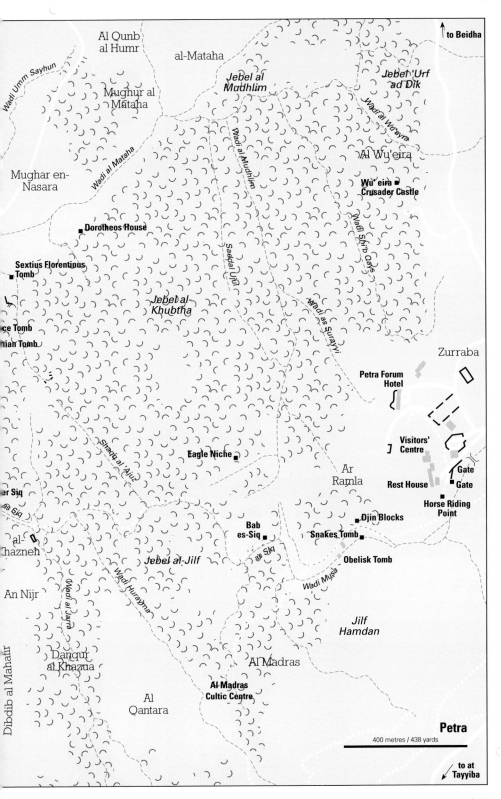

Petra

400 metres / 438 yards

PETRA

There are a handful of places in the world where the hand of God and the mind of man have joined forces to dazzle the human imagination, and **Petra** in south Jordan ranks high on that list. It is far and away Jordan's most spectacular touristic site, offering a powerful and always invigorating combination of Nabataean antiquities, sensational natural scenery, and – for those with the time and inclination to explore it – a convenient microcosm of the past 10,000 years of human civilisation, represented in a handful of archaeological sites within half an hour of Petra.

Carved in stone: Petra is best known for the dramatic tomb and temple facades that its Nabataean Arab inhabitants carved into the soft Nubian sandstone some 2,000 years ago. Since the city was "rediscovered" for the west in 1812 by the Swiss explorer Johann Ludwig Burckhardt, Western and Arab scholarship has identified over 800 individual monuments in the Petra area; all but a few dozen of them were carved into the pink, red and purple cliff-faces.

A closer look at the monuments, however, quickly reveals their hybrid, trans-Mediterranean nature. Petra was and is a dynamic, peaceful meeting-place of people and ideas from the four corners of the earth, a timeless point of convergence of communication routes, mind-sets, and cultural traditions from the leading Occidental and Oriental civilisations of the Mediterranean basin. Obvious Hellenistic and Egyptian architectural influences blend in with traditional Arab/Semitic local traditions, creating what we now refer to as Nabataean architecture. The Nabataeans also used a combination of languages, mainly their own Nabataean script, but also the Greek, Aramaic and Latin languages that were common among trading cultures in the 300 years before and after the time of Christ.

This cross-fertilisation of ideas that characterises Nabataean architecture and culture reflects the single most impor-tant force that gave rise to Nabataean civilisation: the importance of international trade. Historical knowledge of the birth of Nabataea is hazy. Most scholars accept that the Nabataeans were a semi-nomadic people from the northern Arabian Peninsula who migrated to southern Jordan in the 6th and 5th centuries BC (to the lands of the former biblical kingdom of Edom). They were particularly successful in this semi-arid climate due to their ability to harness scarce water resources and to make maximum use of camels for transport.

By the 4th century BC, Petra was establishing itself as a centre of Nabataean culture, perhaps first as a combination commercial entrepot/necropolis of a people whose economic base in southern Jordan relied on the income from regional trade in bitumen, aromatics, salt, copper and agricultural goods.

The importance of trade prompted the Nabataeans' heightened sense of diplomacy; this compelled them to resolve disputes with neighbours without warfare, so that security could be main-

tained and trade continue flowing. The result: as Nabataean traders, camel caravans, professionals and public figures interacted regularly with nearby civilisations, they absorbed those cultural traditions that caught their fancy (for example, a Roman Corinthian capital, a Hellenistic pedimented temple facade, an Egyptian obelisk funerary monument, an Assyrian cultic high place for spiritual activities). At the height of its independence in the 1st centuries BC and AD, Petra was renowned for its developed system of justice, humane monarchy, and technological and commercial prowess.

After the Emperor Trajan formally annexed Petra and the Nabataean Kingdom into the Roman Empire in AD 106, Nabataean trade and culture continued to flourish for several hundred years. Petra seems to have declined gradually after the 4th century AD, and was reduced to a shadow of its former urban splendour after a series of devastating earthquakes between the 6th and the 8th centuries AD.

Visiting Petra now: Today's visitors are awed by the magnificence and beauty of Nabataean tombs, temples, theatres, water works, and other monuments, many of which have eroded into fabulous natural striations of white, pink, red, blue and brown. A full week is required to see every important part of the Petra basin, which comprises nearly 100 sq. km (38 sq. miles) of rippled limestone mounds and undulating sandstone heights interspersed by narrow valleys and broad plains that are exploited for their agricultural potential today just as they have been for thousands of years.

Serious visitors should plan to spend at least one night and two full days to see the highlights in the central Petra basin, and to enjoy the particular pleasure of entering Petra on foot or on horseback in the cool quiet of the early morning.

A spate of new hotels has been built in the last few years, offering a wide range of accommodation from 4-star international hotel chains to small hostels catering to students and budget travellers.

Below left, riding along the *siq*. Right, the Obelisk Tomb.

Booking ahead is a must in the spring and autumn high seasons. Those who can spare only a day can rent a car and make the round-trip on their own (about 2½ hours one way from Amman along the Desert Highway), or take an all-inclusive guided trip offered daily by the JETT bus company in Amman.

A walk through the antiquities: Even the area around the visitors' centre and ticket office is rich in remains: small graves and chambers are cut into the ground, a large Nabataean tomb can be seen next to the resthouse, and across the street from the Petra Forum Hotel there is a large water reservoir which fed the city centre through a rock-cut channel.

From the visitors' centre, the route descends into Petra through the **Bab es-Siq** area, passing three **djin** ("ghost") **blocks**, early Nabataean tombs, on the right, and the stately **Obelisk Tomb**, with its four obelisks, on the left. Facing it, on the other side of the path, is a large Greek/Nabataean bilingual funerary inscription. Just before the dam, you can walk up into the hills to the south to the **al-Madras cultic centre**, with its altars, inscriptions, rock-cut monuments, water installations and many niches.

Today, as in Nabataean times, the dam at the entrance of the *siq* prevents winter floodwaters from damaging the *siq* and the city centre, by diverting water through the al-Muthlim tunnel. The traces of the monumental arch just beyond the dam mark the start of the main route into Petra through the 1¼-km (¾-mile) long *siq* – a natural fissure in the mountain which the Nabataeans developed into the stately entrance into their capital city. It still sports remains of the paved Nabataean/Roman road, two water channels, and innumerable religious niches, stone god-blocks, and inscriptions.

The end of the *siq* opens suddenly to the drama of **al-Khazneh** ("the treasury"), Petra's most famous monument; its name reflects the local legend that the urn on top of the monument held the Pharaoh's treasure. This monumental tomb was probably built for the Nabataean King Aretas III in the 1st century

Outside
al-Khazneh.

BC. Its facade still shows a variety of classical and Nabataean architectural elements, including statues of gods, animals and mythological figures. The Outer Siq leads from here towards the theatre and the city centre, passing several large tombs and tricilinia (singular: triclinium, a funerary banqueting hall with benches along three sides).

On the left just before the theatre are the 44 tombs that make up the eerie **Street of Facades**. The 7,000-seat **theatre** was first constructed by the Nabataeans, probably in the early 1st century AD, but was refurbished by the Romans soon after their conquest of the city in AD 106; the Romans obviously did not respect the Nabataean tombs, which they sliced through to expand the rear wall of their theatre.

From the refreshment stands beyond the theatre, a rebuilt Nabataean staircase ascends to the **Royal Tombs**, a dozen large tombs thought to have held the remains of Nabataean kings. The stairs lead to the most striking one, the **Urn Tomb** with its subterranean vaults

and its large internal chamber that was converted into a Byzantine church in AD 446–47. The southernmost of the Royal Tombs is the very well-preserved **Tomb of Uneishu**, a minister to Nabataean kings. North of the Urn Tomb is the heavily eroded but very colourful **Silk Tomb**, set back in a recess.

Beyond it is the equally eroded but busy-looking **Corinthian Tomb** (combining Nabataean and classical architectural styles, including a replica of the Khazneh in its upper storey). Immediately north of it is the huge, three-storey **Palace Tomb**, with parts of its upper storey built rather than carved. Just north of the Palace Tomb is a large cistern into which flowed the water that came from the pool near the Petra Forum Hotel.

North of the pool is the **Sextius Florentinus Tomb**, built around 130 AD for the Roman governor of the province of Arabia (note the faint Latin inscription and imperial eagle on the facade). A sacred processional way of staircases and corridors started from here and wound its way up to several **The Street of Facades.**

religious High Places on the summit of the mountain.

As you walk from the theatre towards the city centre, three minutes after passing the refreshment stands you come upon (on your right) the remains of the **Nymphaeum**, the public water fountain dedicated to the mythological Nymphs who lived near rivers and water sources. Here you can pick up the remains of the ancient colonnaded street that was built around AD 106 along the line of an earlier Nabataean gravel-surfaced roadway lined with buildings (probably shops). The street was used well into the 6th century, from when the existing street-side shops date.

The street leads directly to the arched gate that was the formal entrance into ancient Petra's most important temple precinct. Before you reach the arched gate, note a staircase leading south from the street towards an open area that scholars have called the "markets" of Petra. Also on the hill overlooking the street from the south is the collapsed Great Temple that is now being excavated. Some scholars think this was the city's Forum or Agora, the heart of its business and administrative dealings.

The slopes north and south of the colonnaded street are covered with broken pottery shards, cut stones, wall lines and architectural elements that indicate the presence of many unexcavated structures – most probably public buildings that once formed part of the city centre. Overlooking the colonnaded street from the north side of the *wadi* are two recently excavated structures: a large, triple-apsed **Byzantine church** with beautiful and well-preserved mosaic floors; and, almost parallel with the Arched Gate, the **Temple of the Winged Lions**, first built around AD 27 and dedicated to a consort of the supreme Nabataean male deity Dushara.

The **Arched Gate** – a common, three-entrance Graeco-Roman structure – had wooden doors that gave on to the temenos (the holy precinct) of the still-standing Qasr al-Bint Temple, the city's leading sanctuary. Note the small carved panels flanking the central doorway of

Below left, the Theatre. Right, hiking to High Places.

the Arched Gate, with their human busts, soldiers, animals and geometric designs, and the capitals on the ground which bear animal head decorations. The **baths of Petra** (these are not safely accessible to visitors) stand immediately above and south of the gate; giving on to the corner of the temenos, they may well have been used in association with religious rites in the temenos.

The 200-metre (656-ft) long temenos, parallel to the *wadi*, originally included a low platform, shallow steps, a long double row of benches along its south wall, and fine stone paving, all dating from the early 1st century AD. The 23-metre (75-ft) high **Qasr al-Bint Temple** (or Qasr Bint Pharoun, "Palace of Pharaoh's daughter") is Petra's most impressive built (as opposed to carved) structure, and dates from just before or after the time of Christ. Its open-air altar was used for public religious ceremonies. The temple faces north towards the Sharra Mountains, which gave rise to the name of the leading Nabataean god Dushara ("He of Shara"). The external walls were decorated with painted stucco, plaster panels, a Doric frieze, rosette medallions and bust reliefs, some of whose remains can still be seen. The temple was destroyed in the late 3rd century AD, perhaps when the forces of Queen Zenobia of Palmyra marched south to Egypt.

High places: The small mountain overlooking Qasr al-Bint from the west is al-Habees. A winding staircase leads up to a small, impressive museum that reveals Nabataean skills in ceramics, hydrology, metalwork and sculpture. The museum is housed in an unusual Nabataean rock-cut structure with five windows over the door; it may have been associated with religious rites along the processional route that passed in front of it, leading to the **Habees High Place**, about 250 metres (275 yds) to the west. This is the easiest high place to reach for visitors who cannot make more demanding climbs on foot. Like most high places, this one has benches, a water basin or tank, an altar, an approach staircase and a dramatic, perch-

Overlooking the Royal Tombs.

like setting overlooking a *wadi*, in this case the Wadi Siyyagh (the site of a massive Nabataean rock quarry and the important Wadi Siyyagh spring).

On the east face of al-Habees (facing Qasr al-Bint) are two interesting monuments that are easy to reach. The large **Unfinished Tomb** shows how the Nabataeans carved from the top down; the adjacent **Columbarium**, a former Nabataean tomb retooled with hundreds of small niches, was used either to hold cremation urns or to raise pigeons and doves. A small, 12th-century **Crusader fortress** on the summit of al-Habees can be reached easily in five minutes along a pathway and stairs from the south. The aerial view into central Petra is well worth the short climb to the fort's keep. The fort was a subsidiary lookout post for the bigger Crusader fortress at Wu'eira (near the Petra Forum Hotel).

Overlooking al-Habees from the southwest is the towering massif of **Umm al-Biyara** ("Mother of Cisterns"), whose east face sports a variety of Nabataean tomb styles. The trek to the summit along an ancient processional way is very demanding and requires a guide, but provides breathtaking panoramas of the entire Petra region. The summit retains the excavated remains of a small Edomite village from the 7th century BC Old Testament period, with impressive rock-cut water channels and cisterns. The Nabataeans also used the summit and built a small temple and other structures along its east rim.

The 45-minute ascent from the museum area to **ad-Deir** is best made in the afternoon, when much of the route is in shade. On the way up, you can visit several interesting monuments amidst stunning scenery: the **Lion Triclinium**; the **Wadi Kharareeb biclinium** (room with two benches); the **Qattar ad-Deir** natural rock ledge and water source which the Nabataeans used as a sanctuary; and the **Hermitage**, a perch-like chamber with many carved crosses. At the summit of the mountain is the open plain where the Nabataeans carved ad-Deir. This mid-1st century AD Nabataean temple or royal tomb has Petra's

eft, the olonnaded treet. Right, top ad-Deir.

largest facade (45 x 50 metres/130 ft x 164 ft), and boasts some classical Nabataean capitals. Like Qasr al-Bint, it also has an open-air altar (just north of the courtyard, near the steps to the urn on top of the tomb). The name ad-Deir ("the monastery") derives from the crosses scratched in its rear wall. The adjacent plateau has many other monuments and installations, including tombs, water works, tricilinia, decorated niches, and a relief of two men with camels.

Petra's most important and perhaps oldest major cultic facility is the **High Place of Sacrifice**, or al-Madbah in Arabic, located atop Jebel (Mount) Madbah, 200 metres (650 ft) above the theatre. Those who have the time should make the three-hour circular trip to the High Place, to complement their walk through the city centre. Such a trip is best made in the early morning. The route up via the Wadi Mataha starts near the theatre, and follows the Nabataean processional way that passes by two huge stone-carved obelisks (probably representations of deities) just before

reaching the High Place. The remains of the fort you have to walk through to reach the High Place are probably those of a Nabataean defensive/lookout facility, or perhaps the stately entrance to the High Place of Sacrifice itself.

The Nabataeans may have inherited the High Place of Sacrifice from the Edomites. This important religious facility comprised two adjacent altars and associated cultic installations, an open central court with a small raised platform for offerings and shallow benches around three sides, and a nearby pool, water channels and drains – probably used for animal sacrifices.

From the High Place, you can return to the city centre via the **Wadi Farasa**, with its collection of fine monuments. You can see several Nabataean inscriptions (near ground-level) in the rocks to your right just after starting down from the High Place. The first major monument you come upon is the **Lion Monument**, a 5-metre (16-ft) long, rock-carved cultic fountain; a few metres away is a small stone-cut altar. The

water that emerged from the lion's mouth reached the city centre in a water channel that runs parallel with the staircase from the Lion Monument that winds down to the Wadi Farasa.

The first monument you come upon in the *wadi* is the **Garden Temple Complex**. It includes a small shrine, and an associated terrace complex above the temple with a once-arched room and a large plastered cistern. Water reached the city centre from here through a distribution system of cisterns, channels and ceramic pipes.

The next complex you reach in Wadi Farasa is the **Roman Soldier Tomb** and its Triclinium. Note the three statues in Roman military dress in niches on the tomb facade. The Triclinium sports Petra's most spectacular interior today, due to the weathering of the rock. Further down Wadi Farasa on your right is the **Renaissance Tomb**, with its delicate facade of Nabataean capitals and six urns, and then the **Broken Pediment Tomb** perched on a raised recess.

The Wadi Farasa trail towards the city centre passes through an area full of rock-cut tombs and houses, crosses the low remains of a small gate within the South City Wall, and finally meanders through the area of **al-Katuteh**, which is thought to have been used as the town garbage dump in the 2nd century AD (that's why there is so much broken pottery on the ground).

The path then passes the rocky summit of ez-Zantur before reaching **Pharoun's (Pharaoh's) Pillar**, one of two pillars which marked the entrance to a Nabataean temple that lies unexcavated in the hillside. It is possible that this structure was located next to a road that entered Petra from the south and that brought camels and goods to the so-called "markets" above the colonnaded street. Recent excavations in this region have uncovered domestic and cultic structures, including a Byzantine church, dating from the 1st to the 6th centuries AD.

From this area south of the city centre, the hardy can head off on foot or horseback to visit two distant sites, each

High Place and high views.

requiring over two hours to reach. The Nabataean suburb of **Sabra** still shows the remains of a small theatre, several major buildings, a possible baths, a water catchment system, cisterns, tombs, niches and other remains from the Nabataean and Roman periods.

At the highest summit in the Petra region – 1,350 metres (4,429 ft) above sea level – is the shrine and 14th-century **mosque of Nebi Haroon** (the Prophet Aaron), which enjoys a marvellous view of the region. The white dome of the mosque can be seen from most areas in and around Petra.

On the opposite, north side of the city centre, visitors can also explore slightly out of the way districts of Petra such as **Mughar an-Nasara** (the "Christian" or "Nazarene caves", so called because of the crosses that are carved into some tomb walls). This unspoilt area has many tombs, cisterns, and altars, traces of the ancient northern entrance to Petra, a rare triclinium adorned with four shields and two Medusa heads, and some of Petra's most bizarre and colourful natural rock formations. (The adventurous and fit can exit Petra from Mughar an-Nasara by walking for about an hour to the north and then east, around Jebel Khubtha and parallel to the rock-cut water channel that linked the pools near the Petra Forum Hotel and the Palace Tomb.)

A kilometre north of Mughar an-Nasara is the new Bdul village at **Umm Saihun**, near an ancient quarry, cultic altars, tombs and hydraulic installations. And 15 minutes by foot west of Mughar an-Nasara, on the other side of Wadi Nasara, is **Conway Tower** (al-Mudawwara in Arabic). This 25-metre (82-ft) diameter tower fortified the northwest corner of the Nabataean town walls and overlooks the entire region.

Two other outlying districts well worth visiting are located immediately west of Mughar an-Nasara. **Wadi Turkmaniyya** has the very important **Turkmaniyya Tomb**, whose upper facade boasts the longest known Nabataean inscription. It mentions the facilities that a proper Nabataean tomb complex

Schoolgirls pose.

should have: tomb, triclinium, cistern, courtyard, portico, gardens, houses, terraces and other facilities (most of which can be seen at the Roman Soldier Tomb or the Tomb of Uneishu). West of Turkmaniyya are the **M'eisrat Mountains**, a rarely visited area full of tombs, water works, cultic installations, and processional ways.

Ten thousand years of history: Within half an hour's drive from Petra are several interesting archaeological sites that fill in important periods in the last 10,000 years of human civilisation in the Middle East. Three of these sites are located alongside the paved road that heads north from the visitors' centre and past the Petra Forum Hotel.

Wu'eira Crusader Castle, west of the road about a kilometre north of the hotel, was built in the early 12th century and abandoned when Salaheddeen (Saladin) defeated the Crusaders in Jordan in 1189. The Crusaders called this region La Vallée de Moise (the Valley of Moses), a name that retains a link to the present Arabic name of the town of

Wadi Moussa (which also means the Valley of Moses).

The dramatic entrance bridge over a precipitous moat (not for the faint-hearted) leads into a roughly rectangular fortress, still sporting some of its defensive walls, towers, vaults, cisterns and internal structures, including a possible church.

Siq al-Barid, 10 minutes by car to the north, was a prosperous "suburb" of Petra located at the junction of ancient caravan routes that linked Petra with the Wadi Araba/Dead Sea region, Gaza, the Palestine coast, Egypt and the Mediterranean basin. Several immense cisterns carved into the rocks are still used today by local livestockers. The name Siq al-Barid comes from the miniature *siq* (fissure) that gives access to a splendid collection of tombs, temples, triclinia, houses, cisterns, water channels, niches, cultic installations, staircases and other structures. One small biclinium (room with two benches) still has the remains of 1st-century fresco paintings with floral motifs, birds, and classical mytho-

logical figures including Pan and Eros.

Five minutes to the southwest (by rough dirt track) is one of Jordan's most compelling attractions – the Neolithic (Late Stone Age) village of **Beidha**. This early farming and livestocking settlement still retains standing walls, staircases, hearths, grinding stones, plastered floors, upright doorways and cultic installations from the period 7000–6500 BC, when humankind was making the transition from nomadic hunter-gatherer to year-round settled villager, farmer, and livestocker. Neolithic fans can also visit a similar excavated site at **Basta**, half an hour to the southeast.

Fifteen minutes by car east of Petra is the important ancient site at **Udruh**, whose spring and strategic location were the main reasons for its almost uninterrupted settlement since the Iron Age, nearly 3,000 years ago. The main remains above ground today are the external walls and towers of a Roman legionary fortress, though the site was also important in the Nabataean and early Islamic eras.

Another Roman fortress can be visited at **Daajaniyya**, a 10-minute drive over a desert track southwest of the junction of the Desert Highway and the east–west road to Shobak and Petra. Its standing fortifications and water system are particularly impressive. Like most of the forts along the southeastern frontier of the Roman Empire, it was probably built in the 2nd century AD, and abandoned during the decline of Roman power in this area during the 5th and 6th centuries.

The most recent historical period – the late Ottoman era of the end of the 19th/early 20th century – is well represented at **Taybeh**, 10 minutes south of Petra. This traditional Jordanian village has been recently renovated into a tourist village equipped with modern amenities, but still retains the lifestyle and buildings of turn-of-the-century Jordan. Similar traditional village architecture is visible throughout the Petra area; a good, easily accessible example is **Khirbet Nawafleh**, on the north side of Wadi Moussa town.

Goat train near Beidha

258

BURCKHARDT

I t was with some reticence that a young Swiss explorer summed up his visit, on 22 August 1812, to one of the legendary sites of the Middle East. "It appears very probable," he said, "that the ruins in Wady Mousa are those of the ancient Petra." Johann Ludwig Burckhardt was the first Westerner for 600 years to see the capital of the ancient Nabataeans.

Burckhardt was born in Basle in 1784, the son of a wealthy merchant. After university in Germany, he endured two painful years in London, with no work and dwindling finances, before a fruitful introduction to the scientist Sir Joseph Banks, a member of the Association for Promoting the Discovery of the Interior Parts of Africa. The Association had hit on the idea of exploring caravan routes as a means of finding the source of the River Niger. Undeterred by the death or disappearance of everyone so far sent on this mission, Louis offered his services and was accepted.

After a crash course in Arabic at Cambridge University, he set off in March 1809 for Syria, where he perfected his Arabic and adopted the clothes and manners of his chosen alias, Ibrahim ibn Abdullah, a Moorish trader. Once master of the local dialect, Burckhardt began travelling with the Bedouin. He explored large areas of Syria and Lebanon, taking copious notes as he went – secretly, for discovery could have cost him his life. So too could any inappropriate gesture. During interludes in Aleppo he studied Islam and religious law; learnt by heart large sections of the Koran; and wrote a treatise on Bedouin customs, a classification of the Bedouin tribes on the Syrian borders and notes on geography.

In spring 1812 "Ibrahim ibn Abdullah" finally left Syria for Cairo. En route he visited the ruins of Jerash and Amman and then Kerak where he was delayed for 20 days by the sheikh, who insisted on accompanying him, only to demand protection money. At Tafileh he detached himself from this "treacherous friend", and continued with a Bedouin guide called Hamid.

After leaving Shobak, Burckhardt wanted to deviate from the agreed route in order to see some ruins in the valley of Wadi Moussa which the local people had spoken of with admiration. Knowing that this would arouse suspicion, he feigned a vow to sacrifice a goat at the shrine of Haroun (Aaron) at the far end of the valley. The subterfuge worked. With a local guide and a goat for the sacrifice he made his way through the ruins towards Jebel Haroun (Mount Aaron), hiding his interest in the monuments lest he was taken for a magician seeking treasure. He went into the Treasury, passed the theatre and observed the Royal Tombs. Secretly he noted everything in his journal.

The sun was setting as they approached Jebel Haroun, and the guide became so agitated that they might be seen by unfriendly eyes that Burckhardt reluctantly agreed to sacrifice the goat there and then. The next day he resumed his journey south. He regretted not going to the top of the mountain – as he wrote, "a traveller ought, if possible, to see everything with his own eyes." He added, with characteristic modesty, "Whether or not I have discovered the remains of the capital of Arabia Petraea, I leave to the decision of Greek scholars." The Greek scholars agreed. ∎

WADI RUM

From the heights of Ras an-Naqab the land falls away abruptly to the south into the Quweira plain, an expanse of pinkish sandy desert some 600 metres (1,970 ft) below. Pinnacles and broken ramparts of rock thrust upwards from the desert floor, stacked one behind another to a distant hazy vanishing point.

Coming from the north, this is the first view of the vast tract of southeastern Jordan known as Wadi Rum. The area takes its name from the largest and grandest of a whole network of *wadis* (valleys) which for millennia offered the easiest passage to the nomadic Bedouin and to trading caravans en route to or from the Arabian peninsula. Breathtaking as this distant view is, it is a pale shadow of the towering magnificence of the interior of Rum.

"Vast and echoing and God-like," T. E. Lawrence called it, in one of several lyrical passages on Wadi Rum in *Seven Pillars of Wisdom*. Today Lawrence's own echo is one of the most potent in Wadi Rum. Lawrence returned here time and again during the Arab Revolt of 1917–18, sometimes because tribal politics or logistics demanded it, but at other times to find solace – "to clear my senses by a night in Rumm and by the ride down its dawn-lit valley towards the shining plains... Rumm's glory would not let a man waste himself in feverish regrets."

Visiting Wadi Rum: There are various options for visiting the area. Ordinary cars can reach the village of Rum, the springboard for visiting the area, from the Desert Highway. Ten km (6 miles) south of the little town of Quweira, and about 45 km (28 miles) north of Aqaba, a sign points eastwards along a narrow asphalt road which reaches the **village of Wadi Rum** after 30 km (18½ miles) of increasingly spectacular scenery. The village has a small fort, one of a string built in 1933 by Glubb Pasha as an outpost of the Desert Patrol (now the Bedouin Police) and a government resthouse with a café, bar and basic

camping facilities. It is possible to hire a pick-up, complete with Bedouin owner-driver, at the tourist office beside the resthouse to drive for an hour or more into the *wadi* system and see a few places of particular interest, or alternatively to hire a camel and guide.

The length of time, sites to be visited, and cost, should all be established with the tourist office before setting out (for example, if you want to go as far as the rock "bridge" featured on postcards, it will take several hours). Those with their own four-wheel-drive vehicle are advised to hire a Bedouin guide. There are also several interesting walks, scrambles and climbs, of varying grades, for which advice and guidance are also available at the tourist office.

Overnight camping under a brilliant starry sky is an unforgettable experience, and can be done independently by those with suitable vehicles, equipment, maps and an understanding of the terrain. Alternatively, a handful of companies in Aqaba specialise in making such arrangements and can provide vehicles,

drivers, camels, equipment, food and guides, for groups of all sizes. It is, however, best to book through a reputable travel company in Amman.

The geology of Rum: The valley floors are some 900–1,000 metres (2,950–3,280 ft) above sea level, and the great sandstone crags rise sheer a further 500–750 metres (1,640–2,460 ft). Jebel Rum, at 1,754 metres (5,755 ft) above sea level, is the highest peak in the area and the second highest in Jordan; but Jebel Umm Ishreen, just across the *wadi*, falls short by a mere metre.

The cataclysm which 30 million years ago created the Great Rift Valley – running from southern Turkey through Syria, the Jordan Valley, the Dead Sea, Wadi Arabah, the Red Sea and into East Africa – also tossed up the layers of rock here, the deposits of a wide range of geological periods. As the rocks settled, they were rearranged in the strange and complex formations that we see today, in a pattern of criss-crossing fault lines. Most lines run NNE–SSW, roughly parallel to the Wadi Arabah rift, but these are traversed by counter-faults running NE–SW, NW–SE, E–W and NS.

Mostly hidden beneath the surface lies a crust of pre-Cambrian granites, at least 2,000 million years old. Above it is a vari-coloured mixture of early Palaeozoic sandstones of different periods, textures and colours – rich red Cambrian sandstones, 600 million years old, pale grey Ordovician and whitish Silurian – each separated by up to 100 million years of primitive life on earth. Between them are occasional bands of quartzite, shales, grits and conglomerates. Exposure to rain and wind has sculpted the sandstones into weird shapes that look at times like domes, giant mushrooms and organ-pipes or dripping candle wax. In **Jebel Burdah**, this process of erosion has created an unbroken arch of rock over a canyon. There is another rock arch on **Jebel Kharaz**, in a remote area some 27 km (17 miles) north of Rum village.

The rocks were thrown up higher in the west, nearest the rift valley, and all the strata tilt down eastwards. In the **On guard in Wadi Rum.**

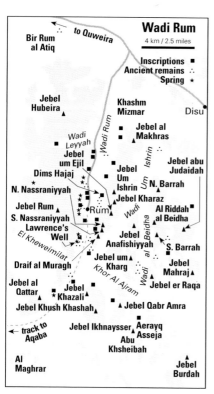

western areas the granite rises above the *wadi* floor beneath a mantle of younger sandstones, and several springs are found here, particularly along the east face of Jebel Rum. These springs were created by winter rainfall penetrating the porous sandstone until hitting the sloping layer of impermeable granite, whence the water seeped down into the open and formed pools and waterfalls surrounded by lush foliage.

Fossil traces are numerous in the sandstones, especially imprints of trilobites (among the earliest known animals on earth, resembling today's wood-lice but with a three-lobed body). These, and other trace fossils of the Cruziana species, were marine creatures, living in the shallow tidal waters of the ocean that recurrently inundated much of Jordan throughout the Palaeozoic and Mesozoic eras.

Human influences: Today, Wadi Rum lies in the territory of the Howeitat, one of the largest Bedouin tribes in Jordan, who claim descent both from the Prophet Mohammed and from the Nabataeans.

They are no longer fully nomadic, for they live in villages in winter, but in the long parched summers they still move around with their flocks and tents in search of pasture.

But early humans, late-comers on to the earth's stage, were in southern Jordan at least 400,000 years ago, in their most primitive Palaeolithic form. Water was plentiful from the springs in Wadi Rum, and they lived by hunting the abundant wildlife with stone-tipped weapons and by gathering fruits and roots in a savannah-like terrain dotted with trees. Very slowly, through the Palaeolithic millennia, the pattern of life evolved from one of almost perpetual motion to a nomadic lifestyle in which temporary camps were re-inhabited periodically, probably on a seasonal basis.

From 9,000 BC on, some Neolithic families and groups introduced agriculture and the raising of domestic animals. Increasingly in the Chalcolithic period (4,500–3,300 BC) semi-permanent seasonal agricultural settlements

A parting shot.

were established throughout the complex network of *wadis*. Other groups adopted only the pastoral aspect, and continued their nomadic life in search of pasture for their flocks and herds. They ranged over a huge territory, in winter often penetrating deep into the Arabian peninsula. Some became traders, and travelled north, south, east and west, exchanging items of value with the more acquisitive sedentary groups.

The Nabataeans may have started coming here in the 6th century BC, but there is no concrete evidence of their presence until the late 4th century BC, when they controlled all the trade routes through their territory in southern Jordan: frankincense and myrrh from Arabia Felix (modern-day Yemen), spices from India, purple cloth from Phoenicia. Through a subtle blend of trade and protection racket, the Nabataeans became immensely wealthy. Though their main centre was at Petra, they also had settlements in the Hejaz at Medain Saleh, in Sinai and the Negev, and here in Wadi Rum.

The Nabataeans were not only inspired traders; these erstwhile nomads had acquired a mastery of water resources that enabled them to create settlements larger than many of their contemporaries might have deemed possible. To provide for their settlement in Wadi Rum, they built an aqueduct from the most abundant spring, Ain Shallaleh, to a reservoir in the valley below.

They also constructed three great dams, the largest at Bir Rum al-Atiq, just south of the road from Quweira, about 6 km (4 miles) west of the Rum-Disi junction; another on the west face of Jebel Abu Jedeideh; and a third just east of Jebel Mahraj. Towards the end of the reign of the last Nabataean king, Rabbel II (AD 71–106), they built a temple, dedicated to the goddess Allat. Its very tumbled remains lie a short distance due west of the resthouse.

Lawrence's pool: Several springs in Wadi Rum have Nabataean rock-cut channels to divert the water into cisterns. T. E. Lawrence found some Nabataean inscriptions when he bathed

The sun sets on a desertscape.

in the **Pool of Ain Shallaleh** after a hot, dusty camel-ride from Rum to Aqaba and back. The moisture, in stark contrast to the surrounding desert, and the "thick ferns and grasses of the finest green made it a paradise just five feet square." As Lawrence delighted in the clear, cool waters of the pool, a Bedouin, gently touched in the head, came and peered at him. "After a long stare he seemed content, and closed his eyes, groaning, 'The love is from God; and of God, and towards God.' His low-spoken words were caught by some trick distinctly in my water pool. They stopped me suddenly... the old man of Rumm loomed portentous in his brief, single sentence... In fear of a revelation, I put an end to my bath."

Coded messages: Something of the story of the nomads and settlers of Rum could be read in images along the faces of the mountains, if only we had the key to decipher them. It is like a coded cartoon strip of antiquity. However, the inscriptions are relatively easy to interpret; some are in the Nabataean script,

Thamudic inscriptions.

an individual adaptation of the Aramaic that was current for many centuries throughout Syria; a few (including one near the Nabataean temple) were written by Minaean traders from Ma'in in Yemen, in a bold angular script. (The Minaean kingdom flourished between the 5th century BC and the 1st century AD.) Most common of all are the Thamudic inscriptions, hundreds of them, scratched on the rock faces by centuries of nomads and traders. The tribe of Thamud lived near Medain Saleh in the Hejaz from around the 5th century BC to the 7th century AD. Some inscriptions are simply a signature to a drawing; others are petitions to the Nabataean deities Allat and Dushara, asking for help; yet others are messages of love or of grief.

For countless centuries, up to the present, the Bedouin have engraved on the rocks representations of the animals, people and events of their world, as enigmatic in their meaning as their date. Outlines of hands and feet, elongated human figures dressed in tunics

and hunting scenes are common; so too are drawings of ibex and camels; rarer are oxen, and local species of lion, wild ass and ostrich, all now extinct. Some interesting and easily accessible drawings can be seen in a gully at the northern end of **Jebel Khazali**.

Another curiosity is the **"topographical stone"** of Jebel Amud, a large stone slab in a cave formed by a rock fall on the south side of the mountain near Disi village. It is scored with grooves and round depressions which appear to form a pattern. In 1978 some local Bedouin showed it to a team of scholars from Florence University, led by palaeontologist Professor Edoardo Borzatti von Löwenstern. After several years of research, Borzatti concluded that the stone was a prehistoric map of the area, the depressions representing the positions of Neolithic and Chalcolithic settlements, or enclosures, while the grooves represented *wadis*. He further suggested that it may have been made by Bedouin of those distant times to keep a tally of the protection money, or taxes, that they extracted from settled farmers in return for not raiding their property. Seeing the outlines of the stone superimposed on a map of the area, it is hard not to be impressed with the similarities. However, many scholars remain unconvinced either that was any kind of map, or that it was ever related to taxes.

Wildlife: Although Wadi Rum does not teem with wildlife as it did even a few decades ago, if you sit still for a while you can usually see animals and birds appearing as if from nowhere. Hyrax, hares, fennec foxes, jerboas and gerbils come out at dusk, as does the Arabian sand cat, an elusive nocturnal hunter. Nubian ibex and gazelle, once abundant, now survive in residual herds. Desert larks, crested larks and pale rock sparrows can be seen, along with bright pink male Sinai rosefinches with their dowdier wives. Chukar partridges also frequent Rum, and Cretzschmar's bunting, redstarts, lesser whitethroats, white-crowned blackchats and yellow wagtails. Three vultures may be seen – in summer the Egyptian vulture, and at any time the griffon vulture and the lammergeier, the latter a rarity.

In the late 1980s Jordan's Royal Society for the Conservation of Nature proclaimed several new wildlife reserves throughout the country, including 510 sq. km (197 sq. miles) of Rum. Within this global area, they plan to make an enclosure of 75 sq. km (29 sq. miles) into which they will transfer some of the Arabian oryx at Shaumari and ibex from the Wadi Mujib Reserve. Another area of the same size will be designated as a park for tourism, and will include the historical and epigraphic sites, and climbing areas.

From the start the RSCN encouraged involvement by the Bedouin, who know better than anyone where to find the animals and have witnessed the reduction in numbers of all species. The RSCN stresses the necessity of an integrated approach, caring for the social and economic needs of the Bedouin as well as environmental protection. Gradually, it is hoped, the Bedouin will become conservationists, responsible for their own environment – and benefiting from it.

Left, man and friend. **Right**, a natural rock arch.

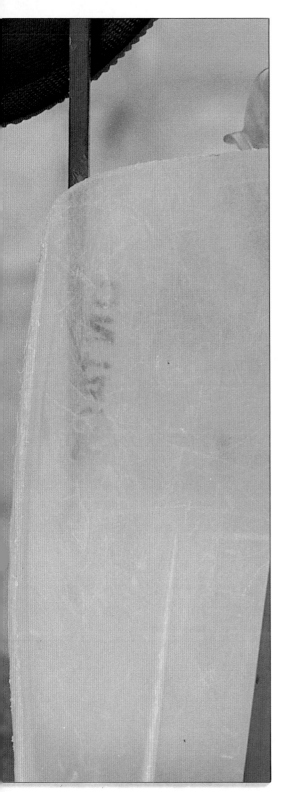

GULF OF AQABA

As Jordan's only outlet to the sea the port city of **Aqaba** evokes a feeling of freedom and a promise of relaxation to most Jordanians, who flock to their country's only real beach resort at every occasion they get. It is known for its clean, sandy beaches and agreeable climate, especially in the spring, autumn and winter. When the temperature in Amman is a chilly zero to 10°C (32°–52°F), the temperature in Aqaba can be a pleasant 25°C (77°F).

But other visitors, especially the growing bands of Italian, German, English and Scandinavian tourists, come for the offshore attractions, for like its Israeli counterpart, Eilat, a pebble's-throw across the bay, and Egypt's Ras Mohammed, Aqaba offers world-class scuba-diving on the coral reefs of the Red Sea.

Aqaba is situated on the tip of the Gulf of Aqaba, the Red Sea's slender eastern finger (about 180 km/112 miles in length and never more than 20 km/12 miles in width), enclosed by barren, pink- and mauve-tinted mountains that are rich in phosphates. To the east a string of dark-golden beaches stretch about 20 km (12 miles) along the length of Jordan's coast, to the Saudi Arabian border, from where there are clear views of the four countries flanking the gulf: Jordan, Saudi Arabia, Egypt and Israel (the tall white building visible on the far shore lies just inside Egypt).

Aqaba is quiet by Mediterranean standards, in spite of the growing numbers of Italian, German, English and Scandinavian tourists. Even its handful of luxury hotels – all parked next to each other like trailers at the northwest end of town – are unassuming. As a consequence you won't find much in the way of nightlife or bars, but you will find water that is a far cry cleaner than anything one encounters in the Med and beaches that are less crowded than at Eilat. Most of the hotels have comfort-

Preceding pages: the Gulf of Aqaba. **Left,** equipment for hire.

able beachside cafés, the most lively being the Aquamarina, which pumps put live music in its outdoor disco until the small hours.

Strategic value: But despite its holiday image, Aqaba's chief importance is as a port. It is Jordan's most strategically important city and has been crucial to other countries in the region (it served as a lifeline to Iraq throughout the 8-year Iran-Iraq War which paralysed the Iraqi port of Basra). As the number and variety of ships docking at the port and the massive truck-park on Aqaba's approach road testify, the city is the hub of sea-to-land transport routes in Jordan and beyond.

Jordan's economy bloomed during the 1980s largely as a result of the transport activity that went through Aqaba's port. When the Allies almost closed access to Jordan's Red Sea port during the 1990–91 Gulf War, the port came to a virtual halt except for ferrying people to and from Egypt. Dependent on exports for about 70 percent of its food needs, Jordan consequently suffered a crushing blow to its economy. It took more than a year after the war for the export-import business to recover.

To first-time visitors, Aqaba's proximity to the Israeli port city of Eilat is astonishing. Indeed, at night the lights of the two cities seem to merge into one twinkling curve. If a peace pact between Israel and Jordan becomes a reality, Aqaba would undoubtedly increase in size and prosperity

A long history: The name Aqaba was given to the port city in the 14th century when it was ruled by Mamluke sultans based in Egypt. Previous to that it was known as Ayla, a name which archaeologists and historians have often interpreted as the twin version of Eilat.

Aqaba's history goes back to biblical times at the very least. According to the Old Testament, King Solomon built a naval base at Ezion Geber, some 3 km (1¾ miles) north of modern Aqaba, next to the Jordanian-Israeli border: "And King Solomon made a navy of ships in Ezion Geber, which is beside Eloth, on the shore of the Red Sea, in the land of **Livestock arrives regularly from Australia.**

Edom." Excavations here have revealed evidence of copper smelting.

From Ezion Geber the Old Testament King traded with the rulers of what is now Somalia and then used his new-found position to oversee trade with the old Kingdom of Saba (Yemen) and Abyssinia (Ethiopia).

The Romans (106 AD), who ruled the region from Bosra in Syria, used the town as one of their main trading stations en route to the sea. In the early 4th century the port city came under the rule of the Byzantine empire and was ruled on their behalf by the Ghassanides, Christian Arab tribes originating from south Arabia.

Ayla came under Islamic rule in 630–631, when the spread of Islam from the Hejaz reached the peoples of the Red Sea. During this time the port was known to travellers as the "door to Palestine" because of its proximity to the holy land. Twelfth-century Crusaders wrested Ayla from the Muslims and built a fort on Far'un Island – then called the Ile de Graye – some 7 km (4 miles) off-shore. When Saladin launched his counter-crusade against Western Christendom he also captured Ayla and the former Crusader castle became known as Saladin's Castle.

In 1182, shortly after Saladin had captured Aqaba, the Crusader Reynald de Chatillon retook the Island of Graye only to lose it during a battle with other Muslim forces in the following year.

With the rise of the Mamluke sultans in Egypt, Aqaba (as they renamed it) came under Mamluke Egyptian rule. A Mamluke fort was built in the 14th century by Qansah Ghouri, one of the last sultans of the Mamluke era. After the Mamlukes, the Ottomans controlled Aqaba for some 400 years, during which the port declined to a relatively unimportant fishing town.

But Aqaba's fortunes revived in the early 20th century. It was of key importance during the Arab Revolt. T. E Lawrence and the Arab forces skilfully prised the port from the Ottoman forces in 1917 and used it to receive arms shipments from Egypt. After World War I,

the British secured Aqaba for Jordan rather than Saudi Arabia, though the new Saudi-Jordan border, originally drawn just a few kilometres southeast of Aqaba, was pushed back in 1965 when King Hussein traded 6,000 sq km of desert for an additional 12 km (7½ miles) of coastline.

Nonetheless, space remains tight and Aqaba has only a little room to expand. Already the demands of tourism, industry and shipping are clashing. When shipments of livestock bound for Saudi Arabia arrive from Australia or New Zealand every few weeks or so, they bring unpleasant odours, insects and fleas. So far, hoteliers have simply held their noses, but as tourism continues to develop complaints are likely to rise. Similarly, fears are being raised about the adverse effects heavy shipping and phosphate dumping is likely to have on the coral reefs.

A conservative society: As the city grew, many of the original inhabitants of Aqaba – generally fishermen or traders – sold their lands to newcomers, hoteliers or transport companies, and migrated to Amman. At least 40,000 of the current 55,000 inhabitants are migrants from other cities in the south, such as Ma'an and Petra. Palestinians too have settled in Aqaba, many working in hotel administration or banking or holding executive posts at the shipping companies. The Kaberity and Madi families, native scions of the city, have run municipal councils and kept Aqaba's seat in Parliament for successive generations. Non-natives usually seek sponsorship from one of the large local families in order to better their social and economic standing in city.

Most of the port labourers are Egyptians, Pakistanis or Indians. Prohibited under the restrictions of a migrant labour law from bringing their families with them, this expatriate community tends to be excluded from mainstream life in the town, which is very family-oriented and deeply conservative, in spite of Aqaba's growing reputation as an international resort. Most of Aqaba's women wear the *hijab* (Islamic head-

Aqaba's beach with Eilat in the background.

dress) and strict social mores dictate a largely indoor life. Family beaches – in effect private or hotel beaches – are separated from the generally all-male public beaches and Arab women who do swim at public beaches invariably do so fully clothed.

Aqaba's sights: The remains of **Ayla**, Aqaba's medieval forebear, can be visited. The excavations, begun in 1987, are opposite the Miramar Hotel in the centre of town. Signs in Arabic and English take visitors on a guided tour of the once high-walled city. Historically Ayla was on important north-south and east-west trade routes, and even Chinese ships where known to dock here. Evidence of Egyptian, Syrian and even Moroccan presence has been found.

At the southeastern end of the corniche don't miss the **Mamluke fort.** The Hashemite coat of arms over the entrance was added after the Turks were ousted from Aqaba during World War I. Sherif Hussein ben Ali, the leader of the Arab Revolt, resided in the fort for a time. Just below the fort, in an attrac-

tively restored complex that also includes the Department of Antiquities and the tourist office, a fine **museum** dedicated to finds in the area, including fragments of lustreware from Samaria and Chinese ceramics. One of the rooms contains an exhibition on traditional Jordanian and Palestinian village architecture by the artist-cum-architect and historian Amar Khammesh.

Sand and sea: But the main appeal of Aqaba to the visitor lies in its offshore coral reefs. Before venturing underwater it is worth visiting the **aquarium** in the Marine Sciences Centre (on the corniche southeast of town) in order to familiarise yourself with the exotic marine life you may encounter.

In town, the **Aquamarina Hotel and Diving Centre** offers the best facilities for water skiing, diving, scuba-diving, snorkelling, fishing and sailing, as well as trips in glass-bottomed boats. The **Al-Cazar Hotel** also organises dives, both during the day and at night – with cameras and lights.

Enjoying a quieter location 15 km (9

Holidaying Jordanians.

miles) out of town (4 km/2½ miles from the Saudi border) is the **Royal Diving Centre**, run by an English couple but set up by King Hussein. It offers scuba-diving lessons on a number of nearby reefs. The centre has a pool, changing facilities and expensive snackbar but no accommodation (the neighbouring holiday homes are for use by high-ranking police officers on vacation); however, a daily mini-bus service transports people to the centre from Aqaba's main hotels and taxis ply the route.

Independent private sailing is not allowed in Aqaba for security reasons – but arranged trips through one of the centres is possible. Boat trips to Saladin's Castle (which lies in Egyptian waters) run daily, providing the number of visitors is sufficient to make the journey worth the while of the boat captain; enquire at the Aquamarina Hotel for further details of sailings.

Aqaba's beaches are generally clean, especially the beaches belonging to the hotels. The public beaches are on the southeastern side of town. If you are not staying at a hotel with its own stretch of beach you will have to pay a fairly steep entrance fee to use a hotel's beach facilities. However, this may be worth it, especially for women travelling without male company. While nothing dangerous ever really happens in Aqaba, staring, giggling men can ruin your enjoyment.

In search of seafood: In spite of the great potential for corniche seafood restaurants there are still only a few upmarket restaurants in town. The Holiday Inn has a good Continental restaurant (at Continental prices) and a live band offers nightly entertainment in its air-conditioned bar – frequented by expatriates and wealthier Jordanians.

Otherwise try **Ali Baba**, a fish restaurant which specialises in *masgoof* (grilled fish), and has an outdoor terrace, or **China Restaurant** (Chinese), in the commercial centre of town.

Below and to the east of the museum is **Mina House**, which was converted from an old tugboat and offers barbecued meats and fish.

Left, take the plunge and enter a different world (**right**).

ROYAL DIVING CENTRE مركز الغوص الملكي

MARINE LIFE

Deep water lies close to the shore in Jordan, creating a fascinating marine environment where skin-divers may encounter a wide variety of species including, on occasion, the largest fish in the world, the whale shark.

This harmless plankton feeder is attracted to the northern Gulf of Aqaba by the upwelling that occurs at its headwaters, which carries nutrient-rich waters to the shallows and fuels planktonic bonanzas that are like manna from heaven to the filter-feeding whale sharks. But one does not need to overdramatise Aqaba's marine life to justify its description as one of Jordan's richest wildlife habitats.

Neither need one make a major expedition out of enjoying its splendours. To explore the underwater world of corals, sponges, sea-fans and multitudes of reef fish, you can simply drive along the coast to a suitable location and swim out a short distance. North of Aqaba the shore tends to slope more gradually and the shallow seabed has abundant sea-grasses where one can find seahorses, cuttlefish and a variety of other well camouflaged species. The grasses also form an important nursery for young fish.

For more dramatic diving, you should make your way to the tip of one of the promontories that project out towards deeper water. Tidal currents that sweep around these headlands help to keep corals free from sediment and thus provide habitats for a range of invertebrates and fish, including clown fish, Picasso trigger-fish, goby and cornet fish.

A marked diurnal tidal range supports interesting shore-life that can be investigated at low tide. Rocks are covered by barnacles, chitons, limpets and periwinkles, all of which are behaviourally adapted to survive the constant change from a submerged existence to one where they are exposed to the air and strong sunlight. At low spring tides the tips of some shallow-water corals may protrude above water. These are most likely to be the bushy *Stylophora pistillata,* which often has damsel fish living among its submerged branches.

Among the most interesting underwater sights along Jordan's coastline are the garden eels. To see them, either go by boat or swim out from the shore, across the sea-grass beds at the northern end of the Gulf. They are not that easy to distinguish at first since from a distance their waving frond-like bodies are easily mistaken for blades of sea-grass. As one swims towards them they slowly and silently reverse into their deep tubular burrows. The garden eel was first recognised by one of Jacques Cousteau's original underwater cameramen, Ludwig Sillner, who is commemorated in their Latin name, *Gorgasia sillneri.*

There are now a number of diving centres at Aqaba and it is possible to take diving lessons here or to rent gear and dive with experienced guides. Although Jordan's coastal waters have come under severe pressure from industrial developments such as harbour construction, land reclamation and leakage of phosphate into the sea, it is remarkable how resilient its marine life has shown itself to be. For such a short stretch of coastline the variety of habitats and the range of species offers much for both the casual holiday diver and the more dedicated underwater photographer. ∎

279

THE WEST BANK

The Old City of Jerusalem, Bethlehem, Hebron and Jericho lie just a couple of hours' drive from Amman, albeit across the Jordan River, a precious if unimpressive waterway that doubles as a formidable border. Together with their surrounding lands these historic cities comprise the West Bank, the area earmarked for Palestine in the 1948 carve-up of the region but annexed by Jordan in the subsequent Arab-Israeli war and then occupied by Israel following the Six-Day War of 1967. The region's history under Israeli occupation, including the rise of the *intifada* resistance in 1987, is recorded in the history section of this guide.

In 1993 gradual Israeli withdrawal from the West Bank in a "land for peace" deal was tentatively promised and the prospect of an independent state of Palestine, beginning with Jericho and Gaza, at last inched its way on to the horizon. The peace process is, however, shaky, with both Jewish settlers (some 250,000 Jews, mainly from the former Soviet Union, have made their homes in the Occupied Territories) and anti-PLO Arab forces such as Hamas and Hizbullah intent on derailing progress. What's more, the ultimate goal of the Palestinians, the return of East Jerusalem, is anathema even to many moderate Israelis.

Tourism pays only passing attention to politics and many organised tours already hop between the banks of the Jordan River. If a state of Palestine ever becomes a reality, this traffic will increase enormously, boosting tourism for the whole region, including Syria and Lebanon (a factor which also puts archaeology on the bargaining table). In the meantime, anyone travelling independently to the West Bank from Jordan must contend with a certain amount of red tape and should heed any sudden political developments. (Advice on surmounting the bureaucratic hurdles and arranging transport is included in the *Travel Tips* section at the back of this book.)

Designed as a taster rather than as a comprehensive survey, the following chapter covers Jerusalem, Bethlehem, Hebron and Jericho, the highlights of any Holy Land tour.

Preceding pages: the Church of the Holy Sepulchre; the Dome of the Rock; the walls of Jaffa Gate. **Left**, intricately embroidered dress from the West Bank town of Ramallah.

WEST BANK: PLACES

Al-Quds, Ur Shalem, Jerusalem. Whatever language one prefers to use, **Jerusalem** is one of the most resonant place names on earth. Closely associated with David, Christ and Mohammed, the city is central to the three monotheistic faiths and contains many of their holiest shrines. Jews mourn the destruction of the First and Second Temples at the Wailing Wall, Muslims revere the Dome of the Rock, the site of Mohammed's ascent into heaven, and Christians from all over the world pilgrimage to the Church of the Holy Sepulchre, where Christ was crucified and buried.

Yet Jerusalem has witnessed some of the most brutal episodes in history. Since the first people of Jerusalem, the Canaanites (*circa* 2000 BC), ruled the city it has been conquered 18 times, by people as varied as the Israelites under King David (1,000 BC), the Muslims of Arabia (7th century) and the European Crusaders (at the end of the 11th century). In the 20th century alone Jerusalem has been ruled by Ottoman Turks, the British Mandate Government of Palestine, the Hashemite Kingdom of Jordan and the government of modern Israel. Divided into East (Arab) Jerusalem and West (Israeli) Jerusalem between 1948 and 1967, the city was "reunited" by Israel in the 1967 war.

It remains disputed territory and the crux of any real Israeli-Palestinian peace agreement. While Israelis say Jerusalem is their eternal capital, the Palestinians (both Muslims and Christians), who cultivated the land, herded their flocks and tended their shrines here for over 1,000 years, stake capital claims too.

Arab East Jerusalem: Home to the Old City, East Jerusalem is a congested cobweb of streets crammed with shops, street vendors, schoolchildren, foreign companies and would-be representatives to the "State of Palestine". The strikes and closures of the *intifada* have engendered the attitude that time is money and thus, as strolling visitors soon notice, the people here move fast.

Most of the action of East Jerusalem takes place on one of the three main thoroughfares leading into the walled Old City: **Salahedin Street** (after Salah-ad-Din), **Nablus Road** (where buses from Jordan deposit their passengers) and **Al-Zahra Street**. There are a number of interesting sights off these main streets. A short walk out of the Old City, along a tree-lined lane signposted off Nablus Road, for instance, is the Protestant Golgotha, the **Garden Tomb**, which British General Gordon, in 1883, identified as the site of Christ's burial and Crucifixion (instead of the Church of the Holy Sepulchre). Two small low rooms contain a 1st-century tomb. Nearby, opposite the American consulate, is the **Palestinian Pottery Shop**, where Armenian pottery is sold and made to order.

Also here is **King Solomon's Quarry**, believed to have supplied the Jewish Temple of Jerusalem, and the 5th-century **mausoleum to the Unknown Soldiers of Armenia**. A 10-minute walk from the quarry, on an unmarked road, is the **Armenian Convent of Polyeucte**.

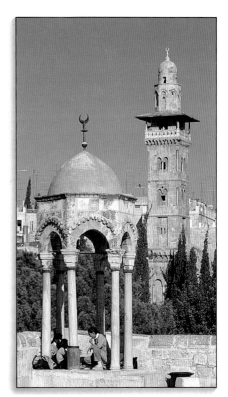

eft, inside amascus ate. Right, quiet corner Haram -Sherif.

Once part of a private home, the convent contains one of the most impressive mosaic floors in Jerusalem.

The **Tombs of Kings**, once thought to be the burial site of the Kings of Judah, is found near the intersection of Salahedin Street and Nablus Road. The subterranean tombs (take a torch if you want to explore) are believed to date from Babylonian times.

History in a nutshell is found at the superb **Rockefeller Museum** (across from Herod's Gate) and the **Palestinian Arab Folklore Centre**, on Obeid ibn Jarrah Street.

The Old City: Set in the middle of a wide plain, the Old City is contained by a 4-metre (12-ft) high wall – built by the Mamluke Sultan Suleiman the Magnificent between 1537 and 1540 – pierced by seven gates. Damascus Gate is the most likely entrance for visitors coming from East Jerusalem, but we begin a tour of the Old City with **Jaffa Gate** (Bab al-Khalil), closest to West Jerusalem. It leads into a maze of mostly British-built churches and hospices, marking the British period in Palestine.

Just inside Jaffa Gate is the **Citadel**, known as Phaesal's Tower, one of only three remaining towers built by Herod. Burned down during the Jewish revolt of 66 AD and again in 70 AD when Titus razed Jerusalem, it was named David's Tower by the Byzantines. Suleiman the Magnificent is largely responsible for its present shape. Its minaret was added in 1635.

A right turn off Omar ibn Khattab Square leads to the Armenian Quarter, one of the most peaceful quarters in the city (also accessible through Zion Gate). The Armenian community, originally from the Caucasus, has lived in Jerusalem for over 1,000 years and still has its own language and alphabet. The first to adopt Christianity as a national religion (310 AD), the community has an important place in the history of Christianity and Jerusalem. Today the quarter numbers some 4,000 people.

The **Armenian Patriarch Road** leads to the **Armenian library**, containing over 50,000 books, many of them hun-

dreds of years old, and the **Mardigian Museum of Armenian Art and History**, charting the history of the Armenian people.

One of the most beautiful structures in the Old City, at the centre of the Armenian quarter, is **St James Cathedral**, which has existed in one form or another since the 5th century. Beyond the Cathedral stands the **Convent of the Olive Tree**, where Jesus was bound before his Crucifixion. Caretakers of the **Assyrian Convent**, on Ararat Street, claim the Virgin Mary was baptised on the site of **St Mark's Church** in the midst of the convent.

East from the Armenian quarter is the Old City's **Jewish Quarter**, which has been destroyed repeatedly through the ages. Although in modern times it appears that Muslims and Jews have always lived in enmity, historically it was otherwise. It was only when Salah-ad-Din recaptured Jerusalem from the Crusaders (1187) that tolerance and coexistence became the rule rather than the exception.

In more recent times, the Jewish Quarter was damaged during the Arab-Israeli war of 1948. Israelis repaired the buildings after they occupied the city in 1967 and today the quarter looks clean and new, if a little sterile compared to the three unreconstructed quarters of the Old City.

Until 1948 most of Jerusalem's Jewish residents were Eastern or Sephardic Jews (today most are American or Russian) and by far the most impressive sights in the quarter are the four Sephardic Synagogues, originally built in the 17th century but altered and embellished numerous times since.

Other highlights of this quarter include the **Ophel Archaeological Gardens** containing finds dating from the 10th century BC onwards.

The gardens border the famous **Dung Gate**, also known in Arabic as the Moorish Gate (alluding to the Moroccan community – Jews and Muslims – that traditionally settled around the gate). It is the only one of the seven operational gates to lead directly into the Jewish Quarter.

Jerusalem from the Mount of Olives.

The present name is a reminder that in past centuries the garbage left the city through here.

To the right of the gate is one of the most famous symbols of Judaism: the **Western Wall** (Wailing Wall), believed to be a wall of the Second Temple. But the Western Wall is a retaining wall rather than the wall of a temple and Jews use the wall to lament the destruction of their two temples (though some ultra-Orthodox Jews believe that praying at the wall is tantamount to idolatry and incompatible with Judaism).

The wall, divided into men's and women's prayer areas, is peppered with prayer notes. The plaza-like area in front was originally quite small but after Israel captured the Old City in the 1967 war, the Moorish Quarter which was adjacent to the wall was bulldozed.

Muslim shrines: Right of the wall is the entrance to the **Haram al-Sherif** (the Noble Sanctuary), known as Temple Mount by Jews, who believe it to be the site of the First (955–587 BC) and Second (515 BC–70 AD) Temples.

Eleven gates, two of which are permanently closed, lead to the Noble Sanctuary. Here are the Dome of the Rock, the Al-Aqsa Mosque and the Islamic Museum. The two mosques are among the most impressive and important shrines in the Muslim world.

The rock enshrined by the **Dome of the Rock** is held to be the spot where Abraham prepared to sacrifice his son and it is holy to Muslims and Jews alike. According to Muslim tradition, the Prophet Mohammed flew to Jerusalem from Mecca on his horse and from the Rock of Abraham ascended to heaven, only to return to Mecca at dawn. Muslims turned to Jerusalem to pray before the direction of prayer was changed to Mecca.

When Omar Ibn al-Khattab, the Second Caliph (634–644), captured Jerusalem, he headed straight for the area around the rock, then used as a dump by the Byzantine Christians. Seeing the decay around it, the Caliph had a small mosque built around the rock to protect it. The Dome of the Rock itself was

The Wailing Wall.

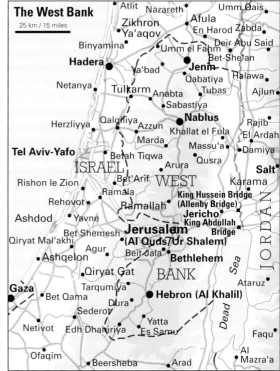

The West Bank

25 km / 15 miles

built in 691 AD by Caliph Abd al-Malik Ibn Marwan.

Apart from during prayer times and on Fridays visitors are allowed inside (shoes must be removed). In a cave-like chamber beneath the rock are small tabernacles dedicated to Abraham and Elijah. The **Well of Souls** lies beneath.

The Al-Aqsa Mosque, first constructed in 715 AD by Walid Ibn Abd al-Malik, has been repeatedly damaged by earthquakes and rebuilt. Its present incarnation dates from 1033. During the Crusades it was known as Templum and both the Crusaders and the Knights Templar set up their administrative quarters in the mosque. It was on the steps of Al-Aqsa that King Abdullah was assassinated in 1951, in front of his young grandson, Hussein.

The **Golden Gate** (in fact, a double gate comprising the Gate of Mercy and the Gate of Repentance), the original entrance to Haram al-Sherif, has been sealed since 1530. Some people believe that a messiah will enter Jerusalem through this gate.

Leaving Haram al-Sherif from either the **Absolution Gate** (Bab al-Hitta) or the **Gate of Darkness** (Bab al-Atm) is the easiest way to enter the **Muslim Quarter** of Jerusalem (unlike the other quarters, this quarter contains both Muslim and Christian houses of worship). Most Palestinians come into the Old City from East Jerusalem through the **Damascus Gate,** which leads directly into the Muslim Quarter, as does **Herod's Gate**.

The Muslim Quarter is worth exploring mostly for its scenic Mamluke (1248–1517) architecture, which contributes so much to the colour of the Old City. It is full of *hammams* (public baths), *madrassa* (Islamic schools), libraries and the tombs of famous Muslims – including that of King Hussein of Jordan's great-grandfather, Sherif Hussein of Mecca.

Palestinian families have lived here without interruption for 1,000 years or more. During the reign of Salah-ad-Din it was common for prominent Muslim families across the Islamic world to

Damascus Gate.

send a son and his family to Jerusalem to establish a branch of the family in the Holy City. Many Palestinian families from Jerusalem can still trace their origins back 1,000 years to places as varied as Syria, Morocco, Samarkand and Sudan. During Ottoman rule the guards of the Haram al-Sherif were all Sudanese Muslims.

In Christ's footsteps: For Christian pilgrims, the highlight of a trip to Jerusalem is to follow the **Stations of the Cross**, along the **Via Dolorosa** (Way of Sorrow) from the traditional site of Christ's condemnation by Pontius Pilate to the **Church of the Holy Sepulchre,** where Christ was crucified and buried. Although the Route of the Cross has been followed, more or less, since Byzantine times when Constantine's mother Helena tried to trace the route, the number of stations has increased over the centuries. Some of what are now 14 stations were added as late as the 19th century.

To trace the supposed route, start at the far eastern end of the Muslim Quarter, at **Lion's Gate**, which is also known as both **St Stephen's Gate** and the **Gate of Our Lady Mariam**, where the nearby **Church of St Anne** is a charming combination of Crusader, French and Muslim architecture.

The **First Station**, where Jesus was sentenced to Crucifixion by Pilate, is located only 250 metres/yards inside St Stephen's Gate. A little further along, on the right, are the **Chapels of Condemnation and Flagellation**, the **Second Station**, where Roman soldiers flogged Christ and set a crown of thorns upon His head. Further down the street you stroll beneath the **Ecce Homo Arch**, said to have been built by Hadrian in the 2nd century. Right next to it is the **Convent of the Sisters of Zion**, believed by some to be the scene of Christ's trial.

Further down to the left of the Via Dolorosa, on Al Wad Road (Valley Road), is the **Third Station**, at a small Polish chapel. This is where Jesus is said to have fallen for the first time. Just beyond the Armenian Orthodox Patriarchate is the **Fourth Station**, where

Dried goods salesman in the Arab Quarter.

Jesus met Mary, his mother. A turn right on Via Dolorosa leads to the **Fifth Station**, where Simon the Cyrene extended his help to a tired Jesus and carried the Cross. The **Sixth Station** is marked by what was once a large column; it was here that St Veronica wiped Christ's face with a cloth. Across the Khan al-Zeit Bazaar, a Franciscan chapel marks the **Seventh Station**, where Jesus fell for the second time.

Up the street and up the steps of Aqabat al-Khanka, the Greek Monastery of St Charalamos marks the **Eighth Station**, where Jesus told the grieving women of Jerusalem: "Daughters of Jerusalem, do not weep for me, weep rather for yourselves and for your children" (Luke 23:28).

To reach the **Ninth Station**, return to the Khan al-Zeit Bazaar and climb 28 stairs to the Ethiopian Coptic Church, where Jesus fell for the third time.

It is inside the complex of the **Church of the Holy Sepulchre**, identified by Queen Helena, Emperor Constantine's mother, in 326 AD as the site of the Crucifixion, that the last five Stations of the Cross are located. On the right near the entrance are two chapels, one Franciscan and one Greek Orthodox. The Franciscan Chapel marks the **Tenth Station**. Here Jesus was stripped of his clothing. At the far end of the chapel is the **Eleventh Station**, where he was nailed to the Cross. The Greek Orthodox Chapel commemorates the **Twelfth Station**, the site of Crucifixion, with a life-sized depiction of Jesus, surrounded by candles, icons and ornaments.

A life-sized statue of Mary, with a dagger in her heart, marks the **Thirteenth Station**, where Christ's body was taken down from the Cross and given to His mother. Jesus's tomb, the **Fourteenth Station**, is in the Church of the Holy Sepulchre itself. It is reached through the **Chapel of the Angels**.

Apart from the last five Stations of the Cross, the Church of the Holy Sepulchre contains at least a dozen points of interest even to the most secular of tourists. The complex – comprising some 60 chapels, altars, churches and other places

A glut of religious trinkets.

of worship – is divided between six denominations (Latins, Greek Orthodox, Armenian Orthodox, Syrian-Jacobite, Copts, and Abyssinians), each jealous of its portion and reluctant to cooperate with the others. They have fought over issues of restoration and prayer times as well as who gets to put a candle where. A Technical Committee, set up in 1954, has attempted to ease some of the rivalry but tensions still run high.

The Monastery of the Sultan – a cluster of mud huts on the roof of the church just above the Chapel of St Helena – is a case in point. This is where the Church of Ethiopia set up its headquarters after losing their right to a section of the church itself when their papers were lost in a fire in 1808. The priests speak Amharic (Ethiopia's official language) and believe that King Menelik, the legendary son of King David of Israel and the Queen of Sheba, founded their church, which has had envoys in Jerusalem since the 4th century. The Church intends to stay – if only on the roof.

Other highlights of the church include the **Chapel of Adam**, officially the burial site for Crusader kings but according to legend the place where the skull of Adam was discovered, and the tiny **Chapel of the Copts**, full of exotic incense and colour. The **Syrian Jacobite Chapel**, next to the chapel, leads into a 1st-century burial chamber.

The Crusader church, the **Katholikon** (now a relatively large Greek Orthodox Chapel) was traditionally believed to stand at the centre of the world (the precise spot is marked by a chalice in the floor). Further down, the Armenian **Chapel of Helena** leads into the cavern where Queen Helena supposedly found the remains of the true Cross.

Christian Quarter: Jaffa Gate and David Street lead to a cluster of churches and *suqs*, including the oldest church in Jerusalem, **St John the Baptist Church**. (If you are coming from the Church of the Holy Sepulchre, walks towards the Armenian Quarter.)

The **Church of the Redeemer**, now a Lutheran church, is believed to have been built in Byzantine times. The zo-

Grotto of the Nativity, Bethlehem.

diac signs on its northern gate are typical of designs used by the Byzantines. The existing structure was built by the German Crown Prince Friederich Wilhelm, who bought the site during an official visit in 1869. The church's tower offers one of the best views of the Old City. East of the Holy Sepulchre is **St Alexander Church**, where prayers for the late Tsar Alexander of Russia are held every Thursday. The **Mosque of Omar**, down the street from the Holy Sepulchre, commemorates where the Caliph Omar prayed in what was then the courtyard of the Sepulchre church.

The Christian Quarter is also home to the **New Gate**, which was hammered into the wall of the Old City in 1887. It is the only gate that leads into the Christian Quarter.

The 19th-century **Notre Dame de France** is one of the most prominent buildings in the Christian Quarter. It houses the papal delegation to the city along with a monastery and a first-class French restaurant.

Outside the Old City: To the east of the Old City lies the most famous hill, the **Mount of Olives**. It is said to be the site of at least a dozen biblical events. It is from here that Jesus made his triumphal entry into Jerusalem, where he wept over Jerusalem, was betrayed and arrested and where he ascended into heaven. At the top is Al-**Tur**, one of many Palestinian villages crowning the hills around Jerusalem. Al-Tur is home to the quaint **Chapel of Ascension**, where Jesus ascended to heaven 40 days after his resurrection. A petrified footprint marks the spot where Jesus stood.

Across the road from the Chapel of Ascension is the **Pater Noster Carmelite Convent**, where Jesus preached. The land around Pater Noster was bought by a French noblewoman in the 19th century. She had the Lord's Prayer inscribed on the walls in over 60 languages. Further down the mountain is the **Russian Monastery**, supposedly containing the head of John the Baptist, and the vast **Jewish cemetery** spreads towards the Golden Gate.

The sorrow of Jesus is immortalised

Bethlehem café.

in the **Church of Dominus Flevit**, which was designed in the shape of a tear by the Italian architect Anton Barluzzi in 1953. Immediately below is one of the most picturesque churches in Jerusalem, the **Church of St Mary Magdalene**, with its seven onion-shaped domes. The adjoining **Garden of Gethsemane** is where Jesus was betrayed.

The Church of All Nations at the foot of the mountain was built in 1924 but contains the remains of at least two other older churches, one from the 4th century and one from the 12th. To the right of the path at the bottom of the Mount of Olives is the **Tomb of the Virgin Mary**, next to the tombs of Crusader kings and their families.

To the south of the Old City is **Mount Zion**, associated historically with both David, who is said to be buried on the hill, and with Jesus, said to have celebrated the Last Supper here. It can be reached through Zion Gate, Dung Gate and Jaffa Gate.

The site of Mary's death is marked by the **Dormition Abbey**, where an impressive mausoleum, built in 1900, is surrounded by 12 columns. Virtually in the backyard of the Abbey is the **Coenaculum** – the room where the Last Supper is said to have taken place.

Beneath is the **Tomb of David**. Again, there is disagreement about whether David was buried to the east or the south of Jerusalem; Jews nevertheless count the tomb as a holy shrine.

BETHLEHEM: The West Bank town of **Bethlehem** lies 17 km (10 miles) from Jerusalem. Hundreds of thousands of pilgrims flock to this ancient village to commemorate the birth of Jesus. Every Christmas millions of people around the world watch the televised midnight Mass from Bethlehem's Church of St Catherine.

The first basilica over the grotto said to be the birthplace of Jesus was built by Constantine between AD 326 and 339. A Samaritan revolt in AD 529 destroyed most of Bethlehem, including the basilica, but the Emperor Justinian (AD 527–565) repaired and enlarged the structure. In 614 the Persians destroyed

The Judaean Hills.

298

almost every Christian house of worship but left the Basilica of Nativity intact. In 638 the Second Caliph, Omar Ibn al-Khattab, prayed in the southern part of the church and while it has not become a place of prayer for Muslims it is revered as a symbol of Christian goodwill towards Islam. The Crusaders renovated the basilica in 1099, and Bethlehem became a site where Crusader kings were crowned. Baldwin I was crowned in Bethlehem in 1100.

In 1187 Salah-ad-Din captured Bethlehem but in 1229 the Muslim Sultan Malik al-Kamil returned the town to the Crusaders, which they held until they were finally ousted from the Holy Land in 1291.

Many Bethlehemites claim to be descendants of either the Beni Ghassan (an ancient Christian Arab tribe from the southern peninsula, known today as Yemen), or the Crusaders, or both. Many are Catholics and have sought commercial, cultural and religious ties with other Catholic countries since the 19th century. In the first half of the 20th century a large number of Bethlehemites fleeing the Zionist encroachment on Palestine settled in South and Central America, where they became known for their skills in business.

Since then, these immigrants have opened hundreds of Arabic language schools all across South America. Every summer descendants of South American Bethlehemites return to their native town to find a bride or a bridegroom for their children.

Today, many of the town's residents are descendants of Palestinian refugees who fled their homes in northern Palestine when Israel was created in 1948. Today the population of Bethlehem stands at about 30,000.

The first sight as one approaches Bethlehem from Jerusalem is **Rachel's tomb**, at the edge town: "Rachel died on the way to Ephrath, which is Bethlehem. And Jacob set a pillar upon her grave." (Genesis 35:19). Rachel, the wife of Jacob, who died while giving birth to Benjamin (Genesis 35:19-20), is the only one of the four Old Testament matriarchs to be buried here rather than in Hebron. The current tomb was built by the Ottoman Turks in the 1620s and the existing dome was added by British Moses Montefiore in 1841. The site is revered by both Muslims and Jews. The Muslim Ta'amre tribe bury many of their kin close to Rachel's tomb.

Manger Square is the centre of Bethlehem and the hub of various pilgrim sites. (It is less biblical and more commercial in character than the old *suq* in Star Street, just off Manger Square, which has a more authentic character and offers more interesting goods.) The **Church of Nativity** (326–339 AD), next to the Church of St Catherine on the square, encases the grotto where Christ is believed to have been born.

Following a complex schedule of worship more than half a dozen different churches – including Catholic, Protestant, Russian and Greek Orthodox, Armenian, Egyptian Coptic and Assyrian – manage to coexist in this grand basilica. Attempts by different denominations to control the church have created constant rivalry and even

provoked war. It is believed that one of the causes of the Crimean War was Napoleon III's insistence that the complex be declared French property.

Most of the existing structure, including the remaining mosaic floor, date from the time of Constantine and Justinian, but the oak ceiling was a gift from King Edward IV of England. Most of the decorative icons around the main altar were gifts of the Russian imperial family in the 19th century.

At the front of the church, two sets of stairs on either side of the altar lead down to the **Grotto of the Nativity** where Christ was born (such grottoes, as part of a rock wall, are common in many older Bethlehem homes to this day). Marked by a 14-point silver star, the site of Christ's birth is inscribed in Latin – "Here Jesus was born to the Virgin Mary." Silver-plated lanterns with precious stones light the spot day and night. Next to the grotto is the **Chapel of the Manger**, where Mary placed her newborn son.

Crosses etched into the walls and columns are the work of pilgrims and, in some cases, the Crusaders.

The traditional Christmas Eve Mass that is televised all over the world is held next door in the Franciscan **Church of St Catherine** (1881). (Tickets are required for the event, but monks roaming about outside the church often carry tickets underneath their cloaks and may pass them on without charge to disappointed visitors.) The church is dedicated to St Catherine in tribute to the vision of Christ that Catherine of Alexandria had here.

Bethlehem's other place of pilgrimage is the **Milk Grotto Church** (down Milk Grotto Street), where, according to legend, some of Mary's milk dripped on the ground and whitened the red floor. Pilgrims have been known to chip off a piece of the floor and take it home.

Nearby Beit Sahur (House of the Shepherd), is believed to mark **Shepherds' Field**, where the angels announced the birth of Jesus to the shepherds. Jews also cherish this location because they believe it to be where Boaz fell in love **Hisham's Palace.**

with the widowed Ruth. Their grandchild was David, King of Israel.

HEBRON (AL-KHALIL): One of the oldest towns in Palestine, **Hebron**, some 16 km (10 miles) south of Bethlehem, was inhabited by the Canaanites as early as 2000 BC. An envoy of Moses returning to Transjordan from an exploratory expedition described Hebron as the "land of milk and honey". In 1200 BC Moses's successor Joshua invaded and destroyed the city and killed all its inhabitants (Joshua:10:37).

A commercially active and industrially important town of some 65,000 Palestinians (half of whom are under the age of 20), Hebron is the hub of some four dozen villages. It is famous for its peaches, apples and grapes and exports agricultural produce to neighbouring Arab countries. It is also known for its stone – most of the more refined homes in the Occupied Territories and Israel are finished with stone and marble from Hebron quarries – and for its lovely glasswork, a craft developed by monks from Italy.

However, Hebron is best known for the Haram al-Khalil, or Tomb of the Patriarch of monotheism, known as the father of all Jews and Arabs – Abraham. As such it is a place of great religious importance to Muslims, Jews and Christians alike and has become a hotbed off religious zealotry. (Discreet and conservative dress for both men and women is recommended.)

The origins of the town's Old Testament name – Qiryat Arba (the village of the four) – is disputed by scholars. Some believe the number four refers to the four patriarchs believed to be buried here while others say it alludes to the four Canaanite tribes that settled the town in pre-biblical times.

According to Muslim and Jewish tradition, Abraham, Sarah, Isaac and Rebecca, Jacob and Leah, as well as Adam and Eve are buried here, and according to Islamic tradition Adam and Eve lived out their old age in Hebron. Muslims also revere Hebron because Mohammed is said to have visited the Haram al-Khalil on his way from Mecca

George's
nastery,
ar Jericho.

to Jerusalem, where he ascended to heaven.

In the opinion of some Jews, Abraham's purchase of the "Cave of Machpelah as his burial place", which forms one part of Haram al-Khalil, made the site exclusively Jewish for all time. Hebron and the holy places in Haram – al-Khalil in particular – have witnessed inter-faith rivalry since time immemorial. According to both Muslim and Jewish tradition King Solomon is believed to have laid the groundwork for the Haram al-Khalil and, according to Muslim tradition, *djns* (spirits) helped Solomon's men to build the edifice. In AD 70 the Jews revolted against the Romans and were expelled from Hebron until the city came under Muslim rule, when the city was again open to all.

The **Haram** (tomb) looks more like a huge fortress than a place of worship. The site of Haram al-Khalil was converted into a Byzantine church in AD 570 by the Byzantine rulers of Palestine. Under Islam in the 7th century the church was converted into a mosque, which was again transformed into a church in 1099 by invading Crusaders. The church replaced both the mosque and the adjacent synagogue, which marked the centre of the Haram at the time, and Jews and Muslims were banned. After the defeat of the Crusaders by Salah-ad-Din in the 12th century, the church was re-converted into a mosque and Jews and Muslims were allowed to return to the city.

Entering the Tomb from the northwestern entrance visitors climb a Mamluke staircase leading to the Mamluke Mosque Djaouliyeh (built in 1380). An adjoining courtyard leads to the synagogues, which house both the 14th-century cenotaphs of Jacob and Leah and of Abraham and Sarah, and the Mosque of Isaac (also known as the Great Mosque), which houses the cenotaphs of the Isaac and Rebecca.

A small Mamluke mosque in the southeastern corner of the Haram is reserved for women; in one corner is a petrified footprint said to have been left by Adam as he left the Garden of Eden.

The Mount ◖
Temptation

302

The exit leads through yet another mosque, which Muslims believe houses the cenotaph of Joseph.

JERICHO: Believed to be the oldest continuously inhabited town on earth (12,000 years), Jericho is a green desert city studded with palm trees ("City of Palms": Judges 3.13), banana plantations and flowers. In September 1993 it also became a town of hope as the first peace accord was signed between Palestinians and Israelis. For the umpteenth time this pre-biblical town made history.

It was in Jericho that the Neolithic hunter turned settled farmer, that the ancient Canaanites made fine pottery and that, at Mount Sultan near Elisha's spring, 23 consecutive cities rose and fell. This is where the prophet Elisha purified the water so the people would not die of thirst (Kings 2:19-22) and where Christ restored the sight of the blind beggar (Luke 18:34-43). Today it is a city of 7,500 people, with another 10,000 people living in the vicinity.

Ancient Jericho, also known as Tel al-Sultan, goes back to the 10th millennium BC. Located about 2 km (1 mile) from today's city centre the existing *tell* (a hill formed by the layered accumulation of settlements) is today a heap of ruined walls.

Archaeological excavation of Tel al-Sultan began in 1867, but the most significant work was conducted in 1952 by British archaeologist Kathleen Kenyon, who traced the transition of Jericho's inhabitants from hunter communities to settled farmers. The town still boasts a Neolithic stone tower dating from 7,000 BC. Ten Neolithic skulls (now on display at the Rockefeller Museum in Jerusalem) were uncovered during Kenyon's excavations.

A centre for Canaanite trade as early as 3000 BC, in Roman times the city was one of Mark Antony's gifts to Cleopatra. Later Herod was "given" the town by the Emperor Octavian. In 550 BC the Persians used old Jericho as an administrative centre, and under Alexander the Great, in 332 BC, the town served as a royal resort.

The town fulfilled a similar purpose

under the Muslims. **Hisham's Palace** (Khirbet al-Mafjar), Jericho's most impressive archaeological site, was built between 724 and 743 AD as a winter retreat from Damascus by Walid Ibn Yazid and named after his uncle, Sultan Hisham Ibn Abd al-Malik.

The ruins (2½ km/2 miles) north of Tel al-Sultan) bear traces of luxurious living-quarters as well as two mosques (in spite of the earthquake in 747, which destroyed most of the palace walls). The bath hall is decorated by elegant colonnades and a blue and pink mosaic floor. The *diwan* (reception hall) contains the famous tree of life mosaic, with its 15 fruits (each representing a governate under the Sultan Hisham's rule). The two gazelles in the mosaic represent friends of the Sultan while the gazelle being attacked by the lion (on the right) represents the enemy.

About 1 km (half a mile) south of the palace is **Elisha's Spring** (Ain al-Sultan), where the prophet Elisha is supposed to have purified the spring's waters with salt. These spring waters have

kept the town supplied since antiquity; today the springs provide water at a rate of up to 1,000 gallons (3,800 litres) a minute.

A 20-minute walk – on carpets of wild flowers in spring – takes one up to the **Mount of Temptation** (Quruntul), the cave, where Christ spent 40 days and nights fasting after being tempted by the devil. The Greek Orthodox Monastery houses the grotto where Christ is supposed to have sat during his fast.

The Arabic name Quruntul is a local version of the old Crusader name of Mons Quaranta – "Mountain of Forty" (in commemoration of the 40 days and nights). The existing monastery was built at the end of the last century, but was by no means the first to be built over the famous cave. Today's monastery didn't receive electricity until 1992, and water is still taken from half a dozen wells inside the monastery walls.

Just 8 km (5 miles) outside modern Jericho lies **the Mosque of Moses**, believed by Muslims to be the burial sight of Moses. Islamic tradition holds that God carried Moses's bones from the east side of the Jordan River, where he died at Nebi Musa Mount, for burial in Palestine. The place is isolated and has a bleak feel about it.

Some 10 km (6 miles) east of Jericho, **Al-Maghtas** by the Jordan River is the supposed site of Christ's baptism by John the Baptist.

Jericho today: Jericho today is a friendly and peaceful town, offering delicious fresh fruit juices and excellent Arabic cuisine. About 10 percent of its inhabitants are descendants of Afro-Arabs who settled in the region over 1,000 years ago. In more recent times Jericho was home to some 185,000 refugees who fled Palestine after 1948. However, almost all these refugees fled to Jordan during the 1967 war.

From Jericho, a road leads 20 km (12 miles) down to **Qumran** on the Dead Sea. It was in a cave here, in 1947, that some local boys discovered the Dead Sea Scrolls. A visitors' centre at the site documents the story of the scrolls and their finding, as does the Archaeological Museum at the Citadel in Amman.

Left, the Palestinian flag. **Right**, the Director of Tourism i‹ Jericho has high hopes for the futur‹

SYRIA

Straying into Syria, a historic land of fabled cities and remote antiquities, is a natural extension for many travellers to Jordan, for the modern border creates an arbitrary disruption to both geographical and historical realities. Yet Syria is little known to the average tourist. Divergent political orientations in recent decades have made travel difficult for some nationalities, while relations between Jordan and Syria have been, on occasions, frosty. In addition, a limited touristic infrastructure tended to discourage the casual or timid traveller.

Now, however, with the breakdown of Cold War alignments and moves towards peace in the Middle East, Jordan and Syria see their economic destinies best served through cooperation. This is already happening in their planning for tourism, where joint efforts are being made in site development, tour organisation and improved transport facilities.

Modern Syria is a 20th-century entity, created in the wake of World War I and the breakup of the Ottoman Empire. Prior to this, the name had historically referred to the whole area covered by Lebanon, Syria, Palestine and Transjordan, a unit whose frontiers were the Taurus Mountains, the sea, the Euphrates, and the deserts. In its present truncated state, it lacks broad access to the sea and associated trade advantages.

Once the commercial centre of a vast trading basin, the arbitrary sub-division and isolation of the country as a French Mandate sidelined the major trading cities of Damascus, Homs and Aleppo. In more recent times, alliance with the Eastern Bloc countries and isolation from the West inhibited development.

Historical Syria was located geographically between the great civilisations of the east (Mesopotamia and Persia), the West (Europe), the north (Anatolia), and the south (Egypt). Syria, in the middle, was a true crossroads of civilisations and cultures, the natural battleground not only of armies but also of ideas. The result is a magnificent heritage of peoples, cultural expressions and monuments that has drawn the most eminent explorers and Orientalists of recent times, from Burckhardt and Burton to extraordinary women travellers such as Lady Hester Stanhope and Gertrude Bell, not to mention a swathe of eminent surveyors and archaeologists. All were attracted by Syria's fabulous ghosts and became intrigued by its present.

Preceding pages: Damascus overview; *norias* (water wheels) at Hama; the Roman Theatre, Bosra. **Left**, fluted columns at Apamia.

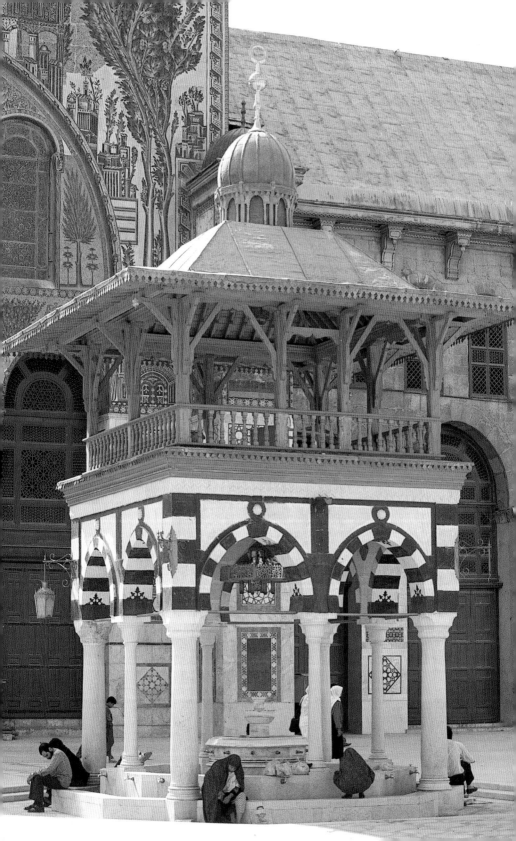

SYRIA'S MAIN SIGHTS

The order in which the following sights have been arranged presupposes an approach from Jordan. It thus begins with the sights closest to Jordan and then moves in a looping arc north to Damascus, anti-clockwise east to the Euphrates, north to Aleppo and its environs, west to the coast and finally south and southeast back to the starting point.

Land of the volcanoes: Having crossed the southern border at Dir'a, follow the road due east across the rich red soils of the Hauran plain towards the rising heights of the **Jebel al-Arab**, known until recently as the Jebel Druze, after the principal inhabitants of the region (and also called the Jebel Hauran, or Mount Bashan of the biblical Psalms).

The Hauran (classical Auranitis) is littered with basalt boulders from the volcanic activity of the Jebel al-Arab. The Jebel itself is not one but myriad volcanic cones which have spewed out lava in several phases over time. The accumulation of lava is sometimes more than 1,000 metres (3,280 ft) thick and the highest point on the Jebel is 1,860 metres (6,200 ft). In winter the Jebel is covered with snow and the higher rainfall catchment provides an important source of water for the Hauran settlements and for artesian basins to the south. Though it is a strange, bare and wild landscape, many sombre black villages dating back to Nabataean and Roman times perch on the edge of the desert to the east. On the eastern slopes, where nothing is grown today, the remains of ancient field systems are evident, attesting to a more populous and vital agricultural society in the past.

The overall use of black basalt building stone is typical of Hauran architecture. Lack of wood encouraged an idiosyncratic system of construction, whereby beams hewn out of basalt were placed on projecting corbels to span the roofs, and transverse arches necessary to support them were placed at frequent intervals. Stone was also used for doors and window screens.

Situated on the plain some 42 km (27 miles) to the east of Dir'a, lies the ancient town of **Bosra**, still inhabited today, although the government is now relocating the population outside the city walls. Settlement dates from the Early Bronze Age, but the town rose to pre-eminence in the late 1st century AD when the last king of the Nabataeans, Rabbel II, moved his capital from Petra to Bosra, which was better placed to take advantage of changing international trade routes. When the Romans established direct control over the region, Bosra was made the capital of the Roman province of Arabia.

One can easily spend a whole day wandering through the extensive and well-preserved ruins dating from Nabataean, Roman, Byzantine and Islamic times, needing little imagination to picture the living city. The most surprising monument within this rich array is the **Roman Theatre**. Like a pearl within an oyster shell, it is completely hidden from view by the medieval citadel which fortified and surrounded it. Such pro-

tection has ensured its preservation as one of the most complete Roman theatres in the world. Clearance and excavation is ongoing, and the most recent discovery of note is an enormous Christian church of a centralised circular form, comparable in size to the great church of Hagia Sophia in Istanbul.

Museums are located in the citadel and in the **Hammam Manjak** (the restored Mamluke bath house). A new luxury hotel has recently made Bosra the most attractive centre for exploring the Hauran and the Jebel.

The main regional centre of **Suwayda** is 32 km (20 miles) northeast of Bosra, on the mid-western flanks of the Jebel al-Arab. The populous modern town has now overrun the classical city of Dionysias, but it does have an excellent regional museum, located along the road out to Qanawat.

Passing through the town, one is struck by the manner and dress of the local Druze population, where, as Robin Fedden, the author of *Syria and Lebanon*, observes, "even the poorest appear chieftens". A secretive religious minority, the Druze fled the Lebanon mountains in the mid-19th century after conflict with the Christians and sought refuge on the depopulated Jebel. They are noted for their beauty, courage, and fiercely independent spirit. The latter has continually brought them into conflict with authority, as the Turks, the French, and even the modern regime can attest. Many still wear traditional costume and the turbaned men take pride in their magnificent moustaches waxed at the tips. The women wear sweeping patterned dresses bunched into a high waist with a scooped neckline, striking quite a contrast to typical Arab attire.

A road northeast from Suwayda leads to **Qanawat** through rising terrain and the remnants of oak forests which once flourished on the Jebel al-Arab. Perhaps the prettiest area in the Hauran, Qanawat commands expansive views westwards across the plain to Mount Hermon/Jebel al-Sheikh (so-called in Arabic because of its year-round snow, which is likened to the white beard of a venerable sheikh).

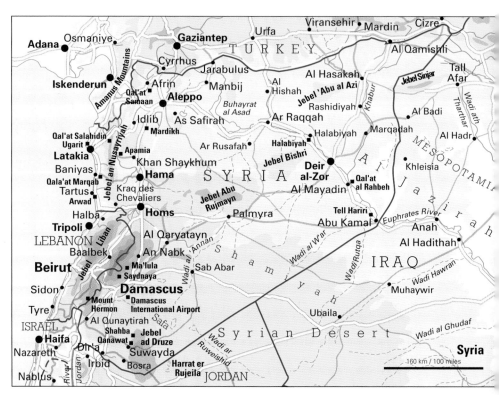

Qanawat was important in Hellenistic to Byzantine times and retains a charming but scattered collection of ruins. The main complex, the Seraya, is next to the central town square. It was originally a Roman temple and civic complex which was later appropriated to accommodate two Christian basilicas, with the addition of a monastery. Fifty metres/yards southwest of the town square are the remains of a small Temple of Zeus with a columned portico.

If one follows the road descending north from the front of the colonnaded courtyard of the "Seraya", access can be gained to the steep *wadi* on the right, containing a small theatre (odeon) and a nymphaeum set within a park of pine trees. Just off the road leading back to Suweida, in the northwest of the town, is a temple dedicated to the sun-god, Helios.

It is a short, 3-km (2-mile) drive southeast of Qanawat to the hilltop sanctuary of **Sia**. Set on a narrow ridge, this beautiful site was originally a Semitic "high place", which later, under the Nabat-

aeans and Romans, was embellished with temples and courts. An important place of pilgrimage for both urban and pastoral dwellers, even the Safaitic nomads have left their inscriptions there. The remains of settlement, fortifications and a large gate spread along the ridge to the east.

The extraordinary product of a "local boy makes good" is found at **Shahba** (the Roman Philippopolis), 26 km (16 miles) north of Qanawat. When Philip the Arab gained the imperial crown of Rome in AD 244, he decided to glorify his roots (and himself) by creating an Imperial Roman city at his birthplace. Unfortunately his reign was shortened by his early and violent death and the major monuments in the town of Shahba can be dated to a few short years (247–49), although a small Christian settlement lasted into the 4th century. Set beside black volcanic cones, the structures and streets which survived the 19th-century influx of Druze settlers, are austere but beautifully built. A museum houses the best Syrian examples

ruze
edding,
hahbah.

of late Roman (4th-century) mosaics, still *in situ* in the private house for which they were made.

To the northwest of Shahba lies a bizarre area of land called **the Ledja**, actually a giant island of solid lava. The indefatigable Gertrude Bell described a similar area (Safa, further to the east), as "like a horrible black nightmare sea, not so much frozen as curdled". And yet the Ledja contains many villages, some still inhabited and dating back to Roman times. From its time as classical Trachonitis until the early 20th century, the Ledja has been feared as a lair for brigands and runaways. The Romans tried to tame it by building a dual-carriage highway across the middle of the lava. This is still visible today – complete with a central reservation.

The oasis capital: Passing the Ledja on the left, the eastern road heads directly north to **Damascus**. Capital of modern Syria, once capital of the Omayyad caliphate whose borders stretched from Pakistan to Portugal, and earlier of biblical Aram, Damascus has risen and fallen with the tides of history since earliest times. It nestles at the foot of Mount Kassiun, on the eastern slopes of the Anti-Lebanon range, within a large basin watered by the Barada River and on the edge of the great Syrian Desert. By careful husbandry of the river, the rich soil of the basin has been irrigated and cultivated, creating a lush oasis (the Ghouta) which engirdles the city protectively. It is one of the traditional candidates for the location of the Garden of Eden, and the city itself has been lauded as the oldest continuously occupied capital in the world. Legends they remain, as such uninterrupted and dense settlement has allowed for little systematic archaeological excavation.

The expansion of Damascus since Turkish times has largely occurred outside the walls, and the old city has retained its mixed medieval character. Artisans and craftsmen still ply their trade and the delights of shopping in the **Suq al-Hamediyeh** could trigger a serious case of shopping fever in the unwary. Silks, embroidered and printed

Azem Palace Damascus.

cloth, wooden inlay, glass, copper, rugs, gold, spices, sweets – and myriad more crafts and goods are located in their specialised areas. The crowd is dense and the hawkers are vociferous. Walk down the **"Street called Straight"** (where St Paul was lodged after his conversion on the road). It is, as Mark Twain quipped, "straighter than a corkscrew, but not as straight as a rainbow". In between, visit the old *khans* (warehouses for trade and traders' accommodation), *madrassas* (schools), mausoleums (especially of Saladin and the Sultan Baybars) and, to appreciate the comforts and luxuries of urban life for the wealthy, visit the **Azem Palace**.

It is a particular delight to get lost inside the Oriental maze of streets, covered alleyways, cul-de-sacs and courtyards lined by half-timbered houses of amazing variety and eccentricity. A walk around the citadel (at present under reconstruction inside), walls and the gates is for the interested but energetic. A major monument is the **Omayyad Mosque**, built on the site of the grand Byzantine cathedral of St John the Baptist (whose head is reputedly still inside), which replaced the Roman Temple of Jupiter (note the arch and columns at the end of the *suq*), which, in turn, replaced the Aramaean Temple of Haddad. The mosque is especially famous for its vast expanse of brilliant mosaics and patterned marble, although what survives is but a pale reflection of the original display.

Beyond the old city, visit the **Hejaz railway terminus**, recently restored with a rich Damascene ceiling, and the **Tekkiyeh Mosque**, a beautiful 16th-century construction by the famous Ottoman architect Sinan. The adjacent handicrafts centre (added later, in similar style) is worth a visit. The **National Museum of Damascus** contains a magnificent collection of archaeological and historical material. Across the river, on the lower slopes of Mount Kassiun, and surrounded by the wealthier section of the modern city, the old quarter of **Salihiyyeh** contains many important monuments and is rich in atmosphere.

elow left, e hand-ome Hejaz ailway tation, amascus. ight, njoying smoke.

Finally, one should not leave Damascus without a trip up **Mount Kassiun** itself, where the whole tapestry of the city is laid out for leisurely perusal.

Legends and Christians: Syria is a repository of many significant monuments and traditions relating to early Christianity. The picturesque village of **Saydnaya**, on the edge of the Anti-Lebanon range 27 km (17 miles) north of Damascus, became the second-most important place of Christian pilgrimage in the east after Jerusalem. The convent derives from the time of the Emperor Justinian and contains an image of the Virgin said to be painted by St Luke and associated with numerous miracles.

A further 26 km (16 miles) north through the hills lies the village of **Ma'lula**. Set in a dramatic ravine, its houses jumble around the lower slopes of the cliffs. The small upper monastery contains a chapel dating back to Byzantine times and the monks make a very creditable local wine. The village has clung so tenaciously to its Christian identity that they still speak Aramaic, the language spoken by Christ. The gorge extending behind the village narrows into a dramatic passage reminiscent of the famous *siq* at Petra.

The caravan oasis: The oasis city of **Palmyra** rises like a mirage from the barren waste, 243 km (150 miles) northeast of Damascus. Strings of honey-coloured colonnades interspersed with elegant ruins march across the vast plain, partially enclosed by bare hills to the north and west, with a backdrop of brilliant green from the palms and gardens of the springs to the south and east. As a source of water in the desert, midway between the coast and the Euphrates, Semitic Tadmor, as it was known, has been settled since Neolithic times.

However, it was not until the late Hellenistic and Roman period that the tribes of the desert organised to provide a safe route for traders from the eastern markets, shipping goods upriver to Dura Europos and cutting the shortest way across the desert to Damascus and the great Levantine trading cities on the Mediterranean coast. The Romans called it "Palmyra", the place of palms, and it grew rich from the taxes on the flourishing caravan trade.

As a buffer between Rome and its successive arch-rivals in the east, the Parthians and the Sassanians, Palmyran troops proved to be successful campaigners. But it was the remarkable Queen Zenobia who exerted such power and independence that she took on the might of the Roman Empire and captured Syria, Arabia, Egypt and Anatolia. This was the apogee of the city's fortunes, as the centre of an Arab empire. However, it was all too brief – Zenobia was defeated and captured and the city was destroyed.

The site is vast but the layout easily visible. From the major complex of the Temple of Bel in the east the main monuments of theatre, baths, agora and other temples are scattered either side of the impressive main colonnaded street. At the western end lies the military camp of Diocletian, and a further climb up the northwestern hill leads to the later Arab castle of Qala't Ibn Maan. The glorious panorama is worth the

An Orthodox nun in Saydnaya, the most important place of Christian pilgrimage in the East after Jerusalem.

effort, and one can see the full extent of the tower tombs stretching to the west, and the southwest and southeast cemeteries (south of the Cham Hotel). The modern town spreads to the east of the site and the museum contains many of the sculptures and objects which adorned the site and the tombs.

Along the Euphrates: Continuing to cross the desert to the east, you finally reach the mighty Euphrates and its fertile floodplain at **Deir al-Zor**. There is little of antique interest in this town, apart from the riverscape itself and the town's role as a base for trips south and north. However, the museum has a good collection of material from the major sites of the region.

Travelling south, one can combine Dura, Qala't Rahbeh, and Mari in one trip. The small castle of **Qala't Rahbeh**, just off the main road south to Abu Kemal, is the first site. Built by the energetic Nur al-din in the 12th century, it contains a five-sided keep established to guard the Euphrates.

Further south, the massive mudbrick walls of the riverside garrison and caravan city of **Dura Europos** are clearly visible from the distant road. A chance discovery by British soldiers in 1920 led to the uncovering of a treasure-trove of wall paintings which revolutionised our understanding of early Christian and Judaic traditions and revealed a fascinating mixture of Parthian and Western art. These have been removed to the safety of museums (including the Louvre and Yale University), and one can see the famous synagogue paintings in the Damascus Museum.

Dura was established as a military colony by the Seleucids in the early 3rd century BC, came under Parthian and later Roman control and was destroyed forever by the Sassanian Persians in AD 256. The frantic thickening of the city walls, by filling in buildings adjacent to the walls, ensured the survival of the unique representational paintings in the synagogue, various temples, and the house-church which is earliest Christian cult centre found in Syria.

Twenty-four kilometres (15 miles)

downriver the ancient city of **Mari** (Tell Hariri) has produced crucial information on the history of Syria/Mesopotamia in the third and second millennia BC. The 60-hectare (148-acre) mound is surprisingly low and unprepossessing for the discoveries it has produced. The structures are predominantly mudbrick, dominated by the labyrinthine palace of its last ruler, Zimri-Lim. Mari was destroyed by Hammurabi of Babylon in 1759 BC. Thousands of cuneiform-inscribed clay tablets from the palace archives have revealed the political, social, religious and economic systems of its inhabitants and neighbours.

It is tempting to cross the river at Deir al-Zor and enter the most remote, but agriculturally rich, region of Syria, the Jezira. It is a landscape riddled with ancient tells, and well-watered by the Balikh and Khabur rivers. But time and space restrict us to the Euphrates boundary, and we turn northwards to explore the fortified garrison town of **Halabiyeh**, less than an hour's drive from Deir al-Zor. Perched on the edge of the river, the great stone walls built in the time of Justinian climb the hill westwards to a citadel built at the apex of a triangle. Much of the interior is buried or collapsed, but the magnificent walls, bastions and associated vaulted rooms are largely intact.

The modern provincial centre of **Raqqah**, on the east bank of the river (86 km/53 miles north of Halabiyeh), was historically important from Hellenistic to Ayyubid times, famed as the summer capital of Harun al-Rashid (the caliph immortalised in *A Thousand and One Nights*) and from the late 12th century a centre for the glazed ceramic industry. Remnants of this past can be found in the Bab Baghdad (Baghdad Gate), the Qasr al-Banat (Palace of the Maidens), the Great Mosque, and the museum.

Continuing north, turn left at al-Mansura and cross a bare plain for 28 km (17 miles) to arrive at yet another impressively walled city in the middle of apparently nowhere. **Rusafah** was part of the Roman defences against the **Palmyra.**

322

Sassanians and lies on a caravan route from Damascus, via Palmyra, to the Euphrates ford at Thapsacus. Its remarkable ascendancy in Byzantine times was due to the gruesome martyrdom and subsequent cult status of a Roman court official called Sergius, who refused to renounce his Christian beliefs during the persecutions of Diocletian in AD 305. After Constantine legalised Christianity, the city changed its name to Sergiopolis, and St Sergius eventually became the patron saint of Syria. Much of the city is collapsed and buried and pockmarked with treasure-hunting holes made by the Bedouin. Of the main monuments emerging above ground are three churches, a *khan*, and the magnificent cisterns, which held enough water to last two years.

The medieval bazaar: The culmination of a journey to north Syria must surely be **Aleppo** (Haleb). Set in a dry plain halfway between the Euphrates and the Mediterranean, Aleppo was one of the Near East's great commercial cities in the Middle Ages. It operated at the hub

of world trade converging from Central Asia, India, Mesopotamia and Europe.

Political realignments strangled most of these trade routes and Aleppo has been largely bypassed by the 20th century. Herein lies our good fortune. Aleppo, even more than Damascus, is a hidden doorway into a fabled past. Its old walled city preserves medieval practices and trades and it richly repays a thorough exploration of its nooks and crannies. Be sure to seek out the specialist quarters of its famous *suqs*, it mosques, *khans* and *hammams* (baths) and, of course, its citadel, a military masterpiece set high in isolation like a cup face-down on the saucer of the surrounding city.

The *suqs*, parts of which date from the 13th century, are a labyrinth of vaulted streets reaching 7 km (4½ miles) in length, unsurpassed in size and atmosphere. Quarters outside the old walls, such as Jdeide ("new", dating from the Mamluke period) and the old *madrassas* (schools) to the south also charm the wanderer. The **Aleppo Museum** con-

tains important collections from many periods and sites.

Aleppo is a melting-pot of Arabs, Turks, Kurds, Armenians and Assyrians and this is reflected in the wonderful variety of cuisine that can be sampled in the restaurants of the surrounding modern town.

The Dead Cities: Aleppo is an excellent base from which to venture to the region of the **"dead cities"** and other sites of interest. This evocative term refers to the bare mountainous limestone region in the north, populated by the remarkably well-preserved ruins of elegant country villas, towns, monasteries and churches, now abandoned. During the Roman and Byzantine periods they were the centre of a thriving olive oil and wine industry, which relied on the careful conservation of winter rains and commerce with the Mediterranean world. This economy collapsed with the disruptions of the Muslim conquest but the monuments of daily life remain, largely unpillaged and undisturbed except by earthquakes. The buildings,

standing up to three storeys high, are of well-cut limestone, marrying Graeco-Roman architecture with an individualistic Syrian interpretation that is unique to this area.

Of the multitude of sites, **Qala't Semaan** (the Church of St Simeon) and the related monastery and pilgrimage centre is perhaps the most striking. A great cruciform church was built around the pillar of the 5th-century ascetic, Simeon Stylites, who chose to isolate himself from the world by living on top of a giant column for the final 40 years of his life. He was revered for his piety and wisdom all over the Byzantine world, attracting hordes of pilgrims, as well as many imitators. The remnants of the pillar form the centrepiece of the church today. The hilltop setting is dramatic and the honey-coloured buildings are extraordinary not just for their beauty but for the numerous architectural innovations employed.

The ruins of the classical city of **Cyrrhus**, perched on the Turkish border, are not as well preserved as other

Blacksmith, Aleppo.

such sites in Syria, but the location is one of the most romantic in its isolation and beauty. The approach to the site crosses two Roman bridges, both still in use today.

Another site with less to see on the surface but of enormous significance in recent scholarship is **Ebla** (Tell Mardikh). Located south of Aleppo on the sweeping north Syrian plain, Bronze-Age Ebla was a major urban centre with wide international links at the time of the great cities of Sumer and Akkad in Mesopotamia. In 1975 the Italian excavators discovered the archives, full of cuneiform tablets in the local language and a repository of invaluable information for archaeologists. Parts of the enormous tell have been excavated, revealing sections of the royal palace, sanctuaries, and city fortifications.

The Central Plains: A good base for visiting central Syria is the river town of **Hama**, which straddles the curving banks of the Orontes. The town is famous for its wooden *norias* (waterwheels), which lifted water into aqueducts for town and agricultural supplies. Despite the destruction wrought on the old city by the internal troubles of 1982, some of its treasured buildings have survived and are being reconstructed. As well as the old mosques and *khans*, the museum in the gracious Beit al-Azem and the waterfront restaurants to the east are recommended. A new luxury hotel overlooks the 12th-century **Mosque al-Nuri** and some of the 17 waterwheels.

The impressive ruins of Hellenistic-Byzantine **Apamia** are reached by an easy drive northeast of Hama. In contrast to the dramatic desert scape of Palmyra, its colonnaded streets, walls, and citadel are beautifully set in lush farmland, overlooked by the range of the Jebel Ansariyeh to the west. A collection of superb mosaics have been recovered from the site and region, some of which are housed in the museum, a converted Ottoman caravanserai.

The Northern Coast: Since Syrian independence in 1946, **Latakia** has grown from a modest fishing village to being the major Syrian seaport. The town has had a long and chequered history since its Seleucid foundation as Laodicea, but continual redevelopment has left few remains of its glory. However, it now functions as a beach resort, with a number of large coastal hotels out of town, and forms a convenient base for visiting the surrounding area.

To the north lies the great Bronze-Age port of **Ugarit** (Ras Shamra). Unlike many contemporary Syrian cities, such as Ebla and Mari, which were built of mudbrick and vulnerable to erosion, Ugarit is largely built of stone. The layout is therefore far more comprehensible to the casual observer. It has been excavated by the French almost continuously for the last 50 years, and has provided a wealth of information and artifacts, including written records. Various palace complexes, temples and housing on the acropolis have been exposed amid an attractive setting of fruit and olive groves.

Crusaders and Saracens: The mountains of the **Jebel an Nusayriyah** stretching behind Latakia have long been a

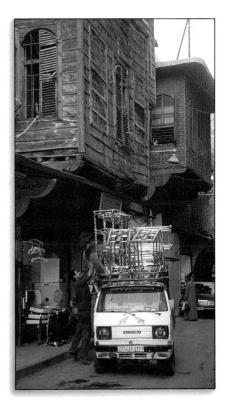

Ottoman architecture, Aleppo.

refuge of breakaway sects and minorities, and today contain populations of Alawites (whence springs Hafez al-Assad, Syria's president) and Ismaelis (once the feared Assassins of medieval times). Hiding within this wild and difficult landscape are myriad Crusader, Saracen and Assassin castles, the journeys to which are rewards in themselves.

One of the most splendid is **Qala't Salahidin**, 24 km (15 miles) east of Latakia. Set on a ridge between two precipitous ravines, it is one of the unchanged survivors of a number of early 12th-century Crusader fortresses. It was lost to Saladin in 1188 and never recaptured. Its history goes back to Phoenician times and covers the largest area of any castle in Syria.

Further down the coast, in the hills southeast of Baniyas, lies the black brooding mass of **Qala't Marqab**, dominating the narrow passage of the coastal plain, with superb views of both sea and mountains. Built by the Muslims in the mid-11th century, it fell into Crusader hands and eventually went to the Knights Hospitallers. They applied novel concepts on a grand scale in their extensive refortification of the structure, pre-empting 13th-century developments in Europe.

The coastal road continues south to **Tartus**, until recently a quiet, charming fishing town but now elevated to the second port in Syria. Originally a Phoenician foundation, it became important in Byzantine times and was the stronghold for the Knights Templar during the Crusades. Remnants of the multi-period fortress can still be traced, and the Crusader cathedral, which is now the museum, is impressive in its simple, massive beauty.

There is much character in the old city and port, and from here one can take the ferry to the island of **Arwad**. Arwad/Arados has a historical importance far exceeding its tiny size. It was a fortress, trading port and centre for ship-building. Today the harbourside fish restaurants are popular with daytrippers (making it hard to squeeze on to the ferries on Fridays and holidays).

Turning inland from Tartus, you can travel via the picturesque hill town of **Safita**, which has a fine luxury hotel with sea views and the remains of yet another Crusader castle, to reach what is undoubtedly the supreme monument to this extraordinary period of European intervention in the Levant.

The magnificent castle of **Krak des Chevaliers** (Qala't al-Husn) is located on a hill near the vital east-west gap that runs through the ranges from the sea to Homs. Already an important defensive site before the Crusades, it was greatly expanded and remodelled by the Knights Hospitallers into the massive impregnable structure we see today. Attesting to the planning and engineering skills of the Crusader architects, the castle was never taken by force, and it remains, as T. E. Lawrence observed, "perhaps the best preserved and wholly admirable castle in the world". It requires a good three hours to wander through the full extent of the complex. From here it is just 50 km (31 miles) to complete the loop to Homs and take the highway back to Damascus.

Left, Krak des Chevaliers. Right, the Citadel, Aleppo. Overpage, a Bedouin saddle-bag.

INSIGHT GUIDES
TRAVEL TIPS

FOR THOSE
WITH MORE THAN
A PASSING INTEREST
IN TIME...

Before you put your name down for a Patek Philippe watch *fig. 1*, there are a few basic things you might like to know, without knowing exactly whom to ask. In addressing such issues as accuracy, reliability and value for money, we would like to demonstrate why the watch we will make for you will be quite unlike any other watch currently produced.

"Punctuality", Louis XVIII was fond of saying, "is the politeness of kings."

We believe that in the matter of punctuality, we can rise to the occasion by making you a mechanical timepiece that will keep its rendezvous with the Gregorian calendar at the end of every century, omitting the leap-years in 2100, 2200 and 2300 and recording them in 2000 and 2400 *fig. 2*. Nevertheless, such a watch does need the occasional adjustment. Every 3333 years and 122 days you should remember to set it forward one day to the true time of the celestial clock. We suspect, however, that you are simply content to observe the politeness of kings. Be assured, therefore, that when you order your watch, we will be exploring for you the physical—if not the metaphysical—limits of precision.

Does everything have to depend on how much?

Consider, if you will, the motives of collectors who set record prices at auction to acquire a Patek Philippe. They may be paying for rarity, for looks or for micromechanical ingenuity. But we believe that behind each $500,000-plus

bid is the conviction that a Patek Philippe, even if 50 years old or older, can be expected to work perfectly for future generations.

In case your ambitions to own a Patek Philippe are somewhat discouraged by the scale of the sacrifice involved, may we hasten to point out that the watch we will make for you today will certainly be a technical improvement on the Pateks bought at auction? In keeping with our tradition of inventing new mechanical solutions for greater reliability and better time-keeping, we will bring to your watch innovations *fig. 3* inconceivable to our watchmakers who created the supreme wristwatches of 50 years ago *fig. 4*. At the same time, we will of course do our utmost to avoid placing undue strain on your financial resources.

Can it really be mine?

May we turn your thoughts to the day you take delivery of your watch? Sealed within its case is your watchmaker's tribute to the mysterious process of time. He has decorated each wheel with a chamfer carved into its hub and polished into a shining circle. Delicate ribbing flows over the plates and bridges of gold and rare alloys. Millimetric surfaces are bevelled and burnished to exactitudes measured in microns. Rubies are transformed into jewels that triumph over friction. And after many months—or even years—of work, your watchmaker stamps a small badge into the mainbridge of your watch. The Geneva Seal—the highest possible attestation of fine watchmaking *fig. 5*.

Looks that speak of inner grace *fig. 6.*

When you order your watch, you will no doubt like its outward appearance to reflect the harmony and elegance of the movement within. You may therefore find it helpful to know that we are uniquely able to cater for any special decorative needs you might like to express. For example, our engravers will delight in conjuring a subtle play of light and shadow on the gold case-back of one of our rare pocket-watches *fig. 7*. If you bring us your favourite picture, our enamellers will reproduce it in a brilliant miniature of hair-breadth detail *fig. 8*. The perfect execution of a double hob-nail pattern on the bezel of a wristwatch is the pride of our casemakers and the satisfaction of our designers, while our chainsmiths will weave for you a rich brocade in gold *figs. 9 & 10*. May we also recommend the artistry of our goldsmiths and the experience of our lapidaries in the selection and setting of the finest gemstones? *figs. 11 & 12*.

How to enjoy your watch before you own it.

As you will appreciate, the very nature of our watches imposes a limit on the number we can make available. (The four Calibre 89 time-pieces we are now making will take up to nine years to complete). We cannot therefore promise instant gratification, but while you look forward to the day on which you take delivery of your Patek Philippe *fig. 13*, you will have the pleasure of reflecting that time is a universal and everlasting commodity, freely available to be enjoyed by all.

Should you require information on any particular Patek Philippe watch, or even on watchmaking in general, we would be delighted to reply to your letter of enquiry. And if you send

fig. 1: The classic face of Patek Philippe.

fig. 4: Complicated wristwatches circa 1930 (left) and 1990. The golden age of watchmaking will always be with us.

fig. 6: Your pleasure in owning a Patek Philippe is the purpose of those who made it for you.

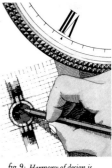

fig. 9: Harmony of design is executed in a work of simplicity and perfection in a lady's Calatrava wristwatch.

fig. 10: The chainsmith's hands impart strength and delicacy to a tracery of gold.

fig. 2: One of the 33 complications of the Calibre 89 astronomical clock-watch is a satellite wheel that completes one revolution every 400 years.

fig. 5: The Geneva Seal is awarded only to watches which achieve the standards of horological purity laid down in the laws of Geneva. These rules define the supreme quality of watchmaking.

fig. 7: Arabesques come to life on a gold case-back.

fig. 11: Circles in gold: symbols of perfection in the making.

fig. 3: Recognized as the most advanced mechanical regulating device to date, Patek Philippe's Gyromax balance wheel demonstrates the equivalence of simplicity and precision.

fig. 8: An artist working six hours a day takes about four months to complete a miniature in enamel on the case of a pocket-watch.

fig. 12: The test of a master lapidary is his ability to express the splendour of precious gemstones.

PATEK PHILIPPE
GENEVE
fig. 13: The discreet sign of those who value their time.

your card marked "book catalogue" we shall post you a catalogue of our publications. Patek Philippe, 41 rue du Rhône, 1204 Geneva, Switzerland, Tel. +41 22/310 03 66.

THOMAS COOK
MASTERCARD
TRAVELLERS CHEQUES...

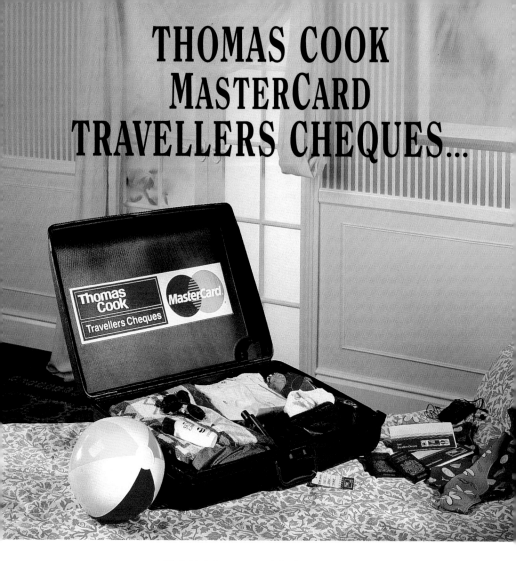

...HOLIDAY ESSENTIALS

Travel money from the travel experts

THOMAS COOK MASTERCARD TRAVELLERS CHEQUES ARE
WIDELY AVAILABLE THROUGHOUT THE WORLD.

Getting Acquainted

To the east of the Mediterranean and northwest of the Arabian Peninsula, Jordan lies between 29°11'–33°22' north and 34°59'–39°18' east parallels. It is bordered in the north by Syria, in the east by Iraq and in the south by Saudi Arabia. To the west lies the Israeli-occupied West Bank and Israel, with which Jordan has the longest ceasefire line of any Arab state. This fact has been of crucial importance in the modern history of Jordan.

Size

Jordan covers an area of 89,411 sq. km (55,900 sq. miles) excluding the West Bank which comprises 5,440 sq. km (2,100 sq. miles). (King Hussein formally renounced his claim to the West Bank in July 1988.) It is only 414 km (257 miles) from Ar-Ramtha at the border with Syria to Aqaba in the south and 387 km (240 miles) from the King Hussein Bridge on the Jordan river to the Iraqi border in the east.

Topography

The kingdom is divided into three natural regions from east to west, which converge in the south at Aqaba, Jordan's only outlet to the sea. The first consists of the eastern depression of the Jordan Valley from the southern end of the Sea of Galilee in the north, along the Jordan River, the Dead Sea (at about 395 m/1,300 ft below sea level the lowest point on earth) down to the Red Sea at Aqaba.

The second natural region is the upland area above the Jordan Valley, which begins at the Yarmouk River in the north. Stretching down to Aqaba, this region is intersected by wadis (valleys and gorges) that subdivide it into three distinct areas. The first lies in the area between the Yarmouk and Zerqa rivers, the second runs from the River Zerqa to the spectacular Wadi Mujib and the third consists of the upland regions around Kerak. The desert to the east of these uplands is the third and largest region, forming more than 75 percent of the total area. Azraq, whose black stone fort was for a short time the headquarters of Lawrence of Arabia, is the only major oasis in this inhospitable region. Throughout history, the line between the desert and the settled uplands has fluctuated according to the strength of central authority, local villagers and the Bedouin.

Geology

Soil types and climate vary between these different regions. Most of the Jordan valley to the north of the Dead Sea consists of alluvial soil and is very fertile. But low rainfall and high temperatures necessitate irrigation, which comes by way of a canal running through the valley from the north. Around the Dead Sea and to the south the soil varies between high salinity and a desert of gravel and sand.

The uplands to the east have attracted settlers throughout history. The dry temperate climate and soil, which varies from shallow and light to deep and rich, favour the production of grains and fruits. The desert to the east, which has almost no rainfall, is suitable only for animal husbandry. The cultivated area around the oasis at Azraq has shrunk in recent years as a result of excessive use of local water resources. In the north the desert region comprises grey basalt; further south granite and sandstone create the beauty of Petra and Wadi Rum. The area of Wadi Araba is rich in potash and Wadi Al-Hesa has phosphate: both are mined primarily for export.

National Parks

The **Dibbeen National Park**, between Jerash and Ajlun, has 48 km (30 miles) of pine woodland and a resthouse with bungalows and a picnic site. A Friday favourite with Jordanians it is a great place for a picnic after a trip to Jerash and for walks, especially in spring when the wildflowers are out.

The **Zai National Park**, on the road from Salt to the Jordan Valley is also covered with pine trees and commands beautiful views of the valley. A small road winds through it and a resthouse (istiraha) offers fine views. Both parks have play areas for children and are ideal for half-day outings from Amman. Unfortunately litter collection is spasmodic and much of the green is littered with plastic containers.

Nature Reserves

The **Shaumari Wildlife Reserve** near the eastern town of Azraq was established by the Royal Jordanian Society for the Conservation of Nature to reintroduce animals that had become extinct in the region, such as the Arabian oryx (an antelope species), ostriches and gazelle. The nearby **Azraq Oasis** hosts many bird species migrating from Europe. The **Dana Nature Reserve** is a little to the south of Tafila off the King's highway and offers camping. The **Gulf of Aqaba**, with a huge variety of tropical fish and coral, offers world-class scuba-diving. **Wadi Rum** is one of the most magnificent desert landscapes in the world.

Time Zones

Jordan is two hours ahead of Greenwich Mean Time and 7 hours ahead of US Eastern Standard Time from the beginning of October to the end of March and three hours ahead of GMT from April till the end of September.

Climate

Jordan enjoys almost year-round sunshine and blue skies. Rain falls only from late autumn to mid-spring. Quantity is unpredictable, however, and when the time comes, farmers and other Jordanians often pray for rain. Aqaba, the south and the desert have negligible rainfall.

The best time to visit is in the spring (April–May), when the winter rains have turned the country green. In places, even the desert is a mass of colourful flowers. The next best time is autumn, October–November, when the hot summer has given way to milder weather perfect for outside dining.

Average temperatures: January: Amman 7°C (45°F), Irbid 9°C (47°F), Aqaba 16°C (61°F); July: Amman 25°C (76°F), Irbid 25°C (76°F) and Aqaba 31°C (88°F).

The People

The population is about 4 million, of whom nearly one half live in Amman. Most sources agree that the majority are of Palestinian origin. Jordan lays great stress on national unity and officially no minorities exist. Christians have lived in what is now Jordan since the dawn of Christianity. They make up about 5 percent of the population and are concentrated in and around Kerak, Madaba, Salt and Amman. About two-thirds of these Christians are Greek Orthodox, who fall under the authority of the Patriarchate of Jerusalem. Their liturgy is in Greek and in Arabic. Most of the higher levels of the clergy are reserved for native Greeks.

Most of the remaining Christians are Greek Catholics, who broke with the Patriarchate in 1709. They have their own Patriarch and worship in Arabic. They recognise the authority of the Pope. There are also small numbers of Roman Catholics, Protestants, Assyrians (Nestorians), Armenians and Syrian Orthodox (Jacobites) in Jordan.

The Circassians (about 35,000) and Shishanis (about 4,000) are the only ethnic minority of any size in Jordan. They are Muslims (Sunni and Shia respectively), who originated in the Caucusus and Southern Russia. In the mid-19th century, the Ottomans in Istanbul, seeking to reassert their authority, encouraged the Circassians and others to settle parts of the empire which had broken away from central control.

The Economy

Jordan has few natural resources. Nowadays, agriculture accounts for about 7½ percent of GDP and phosphate and potash are among the kingdom's principle exports. Tourism and light manufacturing also figure; but until recently, Jordan's main natural resource and earner was its highly-educated population. In the 1970s Jordan benefited from the oil boom in the Gulf and the civil war in Lebanon. Within a short time 28 percent of the labour force was working in the Gulf and their remittances were the largest single contributor to the balance of payments. At home the service sector expanded and became more efficient. Improvements in the infrastructure, in banking and finance permitted Jordan to take over Lebanon's role as the regions entrepot.

From the outset, Jordan has also relied heavily on foreign aid, first from Britain, then the US and the Arab states. The Jordanian economy enjoyed rapid growth between 1975 and 1983 at 13.9 percent per annum. However, the collapse in oil prices in the 1980s, among other things, reduced this figure to about 3 percent. More recently, the expulsion of more than 350,000 Palestinians and Jordanians from Kuwait following the 1991 Gulf War created further problems.

Jordan's economy is burdened by a huge foreign debt which in 1993 stood at US$6.5 billion. Nonetheless in the early 1990s the World Bank and the International Monetary Fund were talking about Jordan as a success story. The country has implemented many of the structural adjustment measures demanded of it and the US and other powers are beginning to forgive what they simplistically perceived as Jordan's support for Iraq in the Gulf War. Infact, 1992 was a boom year for Jordan, with GDP growth of about 11 percent.

However, much of this growth reflects the savings of those who were expelled from Kuwait and the boom in the construction sector following their return. Experts predict that GDP will soon return to 2–3 percent. While the Gulf remains closed to Jordanian workers and Iraq is penalised by UN sanctions, it is difficult to be optimistic about the long-term prospects of the Jordanian economy.

Government

Jordan is a constitutional monarchy and succession rests on male descent. The 1952 constitution is the basis for the political system. Jordan has a two-chamber National Assembly, comprised of a senate of 40 members who are appointed by the King and a Chamber of Deputies of 80 members which is elected by direct universal suffrage. The King has extensive powers. He appoints the prime minister and is Commander in Chief of the armed forces. He approves laws, convenes and adjourns the Chamber of Deputies and can postpone elections for up to two years. One expert has referred to him as "patriarchal rather than autocratic".

The first free elections since the 1950s were held in 1989. In September 1992, a new law legalised political parties which had been banned in 1957. Twenty parties participated in the 1993 elections, and the most significant of these was the Islamic Action Front, in which the Muslim Brothers play the dominant role. In 1993 the first woman MP was elected. Christians, Circassians and Shishanis have their quotas in parliamentary seats.

Islam

Islam, meaning submission in Arabic, is the religion propagated by the Prophet Mohammed in Arabia in the 7th century AD. Those who accept it are called Muslims. For them, Islam is the consummation and correction of its monotheistic predecessors, Judaism and Christianity. The basic principles of Islam are that there is one God who must be worshipped by man and that the Prophet Mohammed was the ultimate messenger of God's wishes to mankind. The Koran, the Word of God, revealed to the Prophet Mohammed and the *Hadith*, the words and actions of the Prophet, are the main sources of Islam.

Every Muslim has five basic duties called the pillars of Islam. These are testifying that "there is no god but God and that Mohammed is the messenger of God", praying five times a day (at dawn, midday, mid-afternoon, sunset and evening), setting aside a certain amount of money for the poor, fasting from dawn to dusk in the month of Ramadan and making the pilgrimage to Mecca at least once in a lifetime. As with other religions, practice and interpretation vary widely. And like Christianity, there have been schisms from the Sunni or Orthodox line. The most important of these were the Shia, who believed that the leadership of the early Islamic community rightfully belonged to Ali, the cousin of the Prophet and the father of his grandchildren through his daughter Fatima.

In the 19th century, Islam began to play a more political role, largely in response to the confrontation between European domination and local forces. For many Arabs Islam now represents a form of cultural assertion and regeneration.

Jordan is overwhelmingly Sunni Muslim and Shiism is largely confined to the small Shishan community who number only 2,000. King Hussein enjoys considerable prestige as a Hashemite, a descendant of the Prophet Mohammed, and he has managed to contain political Islam. The Muslim Brothers, for instance, were co-opted by the regime from the 1950s onward. However, shortly before the 1993 elections, the King changed the electoral law in a move which many observers said was directed against the power of political Islam in Jordan.

Planning The Trip

What To Bring

Comfortable, hard-wearing walking shoes are a must. In the cold months (November–March) bring warm and waterproof clothing. In the warm and hot weather you will need a pair of dark sunglasses, cotton clothes (avoid synthetic materials that do not breathe) and a hat. Even in the summer, the temperature drops significantly after sundown and you will need something to keep yourself warm in the evenings. If you plan to swim, bring a swim suit and suntan or sunblock lotion as these items are very expensive locally. Also bring insect repellent.

Jordan is a conservative country as far as dress code is concerned. You should avoid wearing tight clothes, sleeveless blouses, shorts, mini-skirts, and see-through materials, and refrain from exposing your back (see also *Women Travelling Alone*).

Jordan operates on a current of 220–240V. Most places have two-pin European-style plugs but a few have British-style three-pin plugs. You may find adaptors as well as transformers for American electrical goods in electrical stores.

Camera film and video cassettes cost a lot more for them than you would at home. Tampons are also expensive and not always easy to find.

Maps

Maps are available in most hotels, bookshops and shops geared towards the tourist trade. You can purchase the quite cheap and very adequate Arabic-English maps produced by The Royal Jordanian Geographic Centre (RJGC): *The Tourist Map of Amman*, *Road Map of the Hashemite Kingdom of Jordan* with city plans of Amman, Aqaba, Irbid, Jerash and Kerak, and *The Tourist Map of Petra*. The RJGC also prints the *Map of Jordan*, also produced in English, French, German and Italian. You are advised not to rely on the Amman map supplied by the Ministry of Tourism as it is very out of date.

Jordan, the map produced by GEO Projects (Lebanon), is adequate but its roads badly need updating. If you want the most reliable and frequently updated information on roads in Jordan you should purchase Bartholomew's map of *Israel with Jordan* which unfortunately omits the eastern tip of Jordan that borders Iraq. Foreign maps of Jordan are not available in Jordan.

Entry Regulations

Visas & Passports

All passports require an entry visa which is free of charge for some nationals and quite expensive for others. The price you pay usually depends on the amount your country charges for Jordanians to enter your country.

Apart from obtaining a visa from your nearest Jordanian consular authority you can get one upon arrival at any border entry, including the two new ones between Jordan and Israel, the Sheikh Hussein Bridge and the Wadi Araba border crossing. However, you still cannot obtain an entry visa at the King Hussein (Allenby) Bridge if you are entering from the West Bank, because Jordan does not recognise this to be a border. If you want to enter Jordan from the bridge you must already have a valid visa stamped in your passport (it doesn't need to be a multi-entry visa if you are re-entering).

Visas obtained in Jordanian consulates are valid for 3–4 months from the date of issue and can be issued for multiple entries. You will need to register at the nearest police station if you stay for more than two weeks in Jordan. Tourist visas allow a stay of up to

one month initially; upon expiration this period can easily be extended for another two months. Beyond that date you should exit and re-enter the country or undergo the complicated immigration procedures. If your visa has not been renewed properly by the time you leave Jordan you will have to pay a fine at the border.

Animal Quarantine

There is no animal quarantine in Jordan. In fact there are no regulations about bringing pets into the country and at the very most you may be asked for is a certificate of health for the animal.

Customs

Customs regulations exempt from duty personal effects such as cameras, clothes, typewriters and up to 200 cigarettes, 1 litre of spirits and 2 litres of wine and 200 grams (7 oz) of tobacco. Cars and electrical equipment, from household goods to personal computers etc, are subject to duty which can be very high. However, if you intend to take taxable goods with you when you leave you may ask the customs officials to enter details of these goods in your passport to avoid paying tax. Upon exit you will be asked to show that your goods were tax exempted.

Books are subject to censorship in Jordan and if you carry large numbers do not be surprised if your books fall under scrutiny. Books with a political content hostile to the interests of the state of Jordan, as well as sexually explicit material will be confiscated.

Health

If you come from a country infected by epidemic diseases such as cholera and yellow fever you will have to show a certificate of inoculation. It is advisable to be inoculated for hepatitis (Gamma Globulin), polio, tetanus and typhoid. Jordan is one of the cleanest countries in the region, but it is advisable to take some precautions at least until your system adjusts. Hotels rated 4-star and up have their own filtering systems and their tap water is safe to drink. Elsewhere you should use bottled water which is widely available and, outside hotels, cheap. All fruit and vegetables that you buy should be washed thoroughly and during the warmer months avoid salads and cold meats that have been sitting for a long time on hotel buffets.

Money Matters

The Jordanian currency is called the Jordanian Dinar (JD) and it is divided into 1,000 *fils* or 100 *'irsh*. It appears in paper notes of 20, 10, 5, 1 and 0.5 JDs, silver coins of 500 (new), 250 (rare), 100, 50 and 25 *fils* and in copper coins of 10 and 5 *fils*.

Since the 1988 devaluation of the Jordanian Dinar Jordan has become a relatively cheap country for Westerners to visit.

1 US$	=	0.7 JD
1 £	=	1.05 JD
1 DM	=	0.40 JD
1 FF	=	0.10 JD
1 Yen	=	0.65 JD
100 IL	=	0.04 JD

You can change foreign cash or traveller's cheques in any bank in Jordan, only traveller's cheques will be charged a commission (this varies from bank to bank). When you change traveller's cheques you will be asked to show your sales receipts for the cheques despite the fact that you are not supposed to keep them together.

There are authorised money-changers in Amman, Aqaba and Irbid and generally speaking you get better deals at moneychangers downtown. Exchange rates between banks and moneychangers vary slightly. Hotels of 3 stars or more will also change money but at a less favourable rate. Non-Jordanian nationals are forbidden to buy foreign currency in Jordanian banks but can at moneychanger's.

Credit cards are acceptable in several hotels, restaurants and shops; the most widely accepted being American Express, Visa, Diners Club and Mastercard (in this order). You can also use your cards to draw cash (up to 500JDs only) at any bank linked with your credit card network at no extra charge. The automatic cash machines outside some banks in Amman can only be used by Jordanian bank account holders at present and you should not attempt to use them. However, there are plans to enable foreign account holders to use these machines in the future.

Public Holidays

Friday is the weekly holiday when government offices, banks and most offices are closed. However, some airline offices and travel agents stay open to offer a reduced service and some shops also open. Most businesses and banks have a half-day on Thursday and some businesses and banks take Sunday as a half-day or a complete holiday.

Fixed public holidays:

1 January/Christian New Year
15 January/Tree Day (Arbor Day)
22 March/Arab League Day
1 May/Labour Day
25 May/Independence Day
10 June/Arab Renaissance Day, commemorates the Arab Revolt, and also Army Day
11 August/King Hussein's accession to the throne
14 November/King Hussein's Birthday
25 December/Christmas Day

Holidays that are not fixed:

Muslim holidays follow the lunar calendar, moving back each year by 11 days. The first two holidays in this list last three days, during which Friday services are found. The remaining holidays in the list are one-day public holidays.

Ayd Al-Fitr: the feast that marks the end of Ramadan, the month of fasting.

Ayd Al-Adha: the feast of sacrifice, which falls at the end of the month of the pilgrimage to Mecca (*Haj*). It commemorates Abraham's offering of Isaac for sacrifice. Families who can afford to slaughter a lamb share the meat with their poorer co-religionists. The richer the family the more lambs it slaughters and distributes to the poor.

1st of Muharram: Muslim New Year
Mawoulid An-Nabawi: the Prophet Mohammed's Birthday.

Ayd Al-Isra wa Al-Miraj: the feast celebrates the nocturnal visit of Prophet Mohammed to heaven.

Although Ramadan is not a good month to come to Jordan for business it is a great time to enjoy local customs and the special atmosphere that the shared hardship of fasting creates among Muslims. You should avoid eating, drinking or smoking in public during the hours of fasting because it it illegal and can provoke strong reac-

tions. At sundown everyone breaks the fast with *iftar* and then relaxes until long into the evening. Just before dawn the last meal is eaten before the next day's fasting resumes. Huge amounts of food and sweets are prepared and devoured after dark. As a result most people look exhausted at work next day and government officials may often use this as an excuse to provide a much reduced service.

Christian holidays:

Easter: If you happen to visit Jordan during Easter bear in mind that the local Protestant and Catholic churches celebrate Easter at approximately the same time as the local Greek Orthodox. Three out of every four years the timing will vary, usually by a week but for one year by a whole month. Eastern (Orthodox) Christians regard Easter as a more significant feast than Christmas. If you plan to visit Jordan during Christmas don't be put off by the fact that this is a predominantly Muslim country because thanks to Western commercialism and the local foreign community Christmas and the New Year are celebrated in some splendour. There are also many opportunities for children to enjoy themselves during these times.

Getting There

By Air

Jordan's national airline, Royal Jordanian (RJ) flies direct to Amman from numerous European and Middle Eastern destinations, Chicago, Montreal, New York and Toronto to the west and Calcutta, Delhi, Colombo, Bangkok, Kuala Lumpur, Singapore and Jakarta to the east. RJ has offices in even more destinations with an office in almost any every European capital.

Athens: 80–88 Syngrou Ave, Athens 11741. Tel: 9242600-602
Berlin: Budapest Strasse 14A. Tel: 30-261 7057
Cairo: Zamalek Sporting Club Bldg, 26 July St, Mohandeseen. Tel: 3443114/3467540
Copenhagen: Vester Farimagsgade 6, DK-1606, Copenhagen V. Tel: 33-115858
Damascus: 29 Ayyar St, Damascus, P O Box 2887. Tel: 211267/218681
Detroit: 6 Parkland Blvd, Suite 122,

Dearborn, Michigan 48126. Tel: 800-223-0470

Dublin: 1st Floor, 3 Lower Abbey Street, Dublin 1, Ireland. Tel: 1-8788433

Frankfurt: Munchener Strasse 12. Tel: 69-239 243/4 and 250 868

Geneva: 6 Rue Adhemar Fabri 1201, Geneva. Tel: 22-7328051

Jerusalem: Salah Eddin St, Jerusalem. Tel: 282365/282366

London: 177, Regent Street, W1R 7FD. Tel: 0171-734 2557 (6 lines)

Los Angeles: 6033 West Century Blvd, Suite 760, Los Angeles, California 90045. Tel: 310-215-9627

Madrid: Plaza de España No. 18 Torre de Madrid Building, Ground Floor, 28008 Madrid. Tel: 542-8006

New York: 535 Fifth Ave, New York, N Y 10017. Tel: 212-949-0060

Perth: 7th Floor, Georges Terrace, Perth WA 6000. Tel: 4811166

Rome: Via San Nicola Da Tolentino 82. Tel: 4820369

Sydney: National Mutual Center, 44 Market St, Suite 4, 20th Level, Sydney NSW 2000, Australia. Tel: 2626133

Toronto: 45 St Clair Avenue West, Toronto, Ontario M4V 1K9. Tel: 416-962-3955

Vienna: Hilton Hotel, Am Stadtpark, 1030 Wien. Tel: 712-3242

Washington: 1660 L Street NW, Suite 305, Washington DC 20036. Tel: 202-857-0401

Other airlines operating direct flights to Jordan are Air France, KLM, Alitalia, Turkish Airlines, Austrian Airlines, Cyprus Airways, Air Roumania and a host of airlines belonging to Middle Eastern countries. International flights use the modern and very secure Queen Alia International Airport, which is 32 km (20 miles) south of Amman on the highway to Aqaba.

There are several package tour and airline deals to choose from, especially if you do not mind taking connecting flights via Paris, Istanbul or Amsterdam.

By Train or Bus

By train from Syria: The Hejaz railway train runs once a week between Amman and Damascus on the same single track that was built by the Ottomans at the beginning of the century. A train leaves Damascus every Sunday at 7.30am arriving at Amman at 5pm. Tickets cost 2.500JD and can only be bought on the day of travel.

By bus or service taxi from Syria: Karnak, the Syrian bus company, runs an air-conditioned bus service between Damascus and Amman twice daily (early morning and in the afternoon) which takes about five to six hours counting the time taken to complete formalities at the border crossing from Dir'a 100 km (62 miles) south of Damascus on the Syrian side to Ar-Ramtha 88 km (55 miles) north of Amman on the Jordanian side. Buses leave from the Karnak bus station and arrive at the JETT bus station near Abdali. Book well in advance. One-way tickets cost about US$5 in Syria. In Jordan, bookings are handled by the Jordanian Express Tourist Transport Co Ltd (JETT). Abdali, Amman (tel: 696151, 664146/7).

Service taxis (pronounced *servees*) are shared taxis and they run throughout the day. The taxi rank is near the Karnak bus station. Fares cost S£3 and the trip takes almost as long as on the bus.

By bus and ferry from Egypt: There is a bus service between Cairo and Amman run by JETT and Superjet of the Arab Unity Co, Sharikat Al-Ittihad Al-Arabi, Cairo (tel: 290 9013). The bus leaves Cairo every Saturday, Monday, Tuesday and Thursday at 5pm from the bus station in Masr Al-Gedida, arriving in Amman the next day at around 10pm. One-way tickets cost US$59 for non-Arabs and include the fare for the Nuwayba-Aqaba ferry.

By bus from Saudi Arabia: JETT runs a bus service from Jeddah to Amman three times a week and the trip lasts around 22 hours.

By bus or service taxi from Israel and the Occupied Territories: In East Jerusalem service taxis (*sherouts*) leave from just opposite Damascus Gate (Bab Al-Amoud) for the King Hussein (Allenby) Bridge and fill up from 7.30am onwards. You can reserve a seat at the nearby office or you can ask your hotel to call the taxi company and organise for you to be picked up from your own hotel at a prearranged time. You should try to book in advance and ensure that they will take you all the way to the check-point. Start your trip early as the bridge crossing can take a long time, especially during the high season. The fare is 26 shekels per person if the 7-seat taxi is full. If you cannot get a shared taxi you will need

to pay up to 100 shekels for a private taxi that takes four passengers.

The trip takes 40 minutes to the bridge check-point on the Israeli-occupied side. Upon exit from Israel or the West Bank you will have to pay an exit tax of approximately US$26, payable in dolars, shekels or dinars. From there you have to join the JETT bus that shuttles every hour between the Jordanian and Israeli check-points from 8am, when the bridge opens, till it is closed, at sunset (6pm in winter and 8pm in summer) or at 2pm on Fridays. The JETT bus ticket costs 1.500JD and must be paid in JDs or US dollars. Once you are on the Jordanian side you have to pass through passport control and your bags will be checked by customs officers. For Amman, pick up a shared taxi at the nearby rank where you should pay no more than 2.000JD. The taxi will drop you at Abdali bus station. You can also catch the cheaper public minibus that will drive you straight to Abdali.

As well as the King Hussein (Allenby) Bridge there are two new border crossings between Jordan and Israel, the Sheikh Hussein Bridge at the north of the Jordan Valley near the Israeli town of Bet Shean and the crossing at Wadi Araba near Aqaba and Eilat. Like the King Hussein Bridge these two entry points are open from 8am till sunset from Sunday to Thursday, and till noon on Fridays. On Satrudays, Israeli holidays and some Muslim holidays they all remain closed.

Exit tax from Israel is the same (*see above*) and you will get your passport stamped automatically on both sides of the border – so , clearly, this is not the way to enter Jordan if you plan to make your way to Syria. (See *On Departure, To Syria*. There are bus services operated by the Israeli state company Egged (for information, tel: 02-30455) that can take you to Bet Shean and Eilat, and from there you can take a *sherout* or private taxi to the borders. Massada Tours in Israel (tel: 02-255453 and 03-5444454) runs a bus service from Jerusalem to Jordan via Tel Aviv for $30 one way or $50 return. Israelis have to travel in groups of at least five people when entering Jordan. All travellers entering Jordan through these points must spend at least one night in Jordan.

By Car

To bring your car into Jordan you will need an international driving licence (*carnet de passage en douane*), and insurance, both of which should be obtained before leaving home. You may also have to pay for a local third-party car insurance, which costs very little, or you may want to buy a local comprehensive insurance, the price of which varies according to the make of the car. Your car is free of import duty for up to one year unless you decide to sell it to tax-paying residents, in which case you have to pay the duty.

From Syria: Drive to Dir'a and cross into Ar-Ramtha.

From Egypt: Drive to Nuwayba and take the Egyptian or Jordanian ferry to Aqaba, which leaves in the morning and in the afternoon (check precise timings before you travel). You can buy tickets at the port office in Nuwayba and you must pay for each passenger as well as the car. The ferry journey should take three to four hours but it can take much longer, depending on traffic and weather conditions.

From Israel and the Occupied Territories: The peace treaty between Israel and Jordan stipulates that there will be private car traffic beween the two countries and preparations are under way to allow cars to cross the three crossing points.

Special Facilities

Children

The Middle East in general does not have any of the Western hang-ups about children. Travel in Jordan for children will be as easy and pleasurable as it is for adults. Jordanians take their children everywhere and you will often see them up until late in the evening at parties and in restaurants. Children are allowed complete freedom and are enjoyed by all. Crime against children committed by strangers is unheard of. Jordan is so safe from this point of view that busy parents are known to leave their children to roam around Safeway supermarket on their own for hours instead of hiring a babysitter.

Most restaurants can cater to children's needs and a few in Amman have a play area for children. Some hotels have playrooms and can easily arrange baby-sitting. Amman hotels that cater readily to children's needs include the Amra Hotel, which has a special playroom and organises weekly puppet shows and story-telling, the Marriott which, among other things, arranges entertainment for children over Friday brunch, Christmas and Easter and Al-Maqsura apartment hotel which has a small playground. Almost all hotels of 3-star and up have baby cots. Babies up to two years of age travel free on planes, and up to the age of 12 for half price.

Student

Non-Jordanian students will get no concessions at museums or on public transport in Jordan, but all airlines give discounts on airfares. Royal Jordanian gives discounts of 45–60 percent of the full fare to holders of an international student card. Discounts are also available to students under 31 years old for routes in Europe, to students under 26 for Europe and the Middle East and to students under 25 for Europe, the Middle East and the United States. Young people, between 12 and 24 years old, qualify for discounts of around 45 percent of the full fare. Jordan has no travel agents specialising in youth/student travel.

Disabled

Although special facilities for disabled people are very rare, Jordanians are always willing to help. You are advised to enquire with your travel agent or your hotel before booking. The new Taybet Zaman Village at Petra promises to have ramps available throughout the public areas. As a rule, Royal Jordanian provides wheelchair service when they receive prior notice. In Petra disabled visitors can reach the main sites by horse-driven carriages very easily.

Women Travellers

Sexual harassment in Jordan is less common than in other parts of the Arab world with high numbers of tourists (Morocco, Tunisia and Egypt). However, there will be moments when you will feel uncomfortable – as men try to touch you on the street or by the way they stare at you. The city centre of Amman, where men far outnumber women on the streets, may make you feel particularly uncomfortable. One tip is to avoid looking into people's faces and to concentrate on where you are going. This won't save you from harassment but it will make you less upset. When choosing a place to sit for a coffee or tea look first to see how many other women are present to give you an indication of how comfortable you will be. However, even if you venture into a café full of men without realising, you won't experience any hostility – as Jordanians are too polite for that.

It is sensible to dress modestly, but even modest dress will not save you from some degree of harassment. Modest clothing is a gesture of respect for local culture rather than a safeguard against harassment by men. If you happen to see young Jordanian women in mini-skirts consider the fact that they are more aware of social confines than you are likely to be and would rarely dress like that to go downtown or take public transport.

Although Jordan is a relatively safe country and crimes against women travellers are practically unheard of, be alert and careful. If you take a taxi to a remote area on your own take the name of the driver and the number of the taxi before you get in. Do not sit in the front seat of a taxi. In the countryside and when visiting archaeological sites try to be in view of other people at all times. Hitching will invite the inevitable unpleasant encounter so avoid it. Take special care at hotels of two stars and below, making sure that there are no peeping holes and that your bedroom door locks. Finally, it is best for women to travel together.

Useful Addresses

The Jordanian Ministry of Tourism has no offices outside Jordan but all Royal Jordanian offices will supply you with information and a few brochures.

UK Tour Operators

Abercrombie & Kent, Sloane Square House, Holbein Place, London SW1W 8NS. Tel: 0171-730 9600

Bales Tours, Bales House, Junction Road, Dorking, Surrey RH4 3EJ. Tel: 01306-885991

British Museum Tours, 46 Bloomsbury Street, London WX1B 3QQ. Tel: 0171-323 8895

Egyptian Encounters, 51 Brookley Road, Brockenhurst, Hants SO42 7RS. Tel: 01590-22992

Exodus Expeditions, 9 Weir Road, London SW12 0LT. Tel: 0181-675 5550

Explore Worldwide, 1 Frederick Street, Aldershot, Hants GU11 1LQ. Tel: 01252-319448

Flights of Fantasy, Concorde House, Stour Street, Canterbury, Kent. Tel: 01227-763336

Jasmin Tours, High Street, Cookham, Maidenhead, Berks SL6 9SQ. Tel: 016285-31121

Jetsave Travel, Sussex House, London Road, East Grinstead, West Sussex RH19 1LD. Tel: 01342-328231

Kuoni Travel Limited, Kuoni House, Dorking, Surrey RH5 4AZ. Tel: 01306-740888

Martin Randall Travel, 10 Barley Mow Passage, Chiswick, London W4 4PH. Tel: 0181-742 3355

McCabe Travel, 53/55 Balham Hill, London SW12 9DR. Tel: 0181-675 6828

Noble Caledonia, 11 Charles Street, Mayfair, London W1X 7HB. Tel: 0171-491 4752

Prospect Art Tours, Ltd 454/458 Chiswick High Road, London W4 4TT. Tel: 0181-995 2151

Swan WF & RK (Helenic), 77 New Oxford Street, London W1A 1PP. Tel: 0171-831 1234

Temple World Travel, 13 The Avenue, Kew, Surrey TW9 2AL. Tel: 0181-940 4114

The Imaginative Traveller, 59 Chepstow Road, London W2 5BP. Tel: 0171-792 8494

Tour de Force, Glen House, 200/208 Tottenham Court Road, London W1P 9LA. Tel: 0181-983 1487

Travelsphere, Compass House, Coventry Road, Market Harborough, Leics LE16 9BZ. Tel: 01858- 410456

Twickers World, 11 Church Street, Twickenham, Middlesex TW1 3NW. Tel: 0181-892 7606

Voyages Jules Vernes/Serenissima Travel, 21 Dorset Street, London NW1 5PG. Tel: 0171-730 9841

Diving

Aquatours, 7 Cranes Drive, Surbiton, Surrey KTS 8AJ. Tel: 0181-399 6953

Regal Diving, Station Road, Sutton in the Isle, Ely, Cambs C36 2RL. Tel: 01353-778096

Pilgrimage Tours

Fellowship Tours, South Chard, Somerset TA20 2PR. Tel: 01460-20540

Maranatha Tours, Trafalgar House, Grenville Place, Mill Hill, London NW7 3SA. Tel: 0181-959 5303

Raymond Cook Holidays, Bedfordia House, Prebend Street, Bedford MK40 1QC. Tel: 01234- 349512

Steam Train Tours

TEFS, 77 Frederick Street, Loughborough, Leicester LE11 3TL. Tel: 01509-262745

US Tour Operators

Journeys Unlimited, 150 West 28th St, New York, NY 10001. Tel: (212) 366-6678

Calvary Tours, 1559 Post Road, Fairfield, CT 06830. Tel: (203) 256-1234

Tri-Star Tours, 3432 Richmond Road, Staten Island, NY 10306. Tel: (718) 987-3900

Consolidated Tours, 777 Cleveland Ave, SW, Suite 208, Atalanta, GA 30315

SOLREP International, 3271 West Alabama, Suite 200, Houston, Texas 77098. Tel: (800) 231-0985

Golden Horn Tours, PO Box 207, Annapolis, MD 21404. Tel: (800) 772-7009

LITCO Tours, 5975 Sunset Drive, Suite 505, Miami, FL 33143. Tel: (305) 665-7801

World Pilgrimages, 2300 Henderson Mill Road, Suite 325, Atlanta, GA 30345. Tel: (404) 491-0532

TTI, 401 South Milwaukee Ave, Wheeling, IL 60090. Tel: (708) 520-8087

Rothschild Tours, 900 West End Ave, New York, NY 10025. Tel: (212) 662-4858

Group Wholesale Tours, 200 Main Street, Hackensack, NJ 07601. Tel: (201) 343-3929

Practical Tips

Security and Crime

By general admission Jordan is a very safe country to travel in but obvious precautions should be taken; keep your money in a hotel safe if available and keep an eye on your belongings in public places. It is common wisdom that women travelling alone should stick to places where other people are present and should avoid isolating themselves. If you want to guarantee your complete safety talk to people in the place you are visiting and establish a relationship with them. From then on Jordanians will take care of you better than one of their own.

If you run into serious trouble and need legal advice or representation contact your embassy which may be able to recommend local lawyers. The vast majority of lawyers and doctors speak English. In case of a car accident you should go to the police station with the other party involved and obtain the necessary documents for your insurance claim.

Loss of Belongings

Report any lost belongings to the nearest police station and ask for a certificate of loss for insurance purposes. If you lose your passport you should also contact your embassy/consulate as soon as possible.

Medical Services

All treatment including emergency treatment must be paid for – a certificate of treatment will be issued to enable you to claim back the expenses from your insurance. It is therefore wise to buy health insurance from your travel agent before travelling. Generally speaking Jordan has good medical care and there is a medical centre or clinic in every town and village. Amman has a large number of hospitals and high quality specialists. Outside Amman there are hospitals in Aqaba, Ma'an, Kerak, Madaba, Zerqa, Irbid and Ramtha and there are clinics with a small number of beds in the Jordan Valley.

There are three classes of hospital beds and prices are standardised. Contact your embassy to enquire about hospitals and doctors they can recommend. To find a doctor or pharmacist that is open outside normal hours consult the free monthly *Your Guide to Amman*, which lists doctors and chemists on night duty and hospitals. The *Jordan Times* (Page 2) also lists duty doctors and pharmacists in the capital.

Weights & Measures

Jordan employs the metric system. Length is counted in metres, distances in kilometres, weight in kilograms and volume in litres.

1 inch = 2.54 centimetres (cm)
1 foot = 0.30 metres (m)
1 yard = 0.91 metres (m)
1 mile = 1.61 kilometres (km)
1 acre = 0.40 hectares (ha)
1 ounce = 28.35 grams (g)
1 pound = 0.45 kilograms (kg)
1 British ton = 1016 kilograms
1 American ton = 907 kilograms
1 imperial gallon = 4.55 litres (l)
1 American gallon = 3.79 litres (l)

Business Hours

Government offices: Open 8am–2pm. Closed Friday. During Ramadan: 9.30am–2pm.

Businesses: Open winter (November–April) 8/8.30am–1/1.30pm, 3/3.30–6.30pm and summer (May–October) 4/4.30–7.30pm. Most businesses close Friday and some close Sunday all day or half-day. Some travel agencies stay open during lunchbreak. During Ramadan: 9am–3/6pm.

Banks: Open winter 8.30am–12.30/1pm, 3.30–5/5.30pm, summer 8.30am–12.30/1pm, 4/4.30–6pm, closed Friday all day, Thursday and Sunday afternoons. During Ramadan 9am–1/2pm.

Museums: Generally open 8am–5pm, closed Friday. Consult *Museums* section below as times vary.

Shops: Open winter 9am–6.30/7pm, summer 9am–8/9pm. Most shops close in the afternoon for about two hours any time between 1pm and 4pm. Most shops close Friday except for the Amman downtown *suq* and some close Sunday. During Ramadan: 9am–1pm and after the break of fast most will reopen until 9 or 10pm (see *Shopping*).

Post Offices: Open winter 8am–5pm, summer 7am–7pm. During Ramadan 8am–3/4pm. Some post offices in Amman and around the country open on Friday mornings 8am–1.30pm.

Tipping

In Jordan you will certainly not be pressed anywhere near as much as in Egypt for what is known in Arabic as *baqsheesh* but it is nonetheless a good idea to leave a small tip. The better hotels and restaurants may add 10–12 percent service charge to your bill but waiters do not always get this. Other establishments expect you to leave a tip for all staff or give something to those that worked for you most. Taxi-drivers are generally not tipped but it is customary to pay the nearest round figure to the price on the meter. Anywhere else tip according to will, bearing in mind that tips are always appreciated. One place where you will be pressed very hard to tip is Petra, particularly when you rent a horse. You need not tip more than 10 percent of the price you paid for the horse and in any case no more than 2JD. If you are harassed for more, complain to the Tourist Police at the Visitors' Centre.

Religious Services

There are several churches and monasteries of a variety of denominations in Amman and the rest of the country, including St George's in Madaba, which has the famous mosaic map of Palestine. Amman has Greek Orthodox, Anglican, Roman Catholic, Evangelical Lutheran, German-speaking Evangelical, Armenian Catholic and Orthodox, Coptic, Syrian Orthodox and interdenominational churches. Churches and their telephone numbers are advertised daily on page 2 of the *Jordan Times* and you should ring to find out the times of services. In the same place you will also find information about the times of Muslim prayers (see also *Public Holidays* for Easter timings).

Media

Newspapers and Magazines

Jordanian press is relatively free but the state is the major shareholder in all three dailies. Newspapers often practice self-censorship. There are three main Arabic dailies, *Al-Destour*, *Al-Rai* and *Sawt Ash-Sha'ab* and recently there has been a rash of new weeklies of various political orientations and quality. There are two English language papers, the *Jordan Times*, a daily which covers events in the region quite well and also reproduces analytical pieces from the international press, and *The Star*, a weekly with good feature articles on local news and a French section. Many Amman newsagencies also stock a good selection of foreign newspapers and magazines in English, French, German, Italian and Arabic. Imported press is very expensive and it is subject to censorship, which means that copies carrying articles deemed offensive to Jordan's leadership and the government are not available.

Radio and Television

Jordanian television broadcasts in two channels, Channel 2 being international with English- and French-language programmes and news as well as news in Hebrew. The quality of imported series and feature films varies greatly. The Channel 2 TV programme is advertised daily on page 2 of the *Jordan Times*. In Jordan you can also receive Syrian and Israeli television, the latter being watched very widely. The Jordan Radio and Television Corporation and private companies also sell subscriptions to satellite TV networks like CNN, BBC World Service TV, MTV, TV5 (French) and Super Channel.

Radio Jordan broadcasts in Arabic as well as in English. The English programme is transmitted at 99kHz VHF FM stereo and 350.9 Mhz and 855kHZ medium wave and has news bulletins every hour on the hour. The BBC World Service radio broadcasts to Jordan in English at 1323 kHz, 227 MHz medium wave (3–7.30am and 9am–11.15pm GMT) and 639 kHz, 469 MHz medium wave (3–3.30am, 6–8.15am, 10.30am–12.45pm GMT).

Postal Services

Post offices open winter 8am–5pm, summer 7am–7pm, and during Ramadan 8am–3/4pm. Postal services in Jordan are generally reliable although there have been reports of parcels going missing. Mail is not delivered to addresses but to post office boxes, so if you send letters to an address without a post box number the letter will be returned to you. Registered or express mail sent from Jordan is relatively cheap, but parcels are very expensive to mail and they have to be left open so that they may be inspected by customs officials.

Poste restante service is available

at some post offices but you should enquire first. *Poste restante* letters are kept for only one month from the date of their arrival at the post office.

Telecoms

Jordan has a very good telecommunications system. Public telephones exist inside post offices but many shopkeepers will let you use their telephone for local calls (0.050 fils). International calls are expensive as post offices charge for a minimum three minutes and hotels charge a good percentage more than the actual rates. Faxes are very widely available in hotels and even many of the 1-star hotels have them. Many hotels also have telex facilities.

Actual rates of telephone calls, ie what you will have to pay at the post office and on private telephones (not hotels), per minute are as follows:

Europe (excluding Greece and Cyprus): 8am–10pm 1.650JD, 10pm–8am and Fridays 1.155JD

USA, Canada, Russia: 8am–10pm 2.000JD, 10pm–8am and Fridays 1.400JD

Syria, Iraq, Egypt, Tunisia: 8am–10pm 0.500JD, 10pm–8am and Fridays 0.350JD

Israel: 8am–10pm 0.900JD, 10pm–8am and Fridays 0.630JD

Gulf States: 8am–10pm 0.750JD, 10pm–8am and Fridays 0.525JD

Algeria, Libya, Morocco, Somalia: 8am–10pm 1.000JD, 10pm–8am and Fridays 0.700JD

Greece and Cyprus: 8am–10pm 1.200JD, 10pm–8am and Fridays 0.840JD

Rest of the world: 8am–10pm 2.750JD, 10pm–8am and Fridays 2.500JD

Local telephone codes:
02: Irbid, Umm Qais, the North
03: Wadi Moussa region (Aqaba, Petra, Maan, Kerak)
04: Jerash, Ajlun, Mafraq
05: Salt, Jordan Valley
06: Amman
07: Yaduda (Kan Zaman), Umm Al-Amad
08: Airport, Madaba
09: Zerqa
International network access code: 00.

If you want to call a number outside Jordan you have to dial 00 + country code + local code + number.

Directory enquiries: 121 or 640444 for Amman numbers, 131 for the rest of the country and 0132 for international numbers. Some English is spoken but the service in general leaves a lot to be desired.

Tourist Offices

There are no tourist information offices but the public can visit the Ministry of Tourism in Amman near Third Circle. Tel: 642311. Open 8am–2pm. It operates like a tourist office, supplying visitors with a free map, a few colourful brochures and information. They also run a **Tourist Complaints** service, which deals with complaints about resthouses, hotels and restaurants. Outside Amman there are three Visitors' Centres that are meant to serve the same purpose:

Jerash. Near the South Gate of the archaeological site. Open daily winter 7.30am–7pm, summer 7.30am–8.30pm. Tel: 04-451272.

Petra. At the entrance of the site. Open daily winter 7am–4pm, summer 7am–5pm. Tel: 03-336020.

Aqaba. Near the castle. Open winter 8am–2pm, summer 8am–5pm. Tel: 03-313731.

Your Guide to Amman, a small booklet published monthly and distributed free through airline offices and travel agents, is full of useful although not always accurate information, including the names of tour operators, restaurants, useful numbers, ministries and car rental companies.

Tour operators in Amman and Aqaba organise independent package tours which are generally expensive for individual travellers but worthwhile and convenient for groups and families. If you would like to do something unusual you could enquire about camel caravan trips, desert racing, ballooning (see also *Sports*) or staying with a Bedouin family in the desert - all of which can be catered for in one way or another. It pays to shop around, but if you don't have the time to spare then try any of the following:

International Traders. Shmaysani represent American Express and among other things can organise a Hejaz railway trip with mock Bedouin raid and a meal in a tent in the desert near Amman. Tel: 607014.

Bisharat Tours. Intercontinental, Am-

man and in Aqaba. Friendly staff organise a number of more conventional trips around the country, accommodation, flights and land travel. Tel: 641350, 644355.

Renaissance Tours. Near Third Circle, Jebel Amman. For package tours to Aqaba and Wadi Rum. Tel: 643661.

Guiding Star. Emir Mohammed Street, Jebel Amman. Guiding Star also has an office in Jerusalem and are therefore ideal for booking hotels ahead of your trip to the West Bank. Tel: 642526.

Embassies

All the diplomatic missions listed below are in Amman. Egypt also has a consulate in Aqaba. Other diplomatic missions are listed in the monthly *Your Guide to Amman*, available free at hotels and travel agents in Amman.

American Embassy, Abdoun (no detailed address necessary). Tel: 820101; fax: 813759. Open 9am–noon, closed Friday and Saturday.

Australian Embassy, between Fourth and Fifth circles, Jebel Amman. Tel: 673246; fax: 673260. Open to general public 9am–noon Monday and Wednesday only, but for Australian citizens 7.30am–3pm daily except Friday and Saturday.

Austrian Embassy, Mithqal Al-Fayez Street, near Hisham Hotel, between Third and Fourth circles, Jebel Amman. Tel: 644635; fax: 612725. Open to general public 9am–12.30pm, but will receive telephone calls 7.30am–3.30pm, closed Friday and Saturday.

Belgian Embassy, near Fifth Circle, Jebel Amman. Tel: 675683; fax: 697487. Open 9am–2pm, closed Friday and Saturday.

British Embassy, opposite Orthodox Club, Abdoun. Tel: 823100; fax: 642864. Open 8am–3pm, closed Friday and Saturday.

Canadian Embassy, Philadelphia Bank building, next to Pizza Hut, Shmaysani. Tel: 666124; fax: 689227. Open 8am–4pm, closed Friday and Saturday.

Danish Embassy, Abdel Hamid Sharaf Street, Shmaysani, behind UNESCO. Tel: 603703; fax: 672170. Open 8am–1pm, 3–5.30pm, Friday 8am–1pm, closed Sunday.

Egyptian Embassy, near First Circle, Jebel Amman. Tel: 605202; fax: 604082. Open 8am–2pm, closed Friday.

Egyptian Consulate, Al-Wihdat Al-

Gharbiya, Aqaba. Tel: 03-316171. Open 9am–2pm, closed Friday.

French Embassy, near Third Circle, Mutanabi Street, near Ministry of Tourism, Jebel Amman. Tel: 641273; fax: 659606. Open 8am–2pm, closed Fridays. Visas only on Saturday.

German Embassy, Benghazi Street, behind mosque on Fourth Circle, Jebel Amman. Tel: 689351; fax: 685887. Open 8am–4pm, closed Friday and Saturday.

Irish Consulate, near Ministry of Finance, King Hussein Street (known as Sharia Salt), downtown. Tel/fax: 630878. Open 9.30am–1pm, closed Friday.

Italian Embassy. Jebel Al-Luwaybida. Tel: 638185; fax: 659730. Open 9am–noon, closed Friday and Saturday.

New Zealand Embassy. Khalas Stores building, King Hussein Street (Sharia Salt), downtown. Tel: 636720 (shared with Khalas stores); fax: 634349. Open 9am–1pm, closed Friday.

Norwegian Consulate. Medica Centre, Mecca Street. Tel: 699410. Open 8am–4pm every day except Sunday 8am–1pm, closed Friday.

Saudi Embassy. Abu Bakr As-Siddiq Street (also known as Sharia Rainbow), near First Circle, Jebel Amman. Tel: 814154. Open 8.30am–2pm, closed Friday.

Syrian Embassy. Haza al-Majali Street (behind Ministry of Foreign Affairs), near Third Circle, Jebel Amman. Tel: 641076; fax: 698685. Open 9–11am, closed Friday.

Swedish Embassy. Opposite Salah Eddin mosque on Fourth Circle, Jebel Amman. Tel: 669177. Open 9am–noon, closed Friday and Saturday.

Getting Around

On Arrival

Getting from the airport: The Queen Alia airport, 32 km (20 miles) south of Amman, has a bus service to Amman every half an hour which arrives at Abdali bus station and costs 0.750JD. There are also plenty of taxis. They charge a fixed fare of 8JD on top of which you could add another 1JD as tip. The journey to Amman takes 30–40 minutes.

Getting from Aqaba to Amman: There are six JETT buses every day and the fare costs 4JD. The JETT bus station in Aqaba is on the Corniche opposite the archaeological site of Ayla and is a well-known location. The trip takes approximately four hours. There is also a much cheaper public minibus service that leaves from the main bus station, where you will also find service taxis for Amman, but you will have to wait till one fills up to set off. Royal Jordanian has six to seven flights a week to Amman. These take 45 minutes and cost approximately 25JD one way and 50JD return.

Getting from the King Hussein Bridge to Amman: See *Getting There*.

Public Transport

There are four types of public transport in Jordan: the big blue buses of the JETT company which are air-conditioned and reliable but require booking well in advance; the white large public buses and the public minibuses which are very cheap and go everywhere in the country; the white shared taxis that cover fixed routes and are called service taxis - they leave when they are full – and the yellow taxis that are not for sharing. Amman is the hub of transport in Jordan.

By Bus

JETT runs daily services from Amman to Petra (one way 5JD, round trip 10JD, excursion with horse hire and packed lunch for 32JD). You should book well in advance and can ask to be picked up from your hotel. There are six daily services to Aqaba and one service to the King Hussein Bridge every day except Saturday (see *Moving On*). Public buses and minibuses will take you almost anywhere in Jordan very cheaply. Minibuses leave when they are full. No standing passengers are allowed in any type of bus.

There are two main bus stations in Amman: Abdali and Wahdat. Buses from Abdali go to Ajlun, Beqa'a, Deir Alla, Fuhays, Jerash, Irbid, Suwaylah, Wadi As-Seer and the King Hussein Bridge. Most fares cost less than half a dinar. The Hejazi bus company, whose buses leave from the top end of Abdali, runs a very frequent and cheap non-stop service to Irbid and Yarmouk University. Buses from the Wahdat station go to Aqaba, Madaba, Petra, Ma'an, Wadi Moussa, Kerak and Hammamat Ma'in. If you want to go to Azraq you must first get a bus to Zerqa. Fares do not exceed 2JD.

The Dead Sea is one destination that is hard to get to without private transport as there are no JETT or public buses operating there. You could however take a public bus from Ras Al-Ain in Amman for Shuneh and from there take your chance. Destinations shown on the front of public buses are always written in Arabic, so if you do not read it ask to be shown the bus you need.

Taxis

Service taxis from a number of locations in downtown Amman and from Abdali will take you almost anywhere in Amman. Likewise chances are that any service taxi passing you by can take you to either of these two places. Like buses, service taxis also post their destinations in Arabic so you may find it difficult to familiarise yourself with their routes. If you cannot read Arabic hail a passing service taxi, shout your destination and it may just stop to pick you up. Fares are between 80 and 120 fils (0.080-0.120JD).

Unless you are on a very tight budget the yellow private taxis are a fast and relatively cheap way of getting about Amman. You will rarely have to wait long to get one. They are obliged to use their meter, which starts at 0.150JD. Most rides will cost between 0.400 and 1.500JD. Beware of taxis in ranks outside big hotels: they refuse to use their meter and will ask an inflated flat rate. You will be better off walking a short distance away from your hotel and hailing one of the many passing taxis. Jordanian women would never sit at the front of a taxi next to the driver, so it is wise for women travellers to follow suit and sit in the back in order to avoid any misunderstandings.

Private Transport

Jordan has an excellent road infrastructure which is still expanding and improving. Driving is on the right-hand side. There are highways from the King Hussein Bridge to the Iraqi border and from Ar-Ramtha to Aqaba. From Amman to Aqaba the four-lane Desert Highway is faster than the two-lane King's Highway but less interesting.

Car crime is very rare but you should always keep your car locked. There are several petrol stations in the capital and major towns but not many on the road. Petrol/gas is called *benzeen* and super is called *khas*. On the highway it is easy to miss the turning you want because the sign is right on top of it. Most signs are in English as well as Arabic.

Driving in the city can be a frightening experience as Jordanian drivers rarely indicate. They are very responsive to horns, however. If you have to go through one of the Circles be patient and move slowly but steadily. If you decide to drive in the desert ensure that your car has the right type of tyres and a 4-wheel drive and take a container with extra petrol/gas. Before you venture in the wilderness inform the nearest Desert Police Patrol station.

Car Hire

Car hire in Jordan is expensive in comparison to Europe and the US, but there are plenty of choices available in Amman and to a lesser extent in Aqaba and at Queen Alia airport. Rented cars have green number plates with yellow writing whereas Jordanian private cars have white number plates and service and private taxis have green plates with white writing. The free publication *Your Guide to Amman* advertises several car rental companies. When you ring around to compare prices do ask whether they require a deposit, which can be very high. Prices range from 25JD to 35JD per day for a medium size car and mileage limits vary from 100–200 km (62–124 miles) a day, after which you pay extra. Apart from international names in car hire like Avis (tel: 699420), Budget (tel: 698131/2), Europcar (tel: 601350, 601360, 674267) there are plenty of cheaper (and reliable) local companies such as Amin Jarrar (tel: 603500, 08-51000), Atlas (tel: 697469), Dallah (tel: 827736, 815071, 08-51212), Jerash (tel: 603233), Sabri (tel: 693026) and Safari (tel: 605080).

On Foot

You can walk and hitch everywhere in the country except in the security area at the Dead Sea and between the Jordanian and Israeli checkpoints on the King Hussein Bridge. It is relatively easy to get picked up by cars unless you are in a very remote area. Drivers will often expect a small contribution towards their petrol, especially if you travel with them a long way. From Amman, you can hitch from the Seventh Circle to anywhere in the south and west, from Suwaylah for west and north and from the road to Zerqa to the north and east. Women should not hitchhike on their own. Summertime is not recommended for hitching but if you *have* to hitchhike in the summer at least ensure that you are well equipped to cope with the heat and the sun.

On Departure

Departure tax is 10JD at the airport, 6JD in Aqaba going to Egypt, and 4JD at the land borders going to Syria, Iraq, Israel and the Occupied Territories. If you have not renewed your visa you will also have to pay a fine (see *Entry Regulations*).

To Egypt

JETT buses run between Amman and Cairo every Saturday, Monday, Tuesday and Thursday, leaving at 5am and arriving in Cairo in Masr Al-Gedida at around the same time the next day. A one-way ticket costs US$46 for non-Arab nationals and it includes the fare on the ferry between Aqaba and Nuwayba but not the exit tax. For information and reservations call JETT in Amman (tel: 894872 or 664146/7). Book at least two days in advance. Royal Jordanian and Egypt Air run almost daily flights between Amman and Cairo which cost 84JD one way and 186JD return. You must obtain a visa for Egypt at the Egyptian consulates in Amman or Aqaba before entering Egypt.

To Syria

There are buses from Amman to Damascus twice daily early morning and afternoon run by JETT and Karnak, the Jordanian and Syrian bus companies respectively, and the trip lasts about five hours. They depart from the JETT bus station and arrive at the Karnak bus station in Damascus. Buses are air-conditioned and one-way tickets cost 4.500JD. For information and reservations call JETT in Amman. Tel: 696151 or 664146/7. Service taxis leave from Abdali and the one-way trip costs 5.500–6.000JD. For 15JD a service taxi can take you as far as Beirut (if you have a visa). There is also the Hejaz railway service that leaves Amman (Marka) at 7.30am every Monday, arriving in Damascus at 5pm. If you prefer to fly, Royal Jordanian and Syrian Airways operate flights at 43JD one way and 86JD return.

You must obtain a visa for Syria before travelling, preferably from a Syrian consulate in your country of residence, as the Syrian embassy in Amman often refuses to handle visa applications for those not permanently resident in Jordan. Procedures in Amman can take as little as a few hours and you will have to fill in an application that asks, among other things, whether you have ever visited Occupied Palestine – the answer should be "no". If your stated occupation is writer or journalist your application for a visa will take considerably longer to be processed as it has to be vetted by the Ministry of Information in Damascus. You will be denied a visa or entry into Syria if your passport carries any Israeli stamp or an Egyptian or Jordanian stamp from the border crossings with Israel. Therefore if you plan to visit Syria from Jordan you should not enter Jordan from Wadi Araba or the King Hussein and Sheikh Hussein bridges.

To Israel and the Occupied Territories

JETT buses run between Amman and the King Hussein Bridge every morning at 6.30am and they will collect passengers from their hotels. The fare is 6JD and it is more expensive than the service taxi that will take you to the Bridge for no more than 2JD at any time of the morning or the public bus that leaves from Abdali and charges 1JD. However, apart from comfort, the important advantage of the JETT bus is that it guarantees you a crossing as soon as the bridge has opened at 8am and, moreover, it secures a place on the only means of transport allowed across the bridge itself, namely a bus that shuttles between the Jordanian and Israeli check points every hour between 8am and when the bridge closes, at sunset (6pm in winter and 8pm in summer) Sunday to Thursday and at 2pm on Friday. If you take a taxi it will drop you at the Jordanian check point, where you will have to wait for a place on the next available shuttle bus. The bus fare costs 1.500JD and the last bus leaves the Jordanian check-point half an hour before the bridge closes. The bridge is closed all day Saturday, during Jewish holidays and on some Muslim feasts. It is wise to enquire with the Department of Bridges and Borders or your hotel before planning your travel as sometimes the bridges close at short notice.

From the bridge (called Allenby on this side of the river) you can share a service taxi (called *sherout*) to Jerusalem for a rate that is advertised on a board inside the checkpoint building (currently 26 shekels). There are also less frequent *sherouts* to Ramallah and there is a bus service to Jericho and from there to Jerusalem.

It is advisable to make advanced reservations for accommodation in Jerusalem, especially in the Christmas and Easter periods when hotels in Jerusalem are heavily booked.

There are two new crossings into Israel since the peace treaty was signed, the Sheikh Hussein Bridge at the north of the Jordan Valley, between the Jordanian town of Irbid and the Israeli Bet Shean, and the Wadi Araba border crossing between Aqaba and Eilat in the south. You can reach the Sheikh Hussein Bridge from Irbid in a service or private taxi. On the Israeli side you will have to take a taxi or *sherout* to Bet Shean and from there public (Egged) buses will take you to other Israeli towns. The Wadi Araba border can be reached from Aqaba in service taxis which cost 3JD one way. Also a JETT bus leaves Aqaba daily at 8.30am from the border. Neptune Tours in Amman (tel: 651780) run a bus service twice weekly from Amman to Tel Aviv, Jerusalem and Haifa via the Sheikh Hussein Bridge, and their office in Aqaba (tel: 03-313325/ 315135) can arrange a private bus service from Aqaba to Eilat. These two crossing points are open Sunday to Thursday 8am–sunset and until noon on Friday; they are closed all day Saturday, during Israeli holidays and on some Muslim holidays.

By Bus To Saudi Arabia

JETT runs a bus service to Jedda on Monday, Wednesday and Friday, leaving from the JETT bus station near Abdali at 11.30am and arriving in Jedda at 6-7pm the next day. For information call JETT in Amman (tel: 69615 or 664146/7). One-way tickets cost 25JD. Getting the bus is the easy part – you will first have to get a visa and that can be very, very difficult.

By Bus & Service Taxi To Iraq

Service taxis leave from Abdali as they fill up. The trip costs 15JD one way. A cheaper way is to get the public bus from Wahdat station for only 8JD. A more comfortable way is to hire a private car and driver – enquire at the Intercontinental Hotel.

Where To Stay

Hotels

There are no "Bed and Breakfasts" in the English sense in Jordan and no motels.

All hotels are willing to wheel and deal, especially during the low season (October–March) and for longer occupancies. The smaller hotels are particularly flexible. All hotels except one-star hotels charge an additional 10 percent government tax and 10 percent service charge. If you are a foreign resident in Jordan enquire about favourable rates. Many hotels have different rates for Jordanians and foreigners but would charge foreign residents the same rate as Jordanians.

Prices quoted below may vary according to season. Unmarried couples may be prohibited from sharing a room. Proof of marriage may be required if the surnames on a couple's passports are not the same. Some hotels will even complain if a man visits a woman's room for a short while.

The resthouses listed provide adequate and clean accommodation for the budget traveller and tend to be very popular, so book ahead.

Amman

☆☆☆☆☆ **Deluxe**

Intercontinental Hotel (also known as the Jordan Hotel). Jebel Amman, near Third Circle. Tel: 641361, fax: 645217. A favourite among journalists and media hacks. The hotel boasts an efficient business centre, press office, and Reuters wire service. Almost every summer night at the Intercontinental is filled with joyous sounds of bagpipes and drums as another bride and groom celebrate their wedding. Double room 115JD.

Marriot Hotel. Shmaysani. Tel: 607607, fax: 670100. Well located and with the most extensive sports and health club facilities of any hotel in Amman. Double room US$150. Enquire about special rates.

Forte Grand. Shmaysani. Tel: 696511, fax: 674261. Attached to the Housing Bank Centre and home to over 100 shops and businesses. Double room 115JD.

Al Yasmin Suites. Jebel Amman, off Third Circle. Tel: 643216/8, fax: 643219. Ten luxurious suites exquisitely furnished and equipped with every convenience, including a kitchenette. Rates comparable to five-star hotels but the facilities are superior to what is offered anywhere else in town. In-house business centre and private faxes can be installed in executive suites upon request. Guests have free access to the Intercontinental Hotel swimming pool. Ordinary suite 100JD. Executive suite 125JD.

☆☆☆☆

Amra Hotel. Sixth Circle. Tel: 815071, fax: 814072. The best hotel in its class with services that compete favourably with five-star hotels. Double room 70JD.

☆☆☆

Shepherd Hotel. Behind the Islamic College, near Second Circle. Tel: 639197, fax: 639198. Rooms are comfortable and rates include breakfast. Hotel staff are helpful. Perhaps the best thing about this place is its thriving nightlife. It has three popular bars and a quaint restaurant known for its fondues. Double room 40JD.

Hisham Hotel. Near Third Circle. Tel: 642720, fax: 647540. In a green and quiet neighbourhood of Jebel Amman this hotel has a loyal clientele. Small but always busy. Its summer terrace bar and restaurant are a big bonus. Double room 50JD

Al Qasr Hotel. Shmaysani, opposite Peking Chinese Restaurant. Tel: 666140, fax: 689673. A charming hotel situated on a quiet residential street. Reasonable rates and an unpretentious ambience. Double room 50JD.

Al Maqsura. Shmaysani, opposite Safeway. Tel: 698222, fax: 690671. The only hotel in Amman that would pass as a motel, but the standard is superior to the American equivalents. Kitchenette, satellite TV and in-house movies; suites have sofa beds. There's a small play area for children behind the hotel on the edge of a secure parking lot. Front terrace and restaurant. Alcohol-free zone. Not well known amongst the Western crowd but good value for money. Double room 20-30JD.

The Commodore Hotel. Shmaysani, around the corner from Safeway. Tel: 607185, fax: 668187. On the lower end of 3-star scale, and so are the rooms. Hodge-podge decor, all standard conveniences and access to neighbouring Middle East Hotel outdoor swimming pool free of charge. Double room 35JD.

Ambassador Hotel. Shmaysani, opposite American Express. Tel: 605161, fax: 681101. Offers 97 rooms and suites tastefully decorated and equipped with all standard conveniences, although a bit pricey for a 3-star establishment. Babysitters can be arranged. Nice coffee shop in addition to bar and restaurant. Tourist office and rent-a-car right outside the hotel. Double room 60JD.

Amman International. Jubayha. Tel: 841712/3, fax: 841171. Modest comfortable rooms and suites. Rates include breakfast. Facilities: outdoor swimming pool, billiard room, restaurant and bar. Good for those who want to be in the university area or with their own transportation. Double room 35JD.

☆☆
Canary Hotel. Jebel Al-Luwaybida, opposite Terra Sancta college. Tel: 638353, fax: 661196. Offers 21 comfortable rooms equipped with en suite bathroom, TV and balcony overlooking one of the oldest neighbourhoods in Amman. A couple of larger rooms for four persons and with attached dining alcove are available. Homey communal dining area opposite lobby and pleasant front garden make this hotel a good place for single travellers as well as families on a budget. Double room 28JD.

Caravan Hotel. Jebel Al-Luwaybida, opposite the King Abdullah Mosque (also known as the Blue Mosque). Tel: 661195/7, fax: 661196. Pleasant rooms, most with standing shower only. Small sitting areas outside rooms, cheery lobby and communal dining area. Use of kitchen for light meals with advance notice. Light sleepers beware - The call to prayer is highly audible! Double 28JD.

Hotel Al Remal. Abadali, opposite police station. Tel: 615585. Doesn't look too appealing from the outside but actually not bad inside. TV can be arranged for longer occupancy. Fax and telex. Hotel cafeteria through seperate entrance next door. A bit noisy during the day. Double 18JD.

☆
Cleopatra Hotel. Abdali, opposite bus station. Tel: 646959. Rooms are drab but adequate. Bathrooms en suite (Turkish toilets without toilet paper). Hot water in afternoon only. Not the best value but bearable if you're just passing through and need a cheap place to flop, close to bus station. Double 9JD.

Al Monzer. Abdali, opposite bus station (one flight up from Cleopatra). Tel: 639469, fax: 657328. Same price as the Cleopatra but slightly more inviting thanks to brighter lobby. European-style toliets and hot water 24 hours a day. No alcohol on premises. Double 9JD.

Sunrise Hotel. Abdali, opposite the bus station. Tel: 621841. Rates are slightly cheaper and better than neighbouring hotels. Bathroom facilities vary enormously. If the hotel is not packed guests may use hotel facilities to prepare light meals. Double 8.500JD.

New Park Hotel. Downtown, King Hussein Street. A bit more expensive than the other places on this street but some rooms are worth it. First and second class rooms available. Double: 10-15JD.

The Lord Hotel. Tel: 654167. Downtown, near New Park Hotel. Tel: 612144/5, fax: 648145. Decent for its price range. Most rooms have bath-rooms, although same rates apply for those without bathroom facilities. Unless privacy is a priority, use the showers off the corridor, these tend to be larger and considerably cleaner. Communal fridge. Double 9JD.

Palace Hotel. Downtown, opposite Haifa hotel. Tel: 624327, fax: 650603. One of the largest hotels downtown and probably the most decent in its price range. Rates are comparable to the Cleopatra and Al Monzer, but the place is much cleaner and brighter. Double 11.50JD

ROCK BOTTOM PRICES

Cliff Hotel. Downtown, opposite Khalifah stores. Tel: 624273. Most popular among backpackers and budget travellers and has the closest thing to a youth hostel atmosphere. Rates are charged per bed and showers cost extra. Shared bathroom facilities. Free storage. If you're really broke you can sleep on the roof in summer for half price. Sometimes single men are turned away. Bed 2.500JD; Roof 1.500JD.

The Baghdad Hotel. Downtown, near the Cliff. The hotel lacks character and is slightly more expensive than the Cliff for roughly the same standard. Showers are included, but water is hot only in the morning. Those travelling with sleeping bags or spare sheets might find their stay here more comfortable. Bed 3JD

The Farouk Hotel. Downtown, opposite Arab Bank. Keep climbing up the stairs until you cometo a door which looks as though it leads to the roof – which is exactly what it does. The lobby of this place is literally the roof, definitely a plus during the warm summer months. Overall, it's small and a bit creepy. Women are best off avoiding this place altogether. Double 5JD.

The Yarmouk. Downtown, near the Farouk Hotel. The price depends on nationality and appearance. With the right combination (though it's unclear what is ideal) you may get the lowest rate in town. Shared bathroom and no lobby area. Bed 2-4JD.

Haifa Hotel. Downtown, opposite the Yarmouk. This 27-year-old hotel has certainly seen better days but it still bears traces of its past grandeur. Rooms are a bit larger and sunnier than other places in the budget range. Bed 2JD.

HOLIDAY FLATS

Turino. Suwayfiya. Tel: 818637, fax: 679304. Flatlets are slightly ostentatious by Western standards but management offers every convenience. Services include babysitters, business centre and newspaper delivery, valet parking, AT&T international dialling, and free use of local health club. Apartment average is 80JD for 2 beds.
Darotel. Shmaysani. Tel: 607193, fax: 602434. Offers short-let apartments with hotel services. Prices vary according to standard and space. Ice machine, shoe-shine and small fitness room on premises. Discounts of up to 50 percent during the winter season. Apartment 50JD for 2 people.
Olympia. Abdoun. Tel: 810150, fax: 827113. One-bedroom apartments are surprisingly modest for such a swanky neighbourhood. King-size sofa-bed in living-room offers extra sleeping space. Check the apartment allocated as some need minor repairs. Coffee-shop in lobby doubles as bar in evening. Single apartment (only) 40JD.

YOUTH HOSTELS

YWCA. Jebel Amman, near Second Circle. Tel: 621488. Priority given to Arab women residing in Amman but space is sometimes available for travelling foreign women. Smoking is forbidden in rooms and guests must abide by YWCA rules. The 10.30pm nightly curfew is extended to midnight on Thursdays. Advisable to call in advance.

PENSIONS

La Bonita (tel: 615061, fax: 615060) and the **As-Sabeel** (tel: 630571, fax: 630572), both near Third Circle. Both offer pension-style accommodation above their popular restaurants and give good rates for people staying for long periods. Frequented by employees of international organisations and diplomats. Double rooms 30JD.

Aqaba

☆☆☆☆
Coral Beach. Tel: 03-313521. One of the nicest hotels in Aqaba, suitable for those who want to relax in peace rather than indulge in sports and night-life. Double room 48JD, plus 20 percent tax.
Holiday International Hotel. Tel: 03-312426. Formerly the Holiday Inn, it offers excellent facilities but is the most expensive. Double room 50JD residents, 70JD non-residents, plus 20 percent tax. Rates include breakfast.

☆☆☆
Aqaba Hotel. Tel: 03-314091/2. Situated on the beach with air-conditioned rooms and bungalows, it offers a very good service. There is also a night club and some watersports. Double room 43JD-53JD non-residents, 25JD-30JD residents, inclusive of breakfast and tax.
Aquamarina I, II, III. Tel: 03-316250. This group of hotels specialises in watersports. The best facilities are provided by Aquamarina I, the only one on the beach, but these are freely available to guests at the other two hotels. All three are popular, so book in advance. Double room 24JD without seaview, 29-32JD with seaview, plus 20 percent tax. Room only.
Nairoukh II. Tel: 03-312980. This hotel is not on the beach but it has free access to the beach of the Aqaba and Aquamarina hotels. Rooms have TV, fridge and telephone. Double room 25JD plus 10 percent tax including breakfast.

☆
Al-Jameel Hotel. Tel: 03-314118. In the city centre of Aqaba. Air-conditioned rooms, rare in its price range, with hot water and balcony. Double room 6JD without breakfast.

Azraq

Azraq Resthouse. Tel: 681028 ext. 6. All 24 rooms have their own bathroom, mini-bar, and TV and are air-conditioned - a major consideration. Double room 29JD with breakfast.
Hunter Hotel (Al Sayed). Tel: 06-647611 ext: 94.

Petra

Taybet Zaman Village. Tel: 06-661014, fax: 06-669905. This brand-new holiday complex, built by the owners of Kan Zaman, is located 9km (5½ miles) south of Petra. It claims to be environment-friendly using natural toiletries and chemical-free fruits and vegetables. Mid-19th century village houses have been transformed into bungalows with magnificent views of the Petra mountains. They have under-floor heating and cooling, minibar, satellite TV, direct dial telephones and fax upon request. The Village has its own bakery, steam bath, swimming pool, fitness room and town square. Double room US$88–110 plus 20 percent tax.

☆☆☆☆
Petra Forum Hotel. Tel: 06-634200 fax: 634201. Situated next to the entrance of the site this has been for many years the most comfortable hotel in Petra but also the most pricey. It offers air-conditioned, centrally heated rooms, all with private bathrooms, telephone and mini-bar. There is also an outdoor swimming pool overlooking the mountains and a restaurant inside the site. Double room 70JD plus 20 percent service and government tax, without breakfast.

☆☆☆
Palace Hotel. Tel: 03-336723, fax: 03-336724. Near the entrance to the site. No air-conditioning but rooms have TV. Double room 20JD room only.

☆☆
Petra Resthouse. Tel: 03-336011/4 fax: 336686. Budget accommodation with or without air-conditioning, but all rooms have private bathrooms. Advisable to book well in advance during the busy season. Double room 29–44JD, including breakfast.
Flower City Hotel. Tel: 03-336440, fax: 336448. Near the square, 15 minutes' walk from site entrance. All rooms with central heating, TV, fridge and hot water. Some also have air-conditioning. Double room 25JD with breakfast and tax. Price negotiable in summer.

Irbid

☆☆☆
Ar-Razi Hotel. Tel: 02-275510. Near Yarmouk University. It has a coffee shop, bar and restaurant and rooms have TV and fans. Double room 30JD plus 10 percent.
Hejazi Hotel. Tel: 02-279500, fax: 279520. Well located in Irbid, with small but well-equipped rooms. Four-star facilities. Its downstairs café has music and is very popular with students. Double room 60JD.

Dead Sea

Dead Sea Spa Hotel. Tel: 09-802028, 601554, fax: 688100. The ideal place for a quiet health retreat. It has a private beach as well as a swimming pool, fitness and anti-stress programmes,

Jacuzzi, vegetarian menu, special diet plans, mud packs. Double room 48JD half-board, including tax, for residents; 70JD B&B non-residents.

Jerash

Dibeen Resthouse. Tel: 04-452413. Has 19 bungalows in the heart of the National Park a few kilometres from Jerash and is ideal for those who want to go walking. All the rooms have private bathrooms, telephone, fridge, TV and portable heaters and there is a play area for children. However, it has no restaurant, only a snack bar. Not suitable for those without private transport. Double room 16JD without breakfast.

Ajlun

☆☆
Qala'at Ar-Rabad. Tel: 04-462202. Near the castle. Rooms are simple, with bathrooms, hot water and balconies, the view is beautiful. Double room 15JD.
Ajlun Hotel. Tel: 04-462524. Rooms with bathroom, TV, central heating and balconies. Double room 20JD.

Kerak

Resthouse. Tel: 03-351148. There are 13 rooms with private bathrooms heated in the winter as well as a restaurant and bar and a TV lounge. Double/single room 34JD.
Castle Hotel. Tel: 03-352489. Basic, but really the only option if the resthouse is full. Double 7JD.

Hammamat Ma'in

Ashtar Hotel, double rooms with breakfast cost $90 for non-resident foreigners and $70 for Jordanians and foreign residents (who can also take advantage of special 3-night half-board packages). Prices include use of the outdoor cold-water swimming pool, sauna, indoor hot water pool and gym but not health clinic with its hydro- and mud-therapy and massage services.

Campgrounds

The only site that could qualify under this category is located in Dana, south of Tafila. It has clean and architecturally designed toilets that make a big impression on every visitor. The location is beautiful, inside the Nature Reserve.

Syria

The only hotel chain covering the whole of Syria is **Cham Palaces and Hotels**, which has hotels in all the main tourist destinations, including four hotels in Damascus. Their designation "palace" signifies large, luxurious hotels with all facilities. Their "hotels" tend to be comfortable but smaller establishments.

Aleppo

Chahba Cham Palace, Damascus Road, Aleppo. Tel: (21) 248572/ 215272. Aleppo's only five-star hotel.

Bosra

Bosra Cham Palace, PO Box 7570 Damascus. Tel: (151) 23502. Brand-new hotel in the heart of the city. Tennis courts and swimming pool.

Damascus

Le Meriden, Choukri Kouatly Road. Tel: (1) 718730/229200. Well situated in the heart of the city. Close to the National Museum. All facilities, including swimming pool, tennis courts and nightclub.
Cham Palace, Maysaloun Street, Damascus. Tel: (11) 232300-232320. In the heart of the city. Its many facilities include the only Chinese and revolving restaurants in Syria.
Ebla Cham Palace, Airport Road, Damascus. Tel: (11) 241900. Set in extensive grounds halfway between the city centre and the airport. Offers horse riding and golf.
Techrine Cham Hotel. Tel: 11-225077/ 225142. Damascus. Relatively small hotel, with air-conditioned rooms, one restaurant and bar. Access to nearby tennis courts and swimming pool.
Jallaa Cham Hotel, PO Box 9067. Damascus. Tel: 11-664946/47. Pleasant small hotel in Mazzé area of town. Access to nearby tennis courts and swimming pool. Squash court.
Orient Palace Hotel. Tel: 11-2220501 Comfortable older style hotel near the Hejaz railway station. Less expensive than any of the above.
Sultan Hotel, Moussallam Baroudy Road. Tel: 11-225768. More basic, but clean and pleasant and also near the Hejaz railway station. Inexpensive. Other medium range hotels include the **New Omayyad Hotel** (Tel: 11-2217700), **New Semiramis**, (Tel: 02-

894455), and the lower end has a jewel, the **Al-Bassam Hotel**, opposite the Hamadiya market.

Deir Ezzor

Furat Cham Palace, Aleppo Road, PO Box 219. Tel: 51-25418/25126. At the city entrance, on the banks of the Euphrates river. Every luxury.

Hama

Apamee Cham Palace, PO Box 7570 Damascus. Tel: 331-27429. Five-star hotel overlooking the Orontes river. Swimming pool and tennis courts.

Lattakia

Le Meridien, BP 473. Tel: 41-229000/ 3/4/5. Situated in woodlands on the coast about 7 km (4 miles) from the city centre. Offers windsurfing and jet ski.
Cote d'Azur de Cham, PO Box 1079. Tel: 41-26333/34. On the beach about 10 km (6 miles) from the city centre. A less expensive hotel with self-catering facilities, Cote d'Azur de Cham Residence, is attached.

Palmyra

Palmyra Cham Palace, PO Box 7570. Tel: 31-37000. Luxury hotel right next to the ruins, about 2 km (1 mile) from the city. Facilities include an ancient cave bath with sulphuric waters.

Safita

Safita Cham Hotel, PO Box 25. Tel: 321-25980. Small hotel overlooking the rolling valleys of this mountain resort. Swimming pool.

Jerusalem

East Jerusalem has hotels to suit all budgets. At the top end there is the **American Colony**, Nablus Street (Tel: 02-285171), a small but very attractive renovated 19th-century villa which serves the best food in town, and **Seven Arches** (Tel: 02-894455), in the Mount of Olives, with beautiful views (especially sunsets) of the Old City. Medium range includes excellent places like the **YMCA East**, the **National Palace** and the quaint **Al-Zahra Hotel** all in the same vicinity. For budget travellers, very clean and cheap accommodation can be found with religious establishments and a number of youth hostels.

Eating Out

What To Eat

In culinary terms Jordan is bracketed with Syria, Lebanon and Palestine and as such enjoys one of the world's most sophisticated and elaborate cuisines. (There are very few dishes that are unique to Jordan but one of them is *mansaf*.) If you have been in other parts of the Arab world you will already know that food is a very important part of Arab culture and used to express hospitality and generosity. Jordanian people are very hospitable and often it is a matter of minutes before you are asked to their house or shop for tea and coffee or to a meal with their family. Jordanians will be proud to host you at home no matter how modest their means and they will always try their very best. A Jordanian invitation means that you are expected to bring nothing and eat everything.

At home all dishes, main course and appetisers, are served together but in restaurants the appetisers, which are known as *mezze* or *muqabalat*, are brought first; then, if you are still hungry, you will be asked to order your meat or fish. A meal usually ends with seasonal fruit. Some people eat with their hands at home and some dishes, like *mussakhan*, are also eaten with hands at restaurants.

Mezze or Muqabalat

Hoummous: a purée of chick-peas blended with *tahina* (pulped sesame seeds), lemon and garlic. This is the most common of all the *muqabalat* and for many people it is a meal in itself.

Baba ghanoush: a dip made of the pulp of cooked aubergine which is at its best when it's been cooked over charcoal and has a wonderful smokey flavour. When it is mixed with *tahina* it is also called *moutabbal*, although the distinction is not always made.

Ful moudames: a pauper's meal which somehow made its way to the table of the better off and you will come across it in the Arabic breakfast served at your hotel and at street restaurants. It consists of boiled brown beans served with crushed garlic and lemon juice and topped with olive oil. Dip your bread in it and enjoy.

Koubba (or Kibbe) maqliya: a deep fried oval-shaped ball with a meat and bulgar wheat paste as its crust and an aromatic filling of minced meat and pine nuts in the middle. It must be eaten hot to be enjoyed. Making *koubba* requires a lot of skill and talent so the smaller their size and the thinner their crust, the more skilled the cook that made them. You'll find the best *koubba* at home and not at a restaurant. It is also served in a warm yoghurt-based sauce.

Vine leaves: stuffed with rice and/or meat, herbs and spices.

Fattayer and sambusak: small baked pastries filled with minced meat, or with a white salty cheese from Nablus and herbs, or with spinach and *soummak*, a slightly sour dark-red powdered seed.

Taboula: a salad of freshly chopped parsley, tomatoes, spring onions and fresh mint mixed with soaked bulgar wheat and sprinkled with lemon juice.

Main course

Nothing can beat the taste of Middle Eastern grilled meats cooked on skewers over a charcoal fire. Some of the most common grills available in restaurants are *shish taouk*, a delicious low-fat dish of boneless chicken pieces served with lemon juice and garlic, *kofta kebab*, spicy minced lamb and *shish kebab*, cubes of boneless lamb or beef.

Jordan's national dish *par excellence* is *mansaf* and it is a real fortune to be able to taste it in a Jordanian home. It consists of big chunks of stewed lamb in a white yoghurt-based sauce served with rice. In a Bedouin household it is placed on a low round table with the guests and family gathered around it, and is eaten with the right hand. If your hosts happen to be of Palestinian origin they are more likely to serve *mussakhan*, chicken quarters baked and served on pieces of flat soft bread covered with chopped onions, pine-nuts and plenty of *soummak* or *maghlouba* ("upside-down"), which is made of rice mixed with large chunks of chicken, lamb, or fish with vegetables moulded and turned upside down to serve.

A good supply of fresh fish is a relatively new phenomenon in Amman. As a rule, it is prepared on a charcoal fire, fried or cooked according to traditional recipes, like the famous *sayadiya*, boiled fish served on a bed of rice topped with a lemon sauce.

Sweets

Sweets, home-made or bought, are prominent and devoured in huge quantities during Ramadan, Muslim and Christian feasts and, of course, at weddings. However, beautifully arranged trays of sweets are on display at patisseries all year round and they can be packed especially for you to take back home (see *What to Buy*). One type of sweet that is most common all over the Middle East, albeit with many variations, comprises layers of pastry filled with cream or chopped nuts such as almonds, walnuts or pistachios and soaked in a thick syrup.

Baklawa: thin layers of pastry (filo pastry) with chopped nuts in the middle and covered with syrup.

Konafa: shredded dough which looks like very fine vermicelli filled with nuts or slightly salted white cheese.

Ataif: a medieval recipe for small, deep fried pancakes stuffed with nuts or white cheese and coated with syrup. Eaten in Ramadan only.

Ma'amoul: baked pastries with nuts or dates perfumed with rose water.

Other sweets are based on milk, like *mohallabiya*, a pudding made of milk thickened with rice flour and perfumed with rose or orange-flower water and the elastic *mastic* ice-cream, which is made with the powdered sahlab root and flavoured with mastic or Arabic gum, a resin that gives it its texture. It's usually coated with chopped nuts.

Sahlab: hot milk drink made with the powdered sahlab root and served with chopped pistachios, cinnamon and rose water.

Take-Away Food

You will find a wide variety of cheap, delicious Middle Eastern fast food is sold at street stalls and restaurants.

Shawarma: thin cuts of beef, lamb or chicken cooked on the spit and stuffed into pitta bread with *tahina* and pickles.

Falafel: small deep-fried balls of dried

white broad beans crushed and mixed with chopped onions, garlic, parsley and spices. It is often served as a sandwich inside a hot pitta bread with *tahina* and salad but can also be eaten on its own. This is regarded as pauper's food and is rarely served in good restaurants. You'll enjoy it best on the street where it's served hot and fresh out of the pan.

Ma'ajanat: meaning pastries made with dough (*ajin*), such as *fattayer*, *sambusak* and also *manaeesh* (flat bread with powdered oregano and sesame seeds), or *sfeeha*, a flat dough spread with spicy minced meat.

Where To Eat

Amman has many restaurants that serve top quality Arabic food. When Jordanians go out to eat they expect at least the same high standard of cooking that they would have at home. Unfortunately, the same is not the case with the foreign cuisine available locally. Here quality varies and it is very rarely exceptional, even though Amman has a host of Italian, Far Eastern and 'continental' restaurants.

Although it is difficult to generalise about the standards of restaurant hygiene in Jordan as a whole, it is safe to say that Jordan is one of the cleanest countries in the region as far as food is concerned, but if you have not had vaccination shots before travelling it may be wise to enquire about the reputation of an eating establishment before you make use of it and to go easy with uncooked vegetables. When you are faced with a buffet meal check the freshness of the salads and cold meats and refrain if they look as if they have been sitting there for a while. The restaurants listed below are generally known to be safe choices in this respect.

There are no vegetarian restaurants in Jordan but vegetarians will have a real feast with Arabic food (most of the many appetisers are suitable). Where available, fish makes an excellent alternative to meat dishes for a main course. You can also have excellent vegetarian meals in Amman'sItalian restaurants.

The recommendations that follow include a guide to price, based on the average cost of meal with appetiser and main course per person:

£ – Inexpensive: 4JD and under
££ – Medium: 5JD–9JD
£££ – Expensive: 10JD and over

In Arabic restaurants it is perfectly acceptable to have only a selection of starters (*muqabalat*) rather than a full-blown meal. In this case the price of the meal is lower, and we take this into consideration in the price guide.

During the hot months many restaurants serve in their outdoor terraces and gardens or have air-conditioning. Establishments without summer facilities are indicated. Outdoor eating starts in May and ends at the end of October. Jordanians tend to eat late, with lunch at around 2pm and dinner at 9pm. However, restaurants open earlier, at 12.30pm for lunch and at 7.30pm for dinner. All the restaurants listed below serve alcohol except for lower range restaurants. During Ramadan many restaurants close for the whole month because they are not allowed to sell alcohol and their profits are low. Those that do open serve food only after sunset when the fast is broken; some of these offer fantastic Ramadan specials.

Amman and other towns in Jordan are relatively small and restaurants are generally known. Therefore we give only the general area where restaurants are located - so precise addresses would be of no help - no one uses them let alone understands them.

Amman

MIDDLE EASTERN & JORDANIAN

Al-Bustan. University Road, near Jerusalem Hotel. Probably the best known restaurant in Amman and definitely the best Arabic food in town. Lebanese and Jordanian cuisine at its best served with freshly baked bread. Outdoor verandah in the summer. ££

Kan Zaman restaurant. Yaduda, 12 km (7 miles) south of Amman off the Desert highway. A popular restaurant inside the renovated stables of an old house serving Arabic food from an impressive buffet. Bread is made in front of you and the waiters join up for a brief dance, the *dabkeh*. ££

Al-Baydar (also a branch in Kan Zaman) offers similar food in a more intimate atmosphere, with live piano music. ££–£££

Al-Waha. Al-Waha Circle, at the end of

Gardens Street. Excellent Arabic food eaten at low brass tables with traditional decor, log-fire in the winter and outdoor Bedouin tent in the summer. ££

Sakhan Ad-Dimashq. Shmaysani, opposite Jordan Gulf Bank. Excellent cheap Arabic food served in a Damascene interior. So clean, you could eat off the floors. Famous for its *shawarma* which attracts long queues. £

Mata'am Hashem. Downtown, in a small alleyway off the main street. A favourite with local Egyptian labourers, it serves excellent *ful moudames*, *falaffel* and *hoummous* with tons of oil. No alcohol. £

Ma'atouq. Third Circle, Jebel Amman. Fast-serving Arabic *mezze*, grills and sweets, superb *hoummous*. One of the best cheap restaurants. £

Okaz Restaurant. Intercontinental Hotel. Lunchtime Lebanese buffet for Friday lunch and a mixture of continental and Middle Eastern buffet daily for lunch and dinner. £££

Jabri. Shmaysani and Gardens Street. A good chance to taste a wide selection of local dishes served fast in hearty portions cafeteria-style. Packed during the holidays and excellent value for money. No alcohol. £

Ana Amman. Above the Roman amphitheatre, downtown. Grilled meats and *mezze*. The main attraction here is the view rather than the food. ££

Al-Khadeeqa. Shmaysani, opposite the Mukhabarat (the headquarters of the Security Police). Good Arabic food and a garden in the warm weather. ££

La Terrasse. Shmaysani, opposite Jabri's on second and third floors. Delicious Arabic starters and continental main courses. Outdoor terrace in the summer. ££–£££

Abu Ahmad's. Two branches: the **Orient** at Basman Street, downtown and the **New Orient** at the Third Circle, Jebel Amman, both known as Abu Ahmad's. During the warmer months the Third Circle branch offers the advantage of a garden-setting. Arabic food served with freshly baked bread, good grilled meats but *muqabalat* portions are relatively poor in both size and quality. ££

Qasr Snober. Off the Desert highway 10 km (6 miles) from Amman and well signposted. Good Arabic food combines with a nice outing into the countryside. ££

Filfila. Shmaysani, next to Kentucky Fried Chicken. A small, inexpensive place serving a limited range of delicious dishes. Grilled meats are recommended. Also take-away. No alcohol. £

ITALIAN

Romero's. Opposite the Intercontinental Hotel, near the Third Circle, Jebel Amman. A very popular choice with elegant locals and great for its social scene. The food is very good, the service is excellent and the interior decoration is very tasteful. Its homemade *nociolla* (hazelnut) is the best ice cream in town. Outdoor eating in the summer. ££–£££

Leonardo Da Vinci. Shmaysani, next to the Islamic Bank. Excellent food with a salad bar. Only drawback – for tall people – is the low ceiling. ££–£££

Turino. Suwayfiya. Excellent Italian food in a neoclassical kitsch decor. ££– £££

Cheers. Next to Turino. Good Italian and American food in an informal atmosphere. Satellite TV. £

Milano. Shmaysani. The best pizza in town. Delicious sandwiches and salads. Very popular with well-heeled Jordanian youth. £

Nouroz. Third Circle, Jebel Amman. Italian only in so far as it makes delicious pizza. It also serves fast meat grills, salads and basic Arabic *mezze*. £

Bonita. Near the Third Circle. Some Italian food, Spanish paella and other good international cuisine. Also a bar and outdoor eating in the summer. ££

FRENCH

L' Olivie. Abdoun. The finest cuisine in one of the most expensive restaurants in town. Also the most popular in its price range. Live music. Book in advance. £££

INDIAN

Bukhara. Jordan Intercontinental Hotel, near the Third Circle, Jebel Amman. Wide range of Indian dishes including vegetarian, in a pleasant atmosphere. £££

Bykhara. Behind College de la Salle known as Frères school, Jebel Al-Hussein. Small range of delicately spiced meat and fish cooked in a tandoor oven by an Indian cook. No alcohol. £

Mankal Chicken. Gardens Street and Abdali. Chicken tikka and Arabic starters. £

FAR EASTERN

Taiwan Tourismo. Opposite the Akileh Hospital, near the Third Circle, Jebel Amman. Probably the best Chinese food in town in a very modest setting. No air-conditioning, only fans. ££

Peking. Opposite the Al-Qasr Hotel, Shmaysani. The decor is more impressive than the cuisine but it is one of the most tasteful Chinese restaurants in its price range. VIP lounges for special occasions. £-££

China Town. At the Forte Grand Hotel, Shmaysani. Good food and variety. Beautifully decorated individual rooms (enclosed by Chinese screens) for private parties. ££–£££

Restaurant China. Opposite Ahliya school, near First Circle. The first Chinese restaurant in town and still one of the most popular.

CONTINENTAL

Rozena. Part of the Sabeel Hotel suites, near the Second Circle, Jebel Amman. A homely interior and a pleasant summer terrace. Very good food, except for dessert. Excellent service and a friendly atmosphere thanks to its manager.

PATISSERIES & CAFÉS

In Amman you find Arabic as well as French-style coffee house: cafés where you can enjoy a cake or ice-cream or enjoy a *nargheeleh* (water pipe) and Arabic coffee while watching the world go by. There is a concentration of Western-style patisseries in Shmaysani.

Babiche. Shmaysani. The best treat for a sweet tooth that you are likely to find in Amman. Enjoy its splendid fruit tarts and chocolate mousse cake in a nice ambience enhanced by the gentle rhythms of Greek music. Also sandwiches and *ma'ajanat*.

Jabri (downtown) Shmaysani and Gardens Street. Cakes and ice-cream including mastic ice-cream.

Coffee House El-Farouki. Shmaysani and Jebel Al-Hussein. It grinds its own coffee.

La Patisserie. The Marriott Hotel, Shmaysani.

Vienna. Amra Hotel.

Phoenik. Gardens Street. A hang-out for young returnees from Kuwait, where you can eat, drink and see an exhibition.

The Arab League Café. Faces the King Hussein Mosque. A true Arabic café but a man's domain.

Frosti's. Shmaysani. Ice-cream parlour serving the only frozen yoghurt in the country.

Safeway restaurant (top floor). For the best value-for-money Western-style breakfast in town.

SNACK BARS & PUBS

Salute, Second Circle (near Rozena restaurant). Amman's newest bar offers an exotic menu of alcoholic and non-alcoholic cocktails and coffee liqueurs. Book on Thursday nights.

Al-Hannah Pub at the Intercontinental Hotel. Expensive drinks but a great meeting place. Also famous for its Wednesday night quiz. There is a 3JD minimum charge. Satellite TV.

After Eight. Attached to the Amigo Nabeel restaurant, near First Circle. Very small but with a good atmosphere. A hang-out for local journalists.

Cellar's at Al-Qasr Hotel. Often features live music. Reservations are a must on Thursday nights.

Graffiti. At the Shepheard Hotel, near Second Circle. Live music, graffiti on the walls, outside garden in summer.

The Wall. Also at the Shepheard. Featuring rock and blues music. There is a 2JD cover charge Monday and Thursday nights.

Hisham Hotel Bar. Near Third Circle. Particularly nice in the summer when you can sit outside.

Tapas Bar (Bonita). Near Third Circle. Live music in the winter and outdoor terrace in the summer.

Aqaba

Ali Baba. Known for its fish and Arabic food. Wine are wrapped up in green paper due to local sensitivities. ££

Chinese Restaurant. Aqaba. There are two of these in town; both are good but the most recent is one of the best of its kind in the country. ££

Mina House. Tel: 312699. In an old tug boat moored past the Mamluke fort and museum. Fresh fish and barbecued meat

---

Jerash

Lebanese House (also known as **Um Khalil's**). Half a kilometre south of the hippodrome, off the road to Ajlun. The best Arabic food in Jordan, bar none. A favourite with Jordanians and other visiting Arabs who will drive up from Am-

man just for lunch or dinner here. ££
Ya Hala. Inside the town itself and near the northern end of the archaeological site. A good second to Um Khalil's. Large garden with a water pool and artificial streams. ££
Abu Yehia's. On the road to Amman, marked only with a 7-Up sign. Excellent meat dishes. £
Green Valley Restaurant. Tel: 452093 or 450299. On the Jerash-Amman road. Excellent shish and kofta kebabs, supported by great bread and dips. Alcohol served. ££

Pella

Resthouse in Pella. Run by Romero's in Amman, it is nicely decorated and serves snacks and beverages including alcohol. Wonderful view of the Jordan Valley.

Umm Qais

Restaurant at Umm Qais. Tel: 02-217210 or 02-217081 ext. 59. Run by the owner of Romero's in Amman, it offers delicious Arabic food with the most spectacular view of the ruins of ancient Gadara, Lake Tiberias and the Golan Heights. Advisable to book in advance. ££

There are many other places where one can eat clean, decent food in Irbid, Ajlun, in Petra town and at the Azraq and Wadi Rum resthouses.

Drinking Notes

Most restaurants and hotel bars in Amman and outside serve alcohol except during Ramadan when alcohol sales and drinking are banned. Jordanians can be seen drinking in many central locations in Amman. Jordan has its own beer, the excellent Amstel brewed locally under licence. A big bottle costs just over 1JD to buy in a shop and anything between 50–200 percent more in bars and restaurants. Wine is imported from the "Holy Land", Tunisia, Cyprus and France. The best of the Palestinian wines are the Domaine de Latroun wines, especially the Pinots and Sauvignons, as well as the Caregnano. Alcohol can be purchased at many grocer's and supermarkets. Safeway stocks the widest selection in foreign wines.

Attractions

Culture

Jordan has a rapidly developing fine art scene and, to a lesser degree, theatre and poetry that are indigenous to the country and the Middle East region. Music, ballet and film are imported and, this being a relatively poor and small country, are very costly to operate and therefore appear irregularly and often under sponsorship. Many of the cultural activities in Amman take place at the Royal Cultural Centre, which comprises theatres, conference and exhibition halls. The foreign cultural centres are very active in organising lectures, exhibitions, film shows and occasional plays and recitals promoting the work of Jordanian and other Arab artists and intellectuals as well as their own nationals.

Archaeological Sites

Some of the archaeological sites are open all the time and can be visited during daylight hours without paying an entry fee. Others are enclosed with a fence and access is confined to certain hours which are standard for all sites around the country (except Petra), namely every day of the year, even on feasts and during Ramadan, winter 8am–5pm, summer 8am–6pm. At some of these sites the Department of Antiquities charges an entry fee which varies for Jordanians and non-Jordanians. The prices listed below apply only to non-Jordanians. It is forbidden to camp or spend the nights at any of the sites.

AMMAN

Citadel, Roman Amphitheatre, Nymphaeum, Nuwayjis, Rujm Al-Malfouf and Ain Ghazzal are open sites. The Suwayfiyya mosaic, Quwaysima and the Cave of the Seven Sleepers are open during standard hours and entry is free.
Ajlun Castle. Open standard hours. Entry free.

Aqaba. Castle and Ayla are open sites.
Desert Castles. Open sites.
Jerash. Open standard hours. Entry 2JD.
Kerak Castle. Open standard hours. Entry 1JD including the museum.
Madaba, Mount Nebo, Um Ar-Resas and other sites in the Madaba region. Open standard hours. Entry free. Churches of St George and the Apostles in Madaba are closed on Sunday.

PETRA

Open daily winter 7am–5pm, summer 7am–6pm. Entry fee for non-Jordanians and non-resident foreigners 20JD for one day, 25JD for two days and 30JD for three days; for resident foreigners and Jordanians: 0.250JD. This price includes access to the two museums but not horse rental. To rent a horse you will have to pay 6JD for the return journey, excluding tip. Horse rental is optional. You should buy a ticket at the nearby kiosk which will give you the rota number of the horse you will be renting. You may also rent a horse for the return leg only but beware: you may be asked outrageous rates - don't settle for anything more than half to two-thirds of the official round trip price.
Shobak. Open standard hours. Entry free.
Umm Qais. 1JD.
Um al-Jimal. Open site.

Museums

AMMAN

Jordan Archaeological Museum. Citadel. Tel: 638795. Finds from excavations all around Jordan dating from prehistoric times to the 15th century. Open 8am–5pm, closed Tuesday. Entry 2JD for non-Arabs.
Jordanian Museum of Popular Tradition. At the Roman amphitheatre. Tel: 651760. Founded by Sa'adiya At-Tell, wife of Wasfi At-Tell, the Prime Minister who was assassinated in 1971, this is probably the most impressive little museum in Jordan, with fragments of Byzantine mosaics and old costumes and jewellery well displayed. Open 9am–5pm, closed Tuesday. Entry 1JD for non-Arabs.
Jordanian Folklore Museum. At the Roman amphitheatre. Tel: 651742. An effort to recreate traditional life in Jordan with various artifacts such as a

tent, home furnishings, musical instruments and handicrafts. Open 9am–5pm, closed Tuesday. Entry 1JD for non-Arabs.

Jordan University Archaeological Museum. University Campus. Tel: 843555, ext. 3412. Artefacts dating from the Bronze Age to the Islamic period found all over the country. Open 8am–5pm, closed Thursday and Friday. Entry free.

Jordan University National Folklore Museum. University Campus. Tel: 843555, ext. 3739. Open 8am–5pm, closed Thursday and Friday.

Jordan University Biology/Medical Museum. University Campus. Tel: 843555, ext. 2300. Open 8am–5pm, closed Thursday and Friday.

Jordan Postal Museum-Ministry of Communications. Ministry of Communications (the very modern building on Eighth Circle, Jebel Amman). Tel: 624301. Old and new Jordanian stamps. Open 8am–2pm, closed Friday. Entry free.

Coin Museum. Central Bank of Jordan, King Hussein Street (Sharia Salt), downtown. Tel: 630301. Ancient and modern Jordanian coins. Open 9am–2pm, closed Tuesday and Friday.

Military Museum (Martyrs' Memorial). Sports City (Medina Riadhiya) University Road. Tel: 664240. Military memorabilia from the Great Arab Revolt of 1916 to more recent wars. Open 9am–4pm, closed Saturday. Entry free.

Children's Heritage and Science Museum. Haya Arts Centre, Shmaysani. Tel: 665195. Open 9am–1.30pm, 3.30–5.30pm, closed Friday. Entry free.

Museum of Aqaba's Antiquities. Near the Mamluke fort. Tel: 03-313731. Displays from excavations in Ayla. Open daily 9am–5pm. Entry 1JD for non-Arabs.

The Aqaba Marine Science Station. Aquarium hosting the marine life of Gulf of Aqaba. Tel: 03-315144/5. Open daily 8am–5pm. Entry 0.500JD for non-Jordanians.

Archaeological Museum. Tel: 02-277066. Open 8am–5pm, closed Tuesday. Entry free.

Museum of Archaeology and Anthropology. Institute of Archaeology and Anthropology, Yarmouk University. Tel: 02-271100, ext. 3746. Open 10am–3pm, closed Friday.

Archaeological Museum. Situated inside the site, off the cardo. Tel: 04-452267. Open winter 9am–5pm, summer 8.30am–6pm, public holidays 10am–4pm. Entry free.

Archaeological Museum. Tel: 03-351149. Open winter 8am–2pm, summer 8am–5pm, closed Tuesday. Entry included in entrance fee to the castle.

Mazar Islamic Museum. Mazar, near Kerak. Tel: 03-371042. Islamic antiquities. Open 8am–2pm, closed Tuesday. Entry free.

Archaeological Museum. Tel: 08-544056. Open 9am–5pm, closed Tuesday. Entry 1JD for non-Arabs.

Archaeological Museum. Tel: 03-83029. Open daily 8am–4pm.

Archaeological Museum. Tel: 05-555653. Open 8am–2pm, closed Friday and public holidays.

Archaeological Museum. The building that houses the museum is as interesting as its Roman, Hellenistic and Byzantine exhibits. Open 9am–5pm, closed Tuesday. Entry free.

Cultural Centres

Royal Cultural Centre. Tel: 661026. In Shmaysani, near the Sports City, Amman. Opening hours depend on activity.

American Centre. Abdoun, Amman. Tel: 822471. Inside the American embassy complex. Open: office and video library 8am–5pm; library 8am–7pm, closed Friday; feature films Sunday and Thursday 7pm; documentaries Tuesday 7pm.

Goethe Institut. Near Third Circle, Jebel Amman, Amman. Tel: 641993. Reference library, German teaching, film shows, lectures, exhibitions and concerts. Open 9am–12.30pm, closed Thursday and Friday.

French Cultural Centre. Jebel Al-Luwaybida, Amman. Tel: 637009, 636445. French, Arabic, music and computer teaching, exhibitions, film shows. Open: office 9am–1pm, 4–7pm, closed Friday; library (books, video, cassettes) 9am–1pm, 4–7pm, closed Friday and Saturday mornings.

British Council. Abu Bakr As-Siddiq Street (known as Rainbow Street) near First Circle, Jebel Amman. Tel: 636147/8, 638194, 624686. English teaching, library (books, video), film shows, exhibitions. Open: office 7.45am–2.30pm Saturday–Tuesday, 7.45am–1.45pm, 3–6pm Wednesday, closed Thursday and Friday; library 8am–1.45pm, 3.30–6.30pm Saturday–Wednesday, 9.45am–1.45pm Thursday, closed Friday.

Abdel Hamid Shoman Foundation. Near First Circle. For exhibitions and lectures (Arabic) and library in Shmaysani with periodicals and books in English as well as Arabic as well as several foreign newspapers. Entry free.

Art Galleries

The Jordan National Gallery of Fine Arts. Montaza, Jebel Al-Luwaybida, Amman. Tel: 630128. Paintings and a few pieces of sculpture and ceramics by contemporary Arab artists. A good place to start your educaton on modern Arab art. The collection of 19th-century Orientalists is not always on display. Open 9am–5pm, closed Tuesday. Entry free.

If you are interested in buying as well as seeing art, then Amman has a lot to offer as it hosts the work of numerous Arab artists and sometimes of non-Arabs who have been inspired by Jordan. Check the listings in the *Jordan Times* for current events.

Darat Al-Funun. (Tel: 643251/2), meaning the Little House for the Arts, is the most impressive, most attractive and most interesting of all of Jordan's galleries. It is housed in a beautifully restored old house in Jebel Al-Luwaybida (see also *Amman chapter*). Open 10am–7pm, closed Friday.

Baladna. Gardens Street, near Safeways, Amman. Tel: 687598. Specialises in local artists, paintings and sculpture. It has a small gift shop selling crafts. Fastest turn over gallery in Amman. Open daily.

Riwak Al-Balkaa for Arts. Near the Municipality building, Fuhays, near

Amman. Tel: 720677. Exhibitions by foreign and Arab artists, poetry readings, outdoor theatre in the summer and music performances in an old house with a lovely courtyard (the *riwak*). Also has a small complex of craft shops. Open daily 10am–1pm, 3–8pm.

The Gallery. Jordan Intercontinental Hotel, Amman. Tel: 641361, ext. 2183. Paintings and photographs by local and foreign artists, pottery, artistic cards, old prints, books on Jordan and many other ideas for gifts. The owner has many more exhibits stored away. Open 8am–7pm, closed Friday.

Alia Art Gallery. Abu Bakr As-Siddiq Street (known as Rainbow Street) near First Circle, Jebel Amman. Tel: 639350. Open 9am–1.30pm, 3.30–6.30pm, closed Friday.

Jerash Art Gallery. On the main road, halfway between the Tourist Visitors' Centre and Hadrian's Arch, Jerash. Open daily 9am–4.30pm.

In addition, the foreign cultural centres and the Royal Cultural Centre, near Sports City, Shmaysani, often organise exhibitions for Jordanian and foreign artists.

In Jerusalem a visit to **Gallery Anadiel**, 27 Salah Eddin Street, is a must. A small gem of a gallery presenting and selling the work of contemporary Palestinian artists. Open daily 9am–2pm, 4.30–7pm except Sunday 10am–2pm. The gallery may also open on special request (tel: 02-288750).

Music/Ballet/Theatre

Recitals, concerts (classical or pop) and, less frequently, ballet performances take place at the Royal Cultural Centre, the foreign cultural centres and occasionally are organised by the 5-star hotels in Amman. Two theatres have been operating with enormous success since democratisation as they show political satires in Arabic.

Cinema

There are two modern cinemas in Amman: the **Philadelphia** at the Tower building, Emir Mohammed Street, near Third Circle, and the **Concord**, near the Housing Bank Centre in Jebel Al-Hussein. They both show popular films from the West, albeit rather later than in the States or Europe. Shows are advertised in the *Jordan Times* daily. Tickets cost 2JD and each show is prefaced by a picture of the King and the national anthem. All films are censored for kissing and sex scenes. The fastest way to see the latest Western releases is to hire videos but these may also be censored. Other cinemas downtown show karate and low-quality action movies. The foreign cultural centres organise film shows regularly and advertise in the *Jordan Times*.

Diary Of Regular Events

Jerash Festival. Always held in the summer (often in July). It attracts national and international drama, ballet, folklore shows and singers.

Film Festival. Held in May, in Amman. European films are shown at the Royal Cultural Centre for free and in some of the major cinemas for a fee.

Discos

There are virtually no discos outside Amman, though some hotels in Aqaba have nightclubs. In Amman try:

Talk of the Town, Middle East Hotel. One of the most popular discos in Amman. Couples only. Reserve for Thursday nights.

Scandals. Near Eighth Circle. You wouldn't know you are in Amman. Reserve on Thursday nights. The place to be seen but very pricey.

Shopping

Shopping Areas

Gift and souvenir shopping in Jordan can be an exciting experience. If you do not have much time to devote to it, head for the following:

Al-Aydi ("The Hands"). Occupies the ground-floor of a house behind the Lebanese Embassy on Second Circle, Jebel Amman. Tel: 644555. Look out for the sign with the palm of a hand, logo of the Jordan Craft Development Centre (established in the early 1970s to provide a living for craftspeople and to salvage craft skills). Fixed prices. Open winter 9am–1pm, 3–6pm, summer 9am–1pm, 4–7pm, closed Friday and public holidays.

There are a number of well-stocked souvenir shops with a great variety of goods and negotiable prices:

Al-Shami Bazar and Gifts. Between Third Circle and Intercontinental.

Oriental Souvenirs Stores. Emir Mohammed Street, near Third Circle.

Boys' Town. At the Intercontinental shopping arcade.

Al-Afghani. In Jebel Al-Luwaybida, opposite the post office near Al-Hawouz Circle.

Gallerie Mesopotamia. Ground-floor of Jordan Insurance building, off Emir Mohammed Street, near Third Circle.

Arabic and Islamic Heritage House, Baouniya Street, Jebel Al-Luwaybida.

There are also plenty of souvenir shops near all major tourist attractions. However, Jordanian crafts deserve some attention and you should sample the best available.

Two projects, the **Noor Al-Hussein Foundation** (near Safeway) and the **Jordan River Designs**, in the Save the Children building on Jebel Al-Luwaybida, produce a huge variety of beautiful and high quality crafts handmade by local women. Prices are fixed but high.

The **Nazik Al-Hariri Centre for the Handicapped**, near Eighth Circle on the way to Fuhays, has a nice selection of rugs and basketwork. **Kan Zaman** has numerous craftshops stocking the work of several different projects at fixed prices; in particular look out for the **Bridal Chest** shop. Finally the **airport duty-free shop** is an excellent last minute choice.

Shopping Hours

Shops open 9am–8pm – but many close in the afternoon for about two hours (this can be any time between 1pm and 4pm). In Ramadan they are open 9am–1pm and around 7–10pm. Most shops close on Friday with the exception of the *suq* downtown. Some shops close on Sunday.

Markets

A typical Middle Eastern market is the downtown *suq* where you can buy almost anything. Shopping in Amman is less concentrated now than it used to be, with new neighbourhoods developing and establishing their own shopping areas. The following areas should cover almost all your shopping needs: downtown, Emir Mohammed Street (from Third Circle to the city centre), Abu Bakr As-Siddeeq Street (known as Rainbow Street), Wasfi Tell Street, better known as Gardens Street (from Safeway to Al-Waha Circle) and the shopping areas of upmarket Suwayfiyya and Shmaysani

Bargaining is gradually losing ground in Jordan as more and more shops have fixed prices. You should, however, certainly attempt it in souvenir shops and in the *suq* downtown.

What To Buy

Palestinian Ceramics: For mugs, plates, bowls, cups and tiles try **Boys' Town** and **Al-Shami Bazar** in Amman. Jerusalem, however, can offer better variety and prices. The **Palestinian pottery workshop** beside the American Consulate in East Jerusalem has some of the most artistic (and pricey) ceramics. Other ceramicists are to be found in the Arab and Armenian quarters of Jerusalem's Old City.

Palestinian Embroidery: In Amman, one shop worth searching for is **Zakaria Ar-Ramadi's** (tel: 629719, 647719), which has low prices and excellent quality work. It specialises in embroidered cushion covers, jackets, dresses, slippers and hair-bands. It is at No. 10, Alleyway 2, off Omar Al-Khayyam Street, where the service taxis for Jebel Al-Luwaybida have their taxi rank. Another place where you can actually pick out your design and be fitted for items of clothing is the **Olive Branch** opposite the French Cultural Centre in Jebel Al-Luwaybida. Also try **Al-Dalal Co** (tel: 603217), inside the Forte Grand Hotel, **Boys' Town**, **Al-Aydi**, the airport duty-free shop, and Kan Zaman. Prices for small embroidered cushions range from a low 12-15JD to a high 20–25JD and dresses cost between 100–200JD. Quality varies so be careful.

Pottery: Bowls, vases, plates and lamp-bases. The common pattern of pale-coloured pottery with Arabic script designs is produced mainly by two workshops. The first is **Silsal Pottery** (tel: 680128). Its products are on sale at the workshop (third turning right between 5th and 4th circle) as well as at Al-Aydi, the Noor Al-Hussein Foundation (near Safeway), the Marriott souvenir and newspaper shop, The Gallery at the Intercontinental Hotel and at the airport duty-free. The second workshop is **Hazem Zoubi's gallery and studio** (tel: 680908), in Shmaysani, behind Safeway – call for directions – where you can find bowls and plates as well as ceramic wall pieces with abstract designs.

Bedouin kilims: Visit **Bani Hamida House** (tel: 658696), off Abu Bakr As-Siddiq Street (Rainbow Street), near First Circle, Jebel Amman. Sells the famous Bedouin-made rugs to modern design. Open 8am–6pm, closed Friday. **Al-Aydi** also has a large stock of Bedouin rugs in authentic patterns and colours and there are a number of shops in Madaba where many are actually produced.

Hebron hand-made glass: Look out for carafes, bowls, jars, vases and mugs made in Jordan by a family originally from Hebron who now live and work in Na'ur, near Amman. Apart from the traditional dark-blue glass there is also clear glass, light brown, green and yellow. It is sold at **Al-Aydi**, where you will find a variety of colours, but many souvenir shops also stock it. For the best prices go to the workshop in Na'ur where you can see the glass-blowers at work.

Basketry: Produced in Mukhayba, north of the Jordan Valley. Available at **Al-Aydi**, where you will find some of the finest new and old pieces, and at the museum shop in Umm Qais.

Gold: Cheaper here than in the West and there is a huge variety of quality available in the *suq* downtown. Know your stuff and bargain with reason. Look out for silver jewellery and amber. Silver from Yemen is particularly attractive.

Sand-filled bottles: Bottles containing various designs and pictures in coloured sand. Made in Aqaba and Petra and sold everywhere. Quality varies.

Oriental Sweets: These will keep fresh if packed airtight. The patisserie **Jabri** has branches in Shmaysani, Gardens Street, on the main street in Jebel Al-Hussein, on the main road between Fifth and Sixth circles as well as downtown. **Zalatimo** is another famous brand in oriental sweets. Their shop is in the Amra Hotel shopping arcade and they also sell at the airport.

Wood inlaid with mother of pearl: In most souvenir shops you will find boxes with Dome of the Rock designs, mirror and picture frames and sometimes chairs and chests of drawers, most of which are produced in Palestine and Syria.

Olivewood: From kitchen utensils to Christmas Nativity scenes, eggs and other miscellaneous kitsch. On sale all over the country as well as in the West Bank where it is produced.

Copperware: Stocked at most souvenir shops.

Antiques: Try **Al-Afghani** (tel: 625992, 635758, 676670). Branches in Jebel Al-Luwaybida, opposite Khalaf Supermarket, Al-Hawuz Circle, and Jebel Al-Hussein. Only some items are antique.

Art: See *Art Galleries*.

Export Procedures

There are no export restrictions except for antiquities, i.e. items more than 100 years old. Shopkeepers can post your purchases to the US and Europe.

Complaints Procedures

After you have tried to reason with the shopkeeper go to police. Take a receipt, otherwise you will have no evidence of how much you have paid.

Sports

Participant Sports

Sports City (Al-Medina Ar-Riadhiya), on the University Road, Amman. An impressive complex of sports facilities with a gym, indoor and outdoor swimming pool, tennis and squash courts. **Orthodox Club**, Abdoun. This has indoor and outdoor swimming pools, basket and volley-ball grounds, tennis and squash courts and a gym.

Tennis and Squash

There are tennis and squash courts at Sports City, and the Orthodox Club. The YWCA (near Third Circle), the Forte Grand, Crown, Jordan Intercontinental, Marriott, Philadelphia and Amra hotels also have tennis courts.

Weight-training and Aerobics

Gyms are mushrooming all over Amman, health clubs also offering sauna, steam bath, Jacuzzi, massage. You can pay per visit, which can be expensive, or get a short-term or long-term membership, which work out a lot cheaper. The best value for money in this field is Body Must Fitness and Beauty Centre, at the Amra Hotel, and the Plaza Fitness centres in the Housing Bank building and in Suwayfiyya which offer a wide range of aerobics classes. Good facilities are also available at the Marriott Hotel Health Club (the most luxurious but also the most expensive), Regency Palace Hotel Health Club, Power Hut in Shmaysani, Sports City and the Orthodox Club.

Bowling

At the Brunswick Bowling Centre, Abu Bakr As-Siddiq Street (Rainbow Street) near First Circle, Jebel Amman.

Swimming

Most outdoor swimming pools open at the beginning of May and close at the end of September. Most hotel pools are open to non-residents but they must pay an entrance fee. Sometimes monthly and season tickets are available. The best swimming-pools are at the Jordan Intercontinental, the Orthodox Club and Sports City, but they all get overcrowded on holidays and Fridays. Other hotels with outdoor swimming pools of varying sizes include the Marriott, Forte Grand, Amra, Philadelphia, Crown Hotel, Amman International, Grand Palace, Crown Hotel, Middle East and Al-Manar. Many of these places have children's pools. In the winter you can swim indoors at the Marriott Hotel Health Club, Regency Palace Hotel Health Club, Plaza Health Club in Suwayfiyya, Orthodox Club and Sports City, where you can pay by the visit or get a membership.

Jogging

The Hash-House Harriers meet on Monday evenings. A jog is followed by hearty drinking and eating. For details of upcoming venues, contact the British Embassy or British Council in Amman and the Al-Cazar Hotel in Aqaba.

Scuba diving and snorkelling

Aqaba offers some of most spectacular diving in the world on the coast towards Saudi Arabia, but try to avoid March and April when the water contains a lot of algae. Shop around the following diving centres (they offer instruction at all levels and rent out gear):

Aquamarina I Hotel. Tel: 03-316250. Offers snorkelling, diving from a boat or the beach, equipment, water-skiing, windsurfing, fishing trips, pedalo, speed-boat and marine camera hire and half-day boat trips to Far'un Island and its coral reef.

Al-Cazar Hotel. Tel: 03-314131. For diving trips, instruction and equipment.

Royal Diving Centre. Tel: 03-317035. Situated outside Aqaba, en route to the Saudi border. For snorkelling, diving and marine photography equipment hire and instruction.

Red Sea Diving Centre. Tel: 03-318969. Professional but friendly, with reasonable prices. Situated near the Aqaba Gulf Hotel.

Larger hotels also offer trips in glass-bottom boats.

Ballooning

The Jordan Tourism Investment Co., PO Box 811640, Amman 111 18. Tel: 06-668606 (Amman), tel: 03-316324 (Aqaba), tel: 03-83665 (Petra). This company organises hot air balloon rides in Wadi Rum at dawn and in the late afternoon. Trips last between 45 minutes and 1½ hours but are expensive at 120JD per person. However, this price includes transportation from Amman, Aqaba or Petra and champagne breakfast or tea. The entire trip lasts 8–9 hours from Amman and 4–5 hours from Petra and Aqaba (including return travel).

Hiking, Climbing, Trekking

Wadi Rum and Petra are ideal locations for all these, but avoid the summer months. In Wadi Rum aim for the rock bridge. Two useful books on the

subject are: Tony Howard's *Treks and Climbs in the Mountains of Rum and Petra*, Jordan Distribution Agency/Cicerone Press, 1987 (new edition 1993) and Tony Howard & Diana Taylor's *Walks and Scrambles in Wadi Rum*, Al-Kutba, Amman, 1993. For climbing bring your own gear.

Spectator Sports

Apart from **football** and **basketball** matches you can watch **horse- and camel-racing** in spring and summer in Marka (east of Amman city centre) under the supervision of the Royal Racing Club.

Health Resorts & Spas

The Dead Sea

The Dead Sea has considerable potential as a health resort. The minerals contained in Dead Sea mud (sulphur, zinc oxide and magnesium carbonate) are considered highly beneficial for the skin and the warm water of the sea itself is said to help alleviate arthritis and circulatory problems. So far, treatments centre upon the Dead Sea Hotel (see *Hotels*) and the Dead Sea resthouse, but more health facilities are planned. There is no public transport to the Dead Sea.

Hammamat Ma'in

The spa village at Hammamat Ma'in is ideal for a quiet health retreat, if you avoid Friday and Saturday in high season when it's packed. It is built around the natural mineral sources of Zerqa Ma'in and features two hotels (the 4-star Ashtar and a 2-star), portakabins (11JD for two) for camping, outdoor swimming pool, Turkish baths and a grocery-cum-café with limited overpriced supplies of snacks and toiletries. Its most attractive feature is the natural hot waterfall where you can bathe and enjoy a water massage. JETT operates a regular bus service. Ticket prices do not include the entry fee, which is around 3JD.

Himmeh

Himmeh, just below the Golan over the hill from Umm Qais in the north of Jordan, offers piping hot mineral baths. Men and women are admitted at different times.

Language

Nothing pleases Jordanians more than meeting a foreigner who can speak their language, or even a few words, so it's very well worth the try.

Pronunciation

a/as in/look
í/as in/see
ya/as in/Soraya
ai/as in/eye
ay/as in/may
aw/as in/away
kh/as in the Scottish/loch
gh/as in the Parisian/r
dh/as in/the

Double consonants: try to pronounce them twice as long. An apostrophe ' indicates a glottal stop.

Greetings

Hello/Márhaba, ahlan
(reply)/Marhabtáyn, áhlayn
Greetings/As-salám aláykum (peace be with you)
(reply)/Waláykum as-salám (and to you peace)
Welcome/Áhlan wasáhlan
(reply)/áhlan fíkum
Good morning/Sabáh al-kháyr
(reply)/Sabáh an-núr (a morning of light)/Sabáh al-wurd (a morning of the smell of flowers)
Good evening/Masá al-kháyr
(reply)/Masá an núr
Good night/Tisbáh al-kháyr (wake up well)
(reply)/Wa ínta min áhlu (and you are from His people)
Good bye/Máa Saláma or alla Máák (with peace or God be with you)/Ya'atik aláfia (may God give you health)
How are you?/Káyf hálak? (to a man)/Káyf hálik? (to a woman)
Well, fine/Mabsút or mneeh (for a man)/Mabsúta or mneeha (for a woman)
Please/min fádlak (to a man)/min fádlik (to a woman)
After you/Tafáddal (to a man)/Tafáddali (to a woman)/Afáddalu (to more than one)
Excuse me/Samáhli or Idha láwu samánt (to a man)/Samáhili or Idha láwu samánti (to a woman)
Sorry/Áfwan or mutaásif or ásif (for a man)/Áfwan or mutaásifa or ásifa (for a woman)
Thank you (very much)/Shúkran (jazilan)
Thank you, I am grateful/Mamnúnak (to a man)/Mamnúnik (to a woman)
Thanks be to God/Al-hámdu li-llá
God willing (hopefully)/Inshá allá
Yes/Náam or áiwa
No/La
Congratulations!/Mabrúck!
(reply)/Alláh yubárak fik

Useful Phrases

What is your name?/Shú ismak? (to a man)/Shú ismik? (to a woman)
My name is.../Ismi...
Where are you from?/Min wáyn inta? (for a man)/Min wáyn inti? (for a woman)
I am from: England/Ána min Ingíltra
Germany/Ána min Almánia
the United States/Ána min Amérika
Australia/Ána min Ustrália
Do you speak English?/Btíhki inglízi?
I speak: English/Bíhki inglízi
German/Almámi
French/Fransáwi
I do not speak Arabic/Ma bíhki árabi
I do not understand/Ma báfham
What does this mean?/Ya'áni esh?
Repeat, once more/Kamán márra
Do you have...?/Ándkum...?
Is there any...?/Fí...?
There isn't any.../Ma fí...
Never mind/Ma'alésh
It is forbidden.../Mamnú'a
Is it allowed...?/Masmúh...?
What is this?/Shú hádha?
I want/Bídi
I do not want/Ma bídi
Wait/Istánn (to a man)/Istánni (to a woman)
Hurry up/Yalla/bi súra'a
Slow down/Shwáyya
Finished/Khalás
Go away!/Imshí!
What time is it?/Adáysh as-sáa?/kam as-sáa?
How long, how many hours?/Kam sáa?

Vocabulary

GENERAL

embassy/sifára
post office/máktab al-baríd
stamps/tawábi'a
bank/bank
hotel/otél/fúnduq
museum/máthaf
ticket/tádhkara
ruins/athár
passport/jiwáz as-sáfar
good/kuwáys
not good, bad/mish kuways
open/maftúh
closed/musákkar/múghlik
today/al-yáum
tonight/hadhi-l-láyl
tomorrow/búkra

EATING/DRINKING OUT

restaurant/máta'am
food/ákl
fish/sámak
meat/láhma
milk/halíb
bread/khúbz
salad/saláta
delicious/záki
coffee/áhwa
tea/shái
cup/finján
with sugar/bi súkkar
without sugar/bidún súkkar
wine/nibíd
beer/bíra
mineral water/mái ma'adaniya
glass/kubbaiya
bottle/ázaja
I am a vegetarian/Ána nabbáti (for a man)/nabbátiya (for a woman)
the bill/al-hisáb

GETTING AROUND

Where...?/Wáyn...?
downtown/wást al bálad
street/shária
Amir Mohammed Street/Shária al-amir Mohammed
car/sayára
taxi/táxi
shared taxi/servís
bus/bas
airplane/tayára
airport/matár
station/mahátta
to/íla
from/min
right/yamín
left/shimál

straight/*dúghri*
behind/*wára*
near/*aríb*
far away/*ba'id*
petrol, super/*benzín, benzín khas*

NUMBERS

zero/*sifir*
one/*wáhad*
two/*itnín*
three/*taláta*
four/*árba'a*
five/*khámsa*
six/*sítta*
seven/*sába'a*
eight/*tamánia*
nine/*tísa'a*
ten/*áshara*
eleven/*hidáshar*
twelve/*itnáshar*

SHOPPING

market/*súq*
shop/*dukkán*
money/*fulús*
cheap/*rakhís*
expensive (very)/*gháli* (*jídan*)
receipt, invoice/*fatúra, wásl*
How much does it cost?/*Adáysh?/bi-kam?*
What would you like?/*Shú bidak?* (to a man)/*Shú bidik?* (to a woman)/*Shú bidkum?* (to more than one)
I like this/*Buhíbb hádha*
I do not like this/*Ma buhíbb hádha*
Can I see this?/*Mumkin ashúf hádha?*
Give me/*A'atíni*
How many?/*Kam?*

LOOKING FOR A ROOM

a free room/*ghúrfa fádia*
single room/*ghúrfa munfárida*
double room/*ghúrfa muzdáwija*
hot water/*mái súkhna*
bathroom, toilet/*hammám, tuwalét*
shower/*dúsh*
towel/*bashkír*
How much does the room cost per night?/*Adáysh al-ghúrfa al-láyl?*

EMERGENCIES

I need help/*Bídi musáada*

doctor/*doctôr/tabíb/hakím*
hospital/*mustáshfa*
pharmacy/*saidalíya*
I am ill, sick/*Ána marídh* (for a man)/*Ána marídha* (for a woman)
diarrhoea/*ishál*
operation/*amalíya*
police/*shúrta*
lawyer/*muhámmi*
I want to see/*Bídi ashúf*

Further Reading

General

A History of the Arab Peoples, by Albert Hourani. London, 1991. A landmark history of the Arabs, by the doyen of Middle East studies this century. It spent several months on the US bestseller lists.

The Arabs, by Peter Mansfield. Penguin, 1976. A good survey by ex-London *Times* journalist.

The History of the Middle East, by Peter Mansfield. Penguin, London, 1991. A very readable introduction for the lay person.

Heart-Beguiling Araby – The English Romance with Arabia, by Kathryn Tidrick. I.B. Tauris, London/New York, 1989. A must if you nurture romantic ideas about the Arab world.

The Bedouin, by Shelagh Weir. British Museum Publications, London, 1990.

On the Banks of the Jordan: British and Nineteenth Century Painters, by Jordan National Gallery & the British Council, 1987. Available in English and Arabic.

Biblical

If your visit whets your appetite for some controversial theories about Jesus and the New Testament you should read:

The Dead Sea Scrolls Deception, by Michael Baigent & Richard Leigh. Corgi Books, England. A fascinating account of the controversy surrounding the ancient scrolls discovered in caves by the Dead Sea in the late 1940s.

Who was Jesus? A Conspiracy in Jerusalem, by Kamal Salibi. I.B. Tauris, London/New York, 1986/9.

The Bible Came from Arabia, by Kamal Salibi. I.B.Tauris, London/New York, 1986/9.

History

Nomads and Settlers in Syria and Jordan, 1800–1980, by Norman Lewis. Cambridge, 1989. A fascinating look at the land and people of the area. Scholarly, but also a good read by the man who introduced the concept of a "frontier of settlement".

Pioneers Over Jordan: The Frontier of Settlement in Transjordan, 1850–1914, by Raouf Abu Jaber. London, 1989. A scholarly work on settlement in Transjordan in the 19th century.

Jordan: Crossroads of Middle East Events, by Peter Gubser. Colorado, 1983. One of a series of books which provide profiles of countries in the modern Middle East. Gubser is an old Jordan hand and covers all facets of life in Jordan in less than 150 pages. The statistics are a little dated now, but still the best all-round book on Jordan for the newcomer. Scholarly style.

The Making of Modern Jordan, by Kamal Salibi. London, 1993. The latest and best history of Jordan, by one of the most eminent historians in the Middle East. Very readable and informative. Cheaper in Jordan.

Jordan's Palestinian Challenge, 1948–1983: A Political History, by Clinton Bailey. Colorado, 1984. A look at one of the most sensitive political questions in Jordan today by an Israeli academic. Scholarly rather than a good read.

Biographies & Autobiographies

King Abdullah, Britain and the Making of Jordan, by Mary C. Wilson. Cambridge, 1987. A scholarly book covering the period from the founding of the Emirate to the assassination of King Abdullah. Wilson's book looks more closely at the controversy surrounding King Hussein's grandfather than does Kamil Salibi.

Hussein of Jordan; A Political Biography by James Lunt. London, 1989. The most recent biography of the King. Sympathetic and very readable.

Memoirs of King Abdullah of Transjordan by H. M. King Abdullah of Jordan. London, 1950. The Emir's (and later King's) account of Jordan's early days.

Uneasy Lies the Head: An Autobiography, by H. M. King Hussein of Jordan. London, 1962. Particularly interesting about the King's early life. The King also wrote his own account of the run-up to the 1967 war in *My War with Israel*, London, 1968. A later autobiography is *Mon Métier de Roi* (1975), in which the King brings the story up to and beyond Black September. Surprisingly, this book does not seem to be available in English.

Glubb Pasha: A Biography by James Lunt. London, 1984. A sympathetic account of the life of the British commander of the Jordanian army, by one of the officers who served under him.

Glubb Pasha: The Life and Times of Sir John Bagot Glubb, by Trevor Royle. London, 1992. The most recent biography of Glubb. A good read.

A Soldier with the Arabs, by Sir John Bagot Glubb. London, 1957. Autobiography of the British commander of the Arab Legion. A good read which gives Glubb's perspective on Jordan.

Lawrence of Arabia: The Authorised Biography of T.E. Lawrence, by Jeremy Wilson. London, 1989. The definitive account of Lawrence's life.

A Crackle of Thorns, by Alec Seath Kirkbride. London, 1956.

Travel Literature

Walks and Scrambles in Wadi Rum, by Tony Howard and Diana Taylor. Al-Kutba, Amman, 1993.

Famous Travellers to the Holy Land, by Linda Osband. Prior, 1989. Ranges from William Makepeace Thackeray to Gertrude Bell and Mark Twain.

Archaeology

Al-Kutba Jordan Guide Series in English and French on Petra, Wadi Rum and Aqaba, and in English only on Jerash, the Desert Castles, Amman, Umm Qais, Pella, Umm Al-Jimal, Madaba and Mount Nebo, Kerak and Shobak, and The King's Highway. Written by experts but makes an informative and easy read.

Petra, by Ian Browning. Chatto & Windus/Jordan Distribution Agency, 1989.

Jerash and the Decapolis, by Ian Browning. Chatto & Windus/Jordan Distribution Agency (1982) 1991.

The Art of Jordan – Treasures from an Ancient Land, by Piotr Bienkowski (ed.). National Museums & Galleries on Merseyside, 1991.

The Antiquities of Jordan, by G. Lankester Harding, Jordan Distribution Agency, Amman (1967) 1990.

Archaeology of Jordan: Essays and Reports, by Khair Yassine. University of Jordan, Amman, For the specialist only.

Crafts

Palestinian Embroidery, by Shelagh Weir & Serene Shahid. British Museum Publications, London, 1988.

Weaving in Jordan, by Widad Kawar. The Jordan Crafts Centre, Amman, 1980.

The Crafts of Jordan, by Meg Abu Hamdan. Al-Kutba, Amman, 1989.

Palestinian Costume, by Jehan Rajab. Kegan Paul International, 1989.

Traditional Palestinian Embroidery and Jewellery, by Abed Al-Samih Abu Omar. Al-Shark Arab Press, Jerusalem, 1987. In English and Arabic.

For children

Dig Cats, by Carol Meyer. Al-Kutba, Amman, 1989. A pet cat visits the sites in Jerash.

Colouring Jordan, Al-Kutba, Amman. English and Arabic.

Books on the Butterfly Series of Librairie du Liban, Stories from the Arab World Series: *Prince Jamil and Leila the Fair, Ma'arouf the Cobbler, The Man Who Never Laughed*, and, from the Stage 2 series, *Handicrafts of the Arab World, Farming the Desert*, and *Deserts*.

Middle Eastern Cooking

A New Book of Middle Eastern Food, by Claudia Roden. Penguin, 1985. The most comprehensive work of its kind and unique for its culinary history of the region.

The Complete Middle Eastern Cookbook, by Tess Mallos. Peter Ward, England, 1993. Illustrated and divided into country/regional sections.

Wildlife

Birds of Jordan, by Arslan Ramadan Bakig & Dr Hala Khiyami Horani. Amman, 1992.

Photographic

Amman Yesterday and Today, by Arslan Ramadan Bakig. Amman *Photographs from the Jordanian and Palestinian Heritage*, by Ibid. The Arab Institute for Research and Publishing, Amman, 1991. English and French.

High Above Jordan, by Jane Taylor. Amman, 1991. Aerial photographs of the major sites in Jordan with brief commentary, published in English, German, French and Italian; also *Petra*, Autumn Press, 1993. A tour of the famous site with photographs.

Aqaba: Under-Water Paradise, with photographs by C. Petron and text by J. Jaubert. Editions Delroisse/Jordan Distibution Agency. For scuba fans.

Fiction

There is no fiction in English that deals with Jordan alone and what is available draws from the experience of the Palestinian-Israeli conflict.

Nisanit, by Fadia Faqir. King Penguin, The harrowing story of a young Palestinian refugee woman living in Jordan, who falls in love with a Palestinian guerrilla in the West Bank, runs parallel to the story of her boyfriend's Israeli torturer.

Arab Folktales, by Inea Bushnaq (ed.). Pantheon Books, New York, 1986. A superb and delightful read with insight into popular Arab wisdom.

Blood Brothers, by Elias Chacour. Kingsway Publications, England (1984) 1987. The effort of a Palestinian in Israel to bring about reconciliation between Arabs and Jews.

Other Insight Guides

Other Insight Guides which highlight destinations in this region include *Insight Guides: Egypt* and *Jerusalem*.

Art/Photo Credits

Photography by
Lyle Lawson unless otherwise stated.
(The regional costumes worn on pages
74/75, 114, 240 and 286 were lent by
Widad Kawar, and those on pages
170/171, 196 and 241 by **Al-Aydi**.)

Allan Colclough 277
Rami Khouri 186
Mansour Mouasher 130L
Mary Evans Picture Library 29, 38–42,
46
Jane Taylor 88, 128, 130R, 131
Topham Picture Source 36/37, 59,
62–65, 68L, 68R, 69–71

Maps Lovell Johns

Visual Consultant V. Barl

Index